THE
TRUE
GEN

THE TRUE GEN

AN INTIMATE PORTRAIT OF
ERNEST HEMINGWAY
BY THOSE WHO KNEW HIM

DENIS BRIAN

Delta

A DELTA BOOK
Published by
Dell Publishing
a division of
Bantam Doubleday Dell Publishing Group, Inc.
666 Fifth Avenue
New York, New York 10103

Grateful acknowledgement is made to the following:
Alfred A. Knopf, Inc., for permission to reprint from *How It Was* by Mary Welsh
Hemingway, © 1951, 1955, 1963, 1966 and 1976 by Mary Welsh Hemingway;
Random House, Inc., for permission to reprint from *At Random: Reminiscences of
Bennett Cerf* by Bennett Cerf, © 1977 by Bennett Cerf; Quartet Books Ltd., and the
executors of the estate of Claud Cockburn, for permission to reprint from *I, Claud*
by Claud Cockburn; Mrs. Ellis O. Briggs, for permission to reprint from *Shots
Heard Round the World* by Ellis O. Briggs, © renewed 1957 by Ellis O. Briggs;
Doubleday and Co., for permission to reprint from *Being Geniuses Together* by Kay
Boyle and Robert McAlmon, © 1968 by Kay Boyle and Robert McAlmon; Charles
Scribner's Sons, a division of Macmillan, Inc., for permission to reprint from
Ernest Hemingway: A Life Story by Carlos Baker, © 1969 by Carlos Baker and Mary
Hemingway.

ISBN: 0-385-29738-6

Reprinted by arrangement with Grove Press, Inc.

Printed in the United States of America

Published simultaneously in Canada

June 1989

10 9 8 7 6 5 4 3 2 1

BG

TO
MARTINE
AND
DANIELLE
WITH
LOVE

Many thanks to my agent, Peter Shepherd; editor, Walter Bode; Joan L. O'Connor, Curator, Hemingway Collection, John Fitzgerald Kennedy Library; Malcolm Hayes, who put me in touch with John Carlisle; and all who cooperated in making this book possible, especially Archibald and Ada MacLeish, William Walton, George Seldes, Joseph Dryer, Philip Young, Evan Thomas, Susan Lowrey Crist, Henry Strater, Malcolm Cowley, C. T. Lanham, A. E. Hotchner, J. V. V. Heimbach, Dr. Meyer Maskin, Dr. Philip Scharfer, Dr. Bruce Moskowitz, and many Hemingways.

Many thanks to the following for photographs: Hemingway Collection, John F. Kennedy Library; Susan Lowrey Crist; Henry Villard; Henry Strater; Carol Hemingway Gardner; George Seldes; John Hersey; William Walton; John Westover; Mrs. Meyer Maskin; Thorvald Sanchez, Jr.; Joseph Dryer; John Rybovich, Jr.; Robert Cowley; Lauren Bacall; Betty Bruce.

A few of the interviews in this book first appeared in my *Murderers and Other Friendly People: The Public and Private Worlds of Interviewers*, McGraw-Hill, 1973.

CONTENTS

ix

"The true gen" is believed to have been first used by members of the Royal Air Force during World War II. Before going on operations, aircrews were given Intelligence—abbreviated to "gen"—briefings about expected weather en route and over the target, and expected enemy opposition. A pilot who had raided that same target a few nights before might then give a revised, updated firsthand account of expected enemy opposition. This was called "the true gen" and came to be used to distinguish accurate information from rumor and speculation. Some say that gen is short for genuine or general information. Whatever the case, Ernest Hemingway picked up the expression and used it frequently, even creating his own phrase, "the true, true gen."

THE
TRUE
GEN

INTRODUCTION

·

THE ENIGMA

Ernest Hemingway had an extravagant effect on others, leaving them beguiled, besotted, bruised, or bitter. To everyone he was an extraordinary, unforgettable presence.

His last wife, Mary, said he was the most decent and complex man she had known. "Yes," agreed Hadley, his first wife. "Just so many sides to him you could hardly make a sketch of him in a geometry book." His second, Pauline, came to hate him; and Martha, his third, admired the writer, but despised and finally pitied the man.

Gertrude Stein called him yellow, comparing him with Mark Twain's Mississippi River boatmen who talked big, but backed down if anyone stood up to them. If she witnessed Hemingway do that, it was not typical of him. Army General Buck Lanham, one of Hemingway's closest friends in war and in peace, never met a braver man. Archibald and Ada Mac-Leish loved him despite his faults and fellow war correspondent John Carlisle found no fault and idolized him. Artist Henry Strater scoffed at that; to Strater, Hemingway was a charming but sadistic son-of-a-bitch.

3

English professor William Seward had encountered several U.S. presidents and other so-called great men. Of that distinguished group, Hemingway alone did not disappoint him.

Those who knew him best agree on one thing: he was an enigma.

On the surface Hemingway's life was an open, large-print book crammed with pictures. From the 1920s until his gunshot suicide in 1961, he was the best known living writer in the world. His private life was public property and the heroes of his novels and stories, wounded in most and impotent in one, appeared to be thinly disguised aspects of himself.

His broad, twisted grin and bulging biceps were as frequently displayed in newspapers and magazines as photographs of the latest Hollywood favorites. And he outdid them by appearing not only in news and gossip columns, but also in the literary and sports sections. Yet readers got more myth than man, and that was what he wanted: he consciously created a larger-than-life hero behind which he hid.

So Ernest Hemingway strides through the pages of American literary history, a rugged, battered, and battering playboy of the western world. The Hemingway hero was the face he wanted the world to see, the man he longed to be, and behind this mask of fiction he concealed himself. His Byronic camouflage proved surprisingly effective in this age of revelation and research in garbage cans.

Hemingway in hiding? Would a secretive man befriend gossip columnists and take fellow writers as his third and fourth wives, the last from tattletale *Time?* Only, of course, if he felt he could control them or was confident they would protect him.

Lewis Galantiere, a Parisian friend when Hemingway (born in 1899) was in his early twenties, remarked that beneath Ernest's boisterous gaiety there was something wary and secretive. After being Hemingway's close friend for twelve years, Scott Fitzgerald wrote in 1937 that he wished they could meet more often because he felt he didn't know Ernest at all.

Critic Jackson Benson believes Hemingway assumed an air of bravado to hide his shyness, insecurity, and oversensitivity, and "consciously evolved a mask behind which he could approach his work and wrote with conscious regard for his reader—a conscious regard that was often duplicity. . . . Kafka decided to keep his problems to himself by applying as much skill as possible in keeping them hidden. The complexity of Hemingway's technique can no doubt be traced to this necessity to hide or disguise what he was compelled to express."[1]

Hemingway hides, variously disguised, in most of his fiction. That is one route to him.

A more direct approach could prove hazardous. Writer Max Eastman questioned Hemingway's manliness, not to his face but in print. Soon after, the two met by chance in their editor's office where Hemingway first used Eastman as a duster to clear the editor's desk, then wrestled him to the floor.

Some believe his he-man stance and preoccupations masked a latent homosexual and that his macho manner was the continuous, strenuous effort of a coward to appear brave. To others if Hemingway wasn't a courageous, heterosexual man, then no one was.

It was rare for him not to be wounded or injured in war and peace. He broke his arm, repeatedly smashed his skull, shot himself in the legs, and was burned in a brushfire, as if testing his endurance or immunity to pain.

At his lyrical, satirical best in *A Moveable Feast*, he recalled his early idyllic and struggling days in Paris. Yet even those far-off times were disguised or distorted. He admitted as much, inviting readers to regard his memories as fiction, but implying that his fiction might illuminate what had previously been written as fact.

One part of Hemingway, the reporter, aimed for at least subjective truth; another couldn't resist playing with it as if it were bubblegum.

Why did he lie about his life? For fun? Sure. To burnish the banal? That, too. And he obviously got a kick out of arousing gasps from the gullible. But also, it seems clear, he had to make a myth of himself.

His fantasy life was lifelong, perhaps compulsive. At five he told his grandfather he'd stopped a runaway horse, and the old man predicted fame or a criminal career for the young liar. At nineteen he startled his parents with the news that he was engaged to marry movie actress Mae Marsh. They had never even met.

In his book *A Prince of Our Disorder: The Life of T. E. Lawrence*, psychiatrist John E. Mack wrote: "One of the purposes in writing [*The Seven Pillars of Wisdom*] was to invite the public to create with him a new and different self, a mythological Lawrence, larger than life, a self

[1] *The Short Stories of Ernest Hemingway: Critical Essays*, Edited, with an overview and checklist, Jackson J. Benson, Duke University Press, N.C. 1975.

that would be immune to or beyond personal pain and conflict and that would replace the self he felt he had debased. . . . The irony is that, objectively, the real Lawrence corresponded in many ways to the ideal one he sought to create."[1] So did Hemingway.

Both Carlos Baker and A. E. Hotchner nailed many of Hemingway's self-perpetuated legends: he did not, for instance, sleep with the famous spy Mata Hari as he claimed because she was executed a year before he first arrived on the same continent. Baker set out to deliberately sever fact from fancy, but with Hemingway himself feeding him information, Baker was stymied and frequently admitted defeat. Hotchner simply went along with Hemingway's extravaganzas, thinking, no matter how implausible, they were great entertainment.

Why have I tried to free him from his legend, when his authorized biographer—the widow at his side, Princeton at his back, and all documents to hand—had admitted failure; and Hotchner, with recordings of Hemingway's intoxicated and intoxicating monologues, an eyewitness to much of his life from the 1950s on, hadn't made the attempt?

A dummy run in the early 1970s encouraged me. In my book *Murderers and Other Friendly People*, I interviewed outstanding interviewers to discover how they persuaded the reluctant to come out of hiding and the tongue-tied to talk.[2] One chapter was about Hemingway's interviewers and intimates.

The result amused *Esquire* publisher Arnold Gingrich, who wrote: "All Denis Brian had to do, seemingly, to be the wittiest fellow around, was just to get everybody who ever interviewed Hemingway to talk about everybody else who had interviewed Hemingway. He really didn't have to say a thing himself, once he had got that great idea, to come off as the most sardonic satirist since Mark Twain. . . . Hemingway's interviewers do seem to show an astonishing resemblance to the proverbial blind Hindus describing an elephant from firsthand acquaintance with the subject."[3]

Gingrich failed to mention that I had also interviewed him, and that Mary Hemingway had ridiculed his opinion of her husband as uninformed.

[1] *A Prince of Our Disorder: The Life of T. E. Lawrence*, John E. Mack, Little, Brown, 1978.

[2] *Murderers and Other Friendly People: The Public and Private Worlds of Interviewers*, Denis Brian, McGraw-Hill, 1973.

[3] Publisher's Page, Arnold Gingrich, *Esquire*, February 1972.

I read Gingrich's remarks about me aglow with self-esteem until I tumbled to the truth that at best they were qualified compliments. He described my achievement as a happy accident—which, in fact, it was. But accidents sometimes lead to useful discoveries.

He had a point, but missed the point. Far from being witnesses fumbling in the dark, my reasonably clear-eyed informants had accurately described different, even conflicting aspects of the same man. He *was* both shy and boisterous, extremely kind and diabolically cruel, an ultrasensitive war hater who loved fighting, as well as a hunter with a passion for blood sports.

Previous biographers knew that attempting to find out what really happened to Hemingway by taking his word for it was like trying to bottle sunlight. So, forewarned, throughout my investigation I had to take the approach that whatever was in print, including Hemingway's "nonfiction" writings and his letters, might be lie, legend, wishful thinking, or bullshit. And not all of it had been spread by Hemingway.

But there were living witnesses to key events in his life—among them World War I ambulance drivers and hospital patients, and reporters who were at his side day and night during the Spanish Civil War and World War II. It was to them as well as to his wife and ex-wives, friends and ex-friends, sisters, brothers, sons, and ex-lovers; to his fishing, fighting, hunting and drinking pals I went for "the true gen."

To get the facts I spoke with the most credible of these witnesses and checked one witness's account against others.

For events that lacked surviving witnesses, I needed to use a unique approach—to go beyond the traditional biographical method—and so I invited his major biographers, interviewers, Hemingway scholars and critics to join me in a combined operation. I also asked psychiatrists to try to explain him and why he tried to con the world.

All helped and most cooperated enthusiastically. His biographers willingly returned to mysteries and ambiguities they, too, had faced; assessed one another's portraits of Hemingway and reevaluated their own in the light of conflicting evidence and subsequent discoveries, until we had mutually agreed on the most likely explanations. Mystery solving—the hunt, the detective work, seeming contradictions, blind alleys, and gleams of light—is, after all, one of the great lures for the biographer.

As I sat talking with General Lanham among the fruit trees in his Chevy Chase garden he warned me that Mary Hemingway might prove a major obstacle. She had already taken Hotchner to court in a costly but unsuccessful attempt to prevent publication of A. E. Hotchner's *Papa Hemingway*.

Even worse, Lanham explained, was the experience of his friend Cy Sulzberger of the *New York Times*. He had written a first-class book called *The Resistentialists*. About a third of the book was an account of transactions between himself, Hemingway, and a poor benighted Frenchman in the slammer on a bum rap. During these negotiations to free the man, Hemingway wrote several letters to Sulzberger that were included in the book. The book was in the stores when Mary found it contained letters from Hemingway and threatened to sue Sulzberger and his publisher unless they immediately withdrew it. Sulzberger asked Lanham to try to persuade Mary to relent, but she was adamant. The book had to be withdrawn. And, stressed Lanham, looking steadily at me to see, it seemed, if I changed color, "it cost Sulzberger and his publisher a pretty penny."

I told Lanham my aim, whenever possible, was to keep Hemingway's words out of my book except to paraphrase some of his letters.

He concluded, "Watch out. This is the age of the fast buck and the fast buck lawyers who are on the constant prowl to uncover any possible ground for a multimillion dollar suit."

Nevertheless, and though in the midst of writing her memoirs, Mary Hemingway took time out to answer my questions in her Manhattan apartment, and later replied to queries by mail and phone.

No Hemingway intimate, expert, or acquaintance refused to discuss him, although my opening gambit: "I'm trying to separate the man from the myth," invariably produced a smile or laugh. Impossible, they implied, but go ahead and ask your questions.

An interviewer for a biography has a head or notebook full of questions: say eight hundred and forty two. He asks his first six and they generate four more, which lead to a different line of questioning. Then, if later sources contradict earlier ones, he must return to the earlier contacts. And then back again. And again.

So I pursued my quarry through the years, guided by Samuel Johnson's opinion that more knowledge of a man's true character can be gained from a short conversation with one of his servants than from "a formal and studied narrative begun with pedigree and ended with his funeral."[1] To

[1] James Boswell's Introduction to his *The Life of Samuel Johnson, LL.D.*, George Routledge and Sons, 1892.

the servants, I added his friends, relatives, and lovers as well as those who were allergic to him.

Johnson provides another reason to seek living witnesses rather than dated documents: "If a life is delayed till interest and envy are at an end, we may hope for impartiality but must expect little intelligence; for incidents which give excellence to biography are of a volatile and evanescent kind."[1]

I also took Carl Jung's advice to biographers and followed in my subjects' footsteps to learn more about him—which led me to Paris, Spain, Italy, and Key West.

Who better than his first wife, Hadley, could recall their eventful life together in Canada and Europe? She agreed to an interview in her Chocorua, New Hampshire, home. While my wife and daughter explored a wood at the foot of Chocorua Mountain, I sat facing Hadley, a small table and a tape recorder between us, her treasures within reach. On a sidetable she had made a small shrine of books by her second husband, Paul Mowrer, who had died in 1971.[2] Nearby was her piano and above it a painting by Stella Bowen, Ford Madox Ford's wife.

I thought her shrine to Mowrer meant she had soured on Hemingway. She had not. She remembered him with affection.

A friendly, straightforward, down-to-earth woman with a quick wit, Hadley helped to demolish some myths about Hemingway, frequently laughed at recollected absurdities, and never dodged a question however personal. She also put me on to my next interview with Harold Loeb. He, the model for Robert Cohn in The Sun Also Rises, had visited Hadley the previous day. Almost half a century after the novel's publication, she said he was still hurt by Hemingway's mocking portrait of him. She gave me his Connecticut address and in a few days I was at his home and Loeb was telling me of Hemingway's effect on him and others. Later, Malcolm Cowley wrote to me: "Harold Loeb was trying to tell the truth, I think, in his autobiography The Way It Was. In The Sun Also Rises Ernest wasn't even trying to be fair. But he could be satanically accurate."

One person close to Hemingway at first spoke freely, then requested anonymity. I identify this source throughout as "a friend."

---

[1]James Atlas, Delmore Schwartz: The Life of an American Poet, Farrar Straus Giroux, 1977.

[2]Paul Mowrer of the Chicago Daily News was the first foreign correspondent to win the Pulitzer Prize.

It surprised both Dr. Meyer Maskin and me that until I contacted him no one had asked for his side of his provocative World War II encounter with Hemingway. The confrontation was briefly noted in Baker's biography, based solely on General Lanham's unpublished *Memoir*.

Hemingway was known to deride psychiatrists. Why was a mystery. But here he was brought face to face with one while battle raged around them, and we only had Hemingway's scathing, scatalogical version of their meeting—relayed through Lanham who was not a witness.

Maskin gave me his frank and detailed testimony of what happened. However, I traced another living witness, William Walton. When I repeated Maskin's memories to Walton he said they were inaccurate. I returned to Maskin with this information and he goodnaturedly (he must have been an effective psychiatrist) conceded that his version modified by Walton's was as close to the truth as we were likely to get.

I expected problems with Hemingway's younger brother, Leicester. He was a vigorous keeper of the flame who repulsed those he called "muckrakers seeking the dirt on Ernest." I think he came to believe I was not out to diminish or denigrate the man, but to destroy the mystique that had distorted him, because, after several interviews he said, "I truly wish you the best of luck with the book."

Valuable insight came from two men in their nineties: artist Henry Strater, 91, and writer George Seldes, 96. Strater was still painting and living less than ten miles from me. Seldes, who lives in Vermont, has recently published his remarkable memoirs, *Witness to a Century*. Both men, their memories apparently sharp and detailed, had vivid tales to tell of the Hemingway they knew in the 1920s and 1930s.

When, for a time, I ran out of leads I wrote to the *New York Times Book Review* hoping to hear from anyone who had known Hemingway. Thirteen replied. One correspondent wanted to be my agent. I already had one. Another offered to be my researcher. My wife shared that role with me. A third—a poet, perhaps—sent a postcard with a vague return address and no phone number, claiming to have been Hemingway's drinking buddy. "Drank plenty grappa with Papa," he scrawled. My attempts to find him through the postmark were fruitless. Grappa with Papa was his entire revelation.

Several people who replied had new and interesting information about Hemingway which I used.

The most colorful response was from a woman who told how, as an eighteen year old in World War II, she had traveled from the north to

Key West to meet her sailor husband, due to disembark within a few days. But she couldn't find a place to stay in the overcrowded town. Then a burly, bearded stranger came to her aid and escorted her around Key West while snacking on watermelon. It was a hot day and they stopped for a drink. Trying to appear sophisticated, she ordered a Tom Collins. He laughed in a fatherly way and changed her order to iced tea. Eventually, thanks to his persistence, he found her an inexpensive room. During their peripatetic journey through Key West someone whispered to her that she was being escorted by the great Ernest Hemingway and several people greeted him as "Papa." She still remembered him clearly and with affection. The only flaw in her account was that Hemingway was in Europe at the time.

Why has this portrait of Hemingway taken almost two decades to complete, while my previous biographies of Tallulah Bankhead and J. B. Rhine took about three years apiece? Because to get essential information I had to play a waiting game. There was, for instance, Dr. Howard Rome, the Mayo Clinic psychiatrist who ordered Hemingway's electro-shock therapy. Dr. Rome steadfastly refused to discuss details of his patient's treatment with anyone, even fellow psychiatrists. He told me he had promised to keep their conversations secret forever. Fifteen years after Hemingway's suicide, Mary Hemingway's autobiography, *How It Was*, was published. In it she lambasted those caring for Hemingway in the hospital. According to her description his treatment resembled something Kafka and Lewis Carroll might have concocted. I read Dr. Rome both Mary's complaints and those of a psychiatrist who opposed shock treatment for Hemingway. Only then, to rebut Mary and the psychiatrist, did Dr. Rome give me his version of what took place, while still keeping his promise to Hemingway. I also had to wait until Mary Hemingway died in 1986 after a long illness for some to feel able to talk freely about her effect on Hemingway, as they saw it.

My aim in separating the man from the myth has been to humanize him and free him from his comic-strip image. A contemporary poet whose name escapes me said he intentionally led an uneventful life so that potential biographers would have nothing to write about him. To avoid exposure, Hemingway took the opposite tack, frequently acting as if he was a secret agent, and revealing only his convoluted cover story. This disguise overwhelmed any chance of "the true gen" emerging while he lived or soon after his death.

How did he, under almost constant scrutiny, get away with a lifetime of deception? Susan Lowrey Crist, a school friend, knew the answer. She had seen him in action. "Ernest," she said with affection and admiration, "was clever, mischievous, daring and imaginative."

Did he mean it when he said he longed for "the true gen" to be told about him and dreaded "the shit" that would be written after his death? After all, he made it inevitable by supplying the shovel.

Why? What had he got to hide?

CHAPTER
ONE

•

FIRST WAR,
FIRST LOVE,
FIRST WIFE

First War

Susan Lowrey Crist: Ernie and his sister Marcelline sat a few seats ahead of me for my last three years at Oak Park High School. He and Marc were on good terms and he seemed to share his thoughts with her. He often turned around in his seat, flashed a dimple, and said something humorous to his sister and the rest of us. He was fun, enthusiastic, and always creating situations, always laughing and carefree. I was in the orchestra several years with him, he scraping away on his cello and I tooting my clarinet nearby. Once, in the middle of a serious largo, he broke a string on his cello purposely to cause a commotion. We didn't drink, smoke, or have dope in those days, not like it is today.

Lewis Clarahan: For a while I was his best friend in high school and I never knew him to drink.

Carol Hemingway Gardner: Our family was absolutely teetotal and my mother didn't allow anything in the house.

MADELAINE HEMINGWAY MILLER: We were raised Congregational. We didn't bounce a ball on Sunday. We didn't monkey around or go to the movies as other kids might do. We went to visit other people and we went to church and sang in the choir. When we were home—Ernie, Uncle Tyler, and the maid had rooms on the third floor—we did what we were supposed to do.

SUSAN LOWREY CRIST: Evidently his family didn't approve of his dancing, because he never had dancing lessons [though he did go to some dancing classes], and he never asked a girl out. He was attractive enough, but I don't think he paid that kind of attention to them. He didn't ask for dates. That was all right with me. I did a lot of dating and dancing, but he never went to any of those dances. When the junior prom came his mother fixed it up that he took his own sister, Marcelline, for a partner. If any classmate can say he *ever saw* Ernie take a girl to a dance or a school party I don't know who it is. This seems hard to believe now we know he married four times.

LEWIS CLARAHAN: She's right. He didn't have any dates. He was good-looking and he got along well with his sisters, so I thought he would understand the girls pretty well, but he seemed to avoid girls. I don't think he was shy, but we didn't date as much as they do now; dating then was a very special thing. Ernest's father [Dr. Clarence Hemingway] was our family physician and my father was a U.S. postal inspector and a tennis fan. So we had a tennis court in our yard. Ernest was not at his best at tennis. But he didn't want to be beaten at anything, always wanted to be number one. He spent more time with me than with other friends because we lived on the prairie and he liked to get out there and shoot and box with me. He was bigger than me and knocked me out. After that I decided to quit boxing with him. One time he accidentally pulled the trigger on a shotgun and missed my head by a few inches, so I'm lucky to be here. He loved firearms and gunpowder and he took risks exploding small bombs in fields. His favorite sports were shooting and hunting. I didn't care for that; I don't like to kill things. All through his life he was a great hunter and he got that from his father. He was interested in wildlife, mainly as a hunter, and we often roamed the prairie north of us where there were pheasants, northern owls, ducks, and weasels. Ernest usually carried a rifle on our hikes. One time he was shooting at blackbirds and accidentally peppered a cabin in the line of fire. Out came the owner with a gun and we ran for home. We also roamed the Des Plaines River area near Ernest's home, where we fished and canoed and swam without bathing suits at a secluded spot. We slept out several nights and were evicted from one site. On our longest hike, to Lake Zurich about thirty-five miles north of Oak Park, Ernest called home and was told he had a new brother, Leicester. When we reached the lake some of our group opened a cottage window and slept in the beds there.

SUSAN LOWREY CRIST: Ernest was outstanding even then and Lew can tell you how he would shout things out to the trees—thoughts, ideas, sentences, as they went along.

LEWIS CLARAHAN: Yes, it was on our longest hike that I first witnessed his dramatic instincts. We took a boat to Frankfort and hiked from there to Petoskey and Walloon Lake. The purser on the boat had to quiet us because we were making such a noise. When we were walking along on the hike, Ernest made up startling stories and situations and shouted them up to the trees.

SUSAN LOWREY CRIST: If Ernie wanted Lew to listen to what he had to say, he'd stand him up against a tree and thump him in the chest a little bit to hold his attention.

LEWIS CLARAHAN: He loved drama and I don't think he lied, but he would exaggerate any little incident. He liked to pretend to insult you, but he'd laugh when he did it and it didn't mean anything. He was always looking for excitement and action, and he wanted to stir things up. At Walloon Lake we slept in a small shed and rowed over to Windemere, the Hemingway's summer home, for meals. I caught more brook trout in Horton Creek than he did, but I promised Ernest not to boast about it. Did he ask me to promise? I can't remember. He was a very close friend of Harold Sampson's and had Sampson come up to Windemere with him. I can't recall a single quarrel between us, but Ernie argued frequently with Harold about anything he could make up. The quarrels were always something he trumped up to make it exciting. That was his way. Ernie and I got along fine. He was a very nice guy and popular among the other guys at high school. He didn't ever say he wanted to be a writer, but he took me up to the third floor of his home and pulled out the last page of a story he had just written. Then he read it all to me. He was very excited about it and was sure he'd written something good [probably "The Judgment of Manitou," published in the high-school yearbook *Tabula* in February 1916]. I can't recall what I thought of it.

PETER GRIFFIN [author of *Along with Youth: The Early Years*]: In the very early years I was surprised to find that Hemingway's mother held his grandfather, Ernest Hall, up to him as an ideal, and held her husband, Ernest's father, in contempt. And Hemingway hated his mother for holding his father in contempt. And also for making him try to earn her love—"if you love me you'll do as I say and be like Ernest Hall, my father." I was surprised to find that man played such a powerful role in Hemingway's early life. He writes about it in *For Whom the Bell Tolls*, where he says his mother was a bitch, his father a coward, and his grandfather a hero. And he wished he could talk to his grandfather. Hemingway's mother used to write to him that his Grandfather Hall was the ideal to which every man should aspire, courageous, chivalrous, and idealizing women.

SUSAN LOWREY CRIST: Ernest was a good writer. In high school he turned out the best writing in English classes. He and I were two of the six editors of *Trapeze*, our school paper, in our senior year. [Ernest was editor and Susan and Ernest's sister Marcelline were associate editors.] I was also president of the Girls' Rifle Team. Our motto was "To shoot straight and think straight." Ernest had to fill a hole in the school paper one week, and being clever, mischievous, daring, and imaginative, he invented a Boys' Rifle Club, and listed names of friends as members. Each week he wrote something about the club that didn't exist. Then the school yearbook asked for a photo of club members. Ernie was the only one who owned or had even fired a gun. So he quickly borrowed shotguns for the rest of them and had a photo taken.

LEWIS CLARAHAN: He was a charming, enthusiastic person and so outgoing. He just used to make things exciting. He called me up when a steamer, the *Eastland*, turned over in the river and sank, and he wanted me to rush down with him to see it. We saw the steamer turned over but were too late to see any bodies.

CAROL HEMINGWAY GARDNER: I wouldn't say I idolized him on and on, but I certainly did as a young person and I have very good memories of him.

SUSAN LOWREY CRIST: After high school I went away to college and he went to work as a reporter for six months on the *Kansas City Star*.

LEWIS CLARAHAN: He wanted to fight in the war but his eyesight wasn't good enough. [From birth, Hemingway was virtually blind in one eye.] So he volunteered to be an ambulance driver and was accepted.

DENIS BRIAN: He wrote to his parents from New York during a nine-day stopover telling them that he was engaged to marry a movie star, Mae Marsh. They were in shock and insomniacs until he sent them a telegram explaining it was just a joke.

JOHN MILLER: Soon after, Hemingway and I met on the *Chicago*, the ship taking us Red Cross volunteers from New York to Europe. He earned his several shipboard nicknames: his friends called him Ernie or Hemmy, others called him General Nuisance. I thought he was a garrulous nut and tended to agree with the discerning, elderly chap who called him Blabber-mouth and Loudmouth. He expressed himself in a crude and clumsy way. Some called him witty; if he was it was wit of the brittle, even heartless kind. On the train taking us from France to Italy six of us shared a compartment. Then the door slid back with a bang and Hemingway entered. "Move over guys! Make room for me!" I didn't need to open my eyes to know he was tight; I could smell the evidence. But he didn't act like a drunk. He reminded me of an expression my father used: "he'd been slapped with a beer towel." Hemingway was playacting. Everything about him showed he wanted to impress us with his toughness—like spitting over his shoulder. I was nearest the door and he said to me, "Move over, you son-of-a-bitch, make room for me!" I demanded an apology for calling my mother a bitch. He aimed his fist at me and I dodged it and knocked off his fatigue cap. Suddenly all the other feet in the compartment hit the floor and we were held apart. Someone said, "Beat it, Hemingway. You can see we're full up." Next morning, he came in looking sheepish and confessed to being "drunker than hell last night." He offered me his hand and I took it. That was the start of a brief friendship. What I registered regarding his literary inclinations then was his feverish admiration for the writings of Ring Lardner. I think he copied Lardner's style. When we reached Italy the bulk of our ambulance work was transporting soldiers stricken with malaria and quite a few with self-inflicted wounds. They put a loaf of bread between the muzzle of their carbines and the palms of their hands and pulled the trigger, making a clean hole since the bread absorbed the gunpowder. That way they got themselves a trip away from the war for as long as it took the wound to heal. We were stationed near the Piave river, which was no man's land between the Italian and the enemy—the Austrian—trenches. We couldn't see the river because the land was lower than the river's level and on the Italian side the river was bordered with a ridge of earth about ten feet high. The marshland around us was ebony black and gave off a musty odor reminiscent of the Minnesota swamps where peat moss seemed always to hug the morning mist. I had to drive past an Austrian sniper overhead and about a thousand feet away. He sat in a wicker undercarriage hanging from a sausage balloon and attached to a truck below by a taut cable. This was the single stretch of road where I didn't have to drive the ambulance slowly because of shell holes. I opened her up and sometimes shouted at the sniper: "Kiss my royal rectum!"

I had signed a card at my hometown church, Glen Avon, swearing never to drink intoxicating liquor. My downfall came in Italy. I had lost a lot of weight and grown very weak. They drained our well—where we got our drinking water—and found at the bottom of it a skunk, three cats, seven rats, and various birds. After that, I always washed my spaghetti down with wine. For a few weeks in June shellfire was only sporadic. Then the Austrians crossed the river Piave for their last, ferocious battle.

DENIS BRIAN: After driving the sick and wounded for three weeks, Hemingway volunteered for a job closer to the action—working in a canteen for the troops. Even that was too tame for him. Instead of waiting for the men to leave the trenches for chocolates and cigarettes, he went to them, at first by bicycle and then on foot to the trenches.

JOHN MILLER: Ernest and I shared similar experiences. We civilian, unsalaried volunteers were now in the thick of the fighting without having had an hour's drill. The guns, the tear gas, the bloody soldiers, the stench of rotting horses and human flesh combined to make it a ghastly nightmare. Overnight we became veterans, and were skilled at judging by their whine where shells would burst. If shrill, we knew they'd spin harmlessly overhead. If they stuttered we had to lie flat quickly. When we heard nothing it would be too late to either be afraid or be relieved. It was the silent shell that had your number. Now as I drove the wounded and dying I passed trucks with Arditi, Italian shock troops, some of them ex-convicts released from prison for frontline combat. The air always smelled acid and when the earth was indistinct and shimmering with mist creeping toward us we knew to wear our gas masks. When one shell exploded near me I displayed a bit of shell shock, combined body tremors and tears, neither of which I could control. It hit me spasmodically for years afterwards, once when I was watching Lew Ayres in the World War I movie *All Quiet on the Western Front*.

DENIS BRIAN: Varying accounts of Hemingway's exploits generally agree with the following. It was close to midnight on July 8, 1918, hot and humid, when Hemingway cycled from the deserted farmhouse in Fossalta where he kept his supplies. He handed out chocolate bars and cigarettes to men in the trenches, then moved toward an advanced listening post closer to the river and the enemy guns. A trench mortar exploded near him. He felt as if hurled into a blast furnace, then fainted. He came to, paralyzed with one dead soldier lying near him and another soldier gasping or crying in pain. When he was able to move he somehow managed to take the wounded man with him toward safety. But after about fifty yards a machine gun bullet smashed into his right knee and another into his right foot. That's all he remembered until he found himself lying in a dugout and soaked in blood. An Italian officer told Hemingway that he had carried the wounded soldier back with him. Nobody, Hemingway included, could explain how he had pulled off this seeming miracle—covering the final hundred yards to the dugout, his legs a gory mess, both knees smashed, one by a bullet, the other by shrapnel, and with a bullet in his foot. To do it carrying or dragging another wounded man appeared impossible. After lying among the dead and dying for two hours, Hemingway was given a shot of morphine, then evacuated to the American Red Cross Hospital in Milan. Soon afterwards John Miller caught up with him there. Miller had survived the polluted water and the shell-shock spasms only to be stricken with pneumonia.

JOHN MILLER: I was soon visiting Hemingway and hearing how he had connected with a trench mortar. I sat at his bedside watching him pry out a piece of steel that had wiggled its way to the surface of his skin. When he picked the steel loose he dropped it into a pillbox and tabulated the number recovered on a pad. Eventually, the total count was over two hundred. The pillbox looked harmless but those fragments of steel had played havoc with a number of nerves, damaging them into long-lasting numbness. Hemingway was the first American, or at least one of the first Americans wounded in World War I, and was awarded the Italian Silver Medal for heroism.

AGNES VON KUROWSKY STANFIELD [Hemingway's nurse in the Milan hospital]: Oh, for heaven's sake, he was no hero! He got the injuries because he did something that was against orders. They told him to keep away from the front because he was just a boy giving out cigarettes and stuff like that. He went right up to where the fighting was to hand out chocolates to some of his friends. There was a big explosion and he saw a soldier he knew fall, and he jumped over a fence and got a lot of shrapnel in his legs. But I never heard about him carrying a wounded man to safety.

WILLIAM STANFIELD, JR. [Agnes's husband]: I think the reason my wife didn't know of Hemingway's bravery was that at that time of life every-thing might have been a joke. My wife told me that Hemingway had no business being where he was when he got wounded. He was a Red Cross ambulance driver; he wasn't with the United States Army.

JOHN HEMINGWAY: My father never told me how he got the Silver Medal, just that he won it. I have to mention that he also said he was in the Arditi, the elite Italian shock troops, which I don't think he was. Everybody seemed to think my father had earned the medal. But I was in the Third Infantry Division in World War II, and we had more special medals for valor than any other division in the U.S. Army. I suspect that's because the fellow who wrote the recommendations was a better writer than the rest of them. They were superb troops, but the man who writes the recommendations, and what the policy is at the Division toward how they're handled, makes a difference on what you get. If your senior officer likes you, you've got a chance of getting a medal if something happens. But I think it's quite unusual for someone who's an ambulance driver, stretcher-bearer, and candy distributor to get a serious medal. Someone must have thought he'd done something above and beyond those duties.

PHILIP YOUNG [author of *Ernest Hemingway*]: I can't see how it's physio-logically possible for Hemingway to have carried a wounded Italian soldier back with him after being blown up by a mortar and then shot in the knee. I've never understood how he could carry the other guy, after losing his kneecap.

DENIS BRIAN: Whether or not he lost his kneecap and had an aluminum implant is debatable. Although, in a January 1951 letter to his friend and critic Harvey Breit, Hemingway wrote that, after being blown up, when he put his hand on his knee it wasn't there.

MICHAEL REYNOLDS [author of *Hemingway's First War*]: Carrying a man was an act of heroism and I've no doubt it took place. But his actually being where he was, was accidental. There's a period in the 1920s when Hemingway was very shy about his biography, his own life. His editor, Maxwell Perkins, put out a biographical blurb on Hemingway which infuriated him. He asked Perkins to take it out of circulation and not to write any more.

DENIS BRIAN: Yes, I recall a Hemingway letter to Perkins telling him that if Scribner's publicity department portrayed him as a hero, it would make him look a fool or liar to those who knew the facts. He claimed then to have been only a minor camp follower briefly attached to the Italian infantry, and that he was wounded and given four Italian decorations simply because he was attached to the army. He pointed out that the *Croce di Guerra* was given to him for transporting the wounded under heavy bombardment, when at the time he was a hospital patient hundreds of miles away. In *A Farewell to Arms*, Hemingway's protagonist says he was blown up while eating cheese and he didn't carry anyone on his back because he couldn't move.

MICHAEL REYNOLDS: In the short story called "Soldier's Home," the narrator says: "Nobody's really interested in what happened in the war, and you start making up stories to make it sound more exciting." Hemingway himself probably had done that, because there are some really strange stories that other people heard in the 1920s about Hemingway's war experiences which simply weren't true.

DENIS BRIAN: And perhaps Hemingway was furious with Perkins because he didn't want to perpetuate these lies in print.

ARTHUR WALDHORN [author of *A Reader's Guide to Ernest Hemingway*]: You get an echo of Hemingway's reluctance to be called a hero in *A Farewell to Arms*, where Frederic Henry didn't perform a heroic act, but they wanted to give him a medal for being wounded. And in the short story about the major, "In Another Country," where Nick Adams is given a medal not for any great deed, where he is really just a spectator.

CARLOS BAKER [author of *Ernest Hemingway: A Life Story*]: Hemingway was afraid it might be discovered that he had been giving out cigarettes and chocolates to soldiers on the front lines when the explosion took place. This would not be entirely to his credit, because he had often hinted that he fought with the Italian troops—which was not true. It sounds credible to me that Hemingway's modesty and apparent attempts to play down being called a hero may also have been because he had suffered shell shock and as a result of the wounding had a mental breakdown. Also, he was unconscious during his so-called act of heroism, and he might have felt ashamed to claim or acknowledge heroism for something he didn't even remember doing.

DENIS BRIAN: There's a clue to his uncharacteristic modesty in a 1938 letter to his then mother-in-law, Mary Pfeiffer. He wrote that as a result of being wounded and frightened in World War I, the fear and suffering had given him a sort of humility and understanding and decency. Yet the talk of his heroism persisted.

LEICESTER HEMINGWAY: Ernest's real life was fantastic, but see, everybody in the whole world has got a Walter Mitty complex. Ernest wanted to appear to be something else than he was, just as everyone else does. He always wanted to be a little bit more mysterious, a little bit more honcho, a little bit more of an influence, a little bit more of the guy behind the scenes than he ever really was. He would con distant people and new friends. He didn't try to con his kid brother. As far as I know he invariably played it straight with me. I honestly can't think of a concrete incident in which Ernesto lied to me. He may have exaggerated in a few instances, but I don't think I ran into any actual lie. He wanted to be more than Superman. He wanted to be Superman's older brother. He didn't actually fight in World War I. He carried stuff for the Arditi. He was in there close. He messed with their people. He was useful, he was courageous, he was curious. And we know you're credited a lot of times with courage when you're simply being curious and don't have the brains to be scared. There's no question he realized he had been heroic. I think what he started to do was almost automatic. You know, you grab someone who you think is still alive and you say: "Hey, I'm in the Red Cross business. I have to get this guy to where he can be helped." You grab him up and you carry him. I did hear that he not only took a sniper's rifle away from him, but also killed the sniper. I know he shipped the rifle home and claimed he had accounted for the guy. I don't claim that this is absolutely true.

First Love

HENRY VILLARD [World War I ambulance driver]: I was recovering from jaundice and malaria in an adjoining room to Hemingway, and I often visited him. As the youngest and most severely wounded patient, he was the talk of the hospital. And we often discussed Agnes von Kurowsky, his beautiful nurse with a mischievous sense of humor.

AGNES VON KUROWSKY STANFIELD: Hemingway was a good patient as patients go. He had a lot of leg trouble and he liked to make a lot of it, but I guess it was really painful. He had little pellets under the skin and he was digging them out for a long time. I couldn't tell how his worst wound was because it was dressed, covered up. And he had one operation. [He had two.] That's all I know about it. He was gay and full of fun and he loved to talk to people. Some Italian officers used to come to see him because they thought he was fascinating. I only knew him for about three months. There was nothing serious between us. He and I were just friends, and I was taking care of him. I wasn't attracted to him at first. He was my patient, and I was more on night duty than the other nurses because they hated it and I didn't mind it. I slept well in the daytime and they didn't. I eventually got very tired of him because he was very egotistical, so sure he was always right.

JOHN MILLER: Hemingway had his Agnes in the hospital we were both confined to, and I thought another nurse, Ruth Brooks, was for me. I misinterpreted her tenderness for the real thing. When she bent one night to warm the jacket they'd strapped me in (as a guard against the high fever), she planted a kiss on my forehead. That I took to be affection beyond the call of a nurse's duty. I thought myself desperately in love with her. The night following the kiss, when it was time for lights out I pulled her down to kiss her on the lips. For this I got a most unexpected and un-nurselike slap. Later, I thought I overheard her giggling with Agnes when they were having midnight tea in the medicine room near my room. I was wounded to the quick. Next day I dressed, sneaked out of the hospital, and drank a pint of Martell at the nearest bar. I faced a belligerent Miss De Long, our hospital supervisor, when I got back. "You foolish boy!" she said. "We were about to have the carabinieri make a citywide search for you. You have degraded the standing of my hospital, and now you are just plain goofy-eyed drunk. Get to your room!"

I wove an uncertain way to bed and fell into it without undressing. Ruth didn't attend me that night. Miss MacDonald did. Mac was certainly no beauty to lose your heart over and she undressed me with all the expertise of a dutiful mother. She confided that Miss Brooks was reacting to a broken romance with an airman with whom she'd spent leave on Capri. And I had been party to her rebound. "You'll be laughing over this one day, laddie," she said to me. "Just you mark Elsie's words." She was right, of course. I've often laughed about my first romance. Soon after that, on September 18, 1918, Hemingway and I started ten days convalescent leave together. We went straight from the hospital to the bar next to La Scala opera house. Hemingway's wounds had healed, though he needed a cane when he walked. We were both weak in the knees, but the wine in that bar did wonders for us. We shared two bottles of Asti Spumanti, the same wine he bribed the hospital porter to fetch him many times while bedridden. Agnes used to remove the empty bottles, but I'm sure Miss De Long knew of the smuggling of the wine bottles. In fact, I overheard her lecturing the porter about it. She didn't lecture Agnes because she knew there was a bit of romance going on between Agnes and Ernesto. On our train ride north, girls waved to us from every small-town platform we passed.

The night we arrived at Stresa on Lake Maggiore, after our first meal at the Grand Hotel, Ern and I sauntered out to the hotel's private pier. We stood marveling at Isola Bella, like a jewel in the darkening waters of the lake. Beyond, we saw the purple mountains of Switzerland catching the last rays of the sun. It was breathtaking. "Jeezus!" Ern said. "Who wouldn't recuperate up here! This beats paradise all to hell!" As we walked back to the hotel, pausing to look at a small armada of boats along the pier, I said, "Whaddya say we snitch one of these dinghies, row across to Switzerland, and get ourselves interned for the duration?" "Good idea," Ern said. I like to think I deserve credit for the part of the story in *A Farewell to Arms* where the lovers escape to Switzerland by rowboat. Back in the hotel we became friendly with a bearded gentleman, Pier Vincenzo Bellia, from Torino. He called us his adopted sons. He was there with his wife and three daughters. All the drinks were on him and the second night he invited us to be his guests at dinner. Bianca, youngest of the three girls, sat across from us. She had a rich contralto laugh and black eyes that sparkled mischievously when I fought with my limited vocabulary to reply to her many questions. She had a child's curiosity, wanted to know all about life in America in one dinner hour. Next day we all went to Mottarone. Bianca and I shared a seat in the cable car to the top of the mountain. Ern sat with the Signora and the two of them got along nicely, as Ern had a grasp of French as well as a better Italian vocabulary than I had.

DENIS BRIAN: Bianca Bellia told writer Giovanni Cecchin some sixty years later that Hemingway had proposed to her during his convalescent leave at Lake Maggiore, and wanted her to follow him back to the United States.[1] He was hurt, Bianca told Cecchin, when she declined his proposal. Her father had written to John Miller on February 12, 1919: "I stopped in Milan; I saw Ernest; he was well and he promised me to visit us at the end of the year, having to sail for America in January, but since that day I know nothing about him. It is some day since I sent to the

[1] Reported in *Stampa Sera*, an Italian newspaper, August 17, 1981.

American Red Cross of Milan a telegram asking news of him. They answer to me saying Hemingway sailed for America on January 6. I regret for [not] having seen him any more. If you write to him send for him my best love." Is it plausible that Bianca had second thoughts and decided to accept Hemingway's marriage proposal after discussing it with her parents? That would explain her father's effort to contact Hemingway.

CARLOS BAKER: It's not unlikely that a nineteen year old, abroad and in wartime, should ask an attractive young woman to marry him, even if he was in love with another woman.

MICHAEL REYNOLDS: I'll tell you what I know about the evidence that Hemingway had another girl in Italy apart from Agnes. At Stresa, Hemingway met Count [Emanuele] Greppi but he also met another family. There are letters from Hemingway home to his parents talking about the family: father, mother, and daughter. The parents treated him like a son and were kind to him in Stresa on Lake Maggiore, and apparently they stayed in touch back in Milan. Hemingway does not mention the daughter especially in his letters. She was very attractive and I wouldn't be surprised if Hemingway was attracted to her. Beyond that I don't have any evidence that the relationship went any further. But he was nineteen years old and just beginning to realize he was very attractive to women. That was not what he had experienced at Oak Park at the high school. So I'm sure he was interested in her, but my guess would be that he never really proposed marriage to Bianca Bellia.

LEICESTER HEMINGWAY: I don't believe it. Aggie was the only dame he had anything to do with over there.

DENIS BRIAN: Carlos Baker's detailed biography told of Hemingway playing billiards with and learning politics from Count Emanuele Greppi, also a guest at the Grand Hotel on Lake Maggiore. In a not elaborate attempt at disguise, Hemingway names him Count Greffi in *A Farewell to Arms*. Bianca Bellia told her interviewer, Cecchin, that Count Greffi was an amalgam of the count and her father. If Greppi was in fact at the hotel, John Miller seems to have missed him. But then he also missed Hemingway's romantic interlude with Bianca—if it occurred.

MALCOLM COWLEY: Another mystery in Hemingway's life is what did he do after he finished his convalescent leave and before he returned to the United States.

MATTHEW BRUCCOLI [author of *Scott and Ernest*]: Several weeks are unaccounted for, and the clue seems to be this Gamble figure. I've never been able to find out much about Gamble beyond the fact that he had a great deal of money.

PETER GRIFFIN: Yes. Carlos Baker had mislabeled him as as one of the Gambles of Proctor and Gamble. But he wasn't. He had nothing to do with that family. He was a member of the Voorhees family in Williamsburg, Pennsylvania. They were very wealthy and his grandfather was a railroad president. Gamble was an artist and a Yale graduate. He lived in Florence, Italy, and was about twelve years older than Ernest. Gamble married one or more heiresses. He spoke fluent Italian. He said he loved Ernest and Ernest said he loved Gamble.

DENIS BRIAN: Was he homosexual?

PETER GRIFFIN: The letters I've seen between the two of them do not indicate that in any way. They indicate a very warm intimate, male friendship.

DENIS BRIAN: Captain Jim Gamble had been in charge of rolling canteens for the American Red Cross. A bachelor, he had left his Philadelphia home to live in Florence, Italy. Agnes had talked Hemingway out of accepting Gamble's offer to stay in Italy for a year, ostensibly as his secretary, with a chance to tour Europe at Gamble's expense. Nevertheless, without telling Agnes, he joined Gamble for a brief vacation in Taormina, Sicily, where they shared a small house rented from an English artist. There, pleasantly loaded, they strolled by the moonlit sea and talked far into the night. In *A Farewell to Arms* Hemingway hinted at this surreptitious visit, where Frederic Henry says to Rinaldi: "I went everywhere. Milan, Florence, Rome, Naples, Villa San Giovanni, Messina, Taormina. . . ." He also told his friend Eric Dorman-Smith that he saw little of the Sicilian landscape and that only from a bedroom window, because the woman in charge of the hotel where he stayed stole his clothes. She kept him to herself for a week, he said, feeding him well and showing him considerable affection.

ARTHUR WALDHORN: The epic brag.

DENIS BRIAN: Although, when a selection of Hemingway's letters was published in 1981, one to Gamble established the fact of their joint visit to Sicily shortly after the end of World War I.

LEICESTER HEMINGWAY: He was considered slightly an outcast when he came back from the war because his class had already graduated and most of them were working or away at college.

LEWIS CLARAHAN: I'd written to him when he was in Italy but never got an answer from him. But when he came back home he called me up and asked me to walk over to the high school with him. His old English teacher, Frank Platt, had arranged for Ernest to talk before a group there.

FRANK PLATT [who taught Ernest and Marcelline freshman English]: I was at my desk in the Oxford Room in the autumn of 1919 when he appeared at the door, leaning nonchalantly against the entrance as if to say, "I'm home again. It's nice to be here!" After hearing some of his thrilling war stories, I suggested that he come to the Burke Debating Club that night and talk to the boys. At that session debating was tabled and Hemingway was given the floor. As he related the climax of his adventure, he produced his brown uniform—pants, coat, and shoes—and passed them out with an invitation to count the bullet holes in the riddled garment. It was most amusing to see forty high-school boys, who had known him as an upperclassman, examining with infinite care the deadly rents in his clothes. There was some laughter, but there was an undertone of feeling as to what war can mean to a man. This was a proud warrior's return to Oak Park, showing the dents in his shield.

LEICESTER HEMINGWAY: He was enormously lonely. The people he went and talked to at Oak Park High School were there a year after his class had already graduated. There's nothing worse than talking to your juniors. It's an easy thing to be a hero to people who don't know what it's like to have been out in the big, wide, real world. It also makes you a little bit of a scoutmaster coming to talk to a new class of Boy Scouts. You're not in your own league any more.

FRANK PLATT: Shortly after his talk the Italian Consul and his friends came from Chicago to honor Ernest, bringing Italian food, wine, and musical instruments with them.

CAROL HEMINGWAY GARDNER: The first time I saw any liquor in the house was when Ernest came home from the war and that Italian-American organization came out and gave him a great party and brought wine. I had never seen wine in the house before that. But I'm sure Ernest had quite a few drinks when he was in the hospital in Milan.

FRANK PLATT: After three such parties that rocked the neighborhood with music and noise, Ernest's father said: "No more parties!"

LEWIS CLARAHAN: Although he apparently had all these wounds in his legs he was able to walk all right. He seemed to be just the same as I had known him before, friendly to all, enjoying people, but liking his independence all the time. He didn't seem changed at all. He kind of avoided his mother because she was quite strict, but I don't remember him saying anything derogatory about her.

MADELAINE HEMINGWAY MILLER: I went up to Ernie's third-floor room at his invitation. It was quite a privilege to get that far away from the hubbub in the rest of the house, but you only went by invitation. So when I went to Ernie's room I said, "Oh, I'm dying to see some of your pictures." And he said, "Not yet, Numbones; I can't show them yet." It all came about in a gradual way that we drank, and then he let me smoke a cigar. During that time Ernie longed for Agnes to join him, wrote her long letters, and eagerly awaited her replies.

DENIS BRIAN: When you were Hemingway's nurse in the Milan hospital, Mrs. Stanfield, Carlos Baker says that you called Ernest Kid and yourself Mrs. Kid.

AGNES VON KUROWSKY STANFIELD: He was getting childish and he wrote to me twice a day when I was on night duty. He'd write a note and the girls would bring it to me when I woke up at four in the afternoon.

DENIS BRIAN: In your letters to him you called him "the light of my existence, my dearest and best, most earnest of Ernies."

AGNES VON KUROWSKY STANFIELD: I didn't say all that [laughs]. That's some of his writing.

DENIS BRIAN: No, that's what you called him.

AGNES VON KUROWSKY STANFIELD: I didn't.

DENIS BRIAN: You mean Hemingway and not you wrote that?

AGNES VON KUROWSKY STANFIELD: He was the writer, after all.

DENIS BRIAN: Here's what you wrote in another letter to Hemingway: "Gosh, if only you were here I'd dash in and make you up about now and you'd smile at me and hold out your brawny arms. What's the use of wishing!" [She didn't respond.] Was your feeling then that you were a friend, and not in love with him?

AGNES VON KUROWSKY STANFIELD: He thought it was a romance, but I didn't. I was older than he was. I was twenty-six and he was just nineteen. He was so angry with me because I sent him home. He had an offer from Jim Gamble who had money and offered to take him on a tour of Europe after the war, and I told him to go home and see his family first. This man Gamble was fond of him, admired his vigor and all that. So Hemingway went home and didn't get any trip. And he didn't like it. So he was really down on me then.

DENIS BRIAN: And even more so when you wrote to him saying you were not going to marry him.

AGNES VON KUROWSKY STANFIELD: When I was going home to the United States I wrote to an elderly nurse who had gone ahead of me, and she wrote to Hemingway and told him I was coming home. And he said, "I hope she falls down and knocks her front teeth out on the dock!" That was the way he felt about me. It adds a funny touch.

DENIS BRIAN: He felt that you had jilted him and now you, in turn, had been jilted by an Italian officer, Domenico Caracciolo. And Hemingway told a friend he felt sorry for you.

AGNES VON KUROWSKY STANFIELD [laughs]: I don't believe that.

DENIS BRIAN: When he got that letter from you, saying you were not coming home to marry him and he should look for a younger woman, the shock sent him to bed for several days and then into a deep depression. A psychiatrist, Dr. Irving Yalom, believes that your jilting Hemingway caused a profound and enduring emotional injury; part of his evidence is that Hemingway wrote of it not only in *A Farewell to Arms* but in "A Very Short Story."

AGNES VON KUROWSKY STANFIELD: He put everybody he knew in his book *A Farewell to Arms*. Everybody was recognized right away, although I didn't recognize myself in it. I thought Catherine was a made-up character.

DENIS BRIAN: Psychiatrists Irvin and Marilyn Yalom wrote in the *Archives of General Psychiatry* in 1971: "While recuperating from his wounds in the first World War Hemingway fell deeply in love, probably for the first time, with Agnes von Kurowsky. . . . When Agnes chose another man, Hemingway was plunged into despair."

AGNES VON KUROWSKY STANFIELD: I didn't know any other man. I met the Italian army officer, Caracciolo, a long time after I'd broken up with Hemingway. Caracciolo was in love with me, but I wasn't in love with him. I was just a stranger. He was in the Italian army and he was with other soldiers where we nurses were stationed. They were very lonely and they used to come and see us, that was all. Caracciolo was very jealous: he threw away all the letters I had from Hemingway, so I didn't have any of his letters as souvenirs. It's not true, as Carlos Baker wrote, that I went to meet Caracciolo's parents in Naples. I was fascinated by him but never expected to marry him.

HENRY VILLARD: The most I witnessed of any romance between Ernest and Agnes was their brief hand-holding under cover of her taking his temperature. So I was astonished and shocked eleven years later when I read *A Farewell to Arms*. Much of the novel covered the overwhelming Italian defeat by the Austrians at the battle of Caporetto. I knew Hemingway had not even been in Italy when that took place, but the scandalously explicit love scenes came across as personal experience.

In the novel, while everyone else slept, the nurse, Catherine Barkley, and her patient, Frederic Henry, despite his physical handicap which resembled Hemingway's, made love on the hospital bed. I wondered if under fictional guise Hemingway was reporting what actually happened while I was only a few feet away in the next room. I found the part of Catherine dying in giving birth to Henry's child was fictional, because I discovered Agnes was still alive. When I read the book I was U.S. vice consul in Teheran, Iran. I corresponded with Agnes and made several unsuccessful attempts at a reunion, intending to ask to what extent Hemingway's portrayal of the romance had been wishful thinking. I finally met her again in 1975, when she welcomed me to her Gulfport, Florida, home. Now eighty-three, she told me she was the wife of a widower with three children, William Stanfield, Jr. I told Agnes I suspected the love scenes in *A Farewell to Arms* were simply how Hemingway would like things to have been. She said I was right, that she had never been Hemingway's mistress and that they had never made love.

WILLIAM STANFIELD, JR.: Some years ago a man wrote to Agnes from Chicago trying to browbeat her into admitting to having had a physical affair with Hemingway like the nurse in the novel. This stranger wrote that he knew it to be a fact because Hemingway had told him so, on condition he kept it a secret while Hemingway was alive.

DENIS BRIAN: In talking to his friend Eric Dorman-Smith about Agnes, Hemingway said that it takes a professional nurse to know how to make love to a man with his leg in a splint. The implication is obvious. Dorman-Smith mentioned this conversation in his published memoirs. Perhaps that was the source of the Chicago correspondent's misinformation.

WILLIAM STANFIELD, JR.: The idea of someone asserting that this particular nurse, meaning Agnes, was able to do a job in bed with Hemingway with his bad leg, well that isn't so.

DENIS BRIAN: What I don't understand is why your wife denies writing love letters to Hemingway when such letters exist.

WILLIAM STANFIELD, JR.: I believe in a better mood she would admit it. I have to say that she had written to him, because if there are those letters it is so. You can't get away from that. But when they go to these exorbitant things that are absolutely not so! I don't know how to tell you this but I feel sure in what knowledge I only get secondhand that Agnes had no serious sex intentions with either Hemingway or the Italian officer. I don't think she was very serious with any man until she was around thirty, thirty-two. And that happened in New York, long after this European thing was all over.

PETER GRIFFIN: Bill Horne, who met Hemingway as a fellow ambulance driver in World War I, had been saving his letters from Ernest to write a biography of Hemingway. Those letters clearly show that Ernest was profoundly in love with Kurowsky, that they were sleeping together, and that Hemingway was devastated when she rejected him and after that rejection he began writing like Hemingway for the first time. I think the real explosion that affected Hemingway was the broken heart Kurowsky gave him, not so much, as Philip Young said, being blown up. I think that had a profound effect on him in other ways. But that soul going out of his body experience was something Hemingway had as a young boy and it ran in the family—that out-of-body experience. He was a sleepwalker, too. In that unpublished Jimmy Breen novel he talks about when he was a boy and how his soul used to leave his body and go down the streets of Oak Park and float between the trees and how he partly enjoyed it and partly was afraid of it.

DENIS BRIAN: What's your evidence for saying that Ernest and Agnes slept together?

PETER GRIFFIN: In Agnes von Kurowsky's letters she writes about spending three days with Hemingway and the line is, "Remember how we spent three days together and you became restless and wanted some men friends along to do things with?" Words to that effect. And she writes to him about putting her face in a special place and going to sleep there.

DENIS BRIAN: They were more innocent in those days. She denied they ever slept together. Putting her face in a special place could be his neck.

PETER GRIFFIN: But they spent three days together and she wrote about, "I know what I'm going to give you when I get home." Bill Horne told me, and it's borne out by Johnny Miller's letter about an orgy at the hospital, that relationships between nurses and patients weren't all that unusual. This was wartime, too. Hemingway was an incredibly handsome guy and very appealing. Here are two people in love: Hemingway passionately in love with this woman and she's with him all the time in the most intimate physical way, she's his nurse and things like that are going on at the hospital. It's not that unusual. He wanted to marry Agnes and Bill Horne was to be the best man.

DENIS BRIAN: Another witness Henry Villard was skeptical about a physical affair.

PETER GRIFFIN: Villard was in love with Kurowsky. Bill Horne told me that Villard was in love with Kurowsky from the first time he saw her. Bill Horne is very protective of Hemingway. All the letters he has from Hemingway are in Hemingway's handwriting but there's one Bill Horne has transcribed and then he writes "six lines illegible" and later "ten lines illegible" and those lines were all about Kurowsky.

DENIS BRIAN: So you read between the lines that weren't there.

PETER GRIFFIN: And between the lines that were in some of the other stuff. When he wrote, "I make love to a girl and leave her and she needs somebody to make love to and if the right guy comes along you're out of luck." Maybe. Maybe not.

DENIS BRIAN: You also believe that Hemingway and his boyhood friend Kate Smith, who eventually married Dos Passos, were lovers.

PETER GRIFFIN: I don't think there's any question of that. My God, how could Meyers read Hadley's letters and not believe that? Hadley was jealous of Kate. She said, "Kate was in love with you" in a letter to Ernest. There was a lot of trouble about Kate being her maid of honor at the wedding. There's even a line in one of Hadley's letters about the possibility of Kate having had a child. A fellow named Smith at Trinity in Hartford spent part of his career checking on that. One time he was in Chicago and some woman came to his door claiming she was Hemingway's daughter. Probably a bunch of bullshit.

DENIS BRIAN: So it's likely he had an affair with Kate Smith but not positive.

PETER GRIFFIN: I don't have an eight-by-ten glossy. But come on!

DENIS BRIAN: Though, as Hemingway biographer Jeffrey Meyers wrote, "Hemingway portrays sex with women he never managed to sleep with in real life." So that you can make mistakes in thinking there's always fact in the fiction.

PETER GRIFFIN: Maybe that's true.

DENIS BRIAN: Instead of writing long letters to Agnes, after recovering from his depression Hemingway began writing human-interest stories. The *Toronto Star* printed ten of them at a halfpenny a word. After that they doubled the price. Then he took on what seemed for Hemingway an incongruous job—paid companion. While the rest of the Connable family were vacationing in Palm Beach, Hemingway lived in their luxurious Canadian home with their lame son, occasionally taking him to sporting events. When that job was over he daydreamed of emulating Jack London by shipping out to the Far East as a stoker. Instead, he returned home to celebrate his twenty-first birthday on July 21, 1920. Soon after, he and a pal, two of his sisters, and their girlfriends went on a secret midnight picnic. The girls' parents discovered their daughters missing and were distraught until they returned at three in the morning. Hemingway and his pal were blamed and suspected of intending to seduce the girls. Ernest's mother refused to hear his explanation—that he had gone as a chaperone. She said he was no longer welcome in her home and told him why in a harsh follow-up letter. Among her other complaints she said he was a loafer, a pleasure-seeker who borrowed without thought of repaying, who wasted money on luxuries for himself, traded on his looks to fool gullible little girls, and neglected his duties to Jesus Christ. Grace Hemingway concluded by writing that he would find her waiting for him, in this world or the next, her love restored—when he changed his ideas and ambitions to meet her approval.

LEICESTER HEMINGWAY: Here's the injured war hero who was jilted by the woman he loved, kicked out of his home practically on his twenty-first birthday. It was pretty hard on him, right? He was an oversensitive man. How long do you think this stayed with him? Maybe ten minutes, maybe years. I think he held pieces of it in his heart until the day he died, but I don't know how big the pieces were.

DENIS BRIAN: Hemingway strenuously resisted his mother's attempts to bring him to heel. His admiration for grace under pressure may have originated in his own pressure under Grace. According to more than one family member [who spoke on condition they not be identified] Hemingway had watched her emasculate his doctor father, and was determined not to suffer a similar fate.

CAROL HEMINGWAY GARDNER: That's ridiculous! He could make that up, of course, and believe it for a while. But he knew differently. My father was not all that weak a person by any means. Somehow, it's all been distorted. My father was a very busy, very active, and very interesting person who taught Ernest all he knew about woods and fishing and hunting and all the rest of it.

MADELAINE HEMINGWAY MILLER: Ernie depicts my mother as a nag. She was not. She was an artistic woman who was inclined to be dictatorial. She and my father agreed on how to run the family. Mother would joke with us and encourage us to be funny. Ernie would say some things in jest that could be taken as cruel. I have done the same thing. My mouth would open sometimes and things would come out—and then you realize you've said the wrong thing. Then I apologize. Ernie did the same. To say you're sorry is not wicked. He wanted to write a book about the family, but he said there were too many people still alive. He didn't want to hurt people. You give love and you get love back.

DENIS BRIAN: Banished from home, Hemingway moved to a friend's apartment in Chicago where he continued free-lance writing and looked for a job.

MICHAEL REYNOLDS: After Hemingway recovered from the shock of being jilted by Agnes von Kurowsky, he was involved with two or three girls simultaneously.

ARTHUR WALDHORN: I have seen letters to Hemingway and, allegedly, from women mentioned in Carlos Baker's biography, that speak of his prowess; boasting to the women what their sex life together had been, and the women protesting how dare he leave them for another one.

MADELAINE HEMINGWAY MILLER: I like to believe the nice things about Ernie. I cannot stand to believe the questionable things that writers put out. He was attracted to women and they were attracted to him. They were after him all the time. He was a macho kind of fellow and so handsome. The pictures you see now of this pitiful-looking soul was not Ernie in those days. He was as handsome as any movie star. And he had the carriage and interest in life that attracted people to him.

First Wife

DENIS BRIAN: Hemingway did not take Agnes's advice to look for a younger woman. Hadley Richardson was almost a carbon copy of Agnes von Kurowsky—within two months of her age, same height, similar blue eyes, and wry sense of humor. They met at a party in his friend's Chicago apartment in late October 1920, and married less than a year later. It was an uneventful ceremony except that he found it difficult to kneel because of his knee injury.

MICHAEL REYNOLDS: When he finally married Hadley, two girls wrote him very cold letters because they were surprised he had married her. I don't know whether he was misleading them or not, in the sense of what his intentions were. But, obviously, each felt she was special, and they were somewhat shocked when he got married.

DENIS BRIAN: The honeymoon may have been something of a shock to Hadley. She had already discovered that this tough guy was scared of thunderstorms. During the first week in the cottage, Windemere—Ernest temporarily restored to favor by his mother—they were both sick with influenza. She wrote in one of her letters how at the end of the week Hemingway went into Petoskey for supplies, and returned via a "borrowed" speedboat. But he'd had a few drinks, neglected to free the boat from the dock and so dragged part of it all the way back. Feeling lonely, Hadley had begun to walk through the woods to Petoskey. Part way there she saw Ernest trailing the wooden piling behind his speedboat. But she was glad to see him, even stewed, and she accepted his apology. Hadley was a near-perfect surrogate for Agnes; she also admired and encouraged his writing, and had a trust fund that produced about three thousand dollars a year. With this as a cushion they decided to live in Europe. They had recently become friends of Sherwood Anderson and his wife. Anderson, the successful author of *Winesburg, Ohio*, urged them to live on the Left Bank in Paris, among the lively American and British expatriate writers and painters. They took his advice. Soon after his arrival in Paris, Hemingway wrote Agnes von Kurowsky, telling of his marriage and plans to pursue a writing career aided by Sherwood Anderson's letters of introduction to Gertrude Stein, James Joyce, and Ezra Pound.

AGNES VON KUROWSKY STANFIELD: I was surprised to hear from him, but I wrote saying I was pleased to have an old friend back, and how proud I'd be one day to say I once knew him well. I never heard from him again.

TWO

·

PARIS: VICTORY;
TORONTO: DEFEAT

DENIS BRIAN: Arriving in Paris in a cold rainstorm in December 1921, the Hemingways stayed at the Hotel Jacob, then moved to a cramped, primitive apartment that Ernest called high grade. It was near the top of a hill that led to a lively market square of small stores, restaurants, and bars. They celebrated Christmas with dinner in a restaurant, then found they hadn't the money to pay the check. Hadley anxiously waited while Ernest hurried home to get more cash. She was afraid he'd never return, imagining him a traffic fatality or hopelessly lost in the unfamiliar streets. But he made it. He soon knew his way around, strolling through parks and narrow lanes crowded with carts piled with fruits, vegetables, and cheeses, finding warmth and entertainment in the friendly restaurants and art galleries. He and Hadley frequently called on Ezra Pound, as well as Gertrude Stein and Alice Toklas, who became close family friends. Hemingway met fellow writers at Stein's and Pound's, and fellow reporters at the Anglo-American Press Club and on assignments. Before long he was a presence in the city.

GEORGE SELDES: I was covering the Genoa Economic Conference for the *Chicago Tribune* in April 1922, when Hemingway was there representing the *Toronto Star*. Lincoln Steffens, the great muckraking reporter, as he was called, was also there. He asked me to bring a few people to a pub for conversation. And I brought Hemingway and Sam Spewack.[1] That was when we helped Hem write cablese. Later, he spoke about this as the time he discovered a new language.

MALCOLM COWLEY: Cablese is a curious language in which each word has to do the work of several. You omit everything you can take for granted. It's to save money in sending cables, of course. Well, this cablese contributed to Hemingway's literary method.

GEORGE SELDES: I think it was a coincidence and I rather like it, that the three great men of my time, Theodore Dreiser, Sinclair Lewis, and Ernest Hemingway, all became newspaper reporters to be newspaper reporters and not as a stepping stone to be novelists or something else.

ARCHIBALD MACLEISH: Lincoln Steffens was impressed with Hemingway and asked to see examples of his work. Ernest gave him a copy of the short story "My Old Man" and Steffens sent it off to a friend on *Cosmopolitan*, which was then more of a literary magazine than it is today.

HADLEY [RICHARDSON HEMINGWAY] MOWRER: Ernest had just returned from reporting the Genoa conference when he said he was leaving to cover the war between Greece and Turkey. They were fighting over a border dispute. I didn't want him to go and we quarreled about that and I didn't speak to him for several days. It was a rare thing for us to quarrel, but when we did we were both outspoken. He went and came back three weeks later, ill and exhausted. When Ernest was ill he was very sorry for himself. But then I took good care of him.

ADA MACLEISH: He was an emotional man and he acted up in strange ways from time to time. When he was faced with things, he sometimes just gave way. Ernest wasn't a very good patient; he was impatient, as most men are when they're ill.

HADLEY MOWRER: He suffered long and hard from his war wounds. I forget how many hundred pieces of shrapnel were taken out of his legs. People think his being blown up and those injuries affected him psychologically, but I really think he rose over that.

[1] Sam Spewack became a playwright and is coauthor of *Kiss Me Kate*, a musical version of Shakespeare's *Taming of the Shrew*.

DENIS BRIAN: Hemingway kept fit by shadowboxing and exploring Paris hand-in-hand with Hadley. When not writing his money-making articles for the *Toronto Star*, he whittled sentences into near-cablese, trying for accuracy, simplicity, and impact; toyed with a novel started in Chicago; and wrote bitter, bloodthirsty poems. They shared silent breakfasts: he asked Hadley not to talk then because he was already at work on his next sentence.

HENRY "MIKE" STRATER: Some girl sculptor took me to Ezra Pound's studio in the winter of 1922. Pound was a poet with a lot of influence in the literary world and he had open house at his studio. I was standing around feeling like a fool with this little cup of weak tea, and there was this big, handsome guy right next to me, Ernest Hemingway. He had just arrived in Paris as foreign correspondent for the *Toronto Star*. I said to him, "This is pretty weak stuff, isn't it?" He said, "It sure is. Would you like a drink?" I said, "I sure would." Then he pulled out a hip flask. He was just over from prohibition America, still carrying a hip flask. He asked, "What do you do for exercise in Paris?" I said, "I box." He leaped at that like a salmon at a trout fly and said, "What weight are you?" I said, "A hundred and ninety five." He said, "That's my weight. How about us boxing?" I said, "Sure. I've got two pairs of gloves. Come out to my studio tomorrow." So we hammered one another around for no pay for a couple of hours. And that was the beginning of our friendship.

DENIS BRIAN: Hemingway found another sparring partner in Ezra Pound—after teaching him to box. The ever helpful and somewhat battered poet sent six of Ernest's poems to *Dial* magazine, the leading literary magazine in America, with his recommendation, and almost persuaded the editor of *Little Review* to take one of Ernest's short stories. Though all were ultimately rejected, Hemingway was grateful to Pound for his encouragement. He hadn't much time to brood on these failures; he traveled far and frequently for the *Toronto Star*, as well as with Hadley for fun. He went to Turkey, Bulgaria, Austria, Switzerland, and Spain, rarely returning without succinct human-interest articles, flavored with his humorous and personal touches. He wrote two articles about Mussolini after twice interviewing the ex-reporter turned fascist dictator of Italy.

GEORGE SELDES: After those two interviews with him, Hemingway wrote of Mussolini's weak mouth and ridiculed him for wearing white spats with a black shirt. And he caught Mussolini trying to impress him by being absorbed in a book—which Hemingway noticed was being held upside down. That was all good. He also called Mussolini "the biggest bluff in Europe." He was right! Mussolini's whole life was full of bluff.

When I first met Mussolini in 1919 to 1920, we were newspapermen working together. Two or three times I went from my office to cover an uprising in the Fiat works at Turin, and there was a newspaperman from Milan—Mussolini. He used to call me "my dear colleague." Well, I was in Paris in 1924, and before I went back to Italy, Bill Ryall told me: "Grab all the documentary evidence you can find. Mussolini is changing history. He's suppressing the whole story of his past." I wouldn't have gotten anywhere with my political reporting without the help and guidance of Bill Ryall, who later used the pen name William Bolitho. Hemingway thought a lot of him, too. He was a South African working for the *Manchester Guardian*, who had been severely wounded in World War I. Hemingway and I learned about international politics from him. Now there were many statements in Hemingway's account in the *Toronto Star* for December 24, 1922, I knew to be false. For instance, Hemingway wrote: "Mussolini is often described as a 'renegade socialist,' but he seems to have had a very good reason for his renunciation of the party. . . . When war broke out in 1914, Mussolini was editor of *Avanti*, the socialist daily paper of Milan. He worked so strongly for Italy going into the war on the side of the Allies the management dispensed with his services and Mussolini founded his own paper, *Il Popolo d'Italia*, to set forth his views. He sank all his money on this enterprise and as soon as Italy entered the war, enlisted in the crack 'Bersagliere' as a private. Severely wounded in the fighting on the Corso plateau and several times decorated for valor, Mussolini, a patriot above all things . . ." Most of that is inaccurate.

DENIS BRIAN: But how did you get accurate information about Mussolini? Didn't he expel you from Italy in 1925?

GEORGE SELDES: Mussolini had me thrown out of Italy because I got documents proving he was implicated in the assassination of his opposition—the Socialist Matteotti. That was in the days before xeroxing. These were photographs of signed confessions. I was told: "You'll be killed if you send this out!" I said: "It's one of the biggest stories of the time," and I sent it to my newspaper the *Chicago Tribune*.

After I was expelled, I visited Italy secretly in 1931 and spoke with several American newspapermen in Rome. Then I discovered that Mussolini had been bribed with $50,000 by the French Foreign Office to start a newspaper favoring the Allies. As for his being wounded in the fighting—he wasn't. I had the advantage over Hemingway: I had a very good assistant, Camillo Cianfarra, who had been in the diplomatic service stationed at the Italian Embassy in Washington. He was very well informed and I relied entirely on him for the biographical facts about Mussolini. I'd say: "Cianfarra, how was Mussolini wounded?" And he'd say: "He was injured by the accidental or premature explosion of a shrapnel shell behind the lines—and in his behind," in his ass, or arse as Montaigne would have spelled it, not "in my legs," as Mussolini claimed. They all had a story: "Hurrah for Mussolini! He Abolished the Black Hand of the Mafia!" You know what he did with the Mafia? He *incorporated* them into the Blackshirts. When I interviewed Mussolini he treated me as if I were a police reporter and he was a big man. He would make statements like "The policy of my life is to live dangerously," and "My policy is to live beyond good and evil," and "When you go to a woman, don't forget your whip." Then he would look sideways at me, to see if I recognized that he was stealing from or quoting Nietzsche. Even in an interview he was trying to impress you with his greatness. I don't think for a moment that Hemingway deliberately falsified his report about Mussolini. Later, in fact, in Spain, Hemingway did more for antifascism than a lot of us did. But if he had tried he could easily have found out the facts of Mussolini's past.

DENIS BRIAN: Even allowing for the hype with which publications promote their own, clearly the *Toronto Star* recognized what it had in Hemingway. A blurb for his articles, on April 14, 1923, reads: "Hemingway has not only a genius for newspaper work but for the short story as well. He is an extraordinarily gifted and picturesque writer. His close-up pictures of Mussolini and Tchicherin (a Russian delegate at the Lausanne Economic Conference), his despatches from Genoa, Constantinople, and Rapallo, where he was sent by the *Star*, were followed by [sic] intense interest." What helped the twenty-four-year-old Hemingway become the instant political expert and discerning art critic was his eager willingness to learn from others: Bill Ryall, as George Seldes mentioned, was his political mentor; and Gertrude Stein helped him to appreciate Picasso, Pascin, Miro, Sisley, and Cezanne, to scrimp on clothes—especially Hadley's—and to invest in up-and-coming artists for profit and pleasure.

HENRY STRATER: At first, Hemingway was impressed by the fact that I had been hung in the salon in Paris, which was quite something. In 1922 he was only twenty-three and hadn't had any books published. A year later, things had changed.

HADLEY MOWRER: Ernest was very interested in art. He bought Joan Miró's *The Farm* and presented it to me. I could say things about it that show up Ernest's character. This was a present to me. Later, he suggested that we share it—for so long. "You have it for so long, and I'll have it for so long." He took it and I've never seen it since. That's one of his little tricks. The last I heard it was valued at $185,000. It's in the Museum of Modern Art.

HENRY STRATER: He was crazy about my paintings. Then Gertrude Stein told him that they weren't so good and that cooled him off a little on them.

DENIS BRIAN: Hemingway was in Lausanne, Switzerland, covering the Greek-Turk peace conference and waiting for Hadley to join him. They planned to go from there to stay in Rapallo. Before she left Paris, Hadley collected everything she could find that he had written including his first attempt at a novel and packed the manuscripts in a case. At the Paris railroad station she went to get something to read on the train, leaving the case containing Ernest's lifework in the carriage. When she returned the suitcase had gone. She arrived at Lausanne so distraught, tearful, and incoherent that Hemingway thought she had at the very least to confess having had an affair with a black man. The truth may have been even more traumatic. Ernest immediately returned to Paris to try and recover the manuscripts. He never did.

ARCHIBALD MACLEISH: Hadley had taken the manuscripts with her because Lincoln Steffens was at Lausanne and she knew he wanted to see more of Ernest's work. She lost the lot, including all the carbon copies. They quarreled bitterly over that. It doesn't sound like a terrible catastrophe, but it was. They were poor, and this was years of his work. Things were not easy.

HENRY STRATER: I joined them in Rapallo shortly after that. You know what he said about the lost manuscripts? He said, "You know, Mike, if you had had those manuscripts in your trunk, you would not have left them to go and get something to read." In other words, I was a fellow artist and if he had given them to me I would never have left them in an exposed position. He was very upset because it showed how little she valued what he was doing.

DENIS BRIAN: However, I understood she had thought to bring them to advance Ernest's career, in the hope Lincoln Steffens would read them. Did his lost manuscripts give him writer's block?

HENRY STRATER: No, he was working on those one-page stories which were the basis of his whole style, and later published by William Bird of Paris: *In Our Time*. I was painting. I didn't have a studio, so I painted in my hotel room. The two paintings I did of Hemingway were done in the early part of our stay in Rapallo. I painted him and Hadley in their hotel room. I did a profile of Hemingway with a gray background. He complained it made him look too much like H. G. Wells. Then I did the famous so-called boxer portrait with a red background. He begged me for years to give him the boxer portrait and I said, "I'll leave it to you in my will." I would have, but he predeceased me. Then I painted a beautiful one of Hadley. I gave that to them, very unwisely because it's lost. He was around a lot when I was painting and I was around him a lot when he was writing, but I never gave him outright painting lessons. Later I heard that he had done some paintings and they were remarkably good—though I never got to see them.[1] In those early days together we discussed painting and writing all the time.

DENIS BRIAN: And you kept in shape with tennis and boxing?

HENRY STRATER: He was a bum tennis player and so was I, but we'd do it for exercise. There was always a certain friction with him, and he loved nothing better than to beat up a friend. I disappointed him by giving him more than he wanted. The only way he could lick me was to get me dead drunk first. That was his system. What he didn't like was that someone named Hyacinth could hold his own in fighting him. That's my middle name: Hyacinth. My mother promised her Aunt Hyacinth that she'd name her child after her and when I came out with balls that's what she christened me, Henry Hyacinth.

You know one thing he never discovered? I was born a southpaw. I never boxed southpaw with him, but I did it with others. I'd box southpaw or straight, and the one punch I had that he didn't know—you know the guy that knocked out Corbett, from Down Under? Fitzsimmons. He was a natural southpaw. He could box right-handed or left-handed. Executing the Fitzsimmons shift was a cinch for me. You simply shifted from a right-handed boxing position to left-handed. I wouldn't use it at the beginning of a match, but after it got a little hot I'd pull the Fitzsimmons shift. With that you can clobber a guy any place you want. I'd use that on Hemingway and he never got wise to it. I've used that all my life, because I'm a natural shift boxer. I don't think I'd be very good at it now. At ninety-one I'm getting a little over the hill. Hemingway and I boxed

---

[1] No one else I contacted, nor any works on Hemingway mention them.

one time at Rapallo with no call-out of rounds steadily for an hour with no stop. After that he complained to Hadley that he couldn't chew meat for a week because I'd punched him on the jaw. She thought it was funny, because I'd boxed him with a sprained ankle. I was in bed with a sprained ankle and Hemingway hauled me out of bed to box with him. He figured it would be a good chance to lay me low; instead he couldn't eat meat for a week because I'd cracked his jaw.

DENIS BRIAN: You had boxed at Princeton?

HENRY STRATER: Yes, though there wasn't a team there.

DENIS BRIAN: And Scott Fitzgerald, also a student there, hero-worshipped you?

HENRY STRATER: Well read *This Side of Paradise,* his first best-seller. He told me, "The hero, Burne Holiday, is you; but I've thrown in a little of Dave Bruce and a couple of other people." Dave Bruce was head of American Intelligence in Europe [OSS] during World War II.

DENIS BRIAN: Who was the more impressive personality, Fitzgerald or Hemingway?

HENRY STRATER: They were completely different. Hemingway was a big, roaring, very aggressive person and Scott Fitzgerald was very quiet.

DENIS BRIAN: Some say Hemingway was very shy.

HENRY STRATER: He was shy like one of these police dogs. In *Moveable Feast,* he had a lot of disparaging remarks to make about certain people, but in the preface he wrote that there were three people he had omitted to say anything about. I was one of the three. He knew that he couldn't have got started on a thing like that about me [laughs]. He could have put in some dirty cracks about me, but he didn't. And I felt very pleased and flattered. He certainly put in a lot of dirty cracks about Scott Fitzgerald.

DENIS BRIAN: And he described the artist Wyndham Lewis as looking like an unsuccessful rapist. Did Hemingway have a good sense of humor?

HENRY STRATER: If it didn't touch his vanity. He had no humor about himself.

DENIS BRIAN: Hemingway had not been entirely cleaned out of his three-years output. His short story "Up in Michigan" was in the mail to him with a rejection slip. And he found the short story "My Old Man" stuffed in a drawer. Edward O'Brien, editor of the annual *Best Short Stories,* was staying in a village near Rapallo. He listened sympathetically to Ernest's account of his stolen manuscripts and said he'd consider "My Old Man" for inclusion in the 1923 edition of *Best Short Stories.* Soon after, Hadley had more surprise news for Hemingway: she was pregnant.

HADLEY MOWRER: He complained bitterly to Gertrude Stein that he was too young to be a father. She thought it was hilarious. Ernest had been offered the chance to work full time for the *Star* in Toronto. We wanted the baby to be born on that side of the Atlantic, and he felt we needed a regular income for the first year or two after the baby was born. So he accepted the offer, and we left for Canada in August 1923. A big mistake. Harry Hindmarsh, Ernest's boss on the *Toronto Star,* overworked him and gave him mostly unimportant little assignments. I think he was jealous of Ernest's talent. Then he sent Ernest to New York City to cover a story about the arrival of Lloyd George, the British prime minister. Our son was born while Ernest was on the train coming back. He wept with exhaustion and strain when he arrived at the hospital. Then Hindmarsh bawled him out for stopping off to see me and the baby, instead of going straight to the newspaper office. We soon both agreed that coming back to Canada had been a big mistake. But there was one bright spot. Edward O'Brien told Ernest he was including "My Old Man" in *The Best Stories of 1923,* and dedicating the entire book to him. Ernest was elated. But because of Hindmarsh his elation didn't last.

HARRY HINDMARSH [son and namesake of Hemingway's boss and *bête noire*]: Pa used to talk about prima donnas at the *Star* and he felt Hemingway was one of them. Pa's way of handling the situation was to make sure that all reporters did everything. But there were certain jobs that Hemingway didn't feel he should have to do, like writing obituaries.

MORLEY CALLAGHAN: I was nineteen when I first met old Hem and he encouraged me to be a writer when nobody else did. He told me he was seven years older than I was. [He was four years older.] Later, he changed his age a little. But I was sitting in the newspaper library one day. . . . I knew about him but I had never spoken to him. He came into the library and sat with me and it was wonderful. We became friends right then and there. Hem knew I was only in my second year at college and working part-time at the newspaper then.

GORDON SINCLAIR: I was more or less a copyboy in those days, occasionally going out to report stories. Morley Callaghan liked Hemingway, but I didn't like the bugger. Hemingway demeaned me by paying no attention to me. He was a *poseur.* He wore heavy boots and frequently came into the office with cow or horse manure on them, it seemed deliberately, and he walked with a heavy sound. Then he just happened to have those goddamn Italian medals with him so often, in his pockets. He sort of accidentally had them around. I saw them often.

MORLEY CALLAGHAN: Gordon Sinclair never knew Hemingway, really; he imagined he did. It's probably true that Hemingway paid no attention to him; he probably didn't notice him. Maybe listened to him for a minute and wasn't interested in him. What can you say about these things? I never saw Hemingway in heavy boots or with manure on them. So obviously the fellow I met at the *Star* wasn't exactly the same fellow Sinclair met.

GORDON SINCLAIR: Hindmarsh tried to pull prima donnas down a peg or two. He did that to me and to Hemingway.

MORLEY CALLAGHAN: And to me. He tried to humiliate us. I didn't like the way he treated Hemingway, as if Hemingway had no vast experience at all as a newspaperman. He had the kind of talent Hindmarsh couldn't comprehend. Hindmarsh was a tyrant, trying to break Hemingway's spirit.

GORDON SINCLAIR: Hemingway called Hindmarsh untrustworthy, a son-of-a-bitch, and a liar. I didn't get that impression of Hindmarsh at all, and I was with him a hell of a lot longer than Hemingway—twenty-one years. I know they disagreed strongly.

HADLEY MOWRER: Ernest once said: "I'm going to kill Hindmarsh!"

HARRY HINDMARSH: Hemingway was a very, very unhappy man, because he had been disciplined. He wanted the choice assignments and his dignity was hurt by being put on obituaries. But every reporter had to do them. My father didn't want stars.

MORLEY CALLAGHAN: Hindmarsh told me frankly he was going to put me in harness. He expected all reporters to wish him a bright "Good morning!" as he walked passed our desks. Once, when I failed to say "Good morning!" he called me into his office and fired me. He could be childishly petulant and moody, and when he got angry you'd think he'd burst a blood vessel. [He soon rehired Callaghan.]

HARRY HINDMARSH: My father had a temper, that's true. With Hemingway it was a case of two strong temperaments. Hemingway had never had any discipline and he didn't intend to have any. My father never spoke of Hemingway with contempt; he wasn't that way at all. He was very, very hard and very stern, but he was always looked on as one of the most just people in the business. It all depends on what side of the fence you're sitting.

GORDON SINCLAIR: Hemingway said that working under Hindmarsh was like being in the German army with a bad commander. Hindmarsh often got slapped down by his father-in-law, the publisher, Atkinson. This is where Hindmarsh had to eat crow from time to time, and he would take it out on those around him. He fired me several times because of different bits of disobedience. Despite that I liked him. I used to laugh at him. He was almost a typical *Front Page* editor. He saved several reporters from alcoholism. He would nurse them along and send guys to get them out of their DTs. He never fired anyone for alcoholism. That seemed to be a crusade with him, to get them back in good shape.

MORLEY CALLAGHAN: We were discussing writing, and Hemingway said a writer should have the dedication of a priest. He looked at a short story of mine and said, "You're a real writer." He was a strange, warm, beguiling man.

GORDON SINCLAIR: I worked only one assignment with him, about the Japanese earthquake in 1923, when there was big destruction in Tokyo and Yokohama. The *Star* was very anxious to get a firsthand account from people who had been on the Canadian Pacific ship that had just cast off when the earthquake hit. The *Star* was turned down in interview after interview attempt, but they persisted and sent Hemingway, me, and a girl, Mary Lowrey, to Winnipeg to get on the train as the people came back from the West Coast. They still wouldn't talk to us. When we got back to Toronto the earthquake was now about three weeks over, yet for some reason they were damned insistent about this. So the three of us went to a house in nearby Rosedale, and were admitted by a girl in a brilliant red kimono, which she'd apparently just unpacked. We were standing in the hall when we heard water running in a tub upstairs and the mother came and leaned over the balcony screaming: "Who the hell are those bastards down there?"[1] As she leaned over the bannister—she was in a robe, too—her breasts hung out.[2] I was about eighteen months younger than Hemingway and along as a sort of coolie. After we'd been chased out of the house—and got the story, although the two women insisted their names not be used—Ernest and Mary had a discussion as to which one

[1] Not in Hemingway's account.

[2] Not in Hemingway's account.

of them would write the story. Ernest wrote it. The *Star* at that time had a mad on him, so they didn't give him a by-line. But it was a good story.[1]

DENIS BRIAN: Did he quit or was he fired?

GORDON SINCLAIR: He quit. Hemingway was asked to do some promotion for the paper. They had asked the kids of Toronto would they like the *Star* to buy animals for the zoo. It was one of these continuing campaigns. Because it was cheap, they steered the kids toward a white peacock. The kids didn't go for that, they wanted a baby elephant. The votes went so strongly for the elephant, and the campaign had been so successful, that they bought both. The elephant, called Stella, got a big welcome and was ridden by Fred Griffin, the best reporter we ever had.

Then they assigned Hemingway to do an equal welcome to the peacock. He felt it was beneath him, because it was for promotion. And he quit. When he quit, he pinned a long list of grievances to the noticeboard close to Hindmarsh's office. He wrote it on pieces of copy paper and fastened them together with paste, and it got to be one long piece trailing to the ground. Hindmarsh walked right by it once when I was there. Nobody even picked that damn thing up. It would have been worth a lot of money today. It included the complaint that Hindmarsh treated him like dirt, overworked him, and lied to him. The very first sentence was, as I remember it: "I Ernest Hemingway will not now or ever write about any goddamn peacock."

HARRY HINDMARSH: Dad felt it was best that Hemingway go his own way, because a man like that can be very disturbing in an organization.

MORLEY CALLAGHAN: I saw Hemingway the day he went away and we said goodbye to each other. He gave me an autographed copy of his first book, *Three Stories and Ten Poems*, privately printed in Paris. I never saw his list of grievances pinned to the noticeboard, but you hear so many stories about it. People still talk about him in Toronto and taxi drivers point out where he lived. He told me he planned to write a novel about Hindmarsh called *The Son-in-Law*, but he never did. He explained why, later. He said you should never write a book with the principal character someone you detest, because the emotion would distort your perspective.

HARRY HINDMARSH: Hemingway turned out to be a first-rate reporter, and

[1] The report, "Japanese Earthquake," appeared in the September 25, 1923, issue of the *Toronto Daily Star*, and was reprinted in *Byline: Ernest Hemingway*, Scribner's, 1967.

my father turned out to be a first-class newspaperman, rated one of the best across Canada. He became president of the *Toronto Star.*

DENIS BRIAN: The Hemingways returned to Paris in January 1924, with their infant son, John Hadley Nicanor, nicknamed Bumby. They lived on Hadley's income while Ernest worked for nothing as subeditor on novelist Ford Madox Ford's new literary magazine the *Transatlantic Review,* hoping to get his own work published in it, plugging James Joyce as the world's greatest writer, and enthusiastically rewriting the stories submitted by others.

HADLEY MOWRER: We lived in the rue Notre Dame des Champs over a sawmill. On the opposite side of the street were back entrances to shops on Boulevard Montparnasse. There was a back door into a cellar underneath a bakery and that's where I had my piano. It was so cold in the winter, I played the piano wearing several sweaters while Ernest wrote, or read manuscripts in a nearby café and kept warm with coffee. Ernest and I were very poor at times in Paris but that story by Hotchner [in his book *Papa Hemingway*] about Ernest wringing pigeons' necks in the Luxembourg Gardens and hiding them in the baby carriage—if he did he killed and ate them himself without giving me a bite. I just don't believe it. That's Ernest's very inventive mind.

HAROLD LOEB: Ford Madox Ford had invited me to a tea party early in 1924 and Ernest was there, just returned from Canada. He was helping Ford on the magazine. Hemingway and I took to each other at once and played tennis, and boxed thereafter. At that party he wore my favorite footgear, sneakers. And a patched jacket. I had never met an American so unaffected by living in Paris. I liked his combination of toughness and sensitivity, his love of sports and his dedication to writing. He was conspicuous for hard work and being faithful to his wife.

He made himself out to be a sort of bad boy; he certainly wasn't. He was a bit of a Puritan, if anything. He was searching for a good time and life was a pretty dreadful business. We boxed several times a week and it was important to Ernest then. I was pleased, because I had grown up with the impression that writers were not quite virile, along the lines of Oscar Wilde, and to come across Ernest who liked the outdoors, sports, and boxing, was a great relief.

HADLEY MOWRER: I played tennis better than Ernest did. He couldn't run very fast because of his injured knee, it was still stiff from the war wound. Some of his shots were quite awkward because of his blind eye and every time he missed a shot he would sizzle. His racket would slash to the ground and everyone would stand still and cower—until he recovered with a laugh.

HAROLD LOEB: He was a lousy tennis player and hated to miss a shot. But he was so exuberant you never had a lackadaisical game. He was fun to be with and a very charming person.

HENRY STRATER: He liked to win everything. At boxing he was very dangerous in the first minute or two. He had a very wicked overhand right, but, as I said, all you had to do was block it a couple of times and counterpunch from the inside. That would slow him up.

HADLEY MOWRER: Ernest was always looking for someone who could really talk with him and on his level, and with the same interests. John Dos Passos was one of the few people at certain times whom Ernest could really talk to. He lived in a funny little hotel near us. Dos had this dictionary at his side, trying to increase the sight of his eye by studying it. [Both men were virtually blind in one eye.] They had a lot to say to each other. There wasn't anyone else around for Ernest like that.

GEORGE SELDES: In Paris there were Saturday night literary parties at Gertrude Stein's, Thursday nights at Natalie Barney's, and Sunday nights at Ford Madox Ford's. Writers and critics belonged to those groups; being a newspaperman I was an outsider. But the one person who did take me in was Ford Madox Ford, and I never missed a week there. I knew Ford very well.

HADLEY MOWRER: Although Ernest had a good many fits of depression there was generally some good cause [laughs]. One cause was Ford Madox Ford. Ernest would sit over coffee in solitude all morning, working, and then Ford would appear and interrupt him. I imagine Ford said something like, "Ah, Hemingway! Just the man I want to see!" And Ernest was probably sorry he didn't have a gun with him.

GEORGE SELDES: I wonder why Hemingway hated him. Maybe because Ford had enough to live on, and could give a party every week. Ford breathed heavily and talked in a mumble, and he was a difficult person to get along with.

HAROLD LOEB: I was very fond of Ford. He was very generous and very kind to me and to everybody else. Hem accused him of bad breath. I crossed the ocean with Ford. I don't think he had bad breath, not that anyone can help it. Ford was not good to look at. He had asthma or something and was always a little watery about the eyes. But he was a nice person and a great raconteur. I know Hem called him a phony, but Hem was so nasty to people who helped him.

ADA MACLEISH: Ernest probably didn't like Ford because he didn't agree with Ernest [laughs]. Ernest didn't necessarily have to be agreed with, but he had strong opinions.

MORLEY CALLAGHAN: Ford Madox Ford was one of those Englishmen who look as though they've just come from the port wine. Hemingway thought he was letting him do all the work on the *Transatlantic Review* and taking all the credit.

GEORGE SELDES: Ford had a terrible deal from people he helped like Conrad and Hemingway. Ford broke down and cried one evening—the late twenties or early thirties—when we were alone together. He told me, "I started Joseph Conrad when he was a sea captain and couldn't even write English." Ford gave me the full story of his collaboration with Conrad and the names of the books of which he wrote at least half, like *Romance.* Then he said, "I gave Hemingway his first literary job when I made him editor of the *Transatlantic,* when I went away for a trip. Now every one of them is famous and famous and famous—and I'm forgotten, and nobody cares about my work." He brought out half a bottle of Napoleon brandy with a label on it from the 1840s or 50s. It was like lightning with honey mixed. Eventually we drank the half bottle and he told me the story of the misery he'd had, and the crowning misery was "And now the Conrad set has come out with Joseph Conrad's name on it, and my name is no longer on the back of each of the novels." And he cried, he really cried. He did have watery eyes as Hemingway said. Ford said it was the result of being gassed. I don't think so. I was gassed, too, but it had no effect on my eyes.

DENIS BRIAN: Ford wasn't gassed. But as a British officer on the Somme in 1916 he was blown up, in somewhat the same way as Hemingway a couple of years later. As a result Ford suffered shell shock and feared he might go mad. Ezra Pound wrote: "He told stories about himself constantly and as the stories were retold he embroidered them."[1] Robert McAlmon saw Ford as "a Mythomaniac who could step into the Moon Mullins cartoons and double for Lord Plushbottom."[2] Ford also boasted of being an English gentleman and told Hemingway that a gentleman was something he could never hope to be.

[1] *New Directions,* 1942.

[2] Kay Boyle–Robert McAlmon, *Being Geniuses Together,* Doubleday, 1968.

GEORGE SELDES: Oh la la! Well, British gentlemen do feel that way, there's no question. Ford never pulled that on me.

DENIS BRIAN: Ironically, Hemingway, who said Ford resembled an upended hogshead, himself grew to match that description.

ARCHIBALD MACLEISH: Ernest could be fairly ribald about people he wanted to ridicule.

MALCOLM COWLEY: When I saw Ernest briefly in Paris in 1923 he seemed charming, not charismatic. But by 1924 almost everyone in Montparnasse was talking about him. The charisma began to sprout like wings out of his shoulders. He was a very complicated man, as Hadley says, essentially shy and unsure of himself, as Arnold Gingrich says.

DENIS BRIAN: Two friends agree it was almost impossible to resist Hemingway's evangelic zeal in trying to get them to share his enthusiasms. Although he couldn't persuade John Dos Passos to bicycle around the Paris streets in a striped jumper "with his knees up to his ears and his chin between the handlebars,"[1] he did talk him into attending the six-day bicycle races. Hadley sat watching with Hemingway all through the night. Dos Passos stood it for as long as he could keep his eyes open, then sneaked out back to his rooms. Donald Ogden Stewart soon realized, as he wrote in his autobiography, that "when Ernest was enthusiastic about something it was extremely dangerous to resist, especially friendship."[2] On their first meeting in a Paris restaurant, Ernest was about to catch a train for Switzerland where Hadley and Bumby were staying. He insisted that Stewart stay in their apartment until they returned. Stewart woke next morning in Hemingway's apartment. Hemingway had even left a note telling him where he could get eggs and milk for breakfast.

MALCOLM COWLEY: Our boyhoods were in some ways much the same. I was a doctor's son, too, who felt at home in the country, not the city. He was one of the most truly charming people I've ever met. He could charm a brass doorknob off the door.

ARCHIBALD MACLEISH: He'd do *anything* for people with whom he spent most of his time, people who were not in his world as writers at all. He didn't care for other writers much. Neither do I. There's not much point in going around with writers. You've got yourself to stand, and that's bad enough. But Hemingway was a very good friend of mine.

ADA MACLEISH: I don't believe anyone knew Ernest better than Archie

[1] John Dos Passos, *The Best Times*, New American Library, 1966.

[2] Donald Ogden Stewart, *By a Stroke of Luck*, Paddington Press, 1975.

and I did, and my feelings for him are very deep, very affectionate. He was not the usual cut of person. He had some very strong and splendid qualities, some that weren't. I wouldn't have been surprised at anything Ernest did. He was unexpected and temperamental, a lovable person who needed a great deal of understanding. He was sensitive, although he didn't seem to be. If you didn't know him well you'd think he was rather tough.

HADLEY MOWRER: A lot of his toughness was real, but a lot was put on to cover his sensitivity. Ernest was one of the most sensitive people I have ever heard of, and easily hurt. Most people thought he was too sure of himself, but I believe he had a great inferiority complex which he didn't show. At times he had the nerve of a brass monkey, which embarrassed me. He was so complicated; so many sides to him you could hardly make a sketch of him in a geometry book. Ernest was a good father and Bumby called him Papa. One of our friends began calling him Papa, too. Ernest always felt protective toward people, even people much older than he was. I think he wanted people to look up to him as a sort of protector.

HAROLD LOEB: My friend Kitty Cannell thought he overacted the part of a ruthless, hairy-chested, unintellectual he-man in order to suppress his compassion, pity, and softness, to his own loss.

ADA MACLEISH: Ernest could be a bully on occasion, if he happened to feel like quarreling. He'd make a situation and be rather disagreeable about it, but in a very short time it disappeared.

ARCHIBALD MACLEISH: Despite all our quarrels, I had a deep and ineradicable love of Ernest. He once said to me: "I don't love men." I don't either, but I loved him and I think Ernest did have a considerable affection for me.

HENRY STRATER: He'd occasionally write about his friends when he was in a bad humor. Once, I said, "Hem, what's your next story going to be about?" He gave me this very evil look and said, "About you," which was a species of bullying. So I said, "That's fine, Hem. You know, I was a newspaperman before I became an artist. I've always wanted to go back to my writing. You go ahead and write about me and I'll write about you." And, oh, his face fell because he knew I could do as big a job on him as he could on me.

ARCHIBALD MACLEISH: One of the curious misconceptions about those years in Paris in the 1920s is that there was a group or club of Fitzgerald-like people who were always sitting around on their tails and in and out of each other's beds. There was no group. There were a series of associations.

HADLEY MOWRER: Once, Zelda and Scott Fitzgerald came at about four in the morning. We had a baby and we prized our sleep, especially Ernest because he had to write the next morning. But they would come at these outlandish hours. And they'd been drinking. They did foolish things like taking a roll of toilet paper and standing at the top of the stairs and unraveling it all the way down [laughs]. Some people might expect Ernest to tell them to go home. He didn't, though. We sat around in nightie and bathrobe, talking. I don't think Ernest really enjoyed it, but he was observing an alcoholic. Scott would take one drink and pretty soon he'd turn pale green and pass out. His system just couldn't stand it. In Paris, you know, it's awfully hard not to drink. Ernest decided right away the first time he met her that Zelda was crazy. She craved to show she had talent and she did have it. Her letters were marvelous and showed a lot of feeling about language and emotions.

ARCHIBALD MACLEISH: Zelda called Ernest "bogus," but she wasn't responsible for a lot of things she said.

GEORGE PLIMPTON [who interviewed Hemingway two decades later for the *Paris Review*]: Hemingway was very uncomfortable in Zelda's presence. He thought she was mad and was very down on her. He thought of Zelda as being a destroyer of Fitzgerald and his artistic capabilities.

HADLEY MOWRER: Ernest was too assured a male for Zelda. Perhaps she resented this. He was the kind of man to whom men, women, children, and dogs were attracted. He was scornful of some people and would say outrageous things about them. He had a cruel streak. Yet his kindnesses were just about as far in the other direction. Zelda felt she must show her superiority. That wasn't my idea of perfect love, but I can understand it. Ernest was so brilliant I couldn't compete with him—so I let it go.

MALCOLM COWLEY: The most vivid things I've had said to me about Hemingway were by Nathan Asch, who knew him in Paris in 1924–5. Asch's was the picture of a young man in Paris when Hemingway was already the leader of the young people. And Asch did admire him. This may have been from a letter Nathan wrote me when I was preparing for an interview with Hemingway for *Life* magazine. Go ahead and use it, and credit it to Nathan Asch. "Once in Paris Hemingway had a dinner-table argument with another young writer [Asch] about their respective talents. Later when they were walking toward the Dôme for coffee,

Hemingway fell into a boxer's crouch and began feinting and jabbing. The other young writer began shadowboxing, too. He hit Hemingway accidentally and Hemingway hit back, knocking him down. His mouth gritty, tasting bits of teeth, the other picked himself up and stumbled back to his hotel room. Later that night there was a knock at the door. It was Hemingway. 'I couldn't sleep until you forgave me,' he said. 'You know, of course, that I was wrong in the argument. You've got a lot of talent. You've got more of everything than any of us.'" Hemingway was right. Asch did have talent. But, as he said, he wasn't successful and Hemingway was. Asch continued: "It was an event when this towering figure passed the sidewalk tables at the Dôme. Arms waved in greeting and friends ran out to urge him to sit down with them. The occasions were charming little scenes, as if spontaneous, although repeated. In view of the whole terrace, Hemingway would be striding toward the Montparnasse railroad station, his mind seemingly busy with the mechanics of someone's arrival or departure. And he wouldn't quite recognize whoever greeted him. Then suddenly his beautiful smile appeared that made those watching him also smile. And with a will and an eagerness he put out his hands and warmly greeted his acquaintances, who, overcome by this reception, simply glowed and returned with him to the table as if with an overwhelming prize. . . . I have no criticism of Hem's conduct. I do think it's a crazy situation, though, that the elimination was so brutal; that, of the writers in Paris then, Hem was holding the world by the handle and everyone else is either obscure or dead. But you can't blame it on Hem."

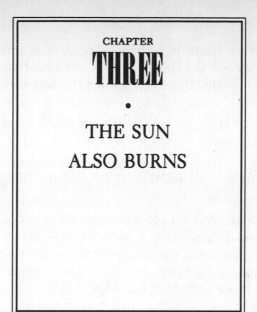

CHAPTER

THREE

•

THE SUN
ALSO BURNS

DENIS BRIAN: Holding the world by the handle, Hemingway decided to shake it up a bit. He'd abandoned the novel born in Chicago to follow his credo: write about what you know. Despite his silent breakfasts he was eager to talk with Gertrude Stein about the progress of his new novel. It exposed the intimate lives of his friends in Paris and their trip to Spain to watch bullfights. The "fictional" characters were so transparently disguised, he might as well have used their real names. Gertrude Stein recognized all the real-life models. So did Hadley. Hemingway titled the novel *The Sun Also Rises*.

HADLEY MOWRER: I lived right through *The Sun Also Rises* and can remember almost the whole thing. The dialogue and situations are very true to what I recall happened. It was a very upset summer for me; I don't know why, because Ernest and I had not started to fall apart at that time. But everybody was drinking all the time, and everybody was having affairs all the time. I found it sort of upsetting. Harold Loeb had a glorious affair with Duff Twysden, a wonderfully attractive Englishwoman, a woman of the world with no sexual inhibitions. Harold came down with her to Pamplona in Spain for the bullfights. A lot of people thought Ernest had an affair with Duff. He just adored her, but I'm sure they didn't have an affair.

HAROLD LOEB: He may have been in love with Duff; I don't know. I don't think they had an affair.

DENIS BRIAN: Kitty Cannell was so upset by Hemingway's picture of her that she took to her bed for three days. And she thought Ernest had crucified Harold Loeb.

HADLEY MOWRER: Harold Loeb will *never* get over the heartache that book caused him. I've talked to him by the hour about Ernest and his ability to create composite characters. Almost none of his characters are pure Loeb or pure you or pure me. He makes a composite that fits his story. But I've never convinced Harold of that.

DENIS BRIAN: I tried the same line with Loeb, asking him, "Aren't almost all novel characters composites?"

HAROLD LOEB: We write about what we know best. In the first draft of the novel I was going to be the hero. I was fond of him until Pamplona. Something happened then. I don't know whether it was because he liked Duff, or what. He took people that went on the fiesta to Pamplona and made a novel about them. I'm Jewish and I played tennis every day with him, so naturally readers connected me with the character Robert Cohn.

DENIS BRIAN: Did you, in fact, write a book and go to New York, and was the book fairly successful—like the Cohn character?

HAROLD LOEB: I suppose that was my first book, *Doodab*.

DENIS BRIAN: In *The Sun*, Hemingway has Cohn spoiled by his first book. You weren't spoiled?

HAROLD LOEB: No, rather not. My book wasn't a great success. I never read Ernest's whole book until long after it came out. Then I read the parts that Cohn spoke, and just got mad because I didn't recognize anything. I've never been offended by it, but I still think it's pretty nasty. I was offended for a day. Cohn had no resemblance to me that I could find. I never did think he was making a portrait and I'd be very unvain if I did. But the fact that he used my background I find offensive. It's not necessary. He could have changed it. He used my Princeton background and my family. He made Cohn a member of the boxing team at Princeton. Princeton didn't have a boxing team. I was on the Princeton wrestling team. He gave an account of my marriage and my editing of a magazine, but then he gave me a character I didn't recognize.

DENIS BRIAN: When I was writing a novel based on my brother, he kept saying, "I wouldn't do this, I wouldn't say this." And I said, "Look, it's only based on you. I've got to be able to use my imagination." Whatever I wrote he was critical of if he didn't feel it was something he would do or say.

HAROLD LOEB: I have somewhat the same feeling. He called my father's family one of the richest Jewish families in New York and my mother's one of the oldest. My father had no money. He did the brokerage for the Guggenheims largely. My mother was a Guggenheim. That isn't inaccurate. But calling them "the richest" is an exaggeration.

DENIS BRIAN: When Loeb asked Hemingway why he had portrayed Cohn as a wimp who cried all the time, Hemingway denied the character was based on Loeb, saying that if Loeb *was* Cohn, then he, Hemingway, must be Jake Barnes. "Do you think I had my prick shot off?" he asked somewhat rhetorically. "And incidentally," Hemingway concluded, "you do cry an awful lot for a man." So did Hemingway.

HADLEY MOWRER: I didn't like what Ernest did to Harold. It was just too easy to ruin his happiness. And I didn't like what he did later to Sherwood Anderson with the satire *Torrents of Spring*.

DENIS BRIAN: Why d'you think he gave a negative picture of Loeb?

HADLEY MOWRER: Harold had a little genius for slightly making a fool of himself. The other boys were rough and tough, and would catch him at these things, so that he appears in the book in very poor style.

HAROLD LOEB: I haven't been upset about it for years and I don't think it's the great book it's made out to be. There are three possible reasons for his animosity. One, I rode on a bull's head, to the admiration of a matador whom he liked. Second, as mentioned, I didn't like bullfighting. And third, I'd outraged his puritanism because I'd been off with Duff [for a weekend together]. Those are my theories. I've never known to this day which is right.

DENIS BRIAN: Wasn't he brought up in a society where it was almost fashionable to be anti-Semitic?

HAROLD LOEB: Anyone that goes to Presbyterian or Episcopalian service is brought up to be an anti-Semite. He'd been brought up in Oak Park and had a do-gooder uncle and a rather puritanical family, I believe.

ARCHIBALD MACLEISH: Ernest's satirizing of Loeb wasn't so much anti-Semitic as anti-Loeb. I know he talked about "kike lawyers," but that was a normal phrase in those days. It was all around in the American midwest at that time. It didn't mean what it's come to mean now. Since Hitler we're much more sensitive about such things.

ARNOLD GINGRICH [publisher of *Esquire*]: Hemingway's anti-Semitism was fairly light, not a brooded thing. In that time and place we talked about the hunkies and the polacks and the wops and the greaseballs and everything else. And the kikes and the sheenies were just part of the language. It didn't mean much. His lawyer, Maurice Speiser, was Jewish. I do know it wasn't a thing that was more than superficial.

DENIS BRIAN: Would you call him anti-Semitic?

HAROLD LOEB: I don't think so. He usually had a Jewish friend or two. I never heard him say anything against them. Kitty Cannell said he called Fleischman a kike, but I don't know.

DENIS BRIAN: In his Hemingway biography, Carlos Baker says you were reported to be looking for Hemingway with a gun. Ernest's response was to let people know around the Quarter that he would be sitting outside Lipp's restaurant between two and four in the afternoon for several days. And, says Baker, he took it as an indication of cowardice among his critics that no one had taken a shot at him.

HAROLD LOEB: That's complete fiction, and so is Hotchner's account in *Papa Hemingway*, where he quotes Ernest as saying I threatened to kill him. I saw him only once after the book came out. I was sitting in Lipp's in Saint-Germain and Hem went to the bar and ordered a drink. We both grimaced as he passed me. And then as he sat there with his back to me I watched his neck go red. Then he walked out. We never spoke.

GEORGE SELDES: Duff Twysden used to boast that she was the bitch "Lady Brett" in *The Sun Also Rises*.

HAROLD LOEB: Duff tried to pretend she didn't much mind his picture of her, but I heard from others that she minded a bit. She was quite something. Hemingway made her into a tramp. I don't think she was at all. He made her promiscuous, a drunkard, all of which I can't support. She was elegant in a way.

DENIS BRIAN: By not being promiscuous do you mean she wouldn't sleep with a man unless she liked him?

HAROLD LOEB: I suppose. I can't prove it.

CHICAGO TRIBUNE. MADRID. JUNE 28, 1924: MacDonald Ogden Stewart and Ernest Hemingway, two American writers, were gored by a bull in the bull ring at Pamplona, where they went to attend a fiesta. Mr. Stewart had two ribs broken and Mr. Hemingway was bruised. Both their lives were saved. Mr. Stewart, Mr. Hemingway, John Dos Passos and Robert McAlmon, all American writers resident in Paris, went to Pamplona, Spain, on account of an old fashioned celebration. It is the custom there to barricade the side streets and drive the bulls for the day's fighting from the station to the arena where the toreadors play leap frog and tag with the animal. Part of the initiation of young manhood in Pamplona consists of being thrown by a bandaged bull. Mr. Stewart and Mr. Hemingway participated in the first day successfully and on the second day Mr. Stewart was thrown. It occurred when he said he could leap on the bull's back and blow smoke in the bull's eyes and then beat him down. The chief toreador presented Mr. Stewart with a scarlet cloak, which he could not refuse, and during the handshaking the bull rushed for Mr. Stewart, lifted him on its horns and tossed him over and then threw him into the air and tried to horn him. Mr. Hemingway rushed to rescue Mr. Stewart and was also gored, but was saved from death on account of the horn bandages.

DENIS BRIAN: In his probably more accurate account—at least he'd get his own name right—Donald Ogden Stewart doesn't mention a rescue attempt by Hemingway. Wanting to please Ernest he had resisted an urge to criticize bullfighting as cruel. Scared but game he joined those running ahead of the bulls in the Pamplona streets. A bull tossed him twice and fractured two of his ribs. But in his euphoria he felt it was worth it especially when Ernest clapped him on the back approvingly. Stewart, who liked Hemingway "tremendously," tells in his book how, when he deserted bullfighting for screenwriting in Hollywood, Hemingway scorned him for selling out.[1]

ARNOLD GINGRICH: As long as people around him were worshipful and adoring, why they were great. The minute they weren't, there was a tendency to find others who were. I think you had here a terribly shy person, dreadfully insecure, who in one instance reflects it by being withdrawn, and in another turns around and is very boisterous. Both are manifestations of the same thing: a dreadful insecurity.

MALCOLM COWLEY: I knew Loeb quite well and he was angry and hurt for a very long time. It was a cruel portrait. Loeb wasn't as bad as he was

[1] Donald Ogden Stewart, *By a Stroke of Luck.*

shown as being and Jake [in *The Sun Also Rises*] who would be identified with Hemingway had more bitterness against Loeb than he admitted to having.

DENIS BRIAN: Over Duff Twysden?

MALCOLM COWLEY: It might well have been. He wrote shocking things about everybody, and he had a mean tongue.

HADLEY MOWRER: Ernest was not perfect. As you know, his admirers like to think he was perfect.

DENIS BRIAN: He called Duff Twysden an alcoholic nymphomaniac. Did he like women?

HADLEY MOWRER: In some ways he didn't have a very deep understanding of women some men have. But if you ask the question, "Did women like Hemingway?"—don't ask [laughs].

GEORGE SELDES: I can certainly understand Harold Loeb and Hemingway being fascinated by Duff Twysden. I met her in Paris when I was working for the *Chicago Tribune,* and living in a two-dollar-a-day room at the Hotel Liberia. No telephone. The concierge yelled up there's a call for me. There were two women there. One was the Countess Modici, who had been a friend of Vincent Sheean, a newspaperman, in Rome. She said, "This is Duff Twysden." And Duff said, "How would you like to join us and Captain Paterson at a nightclub?" Countess Modici had a great love affair with a man with whom she tried to cross the English channel in a rowboat—it's a great story. Duff was fascinating, and I thought I was honored to be invited to her party. As the evening drew on and the third expensive bottle of champagne was drunk, the two women had to go the ladies' room. That didn't surprise me. Then Captain Paterson said he had to go to the men's room. And I sat there. This is an old holdup game. I always thought I was a tough newspaperman, but this had never happened to me before. A half hour went by and the waiter handed me a bill for something like fifty dollars for all the champagne, most of which had been drunk before I arrived. I never saw any of them again. And that's how I got stuck by Duff Twysden. That's my Lady Brett story. She was the kind of gal almost everybody falls for, like a Ziegfeld girl. They're picked for their universal attraction to men.

DENIS BRIAN: Duff Twysden eventually married artist Clinton King and died in Santa Fe, New Mexico, of tuberculosis when she was forty-five. Hemingway told Hotchner that Duff's pallbearers had all been her lovers, one of whom slipped on the church steps, dropping the casket which split open. A likely story! She was cremated.

HAROLD LOEB: After our brief, silent encounter in Lipp's restaurant I never again met or communicated with Hemingway, but I remained in touch with Hadley.

DENIS BRIAN: Hemingway had dedicated *The Sun Also Rises* to his wife and son, but before it saw print in the fall of 1926 he had separated from Hadley over his affair with her friend, Pauline Pfeiffer. *Sun* made him famous.

GEORGE SELDES: My wife used to say of Hemingway, "Forgive him everything—he writes like an angel."

DENIS BRIAN: Hemingway's mother thought the contrary, calling *Sun* one of the filthiest books of the year. He was to write more about his life in Paris in *A Moveable Feast:* fact seen through gauze or a wickedly distorted magnifying glass, or was it simply Hemingway's truth?

CARLOS BAKER: Hemingway's idea about truth was a literary notion and what he meant by truth, I think, was how it looked to him at a particular time, in that particular place. This he wished to get and catch, as it were, in amber, forever, so that it would not be lost. But I think he would have been the first, or at least the second to admit that what he meant was not universal truth in the Aristotelian sense at all.

DENIS BRIAN: He boasted of having a rat-trap memory and nothing to prove, but conceded that all remembrance of things past is fiction. Then why attempt it? One reason was the need to justify himself, "for he felt he had been unfairly portrayed by some of his contemporaries."[1] To put it mildly. Or, as one of his greatest fans, Dorothy Parker, wrote: "Probably of no other living man has so much tripe been penned or spoken."[2]

[1] Jacqueline Tavernier-Courbin, "Fact and Fiction in *A Moveable Feast*," *The Hemingway Review*, Fall 1984.

[2] Dorothy Parker, "The Artist's Reward," *New Yorker*, November 30, 1929.

CHAPTER

FOUR

·

A MOVEABLE FEAST
OR GIVING THEM
THEIR JUST
DESSERTS?

DENIS BRIAN: Ernest Hemingway wrote twenty bitter and bittersweet sketches of his first five years in Paris, from 1921 to 1926. Entitled *A Moveable Feast*, the work was published in 1964, three years after his death when, of course, he couldn't be sued for libel. But by then most of his "victims" were also dead. *Time* magazine called the book "heart-breaking," the *New York Times Book Review* marveled at his "controlled lyricism," and *Newsweek* at the "startling vividness of his feelings" and their "intensity and immediacy," but critics were also disturbed by his mean, even malicious treatment of his friends. He portrays Scott Fitzgerald as a near-hysterical hypochondriac intimidated by his wife into believing he has an undersized penis; recalls his mentor, Ford Madox Ford, as a stupid, pompous snob with foul breath; and expresses shocked revulsion at discovering the lesbian relationship of Gertrude Stein and Alice Toklas. By contrast he pictures himself as a guileless innocent, a devoted husband and father—until the other woman appears on the scene. He also sees himself as the dedicated young writer trying to live the good life, while going hungry, in a city of the decadent, the debauched, and the drug-addicted. Anticipating skeptical readers, Hemingway invited them to view his memoirs as fiction. However, writer George Wickes who was in Paris at the same time estimates that the book is a compound of nine parts fact to only one of fiction. But which is which? That is the question.

MORLEY CALLAGHAN: I was impressed by the extraordinary bitterness toward some of the people in *A Moveable Feast.* Ernest Walsh the editor! Boy! And Ford Madox Ford! I know a little bit about some of the bitterness but I don't understand how he could be so bitter.

DENIS BRIAN: Perhaps as Hadley explained, it went with his being so sensitive.

MORLEY CALLAGHAN: He was a very sensitive, very aware person about other people when he was not excitedly involved, or personally prejudiced; just being aware of people and what they stood for. He was very good at that. I would more or less trust his judgment.

MALCOLM COWLEY: To tell you the truth, Hemingway could not bear rivals, essentially couldn't. And, except for his editor Maxwell Perkins, who was out of his field, he very often couldn't forgive anyone doing him a favor. That was the bad side of his complicated character.

CARLOS BAKER: He loved to make up stories, naturally, being a writer. Also he was given to self-dramatization and then he would sometimes push the truth to a shadow of its former self.

ARNOLD GINGRICH: His picture of Scott Fitzgerald in *A Moveable Feast* was essentially only too terribly true. Sure, it was malicious. But in that trip they made together from Paris to Lyons and back in the car without a top, he showed Scott at his most irritating and infuriating worst. And did it *marvelously.* Made him come alive as very few other things have done. That's what's so paradoxical about this. It's dreadfully unfair in many ways and yet there was this masterful characterization, or caricature if you take caricature as something almost more like the man than the man himself.

HADLEY MOWRER: Ernest was a tragic writer, but I think his account of his trip to Lyons with Scott Fitzgerald is very funny.

MARY WELSH HEMINGWAY [Ernest's fourth wife]: Although we lived under the same roof and were very good friends for seventeen years, I feel I have no right to *assume* things which *might* not be true. I try never to put myself inside Ernest's head. I think it's an intrusion. But in *A Moveable Feast* I think he wrote that piece, especially the funny one about coming up in that car without the top and all that funny stuff, as one sort of crazy memory of his association with Scott.

HENRY STRATER: The treatment he gave Scott in that Paris book was abominable. I'll tell you this: before Hemingway had anything published in America Scott sent a manuscript of Hemingway's to Scribner's and they said they wouldn't publish it. And Scott Fitzgerald, who needed the money, said that if they wouldn't publish the manuscript, *In Our Time*, he would leave them and find another publisher. For a guy who had to eat, that was a terrific thing to do.

ARNOLD GINGRICH: Scott never, never lost his first enthusiasm and admiration for Hemingway, in spite of being terribly badly treated by him in the early days when he was the fair-haired boy and he was pushing Hemingway forward.

ARCHIBALD MACLEISH: Ernest wrote *A Moveable Feast* during a bad time, in the early fifties. He wrote it in retrospect. Ernest wasn't the kind of person to turn on a man to whom he owed as much as he owed Scott.

ARNOLD GINGRICH: The most Scott ever let himself say was, "Ernest was always willing to lend a helping hand to the man on the rung above him." And he certainly had provocation to say worse than that. He never in any way begrudged anything that came to Ernest, whereas Ernest was damned begrudging of anything that came to anyone else.

A. E. HOTCHNER: Ernest also wrote how Scott had confided his anxiety over the size of his penis. [According to Hemingway, Zelda had complained to Scott that his penis was inadequate.] Ernest assured Scott, after inspecting his penis, that it was normal size, and then reassured him by taking him to a museum and showing him the penis on a statue.

BARNABY CONRAD: Hemingway's bullfighter friend Sidney Franklin told me that *Hemingway's* sexual organ was undersized—about the size of a thirty-thirty shell. I wrote about it in my book *Fun While It Lasted*, as retaliation for Hemingway's cavalier treatment of Fitzgerald in *A Moveable Feast*. On the other hand, Franklin was full of bull—if you'll excuse the expression—but he was, especially for a man that lived the wonderful life he led. He didn't have to exaggerate and lie the way he did in his book *A Bullfighter From Brooklyn*. Just about every other third page of that is true, I think.

BENJAMIN NEHMAN [a relative of Sidney Franklin]: I read *The Sun Also Rises* when I was a teenager. Although completely ignorant of sexual emotional problems I had a gut feeling that the author was in trouble. As

I got older and read more Hemingway, and became acquainted with his lifestyle as reported in the press, I became convinced that Hemingway had a problem: his need to be Superman, his need to have the largest gun, hunt behemoths, catch the largest fish, or even write *The Old Man and the Sea*. In the late 1960s I was driving back from Mexico and decided to look up Sidney Franklin who was then living in Mexico. I had not seen him since the 1930s when he was fairly close to Hemingway. Sidney was a distant relative of mine. After renewing our relationship, I asked my question to the point: what was Hemingway's sexual problem? His reply was: "How did you know?" I itemized my reasons as mentioned. He assured me there was nothing wrong with Hemingway except the size of his penis. It was like that of a little boy, Sidney said. Hemingway's ability to function physically and sexually was not affected. It rose to the occasion. Sidney did volunteer that Hemingway was not aggressive with women. I can imagine that women did not give him the opportunity to be aggressive.

BARNABY CONRAD: Sidney Franklin told me he thought Hemingway's lifelong problem was worrying about the size of his "picha." "But he had one, all right," Sidney said. "It isn't true, the way people will try to tell you that he lost it at Caporetto [especially as he wasn't there!], had it shot off, and that he was the model for Jake Barnes in *The Sun Also Rises*.

DENIS BRIAN: If Barnaby Conrad is right, Sidney Franklin is not to be trusted. And if Jeffrey Meyers is right—and he got his information from three sources—Franklin was not a disinterested observer of Hemingway's penis. In his biography of Hemingway, Professor Meyers reveals that, although Hemingway didn't know it at the time, despite his rugged appearance and daring, Franklin was a secret homosexual and a child molester.[1]

ARNOLD GINGRICH: I happen to be in a position to give firsthand eyewitness observations in both instances, of Hemingway's and Fitzgerald's sexual equipment. It's true in neither case that they were undersized. I swam with them and fished with them and all that. They were perfectly normal, ordinary, adequate grown men.

DENIS BRIAN: One Paris friend Hemingway never deserted was Ezra Pound. But he dropped Ford Madox Ford, who over the years wrote pathetic little notes to which Ernest never responded. How about Scott Fitzgerald?

MARY HEMINGWAY: My recollection of their last bits of correspondence

[1] Jeffrey Meyers, *Hemingway*, Harper & Row, 1985.

before Scott died in 1940 (aged forty-four) was that they had an exchange of very gentle and sweet letters.

DENIS BRIAN: In *A Moveable Feast*, Hemingway writes that his friendship with Gertrude Stein soured after he overheard a sado-masochist exchange between her and Alice Toklas, with the massive Gertrude pleading with "Pussy," as she called her, not to force her to do something, presumably of a sexual nature.

EARL ROVIT [author of *Ernest Hemingway*]: I was shocked when I read that, shocked at what had to have been an assumed naïvete. He had known Stein for years when he was supposed to have overheard this conversation, and suddenly to have all the tumblers fall into place. That's nonsense. He liked to play the newspaper reporter, knowing, but at the same time responding to all kinds of impressions. I cannot believe that he hadn't realized—if he hadn't, Hadley would have told him—that Gertrude Stein and Alice Toklas were lesbians and had their peculiar relationship, which inevitably would have assumed a dominant and a submissive partner. To pretend, my God, he'd never heard of something like that!

DENIS BRIAN: Mightn't that be bitterness recollected in anything but tranquility? Wasn't that after she had said he had a yellow streak?

EARL ROVIT: It was certainly an element in his psyche. I wouldn't say it was recollected. I suspect he made it up. He could very well have overheard Alice taking off at Gertrude any number of times, but I can't believe it was this kind of neat fictional stuff. He, unfortunately, wasn't all that nice a guy.

DENIS BRIAN: Was he mythmaking when he explained that his breakup with Gertrude Stein was caused by overhearing the lesbian conversation? Were the pleas of Gertrude Stein that he described authentic? And his shock of discovery?

SAMUEL M. STEWARD [a friend of Gertrude Stein and Alice Toklas]: Not at all: I think it was completely fabricated. It's almost incredible that after he knew them for several years he was just finding out they were lesbians.

ARCHIBALD MACLEISH: During the years when I knew Ernest best, when I knew him as closely as I've ever known a man, he talked to me about Gertrude Stein, whom I never met. I kept away from her as far as I could, simply because I was not interested in her approach to the kind of problems I had, in a very different way, with the art of letters. Ernest never spoke to me of her being a lesbian and he wouldn't allow anybody else to speak of it. Had he lived, I don't think he would have said it in print.

MORLEY CALLAGHAN: When the guy was with me he didn't talk that way at all. Or when he was with my wife. The young Hemingway, the guy who wrote those beautiful books, when he was with me he talked like an intimate friend, never this kind of stuff at all. He was the nicest man I ever knew.

GEORGE SELDES: At Gertrude Stein's weekly literary parties I'm sure there were lesbians and male homosexuals. Hemingway saw them all the time. I always thought his masculine prowess was a cover-up for a feeling that he was exhibiting slightly feminine traits simply because he was an artist and one of the literary set.

ARCHIBALD MACLEISH: I was astonished to learn that Gertrude Stein had talked of Ernest having "a yellow streak." His courage has been questioned because people can't believe he was as courageous as he's been pictured. Of course he was courageous. He had a hell of a lot of courage. He proved it in Italy and he proved it constantly. This is one of the things that sickens me. The people who question his courage are condemning themselves as psychopaths.

ARNOLD GINGRICH: I don't agree with Sherwood Anderson and Gertrude Stein that Ernest was yellow. He had the boy's bluff to show off to the neighborhood and do almost everything, no matter what the cost to himself, just as part of his tremendous pride in showing what he could do. I suppose this was part of his shyness and insecurity, an extreme manifestation of it.

WILLIAM WALTON [journalist and artist]: When Gertrude Stein talked to me she started in about Teddy Roosevelt being Ernest's real hero. "After all," she said, "Teddy's kind of action is what set the pattern of Ernest's childhood." And then she threw off the line I later realized she used over and over again, "Ah, but you see, the trouble about Hem is that he has a wide yellow streak down the middle of his back." She was having her revenge for some trouble between them that I don't understand.

MALCOLM COWLEY: He forced himself to walk forward into danger because of his competitive spirit, and because he was proving to himself that he was not scared.

ARCHIBALD MACLEISH: There was a lot of talk that because there was so much machismo in Ernest he must have been lacking in virility. Absolutely crazy! And he was a terribly funny man. Life with him could be very funny. My wife went with him to a bicycle race and he was extremely protective, being gallant. It was a rough crowd and when a man would brush up against him Ernest would challenge him. And this was a story he told about himself. He said to Ada, "Did you ever notice when I challenge anybody and he stands up, he's only two feet high?"

SAMUEL M. STEWARD: Alice Toklas was interviewed by German radio about this topic and when the interviewer insisted on trying to get an answer from her about Hemingway, she said: "Oh, Hemingway was a horror."

DENIS BRIAN: What did she mean?

SAMUEL M. STEWARD: That he was a horrible man. I don't think Alice ever liked him. I think the statement he made in a letter that he would like to have fucked Gertrude was simply trying to get even with her.

DENIS BRIAN: Hemingway said he sensed a mutual sexual attraction between himself and Gertrude Stein, which Alice of course resented.

SAMUEL M. STEWARD: No sexual attraction on Gertrude's part. She was absolutely lesbian.

DENIS BRIAN: She described him as very attractive.

SAMUEL M. STEWARD: Like all the other young men that hung around Gertrude, most of whom were homosexuals. She thought Hemingway was a secret homosexual and she tried to get him to admit it.

DENIS BRIAN: She went about it a strange way, by saying homosexuals did horrible, repugnant things after which they were disgusted with themselves, but that lesbians did nothing disgusting. How did she expect that by insulting and denigrating homosexuals she'd get him to admit he was one of them?

SAMUEL M. STEWARD: She was trying to get a rise out of Hemingway, to get him to stand up for homosexuals.

DENIS BRIAN: And he didn't.

SAMUEL M. STEWARD: No, he didn't. I don't know who was wiser there.

DENIS BRIAN: Well, her ploy failed. Do you think he was a secret homosexual?

SAMUEL M. STEWARD: I had a conversation with Alice Toklas many years after Gertrude Stein died, in which she said—stating it was gossip—that Hemingway and Sir Francis Rose, an artist, had met in the baths in Paris just off the Place Concorde, and had a little fling together. And then they found out who each other was and never saw each other again.

DENIS BRIAN: Alice Toklas was a great gossip, wasn't she?

SAMUEL M. STEWARD: Oh, yes. She announced this was just gossip.

DENIS BRIAN: His close friends, Archibald MacLeish and William Walton, and his brother Leicester were sure he wasn't in the least homosexual. Was Gertrude Stein also trying to get a rise out of him when she suggested he should run a laundry?

SAMUEL M. STEWARD: She told me the same thing, except she said I should be a butcher. She said that if you were teaching all day, for example in my case, you were using the word-finding part of your brain, and when you started to write later each day that part was all worn out.

DENIS BRIAN: If you think Hemingway's explanation is phony, why do you think they ended their friendship?

SAMUEL M. STEWARD: Gertrude told me the reason for their fight with Hemingway was that neither she nor Alice could stand drunks. One night Hemingway turned up completely drunk and had to be forcibly ejected by two men who were visiting Gertrude. One of them was Professor Clarence Andrews, who taught English at Ohio State University.

DENIS BRIAN: Do you think this is true, Mr. Walton?

WILLIAM WALTON: Yes, probably. I heard dimly about an incident of this kind but nothing firsthand.

DENIS BRIAN: The irony is that one of the two men who forcibly ejected Hemingway was a homosexual.

WILLIAM WALTON [laughs]: That would add to the whole theme. I hope it was true.

DENIS BRIAN: I doubted it because several people, Mary Hemingway among them, told me Hemingway could hold his drink so well he rarely even staggered slightly when walking.

WILLIAM WALTON: Not true at all. He got absolutely cockeyed.

DENIS BRIAN: And would he become aggressive then?

WILLIAM WALTON: Of course.

DENIS BRIAN: That seems to solve one mystery.

MORLEY CALLAGHAN: I'm not so sure. I'm skeptical of these so-called true stories that bob up everywhere. I never saw Ernest rolling around drunk in those days. I saw him drinking an awful lot, but that's all. I know a lot of people didn't like him and never found much evidence to justify their dislike. In his relationship with me he was always splendid. Therefore I just followed my nose and liked him. I had known him well in Toronto and when I met him again in Paris we had the kind of talk, just loafing around, that he evidently didn't have with other people.

DENIS BRIAN: Did you hero-worship him?

MORLEY CALLAGHAN: No, no, no. No. I think he felt both my wife and I were pretty candid with him. You must remember I never had a bad experience with Hemingway, so some of the stories I've heard about him are terribly hard for me to believe. He was supposed to talk in an endless flood of obscenities. This is very strange.

GEORGE SELDES: He began creating the Hemingway myth from the very first days of his success. One aspect of it was the oft-told tale of being rejected when he first began to write fiction. It seemed to please his ego, to build him up as a great writer. I'm sure he knew damn well he was building himself up and enjoyed his story and the enlargement of it about being an overlooked genius in his earliest days in Paris.

MORLEY CALLAGHAN: He did tell tall stories, and it wasn't the normal behavior of a writer who likes to make up stories. He identified himself very strongly with the stories he told, as if he believed them. I also think he encouraged others to make legends out of his life. Max Perkins, for example, told me of Ernest attending a boxing match in France between a champion and an inferior boxer, and the champion was badly punishing the other guy. When the fight ended, said Perkins, Ernest jumped into the ring and knocked out the champion. I never believed it.

DENIS BRIAN: Why didn't you ask Hemingway if it was true?

MORLEY CALLAGHAN: Oh, I would never think of asking him that. It would be embarrassing if it hadn't happened, you see. Louise Bryant, the former wife of William Bullitt, the U.S. ambassador to Moscow, told me that she was with Hemingway and a Turkish boy, an expert knife-thrower who could pin an object—like a man's hand—to a door at twenty paces. And, she said, Hemingway had gone to a door and challenged the knife-thrower to pin his hand to it. I laughed with the others at the Select when she told the story. Ernest might have done it as a dramatic gesture or to test his courage. It was just Louise Bryant's story. Nobody ever presented me with an affidavit.[1]

DENIS BRIAN: In his book, *Writing Lives*, Leon Edel wonders: "What is Hemingway defending himself against, so compulsive is his drive toward

[1]Sportswriter Bill Corum told of meeting Hemingway in the Stork Club in the late fifties when they discussed knife throwing. Ernest borrowed a carving knife from the chef to prove he could throw a knife between his bare toes without harming himself. Strangely, Corum forgets if the demonstration took place—after all they were drinking—but noticed at their next meeting that Ernest was limping. This story is reported in Milt Machlin, *The Private Hell of Hemingway*, Paperback Library, 1962.

action and away from examined feeling, so consistent is his quest to surpass himself, as if he must prove—even after he has the world's acclaim—that he is the best and greatest. . . . Somewhere within resides a troubled, uncertain, insecure figure, who works terribly hard to give himself eternal assurance."[1]

MORLEY CALLAGHAN: That's a kind of rewrite of the stuff in my *Paris* book. That's what I said in effect and he's just dressing it up. It's just that Hemingway had to be this. There's no mystery about it at all. I know many, many people who are driving themselves crazy trying to be Number One.

DENIS BRIAN: What Hemingway hid from his friends like Callaghan and Scott Fitzgerald were his black moods of deep depression, when he was anything but a world beater.

HADLEY MOWRER: I recognized that some of the time. He was very down when he got ill. He did suffer a lot with his throat and we didn't know any particular doctors at the time. We just didn't go in for doctors.

DENIS BRIAN: After reading *A Moveable Feast* I couldn't understand how he could say he was so much in love with you and yet he left you for Pauline Pfeiffer.

HADLEY MOWRER: In a way Ernest felt he had made a mistake in leaving me for Pauline.

HAROLD LOEB: Kitty Cannell and I introduced Hemingway to Pauline and Jinny Pfeiffer. I think Pauline was looking for a man.

HADLEY MOWRER: I liked Pauline. I was a very poor young woman and Pauline was with the Paris office of *Vogue* and from the Hudnut family, which means money. Pauline's Uncle Gus owned Richard Hudnut Perfumes, Sloan's Liniment, and William Warner Pharmaceuticals. I didn't have any money because Ernest hadn't clicked yet. A very great friend of Harold Loeb's, Kitty Cannell—she was a dancer and awfully nice to me—told someone that "Hadley doesn't have any decent clothes and it's such a shame." Ernest, instead of clothes, had just made me a birthday gift, really for himself, of the wonderful Joan Miró painting, *The Farm*.

DENIS BRIAN: Author Kay Boyle was living in Grasse, in the South of France, at the time and she tells that "my sister Joan came down from Paris with a friend who also worked on *Vogue*, a young woman called Pauline Pfeiffer. For a week before their arrival, a letter a day had come for Pauline from Ernest Hemingway. My sister explained to me in confidence

[1]Leon Edel, *Writing Lives: Principia Biographica*, W. W. Norton, 1984.

that Pauline was one of Hadley Hemingway's closest friends, and that Ernest was writing to her about a certain kind of perfume that was bottled in Grasse, and a certain kind of lingerie that could be found only in Cannes. He wanted Pauline to buy these things for him to give as a surprise to Hadley, whom he deeply loved. . . . In the next few months Hadley would be put aside and in her place Pauline Pfeiffer would be Mrs. Hemingway; for the letters that he had written to her in Grasse had nothing to do with a particular perfume or a particular kind of lingerie."[1]

HADLEY MOWRER: At first when I knew he was in love with Pauline I felt alternative relief and rage. I told them they mustn't see each other for a hundred days, and at the end of that time if they were still in love I would divorce Ernest. I felt terribly mean and I'm glad to say I didn't stick to my ultimatum.

ARCHIBALD MACLEISH: Ernest and Hadley were truly in love with each other before the breakup.

ADA MACLEISH: Hadley thought it wasn't going to work out and for the sake of the child and everybody else, it would be better if she just removed herself.

ARCHIBALD MACLEISH: I am very willing to believe that Hadley was shocked when she discovered her very good friend, Pauline, was involved with Ernest. And Pauline knew it too, because she went back to America and put things off for months.

ADA MACLEISH: Ernest came to our apartment a good deal to take a bath or shower, or just to see us. We saw him almost as one of the family. He had very little money and lived a very simple life. He was a dear, affectionate friend and a good companion. I was very fond of him. He had been in love with Hadley. I can't tell when that stopped, perhaps it never did. But life with him was more than she could take. Ernest was very intolerant. I don't think anybody could have lived with him a long time because he was very emotional. It was hard to know how to handle him. He would say terrible things and I think he was probably sorry he'd said them two minutes later. But that was Ernest. Hadley was a sound, straightforward person. I was fond of Pauline, too. She and Hadley were very different personalities. I wouldn't say anybody would have been good for Ernest. It would have been better if he had just occasional ladies and didn't marry them.

HADLEY MOWRER: After we separated, Ernest lived in the Gerald Murphys'

[1]Kay Boyle-Robert McAlmon, *Being Geniuses Together.*

[wealthy Americans and models for Dick and Nicole Diver in *Tender Is the Night*] studio. Then he and Archie MacLeish went everywhere together. They'd come up to see me together in my apartment in the summer. Archie was a great friend, someone he could talk with on an equal basis. Ernest and Pauline were very much in love and that was so upsetting to me, because you can't stand in the way of that. I made them promise to stay apart and not write to each other. She went home to Arkansas. Ernest and I lived apart during that time and we were friendly. He always came around to see me. My heart was not broken. I did love him in a way more than ever, but as though he were a child. Much of our life together had been idyllic but it had been exhausting, too.

JOHN [Bumby] HEMINGWAY: My father was a person of inner turmoil about anything he did to hurt anybody.

A FRIEND: But he could be very cruel. Invariably the real cruelty was to women who he thought had either betrayed him or were not playing straight. He was never as cruel to a man as he was to a woman. He was never cruel to Hadley, except in leaving her for Pauline. I think he always loved Hadley all the way through his life. He not only admitted it but in *A Moveable Feast* there is more show of loving Hadley in spite of everything and forever.

DENIS BRIAN: Marlene Dietrich is supposed to have said to him: "Ernest, I can understand your wanting to sleep with them, but *why* do you marry them?"

JOHN HEMINGWAY: I think he was the kind of person who, if he went to bed with a woman on a semipermanent basis, married her.

ARCHIBALD MACLEISH: One thing that hurt him very much about his divorce from Hadley was his real attachment to his son, Bumby. He was quite mad about Bumby and used to quote him all the time.

JOHN HEMINGWAY: At no time did I ever feel that there had been any bitterness between my parents, either because there wasn't any or because they were super civilized about it so far as not exposing me to anything. Anyway, I held my father in such high esteem I could see him do no wrong.

HADLEY MOWRER: I know he later implied Pauline's money was a big attraction. But it certainly wasn't the reason he married her.

JOHN HEMINGWAY: He really suffered. I think everybody does who breaks up a personal relationship.

CARLOS BAKER: He also suffered a lot physically. He denied he was unduly accident-prone, but his poor eyesight, and physical awkwardness combined to cause a remarkable series of mishaps.

ARCHIBALD MACLEISH: Although he was a remarkably strong, heavy man, he was a bit hypochondriacal. He was always having sore throats. I was there shortly after a skylight fell on his head. I think he'd probably had a good deal to drink and pulled the wrong rope in the can. I was the first one called. Someone dug up a taxi at about half past two in the morning and I went around and picked him up and took him to the hospital. He'd lost a lot of blood by that time so that he babbled a good deal on the way to the hospital. He took a great many stitches with just a local anesthetic and he sat through the whole thing talking to the doctor, telling him the story of his life. I sat in the next room listening. It was a damned painful thing and it wasn't very well done, either.

ARNOLD GINGRICH: He entombed each wife in a book [laughs]. You can't literally cross every *t* and dot every *i*, but to a great extent every novel contains one real-life dead marriage. He wrote things out of his life, got rid of them by writing about them. And that included the women.

MORLEY CALLAGHAN: Scott Fitzgerald thought the same.

ARNOLD GINGRICH: There were always, I felt, the fairly phony crocodile tears and the almost excessive protesting about having loved only one, which grew and grew and grew. In *A Moveable Feast* there's this almost deification of Hadley.

MARY HEMINGWAY: Gingrich, along with a great many people, considers himself *the* final authority on Ernest. He certainly did not know Ernest during Ernest's marriage to Hadley but subsequently, when he married Pauline. And so why he makes these vast, authoritative assertions is a puzzle to me. But everybody and his brother and cousin and his uncle and aunt all think they are the definitive authorities on Ernest. It's kind of amusing. The ordinary life of a healthy and honest-to-himself man would probably, in his generation and this generation, include more than one dame. On the other hand, in those days people were more or less committed to marry the woman they wanted to shack up with. That was the custom. It would seem to me someone of Ernest's wide interests and exuberance, a normally healthy fellow, would be interested in more than one woman. He'd naturally have two or three girls, and the fact that he faithfully got rid of one [laughs] and married another is just a circumstance of this recently past era.

DENIS BRIAN: Hemingway gave his American royalties from *The Sun Also Rises* to Hadley, lived in a small room with a bed and a table and nothing else, ate mostly french fries and leeks, and drank watered wine. He wrote desperate, emotional letters to Pauline, temporarily exiled by Hadley's decree to America, saying he could not stand the strain of their separation.

HADLEY MOWRER: He also broke with nearly all his Paris friends. The Gerald Murphys, for instance, just adored him and he fought with them.

MRS. JOHN DOS PASSOS: My husband never understood why Hemingway described him as "a pilot fish" in *A Moveable Feast*, the pilot fish that destroyed Hemingway's private Eden. They were all mutual friends. It wasn't a question of any one person attracting other people. The Murphys were quite wealthy and were very generous and lavish, and spent a lot of their money. In the earlier days Hemingway had a great sense of humor, then as time went on my husband felt he was always playing a part, shadowboxing, and pretending he was somebody else.

DENIS BRIAN: At this time Donald Ogden Stewart discovered a bitter streak in Hemingway. When, at a party in Archibald MacLeish's apartment, Ernest read his poem concerning Dorothy Parker's abortion, Stewart called it "viciously unfair and unfunny." To Stewart's lasting sorrow his frankness ended their friendship. While Hemingway was breaking up with his friends, Hadley's friends were rallying to her side to help her through the divorce. Ford Madox Ford's wife, Stella, remarked that Hadley didn't want to divorce Ernest but that Pauline, being Catholic, insisted that he marry her. He did, on May 10, 1927, in Paris. With apparent glee the sardonic Robert McAlmon reported a closing scene in Paris, at the Trois et As bar. "Lady Brett was there with her new man; the first Mrs. Hemingway arrived, and soon in came Hemingway with his second wife. Hemingway having turned Catholic was endeavoring to convince his first wife that their marriage had not been a marriage at all as it had not been performed by a priest. Hadley Hemingway had answered, 'All right, then the child is altogether mine.' Hadley was poised and dignified, and her wit and discretion were to be admired. After greeting all the others, she came to sit with Louise Bryant, William Bullitt, and me, and she too saw the high comedy in the situation. None of us had known until she informed us that Hemingway was now a Catholic."[1]

[1] Kay Boyle-Robert McAlmon, *Being Geniuses Together*.

MADELAINE HEMINGWAY MILLER: Mother had been disgruntled with Ernest because of four-letter words. How childish! But to her it was dirty talk. Then, of course, his divorcing Hadley to go with this Catholic person who just stole him from Hadley. And they were good friends, Hadley and Pauline. I went out to my golf lesson with Hadley when she came to visit after this and she said, "If I'd had any sense at all I'd have let him go with Pauline and burn himself out and then we could have begun again."

FIVE

•

KEY WEST AND
OUT WEST

DENIS BRIAN: Hemingway arrived at Key West in the spring of 1928, after an undulating Atlantic crossing in a claustrophobic cabin. But he was in good spirits, having recovered from a deep depression in which he feared he would never write again. He was free, too, from the fear of blindness caused by Bumby poking a finger in his good eye, and from the pain of a skylight falling on his head—though with a permanent scar as a reminder. His chronic sore throat was in remission, as was his remorse for having left Hadley. He was pregnant with his second novel, *A Farewell to Arms,* and Pauline was several months pregnant with his second son.

CHARLES THOMPSON: When he first came through here he thought you could drive a car all the way from Key West to the mainland. He didn't know there was a ferry. So he stopped over and was fishing on the bridges. A friend of mine saw him and said he knew a fellow who liked to fish, and he sent him down to me. We had a bit of luck fishing and he had his friends come down: Waldo Pierce and Mike Strater and Max Perkins and Dos Passos, also Bill Smith. I often went fishing with him. Even if he hadn't been a famous writer I'd have remembered him. In any group, Ernest was the most impressive personality. He was very curious about everything. He would make a joke out of everything. He helped people just to help them, not because it would reflect on him in any way.

LORINE THOMPSON [Charles's wife]: Oh yes, he was very sympathetic and very sensitive. Maybe not always sympathetic, but sensitive to others' feelings. One of his philosophies, which he used always to say to me because I'm a great animal lover and something was always happening to my dogs and I'd get very upset about it, was that you shouldn't become too fond of anything in this world because something's going to happen to it and you're going to be hurt. I think he tried to take the same attitude toward his wife, Pauline, and later to some extent to his children. I don't think any of the books written about Ernest have given Pauline the credit for the part she played in his life. You see, most of his best books were written while he was living in Key West. I felt that Pauline kept Ernest's nose a little bit to the grindstone. I don't mean intentionally. But I think she did everything to keep Ernest at work, to make conditions favorable for him to work. Pauline's Uncle, Gus Pfeiffer—there's no getting around it—with the money he gave Pauline made it possible for Ernest to spend a great deal more time writing than working on other things, and to take his time doing it. Probably the boys don't like the idea and I'm sure Ernest wouldn't. Pauline and her sister Jinny were over there, and although they didn't have money, their father and uncle did. [Two of Hemingway's close friends a few years later were multimillionaire Winston Guest, a distant cousin of Winston Churchill; and another wealthy Palm Beach resident, Thomas Shevlin.] Pauline was a very determined woman in a lot of ways, a very capable person. I was extremely fond of her, and Ernest was very devoted to her for quite a while.

ELSIE BYRON [Helped run her father's ranch in Wyoming]: Hemingway and Pauline went to Kansas City in the summer of 1928 and their son, Patrick, was born there. Then he came to Wyoming. He had been down at Eleanor Donnelley's Folly Ranch. I had been on a pack trip with a bunch of girls when he came to our place, the Wigwam, and I saw him a good deal. He was a nice-looking fellow and I enjoyed talking with him and all. When we closed the camp he and Pauline went to stay with Papa. My father's ranch was out in the Wolf Mountains, thirty miles north of Sheridan. Ernest was working quite a bit on *A Farewell to Arms* at the time. Afterwards I had John Jameison from Chicago on a pack trip. He said he was in Naples with Hemingway during World War I, and he wondered what had gone on that he didn't know about. He thought Ernest was trying to make out that all the adventures and romance in the novel had really happened to him.

There was one thing that happened that Pauline got such a kick out of. She and Ernest were in the car with Papa and they met one of the sheepherders. He was mad about something and he started swearing. Papa said, "Now, now! There's a lady in the car!" The sheepherder looked at Pauline and said, "I don't see no lady." Pauline was dressed in overalls and a denim shirt and had her hair cut short and a little French cap on. He didn't know she was a woman. They thought that was quite a joke. We thought lots of Pauline. We thought she was quite a gal. She was a very enjoyable person and I heard from her for several years afterwards. I've never seen anybody act like Ernest did: he snatched papers and photos from Pauline while she was looking at them. She'd be looking at something and he'd grab it right out of her hands and look at it first, and then hand it back.[1] I used to get mad at him over that, but you couldn't be mad at him for long no matter what he did. My mother thought his books were quite immoral.

FRANCIS GODOLPHIN [husband of Ernest's Oak Park friend and neighbor, Isabelle Simmons]: On the way to Key West from Wyoming Ernest and Pauline went to see his parents, then spent some time with Archibald MacLeish. After that he joined Scott Fitzgerald to see the Princeton-Yale game. On that particular morning when they landed in our apartment together they were both a bit tight and very cheerful, very pleasant and very happy. They seemed very harmonious, enjoying each other and having a hell of a fine time. They were at the apartment for a time, then they went off to the Cottage Club and to the game.

MADELAINE HEMINGWAY MILLER: When Ernest got back to Key West he asked me to type the final draft of A Farewell to Arms. I watched him labor over a sentence to say the thing precisely the way he wanted it. My experience as a nurse helped him, too. In the novel he had the nurse shake the thermometer after giving it to Catherine, and I told him that wasn't right; she should shake it before. Bumby [John] had been living with Hadley in France and he was expected to spend some time with Ernest

[1] Mary Hemingway remarked that Ernest preceded her through doors and she wondered whether this was eagerness or ego.

and Pauline, so Ernest went up to New York to meet him and bring him back.

JOHN HEMINGWAY: I'd come over from France on the boat in December 1928, when I was five. I'm not sure who brought me; I think Jinny Pfeiffer. Papa met me in New York and that's one time he went to see Max Perkins. I remember going to Max's office or house with him. Anyway, we went down to Pennsylvania Station and were on the train. I can't remember if it was there or when we were on the train on the way to Philadelphia that he got the telegram about his father, which I didn't see. [It was at Trenton station.] He just told me that his father was dead and he had to go. I was very sad that he didn't come with me. The porter took care of me all the way to Key West. It worked out fine. Later, my father did tell me about it almost as if I was being let into a great secret. He said his father shot himself. I think his father's death was a great shock to him. At times he said derogatory things about his father, usually in the vein that he had lost respect for him because he toed the line to my grandmother. He just couldn't stand the idea of his father being henpecked.

MADELAINE HEMINGWAY MILLER: Ernest was very tough on our Uncle George, because when father died there was a great disappointment over what he should have done and didn't do when mother was in distress. Uncle George just said, "You get a lawyer." He wasn't helpful at all. He was the one my father asked to borrow money from to pay a debt, and Uncle George said, "No, you got into it, you get out of it."

DENIS BRIAN: John Dos Passos said he was in Key West when a parcel arrived for Ernest from his mother, Grace. In it was a chocolate cake, a roll of her paintings, and the gun with which his father had killed himself. Dos Passos's wife, Katy, remarked: "Mrs. Hemingway is a very odd woman."

HADLEY MOWRER: It was strange, wasn't it? It was a shock to him when he got it. It was almost like suggesting Ernest do the same thing—shoot himself.

ARCHIBALD MACLEISH: Ernest took it as a personal threat.

JOHN HEMINGWAY: There was some point when his mother sent him the pistol. That time he said to me, "One day I'll let you have the pistol," which excited me very much. The significance of it didn't hit me at the time. I really don't know if he had asked for it or whether his mother sent it to him without his asking. But the strength of his feelings against his mother knew no bounds. He never spent hours telling me what a horrible person she was, but there were times when he was talking to adults, and I remember him saying, "Goddamn that woman!" I really think the main thing that bothered him was that she had henpecked his father.

DENIS BRIAN: Hemingway obviously wanted others to think his mother had behaved callously in sending him the gun, when he had actually requested it.

LEICESTER HEMINGWAY: I know for a fact that Ernest asked for the gun. He told me I could have all the other guns, but this one was the gun he wanted, and would I see to it that he got it? And I helped Mother: we both went down to the Cook County Courthouse and made application to get the gun back. It had been seized by the coroner's office and we had to go through paper filling-out and rigamarole, and it finally was returned to Mother. My mother then did, with a certain amount of dignity I'm sure, get it to Ernest. He had indeed requested it. Now what he did with it I do not know. It never showed up again in any further doings with the family. I think he must have destroyed it and I think that's why he wanted it—to destroy it.

MADELAINE HEMINGWAY MILLER: Ernest was on and off with Mother. I have many letters in which he was loving with her.

A FRIEND: Ernest explained his occasional affectionate letters to his mother as role-playing the devoted son to please an old woman. "I hate her guts," he said more than once, "and she hates mine."

CAROL HEMINGWAY GARDNER: He didn't really hate Mother. He's the one who's most like her. They were both very dramatic people. He would have periods of blaming everything in his life on her and yet she was a very big and good influence on him in his early years.

A FRIEND: The main thing he held against his mother was that she dominated the bejesus out of his father. In any household a son hates to see the dominant male not stay dominant. She took his father's balls away. He simply became the providing male. She had so much more push, she was so much firmed in her demands and in her feelings about her rights, and what was right, how things should be, and "No, that's not the way it's going to be!" She just dominated the hell out of him. Ernest's father fell in love with his mother because of her voice. She gave up a possible singing career to marry him. Having fallen in love with her, he was her absolute slave.

CAROL HEMINGWAY GARDNER: No. I think my father really admired and loved my mother very much. She ruled the house in no uncertain terms, but he really kept everything going because she was very much involved in her own affairs.

FRANCIS GODOLPHIN: Grace Hemingway was kind of pretentious and arty, and Hemingway didn't think it was genuine. A couple of his sisters seemed to be the same way. Only one of them he really liked, Madelaine. [He also liked Ursula.] He hated pretentiousness. I thought he was very genuine.

A FRIEND: I once defined tension as being a regular guest at Grace Hemingway's dinner table.

DENIS BRIAN: How about Ernest Hemingway's dinner table?

TOBY BRUCE [Hemingway's general factotum]: He could have quite a temper with someone who bugged him, but as long as he wasn't bugged he was fine. Ernest could find fault with anything he wanted to find fault with, so he could make up some beautiful excuses for being sore about something. Then, after he blew his top about it, he'd cool off.

ARCHIBALD MACLEISH: In Key West Ernest really liked old Bra Saunders, a professional fishing guide, and Charlie Thompson, and he went on liking them—with bad weather in between.

OLIVE NORQUIST: I saw another side to him. He was always being kind and considerate of people and took great care with his son, Bumby. Somebody always had to be with the boy. I think he feared kidnapping. This was the time of the Lindbergh baby kidnapping. The Hemingways were staying at our ranch in Wyoming. We were sitting in the lodge and it was Bumby's bedtime. It was dark and the boy was only five or six years old. We knew he was afraid to walk across the ranch alone, but nobody knew what to say without embarrassing him. All of a sudden, Ernest jumped up. "Damn!" he said. "I forgot something at the cabin. I'll have to walk back with you, Bumby."

JOHN HEMINGWAY: I don't recall that, but, of course, the whole point was that I shouldn't be conscious of it. But I remember being afraid of the dark.

GREGORY HEMINGWAY [Ernest's third son]: He was always considerate of our fears of the dark, and said he'd been so afraid of the dark after he was wounded in Italy he had to sleep with the light on in his room for six months.

DENIS BRIAN: The protective father was even more spirited in defense of his reputation. An article in *Bookman* magazine included him among writers who wrote dirty books. According to Carlos Baker's biography, he threatened the editor of *Bookman*, John Farrar, with a physical thrashing for printing such trash. According to Lesley Frost, the poet Robert Frost's daughter, he went even further.

LESLEY FROST: I think all kinds of artists who live on that ragged edge, between genius and what genius does to people, are on the edge of unreason. If you'd seen the quarrels and the jealousies and the fiendish attitudes of the group around Ezra Pound, it was just wild—they threw each other downstairs and threw things at each other and all over the wording of a poem! I was working for John Farrar in New York City and every few days Hemingway would come storming in. One day, he said he'd kill Farrar. He said he was going to get a gun. So we barricaded John Farrar in his office and he got under the desk. And Hemingway came back with a great long riding whip which he had bought at Abercrombie and Fitch next door and said he was going to have a real . . . Well, we all screamed with laughter, and slammed doors, and finally he went away.

CARLOS BAKER: I know Hemingway didn't like Farrar and occasionally did some storming.

DENIS BRIAN: That same year, 1929, Hemingway spent a month in Spain where he met Sidney Franklin, the Brooklyn-born bullfighter. He persuaded Franklin to let him join the caravan of cars following Franklin's bullfighting appearances throughout the country. They became friends.

ARCHIBALD MACLEISH: On a hunting trip to Montana the following year, Ernest was driving the car with Dos Passos beside him and they went off the road into a ditch. Ernest's right arm was broken just above the elbow, a bad break. Pauline asked me to come out to the hospital because he was in a very unhappy state of mind. Naturally, he would be. I flew out. It was fairly expensive and I didn't have any money. Northwest Airlines then was a fence-hopping operation. I finally arrived and Ernest—surrounded by adoring nurses—took a look at me and said, "You've just come out here to see me die!" This is the kind of thing he was capable of saying. I didn't know if he was serious. You never knew with Ernest. Maybe it was a crack. He felt badly about it afterwards.

LORINE THOMPSON: He wasn't a very good invalid. When anything happened to him, he made an awful lot of it.

A FRIEND: It took several months before he was fit enough to fish again. That was the spring of 1931, when one of his fishing companions off the Keys and the coast of Havana was Jane Mason, the beautiful wife of Grant Mason. She was in love with Ernest at various times.

JANE MASON GINGRICH: I liked Ernest, but I didn't love him. And I liked his wife, Pauline.

A FRIEND: Jane was the woman who jumped or fell out of the second- or third-story window in Cuba, and Ernest remarked that she had fallen for him. Things went on in Cuba that you wouldn't believe.

JOHN RYBOVICH, JR.: Ernest said he liked Cuba because they had both fishing and fucking there. I believe they had him try out all the houses of prostitution.

A FRIEND: Cuba was pure alcohol most of the time. Jane Mason not only drank a bit, but was one of the wildest, hairiest, most drinking, wenching, sexy superwomen in the world, when she was in her twenties and thirties and early forties. She was proud of being the model for the Macomber woman in "The Short Happy Life of Francis Macomber." Her husband, Grant, was not the model for the cowardly husband. He was a hell of a nice guy.

DENIS BRIAN: Hemingway disagreed. In an undated letter to Archibald MacLeish, he described Grant Mason as a wealthy twerp who, while his wife's back was broken in a car crash, spent his time working on a motorboat engine. Ernest told MacLeish that he had tried to write a very short story about Jane Mason similar to the one about Agnes— something to the effect that Jane wanted to marry a different man each spring but couldn't in the spring of 1933, because of a broken back. Hemingway's conclusion was that people earn their own bad luck and that people who marry twerps are liable to repeat the mistake if they marry again.

A FRIEND: I know it's strange that Jane should be proud to be the model for the Macomber woman, but, you see, all her life she came close to being famous without being famous. She married a lot of people, Grant Mason, John Hamilton, George Abel, and finally Arnold Gingrich. She had a lot of money. She'd been in international society since she was a teenager, but she never got the acclaim she wanted. President Calvin Coolidge said she was "the likeliest young lady that ever crossed over the threshold in the White House." That's about the biggest compliment she ever got. "Likeliest," to a New Englander like Coolidge, meant "most beautiful, loveliest."

MADELAINE HEMINGWAY MILLER: People are pleased to have a place in history and "a prize bitch" is better than an absolute nobody.

JANE MASON GINGRICH: Ernest never told me he was writing a character based on me.

ARNOLD GINGRICH: After he'd written the Macomber story, he told me people were flattered to be portrayed in works of fiction.

DENIS BRIAN: Hemingway describes Margot Macomber as having a perfectly oval face. Does Mrs. Gingrich?

ARNOLD GINGRICH: I guess so. Sure.

DENIS BRIAN: He wrote that Margot commanded five thousand dollars for supplying her photograph to endorse a beauty product which she never used.

ARNOLD GINGRICH: That's true. Jane was the first to endorse Pond's face cream. Cecil Beaton took her photograph for it.

DENIS BRIAN: Margot was married to Francis Macomber for eleven years, according to the story. How long was Mrs. Gingrich married to Grant Mason?

ARNOLD GINGRICH: From 1927 to 1938. That's eleven years. He gets it bang on sometimes. Then there was a lot of Jane in the character Helene Bradley in Hemingway's *To Have and Have Not.* There was an awful lot about Jane and Grant Mason and about Dos Passos, oh God, that we took out and had those fights with the lawyer about. Curiously enough, a lot of what I objected to about the rich and about Dos being a pilot fish and so on, showed up almost damn near word-for-word in *A Moveable Feast.* Oh God, if you could get hold of the original manuscript of *To Have and Have Not*—I don't know if it still exists because he tore up whole hunks— but if it exists it should be fascinating to compare the treatment of Dos Passos in *A Moveable Feast* with the stuff that was taken out of *To Have and Have Not.* [In *To Have and Have Not* Helene Bradley is a wealthy woman who lusts after writers as well as collecting their books. She's blatantly unfaithful to her wimp of a husband and raves at her lover for going limp when her husband catches them making love. Gingrich was apparently well aware that Hemingway was writing about his own sexual adventures with Jane Mason barely disguised as Helene Bradley. As Gingrich was attracted to Mrs. Mason, whom he later married, he was an especially keen observer of the scene.]

DENIS BRIAN: Did Hemingway acknowledge to you as his publisher (of *Esquire*) that he lied or romanced about his experiences?

ARNOLD GINGRICH: He'd never come right out and say something was not true, but he would pretty often almost imply that "you have to give them the show they expect." This would be any place, no matter whether in a tavern talking to somebody, pulling his leg or what. A good deal of it was putting people on, indulging in mock modesty, playing things way down in the British way. Or, similarly, the tall tales, all kinds of exaggerations. He was never too concerned with the truth. He loved to arrange it.

DENIS BRIAN: When you went fishing with him in Key West, did you like him?

ARNOLD GINGRICH: Very, very much in those early days. My reaction was that of a tenderfoot scout for his scoutmaster, for God's sake. The guy was marvelous at doing all those things one would like to do, and doing them supremely well. He was great to fish with and shoot with and at that time he was rather impatient of the more social and polite activities. He had a tendency to shun them. I remember his going so far as to show up at the White House with a two-day beard. It was again part of a pose, the rugged he-man, mountaineer, guide-type character. He got away from that to some degree, later.

DENIS BRIAN: I know you and Hemingway used to have drag races, Mrs. Gingrich. Is that how you landed in Doctor's Hospital in 1932?

JANE MASON GINGRICH: No. I was driving the car to nowhere in particular, just for fun. Bumby and Patrick were in the back seat. And I went over a cliff.

ARNOLD GINGRICH: At the moment of the crash, a little voice in the back seat, Bumby, said: "We're perfectly all right, Mrs. Mason. Are you all right?"

DENIS BRIAN: Grace under pressure.

ARNOLD GINGRICH: She wasn't all right, though. She had broken her back.

DENIS BRIAN: It isn't clear whether she did in fact break her back in that crash or merely damage it then and break it shortly afterwards when she jumped from a window. It was one of her several unsuccessful suicide attempts. In the hospital where she recovered from her back injury after spinal fusion, she also underwent several months of psychoanalysis with Dr. Lawrence Kubie, a Freudian, which seemed to have helped her. The Hemingway boys suffered no ill effects from the car crash.

CHARLES THOMPSON: Ernest was very fond of his sons and they were certainly fond of him.

TOBY BRUCE: They could irk him, as all sons do. They'd get on his dirt list and he'd just kind of ignore them. He wasn't the disciplinarian, though. Pauline took care of Patrick and later Gig (Gregory), too. He didn't push them, but he did teach them. Part of their training was to shoot well and not to shoot anything you didn't eat. If they were over-shooting he'd give them hell about it. I'd usually go to pick the boys up from school. If he'd gone the school would have wanted him to make a speech, which he was very reluctant to do. He became very upset and nervous about getting up and making anything in the way of an audience announcement or speech. In a small group he could speak out, but before a microphone he got the jitters and his voice would change completely. There's a record of him speaking; it's nothing like how he spoke normally.

JOHN HEMINGWAY: My father was too far away to collect me from school. Except for summers in the States I'd lived in France and went to school there until 1932, when I was nine. That was the year my father drove me to join Pauline, Patrick, and Gregory for Thanksgiving at the Pfeiffer family home in Piggott, Arkansas. Just before the trip I came down with influenza. I was certain I was going to die because I'd heard that my temperature was 102 and I'd learned in France that no one could live above a temperature of 44. Of course, I was relieved when my father explained the difference between centigrade and Fahrenheit, more from it being told as a family story and then reading about it later in my father's short story, "Fathers and Sons," than actually remembering it, although I'm quite sure it was factual. On another trip I first met Papa's bullfighter friend Sidney Franklin who'd just returned from Spain. He and Patrick and I and Pauline and her friend Lorine Thompson went with Franklin in what was known as the Lincoln Zucker around the Gulf Coast. Franklin was a fascinating fellow with a lot of bullshit, and a tremendous amount of self-esteem. We went to Mexico City. Pauline had friends there and we stopped with them for a few days. Then we went to a place where they raised bulls. There was an informal land revolution going on. The son of the owner of the place had been ambushed in his car and the chauffeur had been released after torture. But the son was burned in the car. So it was a pretty tough time. They had a ring at the ranch and we pretended to be bullfighters with little cows: I did it and then Patrick did it. It was fun. Franklin was a pleasant fellow to be around as long as you paid him a certain amount of homage.

DENIS BRIAN: It was something he had in common with Hemingway, who was looking for more active excitement than the spectator sport of bullfighting.

ARNOLD GINGRICH: Dick Cooper indoctrinated Ernest with the idea of going to Africa on safari and using the same white hunter Jane had, Philip Percival.

JANE MASON GINGRICH: Dick Cooper was my boyfriend in those days. He was a big-game hunter who had a plantation in Nairobi. He came over to see me in the United States and he spoke to Ernest about hunting in Africa. [Cooper later drowned in a shallow pool while drunk.]

DENIS BRIAN: This may be an embarrassing question. Someone said that Jane Mason had a passionate love affair with Hemingway, which she denies. But is it true?

ARNOLD GINGRICH: Yes, that's true. Sure. It's not embarrassing when you know all the husbands and all the non-husbands for, God, forty years. Actually, she also had an affair with Dick Cooper. It was all very incestuous. I got into the picture in June of 1936 and it was a turning point. Dick and Janie and Ernest and Janie were each wondering who was on first base, and it was the end of things in both directions. Dick later married and, of course, Ernest married several times. Janie and I had a total of five marriages between that time and when we finally got married in 1955. The big thing with Janie and Hemingway was between 1928 and 1932.

DENIS BRIAN: Their love affair has never been underscored before though it has been hinted at. In the Carlos Baker biography Jane Mason simply disappears from the story.

ARNOLD GINGRICH: That's true of the Baker book because people came in and went out of Hemingway's life that way. When I was spending so much time in Key West, someone said, "We'll welcome you any day now to a large and I'm afraid not very exclusive society—the ex-friends of Hemingway."

DENIS BRIAN: Among them was his sister, Carol. In 1932, Hemingway became estranged from her when she announced her intention to marry John Gardner despite Ernest's vigorous objections. They were never reconciled, though he said he had once "been nuts about her." After their estrangement, he made extraordinary statements about her, even saying she was dead. Leicester, in one of Ernest's published letters he writes that your sister Carol was raped as a young girl. Was she?

LEICESTER HEMINGWAY: You tell me whether it was true or not. I only know he wrote it. He must have had access to information I didn't have. I only found out about it by reading that letter. I was infuriated, because to a person still alive that is an enormously hurtful, bitter, recriminatory piece of information to be made public. I think it's damned foolish to have published some of those letters.

DENIS BRIAN: Mrs. Gardner, were you raped as a child?

CAROL GARDNER: No, it's just a story.

DENIS BRIAN: But it was published as fact in one of Ernest's letters.

CAROL GARDNER: I heard that from my sister Sunny. She was very worried when she read it and said, "I never heard about that!" Of course not; it never happened.

DENIS BRIAN: His active imagination?

CAROL GARDNER: Yes, I'm afraid so.

DENIS BRIAN: Why do you think he wrote it?

CAROL GARDNER: It might have been something he feared.

DENIS BRIAN: Mr. Gardner, what was your first encounter with Hemingway like?

JOHN GARDNER: He was pleasant in his way and then in the midst of his pleasantries he made the pronouncement that I mustn't marry his sister. I wrote him a note and it was clear that I was going to go ahead and do whatever I was going to do.

DENIS BRIAN: Were you smaller than Hemingway?

JOHN GARDNER: Taller but not heavier.

DENIS BRIAN: Did he try to intimidate you physically?

JOHN GARDNER: He was threatening, but I wasn't intimidated.

DENIS BRIAN: This was in 1932, when he had already married twice, and he was laying down the law about whom you weren't to marry.

JOHN GARDNER: He probably felt that I didn't have any great financial backing and no known prospects, which was true: I was just twenty years old.

DENIS BRIAN: So he was acting like any concerned father or brother?

JOHN GARDNER: From his point of view that is probably correct. I was indifferent. I really was. I didn't hold him in some kind of awe and I was in love with Carol and we were going to do what we both wanted to do.

DENIS BRIAN: Were you surprised by his lifelong silence after that, not even responding to her letters?

JOHN GARDNER: She was probably surprised and upset. I've heard her allude to it once or twice; but hardly, hardly.

DENIS BRIAN: Mrs. Gardner, your husband believes Ernest's opposition to your marriage was because he was young and seemed to have no financial prospects.

CAROL GARDNER: Absolutely true. I had known John in college and John went to see him before we were married and they had a long conversation. When I was studying in Vienna, John came over and we met again in the ski country. Ernest wrote a letter to me there telling me to just come on home and not think about getting married, that I was too young and John didn't know what he was doing. He acted like a father would.

DENIS BRIAN: As your father was dead and he was the eldest son, Ernest was in a way the father of the family, wasn't he?

CAROL GARDNER: Pretty much. My younger brother, Leicester, and I looked to him both financially and as an authority. We really looked up to him. And I hadn't ever defied him before. But I did over this question of getting married. I thought I knew what I was doing.

DENIS BRIAN: But isn't it extraordinary that after you married, Ernest maintained this lifelong separation from you?

CAROL GARDNER: I always felt close to him, anyway. And his first and second wives were very nice to me. And when he got married a third time [to Martha Gellhorn]—I don't know if it was the influence of that wife, he did send me $100. It was as though, you know, I wasn't in his life but he didn't really hold it against me. I didn't feel terrible animosity there. We didn't see each other again, but I often thought of him and I imagine he did of me.

DENIS BRIAN: Professor Meyers, do you understand why Hemingway would be so enraged at the thought of his sister marrying John Gardner that he never spoke to her again?

JEFFREY MEYERS: I think that Hemingway, at that time, acted somewhere between her lover, her boyfriend, and her father. I think he felt sexual jealousy. There's absolutely nothing wrong with John Gardner. He's a perfectly nice-looking, decent man. He's been a terrific husband to Carol; they've been married for fifty years. They're both in terrific shape and seem to get along wonderfully. They have three children. Hemingway completely misread John Gardner. Gardner said he contradicted Hemingway a couple of times and stood up to him, and Hemingway's stupid reaction was to want to punch him in the nose. Then he had this all-or-nothing threat to Carol, which didn't work. Carol said she tried to placate Hemingway on many occasions, with Christmas cards and photos and letters, but he never replied. Hemingway was very poor in that way: he could be shrewd politically about communists and be really dumb about people close to him. I think he had unconscious sexual feelings for Carol. John Gardner thought Hemingway was a big, dumb oaf, and in some ways he was. He was just an irritating person to John Gardner, who was standing in the way of the marriage to Carol that Gardner wanted to make, and made.

DENIS BRIAN: That year Hemingway also quarreled with his friend Archibald MacLeish.

ARCHIBALD MACLEISH: Before he went hunting in Africa, Ernest and I and Mike Strater and Pauline's Uncle Gus took a trip across to the Dry Tortugas in the spring of 1932 and got caught in a northerner. We were marooned for three days. As a result we saw a little too much of each other. Carlos Baker's exposition about our later quarrel isn't quite right. It wasn't Ernest who hauled off with a blast at me; I'm afraid I instigated things. I told him somebody ought to prick his balloon and that led to some ribald observations about my not having a big enough prick to prick his balloon. That began eating at him and he went on and on and on from there. It was a childish quarrel which turned serious, but it didn't start with an attack on me. In fact, I never heard directly or indirectly of an attack on me. There may have been some but I never heard of them. This was a personal face-to-face confrontation and I left his house and went to a hotel and then I went back north.

ARNOLD GINGRICH: In all fairness and trying to be objective, there was always the attitude of being the bully of the high-school class, the one who insisted on winning and was very, very bad about losing. He was essentially a domineering, bullying character.

A FRIEND: When he wanted to be, Ernest could be fucking awful, unbelievably malevolent.

ARCHIBALD MACLEISH: I don't think drink explained Ernest's rages. Not long before he had attacked me to my wife cold sober. This was when I had gotten a job on *Fortune* magazine which I desperately needed. I had a family to support and no job and no income. And he attacked me to her on grounds that hurt her very much. I had "sold out for money"! Jesus Christ, he was making a lot more money than I by selling short stories.

Poems don't sell. These moods of real hatred of people—hatred's too strong a word—rage at people, would come on him from the earliest times I'd known him. I had a series of long letters from him years after our quarrel, which are now in the Library of Congress. One of them, one of the most painful says he always beshat his friends. He suffered for it— knew he'd done it, and suffered. It wasn't always his fault. As between Ernest and me, it was partly my fault, too. We just got on each other's nerves. But it was true that he quarreled with his friends. Why he did, God knows. Maybe the dark night of the soul.

HENRY STRATER: We were friends, but he was a goddamned thankless friend. He never thanked me for getting [Horace] Liveright as his first publisher. I spent a lot of my good money taking Liveright out to a lot of fancy places like the Ritz for lunch, after I returned to Manhattan.[1]

DENIS BRIAN: Several people have called him a son-of-a-bitch.

HENRY STRATER: That's it. I would put it that way, to the point of his taking a fiendish delight in inflicting injury on them when they were completely helpless. He bragged to me about the time he had managed to get somebody drunk. His technique was to get them very drunk and then say, "You need some fresh air." Then he'd take them out in the dark and slug them, and go away, making no provision for anybody even lifting them off the pavement.

DENIS BRIAN: He'd stay sober while he got the other guy drunk?

HENRY STRATER: Right. He had a regular routine.

DENIS BRIAN: Did he do it to you?

HENRY STRATER: Yes, but once there was someone around to rescue me. This was the time I caught a tremendous big fish in Bimini. It was a great feat and I was very much the local hero. Although Hemingway stood in front of me every time the fish was photographed. He'd stand between the camera and fish so he would be visible and I would not. That went on for about an hour and finally somebody in the crowd yelled: "Can't we have just one photograph of the angler and the fish?" [Laughs.]

DENIS BRIAN: And he wasn't doing it as a joke?

HENRY STRATER: Oh, no. It was for the future. One of those photos was reproduced in *Time* magazine and somebody wrote to them, "Wasn't this

[1]His friends Sherwood Anderson, Don Stewart, and Harold Loeb also claimed to have persuaded Liveright to publish *In Our Time*. "This seemed to annoy Hem," said Loeb. "Because apparently it had taken half New York to place his stories."

fish caught by Hemingway the later genesis for his story *The Old Man and the Sea?*" Everyone said to me: "Henry, that's your fish." And I said, "Of course it was." Everyone who was down there in Bimini, fifty or a hundred people, knew this. I was curious whether Hemingway would write in a denial to *Time.* Nooooooo. They had anglers in Bimini for years trying to catch one of those giant fishes, and finally I came in with one and it was a great event for them because it put Bimini on the map. They made a song about me which I hear they still sing over there more than fifty years later!

So when I came in with this first giant marlin caught on rod and reel in the Atlantic, I was completely exhausted. But everyone insisted on bringing me a drink—whiskey and champagne—and I got pretty loaded. I couldn't stand up and by that time there was nobody left but Hemingway, the bartender, and myself. And Hemingway was jealous and hauled off and slugged me in the stomach. Though I was dead drunk, I remember saying, "You're getting weak, old boy. Can't you hit any harder than that?" In other words, he was tonguing the bottle. That was his favorite expression and he lived by it. He'd get a bottle of whiskey when he was with an intended victim and pretend to drink from the bottle, but he kept his tongue against the opening so he wasn't drinking anything. He started tonguing the bottle with me and managed to get one or two more drinks in me until my eyes were nearly closed. The last thing I remember was Hemingway saying, "Come outside." I woke up on the deck of the boat next morning and thought, "By what miracle did I get here?" The owner of the bar was a tough little guy, Irish or Scottish. He told me later what had happened—that I was out on my feet and Hemingway told me I wanted fresh air. This guy had been a bartender for years and knew perfectly well what Hemingway was going to do. He was going to take me out in the dark and slug me. Like bartenders all over the country, he had half a baseball bat, a very effective weapon because he could reach down and grab it and knock unconscious any guy that was giving him trouble. So he grabbed his bat and vaulted over the bar and chased after Hemingway who had just got me out in the dark and was getting ready to slug me. And he said, "Mr. Hemingway, you can't do that to a drunk. That fellow is in a state of exhaustion: he caught a record fish here, the world's record big fish for Bimini and he deserves better treatment than to get slugged in the dark." He was ready to hit Hemingway with the baseball bat—that is quite an equalizer. And he said, "Now be a decent guy for once and take the other side of Strater and I'll take this side and we'll lug him over to your boat and stretch him out." Which is what they did. And I have no recollection of that at all. My only recollection is of Hemingway saying "Come out."

DENIS BRIAN: Did Hemingway ever actually slug you in the dark?

HENRY STRATER: Sure. He knocked me cold one time when I was dead drunk. He was a real s.o.b.

DENIS BRIAN: Yet you remained his friend.

HENRY STRATER: Well, we were friends at times. He and I were both novices on the climb.

DENIS BRIAN: What do you think of Strater's story, Mr. Rybovich?

JOHN RYBOVICH, JR. [fisherman, boatbuilder, writer]: The only photo I've seen is of Strater alongside the fish. The fish—a blue marlin—is badly chewed, so it never counted. It was just like a no-fish. When the fish is shark-bitten like that you might as well leave him out there. It doesn't count. It was a big fish; it looked as if it was seven or eight hundred pounds. In those days, back in the middle thirties, it was a very impressive fish except that fifteen or twenty percent was gobbled up by the sharks. This isn't in any of the fishing records. When a fish has a couple of hundred pounds chewed out of it like that we refer to it as being apple-cored. I don't think Henry was ever again invited to fish with Hemingway after Henry caught the big fish. Hemingway had a tremendous ego and it took a lot to feed it. That was also true in hunting. If anyone was going to shoot a big elephant, big lion, or big anything, to keep the peace in the house it had better be Ernest. I'm pretty sure it was the end of whatever friendship they had. But I do know there were two sides to Hemingway's vanity. He called for and drafted the rules to establish The International Game Fishing Association. So despite his treatment of Strater, Hemingway did have a sense of fair play and responsibility.

DENIS BRIAN: What d'you think of Strater's story of Hemingway tonguing the bottle and then slugging his friends when they were drunk, Mr. Callaghan?

MORLEY CALLAGHAN: I can't imagine it. Now Mike Strater was a friend of Hemingway's and Hemingway did many strange things. But the truth is I can't imagine that.

DENIS BRIAN: Because you knew him as a pretty nice guy basically?

MORLEY CALLAGHAN: Absolutely.

DENIS BRIAN: Except the time you were sparring together and you hit him in the mouth and he spat in your face. What's your view of Strater's story Mr. Walton?

WILLIAM WALTON: It doesn't sound very plausible to me.

DENIS BRIAN: I recall that when he was on location for the filming of *The Old Man and the Sea* one of the film crew, about to box with him, was warned, "Be careful he's been drinking. He'll hit you hard." And apparently he gave the man a black eye.

WILLIAM WALTON: That's probably true.

DENIS BRIAN: After Ernest wore a towel over his head to shield him from the sun while fishing, his friends called him "The Mahatma," switching to "Old Master" when he reverted to the role of dictator whose word was law. Dos Passos recalled that although Hemingway had his crotchety moments "he was a barrel of monkeys to be with. It was a period when life seemed enormously comical to all of us. Nobody ever got so mad that some fresh crack didn't bring him around. If I'm not mistaken, this trip to Bimini was the first time the Old Master really went after tuna. He'd been reading Zane Grey's book about catching the great tuna on the Seven Seas and he wanted to go one better than Zane Grey."[1]

HENRY STRATER: Dos Passos is mixed up on his fish. It was marlin Hemingway was after. Despite his Dry Tortugas set-to with Archie Mac-Leish and with me for catching the big marlin, Ernest invited us to go on that first African safari. Archie couldn't make it. I was going, and then my wife got pregnant. I wasn't going to go off and leave a pregnant wife. So I didn't go, and Ernest's nose was very out of joint that I'd placed my wife ahead of him. The main reason was that I was at last lined up for a one-man show of my paintings. And for Hemingway that was unimportant. He had a low opinion of his friends' achievements. He wanted to be a star that shone alone. So I refused to go to Africa with him. He was going to pay all my expenses.

DENIS BRIAN: He was generous to offer to pay for you.

HENRY STRATER: Sure, for the fun to have somebody to beat up on.

DENIS BRIAN: But weren't you a fairly tough opponent?

HENRY STRATER: Sure. But I didn't want to be at his mercy over there. I would have been a fool to go. He would have tortured me in every way

[1] Milt Machlin, *The Private Hell of Hemingway*, Paperback Library, 1962.

possible. He had been a hobo [not true, but Hemingway said it was] and learned to carry a knife to protect him from being raped by homosexual hobos. He was a lot tougher than me. It was a big blow to him when I refused to go with him. That was when our friendship ended.

ARNOLD GINGRICH: Instead of Strater and MacLeish, the local Key West guy, Charlie Thompson, went along with Ernest. As it turned out, Charlie got all the best trophies and Ernest was mad as hell. Charlie was the real star of the safari. It made Ernest hopping mad because every time the first kudo, the first this, the first that, always went to Charlie Thompson. I don't know if Ernest's idea of a wife accidentally on purpose shooting her husband on safari came entirely from his imagination. Philip Percival was known to talk of the mysterious death of a man on safari some years before. He had been fatally shot and both the wife and the white hunter were suspected. It was hushed up and ruled a suicide, although the white hunter and the man's wife were known to have been having an affair. There is the relationship too of Janie and Hemingway having the same white hunter, Percival: Janie went with him first and Hemingway went with him later.

DENIS BRIAN: Though Hemingway was humiliated by Charles Thompson outhunting him, he soon showed that at sea he was second to none.

JOHN RYBOVICH, JR.: Everything Ernest did was to maintain his macho image. I don't care what he did, it had to be better than anyone else. He delighted in exposing himself to danger. He was a tremendous influence on game fishing by totally revising the system. Before he came along it was a passive type of fishing. To begin with the tackle wasn't strong enough to allow fishing of Hemingway's style—aggressive fishing. He made contact with the fish for hours and hours and hours, until it eventually got tired. Then he'd apply as much pressure as the tackle would take. His method brought on the biggest tackle-busting that ever existed. That in turn brought on better and better tackle. He initiated the aggressive type of fishing, no doubt about it. Incredible! He put it into practice on his *Pilar* in 1935 and so brought the first two tuna to Bimini, one weighing 310 pounds and the other 381. Before that tuna had been destroyed by sharks. Hemingway kept the sharks at bay with machine-gun bullets.

THOMAS SHEVLIN: I was in Bimini in the fall of that year, just after he'd brought in those two fish. I had just come back from Spain and recently read his book on bullfighting, *Death in the Afternoon*. I walked up to him in the Fountain of Youth bar and said, "Aren't you Mr. Hemingway?" He said, "Nobody calls me Mr. Hemingway here." I introduced myself and said I'd spent the summer watching bullfights in Spain and had read his book and thought it was marvelous, "but I have to disagree with you on . . ." and I mentioned a bullfighter, I forget his name. He put down his drink and asked, "How many bullfights did you see?" I said, "Possibly twenty." He said, "You can talk to me when you've seen maybe three hundred." And he turned his back. I said, "I'm sorry, I didn't mean to criticize at all." He said, "Oh, shut up about it and let's have drinks." And that we did. Later we sparred on the beach and he was a hell of a fighter. I boxed quite a lot but he outweighed me. He didn't know how to pull his punches. He'd hit you and knock you flat. There wasn't any question of just getting a workout. He was a puncher, a slugger. He used to say, "You live under your left shoulder."

THORVALD SANCHEZ, JR.: My mother and father met Hemingway at a tuna tournament at Cat Cay in the Bahamas in the thirties. My father was heir to a sugar fortune and owned one of Cuba's largest ice-cream factories. He and Hemingway fished all over the world together. They also did a lot of shooting together and drinking and womanizing.

JOHN RYBOVICH, JR.: He was then at his physical peak, a terribly nice guy who always, I thought, enjoyed being among fishermen and not at all the company of autograph seekers, who annoyed him. He was abrupt with them, rejecting the movie-star image. He fished in the morning off Bimini and then came in for a drink at Helen Duncombe's Compleat Angler Hotel. At the end of a very hot July in 1936, I'd caught my first marlin, a 588-pounder. It was weighed and hanging on the rack when Ernest came in for lunch. I was twenty then and he said to me in a typical macho manner, "What a fish to lose your cherry on!"

THOMAS SHEVLIN: After that first meeting on Bimini, my wife and I joined him at the Nordquist ranch in Wyoming, and Ernest and I went from there to hunt grizzly bears, elk, and antelope in Wyoming and Montana.

DENIS BRIAN: Hemingway thought Shevlin, like all rich boys, couldn't shoot because he'd early on had a few lucky flukes and thereafter didn't practice.[1] He wrote of galloping back four miles to their camp in Cooke, Montana, on horseback during a blizzard over slippery roads. He added how very much he liked his life, then, curiously, added that it would be a "big disgust" when he would have to shoot himself, perhaps soon, but to avoid a bad effect on his sons he'd have someone shoot him. The

[1]A thought expressed in a September 26, 1936 letter to Archibald MacLeish.

previous month he had written to novelist Marjorie Kinnan Rawlings that he felt he was soon going to die, but hoped to live to be a wise old man.

THOMAS SHEVLIN: It's extraordinary the number of times he mentioned suicide. The picture of Hemingway as the very tough, almost bloodthirsty character, because of his hunting and love of bullfighting, is very exaggerated. He was very, very intelligent and read copiously. He was constantly reading a book when he wasn't writing one. He read everything from Sartre to James Bond. And he was always interested in things. He tried to get away from politics and people tried to pull him in. He was a complex, very difficult man with a tremendous zest for life and when he did anything he did it absolutely up to the hilt, no half measures. While we were out West he asked me to read the first draft of the manuscript of *To Have and Have Not,* which he had just finished. I read it carefully and wrote notes telling him exactly what I thought. He read my remarks, became very angry, and threw his manuscript through the window into the snow. He left it there for three days. When he finally got over the thing and we dug it out of the snow, I said: "I don't write. And just because we are good friends, why did you ask me to criticize it?" He said, "Well, I'll be goddamned if I know. I'll never do it again," and he forgot about it from then on. He was obviously very, very sensitive about adverse comments on his writing. That was the first and last time he showed me anything of his before publication. He drank very little when he was writing, when he was hunting, and when he was seriously fishing. But when the fishing was no good, we used to get pretty loaded all the time. Then he'd quit for a week and write a story.

THORVALD SANCHEZ, JR.: He was my father's drinking buddy in those days and my mother wasn't too keen on him, especially when he got drunk.

A FRIEND: There are things he'd say and do drunk he'd never do sober. A couple of times he said to me things like, "Listen, if you object to what's going on just say so and I'll kill you." He said things like that to me twice when drunk, but next morning he said, "I know last night I was a little tight, and if I said anything that hurt your feelings I apologize. I'm awfully sorry, but sometimes I get to talking a little loud." This is a big apology when you get it from Ernest Hemingway. If he said such things when sober it was when his mind was temporarily deranged by fury or frustrations. There were days when he was absolutely a malevolent bastard, full of self-loathing. But the awfulness would leave him after a couple of hours. Generally, before he lost that black mood someone caught hell for it.

DENIS BRIAN: Such as the time he made Carlos Gutierrez weep, perhaps. Leicester Hemingway mentions it in his biography of Ernest.

JOHN HEMINGWAY: I never remember him being cruel to Carlos. There was a point where Carlos could no longer perform his functions as captain of the *Pilar*, and what may well have happened was that my father was incapable of firing him without having something come to a head first.

LEICESTER HEMINGWAY: Not true. Listen, Carlos was good all his life and always knew more about fishing, at least marlin fishing, than Ernest did. Ernest had swiped Carlos away from Jane Mason. Carlos had been Jane's captain on her boat *The Pelican Three*, and when Ernest wangled him away it was simply because he was so much more of a hero to Carlos than Jane Mason was. Carlos was enormously happy to serve Ernesto. You couldn't make Carlos go away. Even all those hurtful words and making Carlos cry in front of people wouldn't make Carlos go away. Carlos would still serve, except it was like spanking a boy in front of all his friends. It absolutely destroyed his dignity. At the same time he still loved Ernesto because he thought Ernesto had the true, inside fire "that I will follow all the days of my life." He sort of carried the Holy Grail with him.

WINSTON GUEST: Ernest had a reputation for being tough and getting into fights, but I never saw him in a fight all the years I knew him—from his early hunting years in Africa to the end. He was a very good friend, delightful company, never aggressive, a charming gentleman. I enjoyed his company very much indeed, and I never witnessed his black temper, never saw him cruel to people.

DENIS BRIAN: Guest must have been a soothing influence. Hemingway broke poet Wallace Stevens's jaw with one punch for denigrating his writing and making his sister, Sunny, cry; knocked magazine publisher Joseph Knapp cold—sending him to the hospital; threatened to beat up Charles Fenton, H. L. Mencken, and Irwin Shaw; taunted William Saroyan and Charles Boyer, among others. And wrestled in Max Perkins's office with Max Eastman, who had called his manliness into question. Hemingway's buddy George Brooks goaded him into violence by using a homosexual as bait. When one entered Sloppy Joe's bar in Key West looking for a willing partner, Brooks steered him to Hemingway with the whispered assurance, "He's as queer as a three-dollar bill." With a fervent cry of "I love you!" the homosexual embraced and kissed Hemingway. Bartender Bill Cates watched Hemingway freeze, blanch, spit and then send the kisser crashing to the floor, a victim of unrequited love and the author's right fist. Despite Brooks' innocent look of startled surprise, Hemingway saw through him, snarling, "You conniving son-of-a-bitch! You put him up to this!" Brooks was vehement in his denial, insisting that the man was a self-propelled and unrestrained fan of the author. Tormenting Hemingway proved irresisible for Brooks who tried the same gag several times. Why Hemingway didn't tear apart the *agent provocateur* was obvious to those on the spot. At 110 pounds, Brooks was literally half a Hemingway. Even enraged, Ernest never physically attacked a bantamweight, especially one like Brooks who was also an attorney.

THOMAS SHEVLIN: Although I greatly admired him, I was always on guard because of his hair-trigger temper. I knew certain things definitely would offend him and I would never, for example, interrupt him when he was writing. He was self-confident about everything in the field and in fishing. But he was terribly shy if he had to go out to dinner. He wouldn't have gone to a Palm Beach society party for anything in the world, partly because he was shy and partly because he didn't give a damn for any of the people. He'd probably have insulted somebody. He had a terrific sense of humor, but he hated jokes on himself. You didn't want to play too many practical jokes on him, or even laugh at him. At times he was very much a bully, mostly when he was drinking, although I never told him so. We used to have a lot of fun shooting pigeons. We'd invite people down and instead of pigeons we'd have lobsters or oysters flying through the air. We'd fool around with guests' ammunition so that instead of pellets sometimes the American flag would come out.

LEICESTER HEMINGWAY: Ernest not only delivered great one-liners, he did them unexpectedly. Most people never had a chance to write them down. I used to wait all day to try to make notes briefly in the evening of what great things he had said. Jesus, the guy would say fifteen or twenty wonderful quotes in a day and you'd think, "Son-of-a-bitch, if there was only some way to keep this stuff!" But he'd say it when the wind was blowing hard, or while the jeep was blowing its horn.

JOHN HEMINGWAY: We took trips across the country in the car in the summer of 1936. As usual, we had periods in the afternoon when scatalogical humor was permitted, which Papa didn't let us do constantly. We had a break-loose period, about four in the afternoon, until we pulled in somewhere. This usually coincided with our mixing him a drink, which he drank while driving. It probably was against the law, but we didn't pay much attention. Usually, he'd get things started. We invented this thing which we called "the famous bathroom," which was a sort of museum of samplings from famous people. It was the sort of thing to really let your imagination go with. The "famous bathroom" was a figment of our imagination and all of us contributed ideas—there would be a case with a gleaming specimen of George Washington's feces, or something. We all contributed, Patrick, Gregory, and I and Papa. There was tremendous laughter. If the car could have shaken from the road, it would have.

CAROL HEMINGWAY GARDNER: If you were in his company and you were accepted by him, it was more fun than anything you can imagine. Every joke got repeated many times and it got funnier every time he repeated it. So that pretty soon there were lots of in-jokes.

HADLEY MOWRER: Ernest had a wonderful wit. One of the most awful jokes that comes to mind was when he was in the hospital and someone rapped on the door, and Ernest would call out, "Friend or enema?" When I first knew him, we went to the Art Institute in Chicago and a sign above the entrance said: "All Passes." Ernest looked at it and said, "Art alone endures." It's absolutely silly, but he did say some awfully funny things.

MORLEY CALLAGHAN: He'd make a lot of what you might call what he hoped were erotic cracks. He wasn't given to telling jokes. He wouldn't sit around and say, "here's a good story."

DENIS BRIAN: Hadley seems to have experienced the lighthearted side, more than Pauline did.

THOMAS SHEVLIN: Apparently Ernest never fell out of love with his first wife, Hadley. On the other hand Pauline, his second wife, was the best one, I think. She was magnificent, but he just overpowered her. Of course, Ernest and Hadley didn't have a nickel [at least from the viewpoint of a Palm Beach millionaire like Shevlin] and when he married Pauline he had some fame.

LORINE THOMPSON: Pauline always tried to be very tolerant of Ernest and any of the girls that sort of made a play for him, or that he seemed entranced with. I don't think he fell in love with other women. He was nice and maybe a lot of women thought he was giving them more attention than what there was; his was in a kidding way. And I think Pauline had a feeling that Ernest's interest in other women sometimes was as a writer, not just as a man.

DENIS BRIAN: Twenty-eight-year-old Martha Gellhorn, a journalist and novelist, appeared at Sloppy Joe's bar in Key West in December 1936. The daughter of a recently deceased gynecologist-obstetrician from St.

Louis, she was with her mother and brother, a medical student. Hemingway was in the bar and they got into conversation with him. When her mother and brother left Key West, Martha stayed on, sometimes as a Hemingway houseguest.

LORINE THOMPSON: Martha definitely made a play for him. Martha was a very charming girl and if I had known her under other circumstances I would have liked her very much. She said she came to see Ernest, she wanted him to read a book she had written, she wanted to know him. There was no question about it: you could see she was making a play for him. Pauline tried to ignore it. What she felt underneath nobody knew.

DENIS BRIAN: When Martha Gellhorn returned by train to St. Louis, Hemingway traveled part of the way with her en route to New York. They were to meet not long afterwards in Spain—by arrangement—to report the Spanish Civil War.

CHAPTER

SIX

•

WAR
CORRESPONDENT
IN SPAIN AND
PARTISAN FOR THE
REPUBLIC

DENIS BRIAN: The Spanish Civil War broke out on July 17, 1936, when rebels attacked Republican government forces. In Key West, less than a week later, Hemingway was discussing the rebellion with two friends, S.L.A. Marshall and a young novelist, Harry Sylvester. Marshall, a journalist, soon to become official historian for the United States Army, intended to report the civil war on the Republican side because emotionally and sentimentally he favored them. Although most Catholics including his wife, Pauline, supported the rebels Hemingway said he was neutral because he had friends on both sides. The war didn't interest him and he wouldn't go to Spain. In his memoirs, published posthumously, Marshall wrote: "Sylvester was shocked and saddened by what Hemingway said. Being a devout Catholic, Harry was committed to the insurrection and disappointed in his great friend."[1]

HARRY SYLVESTER: Not true. I was neutral, too. Marshall got it wrong,

[1]S.L.A. Marshall, *Bringing Up the Rear*, Presido Press, San Rafael, Ca., 1979.

and so has Jeffrey Meyers in his biography of Hemingway.[1] There he says that I was pro-Franco. At no time, under no circumstances, was I pro-Franco. I was what the entire staff of *Commonweal*, a liberal Catholic magazine, was—neutral. The people on *Commonweal* took a middle-of-the-road position, a pox on both your houses. They did not take sides and neither did I. There were just two Catholic publications, the *Catholic Worker* and *Commonweal*, out of all the Catholic publications in the U.S. then that took this position.

DENIS BRIAN: You first met Hemingway in Key West?

HARRY SYLVESTER: I was there on my honeymoon and he had come over from Cuba. He was a generous fellow with his time and I got to know him. He liked to box and so did I. I had boxed at Notre Dame. I think we both had glorified notions of what we were. He was still very badly slowed down by his World War I war wounds, but I don't think his reactions were very good even at his best. He was a big man and grossly overweight for a time. He should have weighed 180 to 185 pounds and he was 200 or more. But he gave off a great feeling of energy. You got the feeling—an intelligent bear is here.

DENIS BRIAN: Did the bear ever knock you out?

HARRY SYLVESTER: No, never came close. He was just too slow with his hands and feet. Morley Callaghan is even smaller than I am, but he was so quick I'm afraid he was able to embarrass Ernest.

DENIS BRIAN: I thought Hemingway had a deadly punch.

HARRY SYLVESTER [laughs]: If you stayed close enough to him, he probably did. Anyone who knew anything about boxing would not get that close to him. He was immensely strong, though not well coordinated. Just horsing around, you were aware how powerful he was.

DENIS BRIAN: Malcolm Cowley said he was like a spirited but surprisingly gentle stallion. Who were his other friends on Key West?

HARRY SYLVESTER: One was Charlie Thompson, the Karl of *Green Hills of Africa*, who ran the marine hardware store. Then there was Jim Sullivan, whom he called "the boilerman." Jim ran a machine shop and there was a lot of boat traffic through there. Hemingway felt admiration for and closeness to working-class or middle-class people which he mentioned to me in his letters from Spain about the Spanish Civil War. He repeatedly—and Sullivan told me this—told Sullivan he was going to kill himself. Of course, nobody took him seriously.

[1]Jeffrey Meyers, *Hemingway: A Biography*.

DENIS BRIAN: John Rybovich was surprised to find Hemingway was hardly articulate, spoke slowly, and searched for his words.

HARRY SYLVESTER: No; he could talk a blue streak. It depended to some extent how well he knew you. This is just an educated guess.

DENIS BRIAN: Did he regard you as competition as a writer?

HARRY SYLVESTER: Oh, heavens no! I was only getting started. I think he envied my contact with athletics. One of the minor disappointments of his life was not having played college football. He didn't go to college, of course. He was very polite about my writing and liked a story of mine about Knute Rockne in *Scribner's Magazine*. It was unusual then to have sports stories in highbrow magazines. I was a student at Notre Dame during Rockne's time there.

DENIS BRIAN: Hemingway was joking, I take it, when he called you a plainclothes Jesuit.

HARRY SYLVESTER: Yes, because I defended the church. At the time I considered myself to be still a Catholic.

DENIS BRIAN: Wasn't he nominally a Catholic?

HARRY SYLVESTER: He sort of weasled if you mentioned it. He and Pauline had a real problem which I never went into very much with him, about birth control. They seemed happy, but then he was on the verge of breaking up with her. They had separated and he was horsing around with Martha Gellhorn. He was pretty angry and he had to "justify" himself. In that mood he called Pauline a whore. My wife corrected him on it. She said, "You know very well she isn't." Ernest's reaction was very funny. He sort of wuffled. When he was corrected—and he was not used to that—he sort of . . . the best word I can think of is "wuffled." He tried to talk and almost couldn't. I guess he was trying to justify himself in contemplation of a new marriage to Martha Gellhorn. His reaction to my wife was like someone caught in a lie. He was a complicated guy and had a certain amount of self-delusion. I guess we all have that.

Before he left for Spain in the spring of 1937, Hemingway wrote to me from Key West. He called the war a bad war in which nobody was right, but said all that mattered to him was to relieve the suffering of human beings. He said it was neither Christian nor Catholic to kill the wounded in a Toledo hospital with hand grenades, or to bomb the working-class area of Madrid simply to kill poor people. He acknowledged that priests and bishops had been shot, but he wondered why the church sided with the oppressors and not with the oppressed. He wrote that his sympathies were always for exploited workers against absentee landlords. And that although he drank and shot pigeons with the landlords, he would as soon shoot the landlords as the birds. He advised me not to worry about politics and religion, and especially not to mix the two. Finally, he said he thought there was a lousy government in Russia, but that he didn't like any government.

DENIS BRIAN: Were you surprised by his change from neutral to pro-Republican?

HARRY SYLVESTER: No, because I knew from his letter, and others he sent me, why he supported them. But I remained neutral. Not a popular position. A few months after he wrote to me, he went to Paris on his way to Spain.

JORIS IVENS [a documentary filmmaker]: I first met Hemingway in the Deux Magots cafe in Paris, and asked him what he intended to do in Spain. He said, "Report the truth about it—that every war is bad." I said, "All right, come." In Spain, he saw what was really happening and became antifascist. He saw that most of his friends there, bullfighters and barmen and others he knew before the war, were fighting on the democratic, the Republican side, against Franco and the rebels.

DENIS BRIAN: In his memoir *Bringing Up the Rear* S.L.A. Marshall wrote that he wasn't surprised at Hemingway's original decision to be neutral, but he was astonished when Ernest changed his mind and went to Spain and wrote as "a passionate crusader for the Loyalist (government) side, blind to its increasingly red coloration and uncompromising ugliness." He was not blind to it. But he thought communists were vital to win the war against the fascists. He reluctantly concluded that their tough, ruthless methods were a necessary evil.

ARCHIBALD MACLEISH: I wrote a piece in the *Nation* to the same effect, stating my own position that in a good cause, and the Spanish Civil War was a good cause, I didn't give a goddamn whom I was working with. The question was whether you could do anything about the Loyalist cause itself. I wish I'd used Churchill's phrase about welcoming the devil himself as an ally in a righteous cause to defeat your enemy.

DENIS BRIAN: Was the war essentially communists against fascists, or haves against have-nots?

MILTON WOLFF: You had to be there to know what had happened. I was there [fighting for the Loyalists with other American volunteers in the

Abraham Lincoln Brigade]. Basically, it was a war waged by the army and monarchists led by General Franco to reverse the 1936 election in which a leftist government of several parties was elected. It was called the Popular Front. Franco brought over Moorish mercenaries, a paid army, to destroy the elected government. In the first weeks of the war, because the British didn't want a Popular Front government in Spain, any more than they wanted one in France, they brought General Franco from the Canary Islands to Spanish Morocco. There was a Popular Front government in France, too, at the time. They keep saying it wasn't the British government but some British adventurer pilot who flew Franco from the Canary Islands, where he had been in exile. If you believe that adventurer-pilot story you believe in Santa Claus. In the very first weeks of the war, long before Moscow decided to help the Spanish government, the Republican or Loyalist side as they were called, Hitler and Mussolini were pouring in stuff to help Franco and the rebels. The final factor was England putting the arm on France to close the border between France and Spain to cut off military aid to the Republicans. And FDR went along.

Joris Ivens: Hemingway liked to accompany me, because my direct connections with the General Staff of the Republican Army and the International Brigades enabled me to get much closer to the front lines than other correspondents could. We became good friends. Because he was strong he carried the movie camera. He also contributed to the story line of the documentary I was directing, *The Spanish Earth,* and later in the U.S. he wrote and spoke the commentary for the film.

Denis Brian: Scouting action scenes for the propaganda film in the spring of 1937, Hemingway and Ivens decided to cover the defense of the Arganda Bridge over the Jarama River. But when they arrived, the action was over. After a furious and bloody battle, the French Battalion of the International Brigades helping to defend besieged Madrid had just retreated from the bridge. Hemingway was told that if he could persuade any of the soldiers to return to the bridge and stage a mock battle he and Ivens were welcome to film them. Hemingway's obvious admiration for the soldiers and generous sharing of his whiskey flasks fired up the exhausted men, some of whom agreed to cooperate.

Milton Wolff: Hemingway said he didn't think much of the Americans who fought at Jarama, which was a stupid thing to say. These men who were thrown into action at Jarama came off the streets and out of the factories. They were disciplined enough to go over the top and get themselves butchered. That, without training, was a remarkable thing in itself. But he doesn't say that. He just says they were no good, full of ideology but no military expertise, though he admits that from Brunete to the Aragon they were much better. Then he says they lost Teruel. That's a crock of shit, because we held Teruel, we were relieved from Teruel, and Teruel didn't fall until several days after we were put in reserve.

ALVAH BESSIE [a former editor of the *Brooklyn Eagle*, adjutant of No. 2 Company of the Lincoln Brigade]: Milton Wolff was a platoon commander in the Lincoln Machine-Gun Company and he wrote an article about Hemingway, calling him a tourist in Spain, which infuriated Hemingway for the rest of his life. Hemingway wrote Wolff a nasty letter: "I commanded troops and was wounded before you were dry behind the ears," or some such idiotic remark. The point is that he never commanded any troops as far as I can find out. [At least, not up to that time.]

MILTON WOLFF: I knew of him vaguely before I met him, but he was not my cup of tea. I would have been more impressed meeting Thomas Mann at that time, or Thomas Wolfe. When I did start reading him I liked many of his things, especially his short stories. He was probably an accurate reporter, but I can't remember reading much of his work. I read his play *The Fifth Column* in Madrid when he was writing it in the Hotel Florida and I thought it was mostly pretty good stuff.

DENIS BRIAN: He spoke well of you, describing you as tall as Lincoln, as gaunt as Lincoln, and as brave and good a soldier as any that commanded battalions at Gettysburg.

MILTON WOLFF: He was a writer. You've got to allow for poetic license. I know I'm as tall as Lincoln, but after that everything's up for grabs.

DENIS BRIAN: But he resented your calling him a tourist in Spain when he tried to create the impression he had an active, secret role.

MILTON WOLFF: I thought in a sense all war correspondents were tourists in Spain because they could call their shots, visit cathedrals when they wanted, and when I say cathedrals I mean whatever action or inaction they wanted. When they were hungry, they could go to Paris to eat and stock up. And they were warm and dry and didn't have to be in the rain. I thought their attitude should reflect that. Well, Herb Matthews, Vincent Sheean, Louis Fischer, Ernest Toller, and a lot of them realized they were playing a different role than men at the front. Hemingway didn't. I just reminded him of that. He wanted to feel he was one of the fighters, and one of the best.

ALVAH BESSIE: We used to call Hemingway the best-equipped soldier in Spain. This was predicated on a map case and military maps, which none of our officers had. I don't know where he got them. He had a compass and binoculars. He had two letters in his shirt pockets. The one in his left-hand pocket was from Franklin Roosevelt, in case he got captured by the Fascists, and the one in the right-hand pocket was written by the prime minister of Spain, if he got captured by the Loyalists. He had two enormous canteens, made to order for him, each of which held about a quart of whiskey. And the guy had access to things we didn't have access to. I was visiting Barcelona on leave, looking for Herbert Matthews, and found him in the Hotel Majestic with Hemingway. Hemingway said, "Look, I've got a case of Scotch I want you to take up to Milt Wolff." I said, "I'll do it, but it's kind of heavy to carry." He said, "You're going back in the truck, aren't you?" I said, "Yeah." He said, "Well, just be sure nobody swipes it from you." It was very well received. The guy had access to everything and since he was a famous name even then and was on our side, objectively, I imagine, the government was extremely helpful to him and lenient with him, and gave him many things we didn't have.

CLAUD COCKBURN: [In his book *I, Claud*] Everyone was happy to have Hemingway there, partly because he was obviously a fine man to have around when there was war and trouble, and partly because to have so famous an author there, writing on behalf of the Republic, made people feel less alone in the world—in a sense, which was no fault of Hemingway, it helped to foster the illusion that sooner or later the 'world conscience' would be aroused, 'the common people' in Britain and France would force their Governments to end non-intervention, and the war would be won."

DENIS BRIAN: As a correspondent for the communist British *Daily Worker* Cockburn was not to be trusted; to aid the Republican cause he faked his reporting. He was, in fact, more propagandist than newsman. But his amusing recollection of Hemingway rings true. "At breakfast one day in his room at the Florida Hotel, Ernest Hemingway was very comforting about the shelling. He had a big map laid out on the table, and he explained to an audience of generals, politicians and correspondents, that for some ballistic reasons the shells could not hit the Florida. He could talk in a very military way and make it sound very convincing. Everyone present was convinced and happy. Then a shell whooshed through the room above Hemingway's—the first actually to hit the Florida—and the ceiling fell down on the breakfast table. To any lesser man than Hemingway the occurrence would have been humiliating.

While we were getting the plaster out of our hair, Hemingway looked slowly around at us, one after the other. 'How do you like it now, gentlemen?' he said, and by some astonishing trick of manner conveyed the impression that this episode had actually, in an obscure way, confirmed instead of upsetting his theory—that his theory had been right when he expounded it and this only demonstrated that the time had come to have a new one." Hemingway also provided more tangible comforts for the troops.

MILTON WOLFF: I was in the Cafe Chicote in Madrid and Hemingway had this gorgeous gal with him. And I left with her. I really don't know how it happened. Next morning, Evan Shipman was in my room. I apparently had left the hotel door unlocked. Shipman, who was a great friend of Hemingway's and a marvelous guy, came into the room and implied that I had walked off with Papa's girl. But I don't think it was his one and only.

DENIS BRIAN: You and many other volunteer fighters were Jewish. Did you detect any anti-Semitism in Hemingway?

MILTON WOLFF: No, I didn't. And, remember, he called himself Hemingstein.

DENIS BRIAN: That was a nickname he adopted in adolescence when he and his friends were pretending to be Jewish pawnbrokers. He also called himself Ernie Hemorrhoid, which I presume didn't show his respect for piles. Anyway, after you walked off with his girl he soon found a permanent replacement.

JORIS IVENS: We were returning from the front one evening when he said to me, "One of these days a nice girl whom I know very well, a blonde with blue eyes and whose legs start at her shoulders will come here." So I was very excited when Martha Gellhorn arrived. She was just as he had described her. She was a good, conscientious reporter, and she learned from Hemingway the clean, cool work of a good journalist.

PETER DAVIS: Martha Gellhorn was in Spain on an assignation with Hemingway. She was in a sense created by Hemingway and Herbert Matthews. They convinced her to write. She had published a novel and a collection of short stories, and had worked briefly as a cub reporter for a Hearst paper. But Spain was the real start of her journalistic career. At the same time, she was overshadowed by Hemingway. She said to me, while I was filming her for my documentary about war correspondents, that the two men had urged her to write and she asked, "What can I write about?" They told her to write about just what she saw. In order to get to Madrid from France she had been given a journalist's accreditation by a friend at *Collier's*.

GEORGE SELDES: But first of all to get from France to Spain she needed a visa from the French. When my wife and I were waiting for our visas in Paris, I called on P. J. Phillip. He was the *New York Times* correspondent there after Walter Duranty. I said we were on the way to Spain and he said, "You should have been a week earlier because Martha Gellhorn was in and she left almost immediately for Spain." And then he said to me, "You know, she told me that she was going to get Hemingway come hell or high water." Now that is what he told me. That was a strange thing for him to say. There never was a secret about Hemingway living with Martha Gellhorn at the Florida Hotel. Although I think Hemingway needed one great love affair for each of his four great or near-great books—D'Annunzio also did—he was no ordinary fornicator or adulterer. No one ever suspected him at the time of being unfaithful to each of his four wives. I knew three of them—his first, Hadley, very well. What I mean is that he was discreet. It's true that during his affair with Martha in Spain he was still married to Pauline, but we knew he intended to divorce her.

A FRIEND: Vincent Sheean was a great admirer of Hemingway, but Sheean's wife, Diana Forbes-Robertson, thought he was domineering and argumentative. She believed he was weak in allowing himself to be trapped by women. Diana also criticized Martha for dressing too showily, especially for a war correspondent, and being too assertive in her relationship with Ernest.

STEPHEN SPENDER: When I was in Spain, the war correspondents in the hotel in Valencia regarded it as a joke that Martha Gellhorn was always looking for Hemingway, and usually he had disappeared with Joris Ivens to the front. They saw Hemingway as being pursued by this tough, aggressive lady. That was their joke.

DENIS BRIAN: Not long after that, you and your first wife, Inez, had lunch with Hemingway and Gellhorn in Paris. What was your impression of her?

STEPHEN SPENDER: She was playing up to him, calling him "Hem" and "Hemingstein." One of the most unfortunate things about Hemingway is that he invented a style which practically everyone imitated. That, in a way, was a sort of achievement—that all the coherent members of the International Brigades talked in a kind of Hemingway style which, of course, they got from his novels. What was rather surprising to me was that people, Martha Gellhorn particularly, actually did it when she was with Hemingway. She talked Hemingwayese to him all the time. [Almost half a century later Martha Gellhorn denied that lunch with Spender ever took place. It is discussed at the end of this chapter.]

DENIS BRIAN: In those days, with Martha talking Hemingwayese, he, ironically, was talking Wodehousese—like a P. G. Wodehouse character. Fellow correspondent Sefton Delmer noticed it when they and Herbert Matthews were driving together in a car. Lacking a rag to wipe the oil dipstick, Delmer used the Union Jack—the British flag—that had been flown as a pennant on the car. Noting Matthews's and Hemingway's looks of disapproval, Delmer asked if they were shocked. "Frankly, old boy, we were," Ernest replied, sounding to Delmer like an American's idea of an upper-class Englishman, and adding: "Millions of men died under that flag." Delmer said that was nonsense, because he'd bought the flag in Madrid and no one had died under it. When Ernest asked if Delmer would use his old school tie for the same purpose, he said he'd wiped many things worse than oil with his old school tie. If Ernest had called Delmer "a cad" he wouldn't have been surprised.[1]

GEORGE SELDES: Hemingway, myself, and other correspondents got to Spain via France. But to leave France and get into Spain, Americans had to get a special permit from the French chief of police. I'd made a deal with J. David Stern, owner of the New York Post for my wife, Helen, and me to pay our own way to Spain because he couldn't afford it. So we were in Paris waiting for them to process our passports when two of the most beautiful people I've ever seen, a handsome man and a beautiful woman came over. It was Errol Flynn and his wife, Lilli Damita. She spoke good French though I understand she was Italian. She was helping him get a visa. As we sat there we introduced each other and he said, "I've got a million dollars which I've raised among the friends of Loyalist Spain in Hollywood. I'm going to Madrid and we're going to build a hospital and buy ambulances for the Loyalists." This was my first meeting with Flynn. To go to Madrid my wife and I had to go to Valencia or Barcelona and wait for vacant places in an automobile. Cars that went to Madrid usually carried only the highest officials or food or medicine. A pint of gasoline, they said, was worth a pint of blood. Although the whole country was starving they raked up a banquet for Flynn in Barcelona and he accepted this. He told them all about the wonders he was going to do, and, believe it or not, they supplied him with a car. He got to Madrid by car and he

[1]Sefton Delmer, Trail Sinister, Secker & Warburg, 1961.

told the same story in Madrid. We met frequently, usually at the entrance to the Hotel Victoria, before going out. Flynn kept talking and everybody bowed to him and said he was one of the great benefactors. He was a goddamned liar! I've met three sons-of-bitches in my life. One was Mussolini, the second was D'Annunzio who betrayed Duse, and the third is Errol Flynn for his betrayal of the Spanish Republic to make publicity for himself for a Hollywood movie. Now this is what he did. He went out with Hemingway and Matthews who were often together at the front in the same building. When they got close to the front, Flynn didn't mind the occasional boomings of the cannon—nobody minded that; but when he heard machine-gun rattles and rifle fire he got scared. He said, and I'll give you his exact words: "Do any of you gents know the address of a good, clean whorehouse?" At that time, April 1937, Flynn was already known as "the grim raper." But all of us seemed to forgive him because of the million dollars he was bringing from Hollywood to establish a hospital and to supply medicines and ambulances for the wounded. But the whole thing was a hoax.

LEICESTER HEMINGWAY: The whole thing was a fantastic fraud and so was Flynn himself. His autobiography, *My Wicked, Wicked Ways*, is a sort of apologia for his entire life. In it he explains over and over how he was in this and that scam, this and that publicity ruse, this and that PR fling, and how he almost didn't have anything to do with it. How they used him. How they set him up. How they put him out front and how he didn't know what was going to come out of what happened. As you read Flynn's book you have the feeling that here must have been the most naïve son-of-a-bitch alive, who constantly kept saying, "Gee, fellers, I don't know what you want with me but go right ahead." Nobody can be that naïve when he's constantly living in Hollywood among the wiseguys, playing gin rummy with them night after night, drinking with them, chasing their dames and they're chasing his dames. Well, Ernest was prevailed upon to give Errol Flynn a special super treatment accorded a Hollywood star who was supposed to be over there to help the Spanish Loyalists.

GEORGE SELDES: After Flynn asked Hemingway and Matthews the way to the nearest whorehouse he disappeared. He did nothing for the Loyalist cause. As for the million dollars he promised, he didn't have a cent on him. When he got back to Barcelona, he had a scratch on his arm or face and a little mercurochrome on it. He said he had been shot in the front-line trenches. Then he sent a very innocent cable: "Everything is set," or "Everything is all right." That was a tip to whomever he was working for to release a story that he was shot at the front. The *New York Daily News*, on the front page, came out with "Errol Flynn Killed at the Spanish Front." That was changed in a later edition to "Wounded." He spread the story that he was wounded because he was about to make a movie [*They Died With Their Boots On*, directed by Raoul Walsh] in which the character is wounded in a cavalry charge. It was all a plot which he and the Hollywood people were engaged in. I think it was one of the dirtiest things in history.

DENIS BRIAN: The *New York Times* confirms Seldes's account. A wire story dated April 4, 1937, said that Flynn, in Spain as a "sort of war correspondent" got a minor bullet wound on his face when he was caught in machine-gun fire. It noted that he had left Lilli Damita behind in Paris. Next day the paper published an official report that Flynn had not been wounded, and that the first false report came from Flynn for purposes of movie publicity. Errol Flynn's ghostwritten autobiography, *My Wicked, Wicked Ways*, says: "On the way out of Spain I mused at length how the Spaniards could have got the idea I was the bearer of a million bucks. Koets [a surgeon and friend who accompanied him in Spain] started to chortle raucously. 'What's so funny?' I demanded. He moved into uproarious laughter. He told me he had set up the idea when he arrived, buzzing the word to the reception committee, but telling them that the money was not available yet. That was why they gave us a car and a chauffeur-guide. 'What I wanted was a chance to operate, to work and operate, that's all,' he said. 'The only way I could do it and get by in style was to use you.' After his thunderous guffaws settled, I said, 'Thank you, Comrade Sonofabitch!' " In the book, Flynn used the pseudonymn Koets for his surgeon-friend, whose real name was Dr. Hermann Erben. After World War II, Dr. Erben spent two years in prison as a Nazi spy. Author Charles Higham reveals this in his *Errol Flynn: The Untold Story*. Higham concludes, with considerable documentation to back him, that Flynn's undercover role in Spain was also to spy for the Nazis.

LEICESTER HEMINGWAY: Ernest not only despised Flynn, he felt the guy was a triple phony. Ernest *never* doublecrossed people. Ernest always kept his word. Flynn you could always count on to let you down.

GEORGE SELDES: In Madrid a lot of the correspondents stayed at the Florida hotel. As a rule you came to Spain and asked the government, "For heaven's sake where can we stay?" Then they put you into the

Florida. We were there. Hemingway was there. As for Hemingway's reportage from Spain, it was not only truthful, it was a brave thing to do at a time when Spain was being red-baited to death. As for physical courage, I tell you his daily or almost daily visits to the wrecked building in no man's land he used as an observation post were an exhibition of courage. From there he could see both the Loyalists as well as the Franco trenches opposite. My wife and I each went to the front-line trenches *once*. But Hem and Herbert Matthews climbed out into no man's land almost every day and lay on their stomachs on the floor near a smashed second-floor window to watch the fighting. And Franco shelled everything, including this hideout.

THOMAS SHEVLIN: You must remember that Ernest was a fatalist. What he felt about death and courage was that it didn't make any difference whether you were running to your left or the right, or away or ahead; if you were going to get it you were going to get it. He was a definite fatalist. If your time is up, it's going to be up. I had a hunch he felt, about himself, "I might as well go ahead as go back, or, if it's more comfortable I'll sit down."

ARCHIBALD MACLEISH: Ernest returned from Spain on June 4, 1937, for a meeting at Carnegie Hall on the Spanish War. I spoke and Ernest spoke—his only political speech. We saw each other that night and were perfectly civil to each other. Our speeches were before the Second Writers' Congress, and I thought Ernest made a good speech that moved the audience. The thing was very successful. But it was difficult all around, because the Writers' Congress had a good deal of communist infiltration and may even have had communist leadership.[1] Part of the attack on me in later years by Joseph McCarthy was based on that.

DENIS BRIAN: Back in Spain Hemingway continued to act as a morale booster. John Gates, a member of the Lincoln Brigade, recalls one such incident in *The Story of an American Communist*. "Suddenly a car drove up, stopped, and out stepped two men. Nobody ever looked better to me in all my life. We hugged one another and shook hands. They told us everything they knew—Hemingway tall and husky, speaking in explosives; Matthews, just as tall, but thin, and talking in his reserved way. The writers gave us the good news of the many men who were safe, and we

[1]The League of American Writers had sponsored the meeting. Donald Ogden Stewart was its president. Among the speakers was Earl Browder, Secretary of the Communist Party of the U.S.A.

told them the bad news of some who were not. Facing the other side of the river, Hemingway shook his burly fist. 'You Fascist bastards haven't won yet,' he shouted. 'We'll show you.' "

GEORGE SELDES: Even during the war he was trying to sustain the Hemingway myth he started in the early twenties about being turned down by all the literary people. [He had, in fact, had his share of rejections.] Here he was, seventeen years later, in the lobby of the Hotel Florida where the war correspondents in Madrid lived. As soon as he had his audience—J. B. S. Haldane and Antoine de Saint-Exupery among them—he told the whole story. Every few years he made the story stronger, telling of his hard time getting published. The worst case, he said, was the *Dial*. It not only sent back "The Killers" but "the editor of the *Dial*, Gilbert Seldes"—Hem pointed his finger at me—"*Your brother!*" had written and told him to make an honest living as a truck driver, "because you will never become a writer." There was no copy of such a letter in the *Dial* files.

DENIS BRIAN: There seems to have been some truth in this "myth." Apparently Hemingway had the right magazine, but the wrong editor. An editor who succeeded Seldes probably rejected the short story, though the truck-driver comment seems unlikely.

GEORGE SELDES: Hemingway had a room on the sixth floor of the Hotel Florida. The seventh and eighth floors had been destroyed by shellfire. My wife and I lived on the fifth floor. When the hotel was shelled our great fun, Helen and I, was to stand at the foot of the stairway where we could see who was running out of what room with what woman. I needn't tell you who came out of Hemingway's room. He and Sefton Delmer of the London *Express* had a half of beef hanging up in a cupboard. My wife and I were there a year and a half and we never had meat or fish or vegetables, but Hemingway and Delmer got these things in somehow. They sometimes had meat dinners in their rooms but they never invited Helen and me.

WILLIAM WALTON: There's another example of Ernest's ability to mix truth and fiction, with his wife saying to Vincent Sheean: "Ernest fought with the Spaniards. He had a brigade. He was in charge of it." And Sheean said: "But, Pauline, how can you believe this? He was a war correspondent as I was." And Pauline said: "Ah, that's what he wanted you to believe."

JOHN HEMINGWAY: It's a tricky subject. He told me he fought in Spain for the Loyalists. My understanding was that—and I don't know if this is possible or not—there was a definite incident at one of the sieges of Teruel where the Franco people came out and surrendered to him because he looked like a Russian, or a bear [laughs]. Then he mentioned having organized an Intelligence thing. So I think he was working for the Loyalists, although he was distressed when he ran into some of the really tough characters like the commies, André Marty and people like that, where he got the picture of them.

LEICESTER HEMINGWAY: He may have done Intelligence work, but that does not constitute fighting. Anybody who is on either side contributes information he or she may have. That's considered part of having your *promisos* validated. "If you're one of our guys, you help us any way you possibly can." He did not fight. He raised money, gave ambulances, did all sorts of things to aid them. This does not constitute bearing arms.

GEORGE SELDES: How could he have fought with the Loyalists unless he was in the Abraham Lincoln or some other foreign brigade?

ALVAH BESSIE: He never fought in Spain. This is part of the Hemingway myth. Whether he ever carried guns during the war, I don't know. I never saw him with one. If he had one he could have gone to the front lines with Matthews and have fired the gun a couple of times and then felt justified in saying, "I fought with the Loyalists." Why not? After all, Errol Flynn is supposed to have done the same thing in Madrid, going up to the front in University City, picking up a rifle and firing it over the barricades.

DENIS BRIAN: On December 29, 1937, a reporter for the French communist paper *Ce Soir* questioned Hemingway at Orsay train station. Hemingway had just arrived from Spain where he had witnessed the successful occupation of Teruel by Republican troops. He claimed not to have slept for five days and nights, but after a bath and change of clothes agreed to an interview in a nearby hotel. The reporter described him as "a tall, robust man with a broad smiling face." Asked if there had been any reprisals against the people in Teruel, Hemingway replied, "As one who was there I can say that not one person was shot. At first some people were shaking with fear expecting Russian troops would enter their town. When they discovered the 'Russians' were all genuine fellow Spaniards, they realized they had been misled by Franco's propaganda, and their attitude soon changed. There were no reprisals and that caused an atmosphere of joy, confidence and cooperation. That wasn't what happened in the city at the start of the war when it was occupied by Franco's troops. I was told of terrible things that happened then. For instance, a young man known to have progressive ideas who had been wounded in the fighting [to defend Teruel] was first given medical treatment. When he had recovered he was taken to the main square of the city and while Franco's regiment played the royal anthem he was shot. Many left-wing Republicans were executed like this by Franco's men."

MILTON WOLFF: Listen, Hemingway was very helpful to the cause of Spain, probably more so than any other prominent public figure. He also wanted to be more in the fight than it was possible for a correspondent to be. He probably gave the impression of being part of the fighting. Many of the Spaniards cooperated with him; they loved him and he had an easy access to leading Spanish commanders and political figures.

GEORGE SELDES: None of his mythologizing takes away from his courage. He stayed on after my wife and I left at the end of 1937. One of the last things I remember is seeing his bullfighter friend Sidney Franklin with him. Hemingway frequently used him as a messenger. "See if you can dig up some hypodermic needles, Sidney! Dr. Bethune's unit is desperate!" Dr. Norman Bethune was internationally famous as chief of thoracic surgery at Sacré Coeur Hospital in Montreal, Canada. A way to store refrigerated blood had just been perfected, so that Dr. Bethune was able to give the wounded blood transfusions from mobile blood banks brought close to the front lines. This saved many lives. My wife and I saw Hemingway again in Paris some time in 1938. Correspondents had to leave Spain about once every three months to get something to eat. There was nothing to eat in Spain. And we were at the Select in Paris with Webb Miller, the poet Robert Desnos, and Hemingway. It was after midnight and each of us had quite a number of those saucers; our bill was getting pretty high. So Desnos said, "I just live around the corner. If we're going to talk all night you might as well come to my house." So we came over there, he served drinks, and we talked for several more hours. It was then that Hemingway, who called himself "Numero Uno," said, "I had to go to Spain before you goddamned liberal bastards knew I was on your side."

DENIS BRIAN: Hemingway made his second journey back to the United States in January 1938, staying mostly in Key West where he again met his friend Harry Sylvester. Had his letters to you, Mr. Sylvester, and his news reports about the war changed you from neutral to pro-Republic?

HARRY SYLVESTER: No, and I nearly got into a fistfight with him about it. A crazy thing. I don't know how spontaneous it was, or if he had it in the back of his mind for some time. He had been away in Spain all that winter and had just returned to Key West. I had gone out to fish. The place was so small then he must have asked someone where I was, maybe my wife, and come looking for me. I was fishing on the bridge. The next thing I knew this car was pulling up in back of me and Hemingway was in it, calling me names, saying this and the other thing. He knew damn well if we began to fight, either we or the other automobiles on the bridge would have to stop. Fortunately, he cooled down pretty soon and drove off. After less than three months at home he returned to Spain in March.

DENIS BRIAN: Sefton Delmer witnessed Hemingway behaving like an unofficial political commissar. Seeing one soldier leading a retreating rabble, Hemingway stopped his car and said, "Look comrade, we all of us got to die once. So we may as well die clean as shitty." Ernest's commanding tone turned the man around. But Delmer saw the same soldier several hours later in Tortosa, thirty miles behind the battlefront. He must have turned tail the moment Delmer and Hemingway were out of sight and *sprinted* for safety. Delmer chose not to tell the self-appointed political commissar of his failure.[1] Because Ernest was always a good man in a tight spot, fellow correspondents were glad to have him along, especially those with him in a boat on the dangerous Ebro river. The boat was out of control and heading for a wrecked bridge when Hemingway grabbed an oar and used his great strength and skill to row them to the river bank. But it wasn't enough for him to be cool under fire and an example to others. He claimed as a noncommissioned officer to have lubricated overheating machine guns during a battle by urinating on them. He told the editor of the newspaper *PM*, Ralph Ingersoll, that while helping to ship art treasures from Spain to Switzerland he had murdered a truck driver. His report of the same incident for his news agency gives a muted and more likely account. He wrote to a friend that on April 15, 1938, on his way from Tortosa to Barcelona, he passed a convoy of trucks carrying art treasures from the Prado, and prayed that they'd escape attack by enemy planes. He may, of course, have had murder on his mind.

Hemingway was back in the United States in June, then made his fourth and final journey to the war in November 1938. The Republicans were retreating. The end seemed near. In Barcelona's Hotel Majestic, Hemingway was discussing the situation with other correspondents and Dr. Edward Barsky, an American physician with the Abraham Lincoln Brigade. How could they prevent Brigade members from capture by Franco's rebels and almost certain death by firing squads? "Why the hell let our guys get trapped by the fascists?" Hemingway said. "If it has to be done, I'll get an American warship and we'll evacuate every single

[1]Sefton Delmer, *Trail Sinister*.

American."[1] Either André Marty, Commissar of the International Brigades, was one of the group or he heard of Hemingway's suggestion, because later when an evacuation plan was being proposed, he said, "And by God, if that doesn't work we'll get Hemingway to get that battleship!"[2]

MILTON WOLFF: I heard from reliable sources that Hemingway acted as liaison between the Spaniards and the British Navy in the last days, in terms of evacuating people. So he did have influence, though he was certainly not on the general staff.

DENIS BRIAN: He had influence but I could find no hard evidence that he got British battleships to do his will. However, a British destroyer did save a close friend, Lieutenant-Colonel Gustavo Duran, a musician turned soldier.

MICHAEL STRAIGHT [who became Duran's brother-in-law]: Gustavo, a Loyalist commander, was holding Valencia on the coast when the war ended. Franco's soldiers surrounding the city had orders to execute Gustavo the day after they captured him. He went to the American consul for help but was turned away, and told he had fought on the wrong side. Gustavo shook hands with the consul and left to wander all night through the city hoping to escape. There was no way. At dawn he returned to the consul, who said, "Although I could have saved your life I refused to, yet you held out your hand to me. Why?" "Why not?" Gustavo said. Then the consul gave him the address of a British diplomat, who drove him through Franco's lines to a launch which took him to a British destroyer and safety.

ALVAH BESSIE: Late in November 1938 the government had decided to disband the International Brigades and repatriate us. I ran into Hemingway and Martha Gellhorn in a little town, Ripall, about fifty kilometers south of the French border. I had just come out of seeing Charlie Chaplin's picture *Modern Times* in Spanish, which is quite an experience. We were waiting to be evacuated. I'd met Hemingway some months before and had liked him immediately. He was aimiable and pleasant to all of us and had cigarettes and whatnot for us. The previous time it had been a case of whiskey for Milton Wolff. On this second meeting Martha Gellhorn gave me a chocolate bar, which was very nice of her. Hemingway

[1] *The Abraham Lincoln Brigade* (Citadel Press, 1967) in which Dr. Barsky is interviewed by Arthur H. Landis.

[2] Ibid.

then said to me, "I'm glad to see you came out of this alive." We were being held in Ripall before being let out of Spain. I said, "So am I." He said, "Because I feel responsible for your being here." I said, "Huh?" "Oh," he said, "you heard the speech I made at the Writers' Congress in Carnegie Hall in 1937, didn't you?" I said, "Yes, I did. It was a good speech." Then he said, "I know that speech influenced a lot of the boys to come over here." Well, this is the kind of egomania the guy suffered from. His speech didn't affect me. I had decided to go to Spain long before that. I was trying to find a way out of my marriage at that time.

MILTON WOLFF: The fact that Hemingway and others were so passionate in their antifascism and defense of the Republic I'm sure influenced a hell of a lot of people to go to Spain, or to support Spain in other ways. It wasn't vanity on Hemingway's part. I mean, he may have been vain about it, but it was true nevertheless that he influenced many people to fight in Spain. I personally never found him to be boastful.

DENIS BRIAN: In the spring of 1939, three months after the International Brigades left Spain, General Franco's Nationalist forces, with continued help in arms and men from Hitler and Mussolini, won the war.

MILTON WOLFF: The British were in touch with Loyalist generals who surrendered Madrid, but whether they used Hemingway and other correspondents as liaisons I don't know.

DENIS BRIAN: It's unlikely that Hemingway helped. Six days before Franco's men entered the city, Hemingway was home in Key West starting on his novel of the war, *For Whom the Bell Tolls.* He explained to Max Perkins that as a nominal Catholic he had accepted communist discipline in Spain because the communists were the most effective fighters against the fascists. But now, back in America, as a writer his only allegiance was to the truth. In a letter to Mrs. Pfeiffer, who was still his mother-in-law, Hemingway described himself as an anti-war correspondent, said he was not scared during the Spanish War, although he had been in World War I. He admitted he had been intolerant, righteous, ruthless, and cruel—without saying to whom. He said the only way he could live was to submit to the discipline of the Catholic Church. At the same time he wrote that it seemed crooked to have anything to do with the church when they were on the side of the enemy.

ALVAH BESSIE: As I said, I don't know if Hemingway carried guns in the war; I never saw him with one. But I do know he brought home to the United States two Spanish pistols. He gave both of them to Edwin Rolf, a friend of mine, who gave me one of them. I left it with a friend for her protection. And she married a man who used the pistol to commit a holdup. He planned to rob a store he knew banked lots of money every Friday afternoon. He made the very sad mistake of holding up a man he thought would immediately give him his car for a getaway car. The guy grabbed him by the wrist to get the pistol from him and was shot. The holdup man hid the body in the woods. He was caught within forty-eight hours. Anyway, this is where one of Hemingway's pistols, which he shouldn't have brought out of Spain, wound up. The holdup man got the death sentence. In the final statement, the judge said: "I regret very much having to impose this penalty, because the story of the man's life is heartbreaking. But there is nothing I am allowed to do under the law except what I am doing." I never saw Hemingway again after Spain and he never knew that a gun he brought from Spain killed one guy and was the death of another.

For Whom the Bell Tolls

GEORGE SELDES: It's one of the greatest things written about the war.

ALVAH BESSIE: I wrote a long review of it for *New Masses* [an American communist magazine]. I don't think the book had anything to do with the Spanish war, and I called it a *Cosmopolitan* magazine love story against the background of the war. At a meeting with the Vets he defended the book: "The greatest thing I ever wrote," and "blah, blah, blah," and, "It's all true. Every word of it is true, and I don't understand politics—it hurts my head."

WILLIAM W. SEWARD, JR.: I was a professor of English who was interested in his writing. That's how our friendship began—by correspondence. Which on the face of it was rather unusual because he had perhaps more of an aversion toward professors of English than he did toward news interviewers, if that's possible. Some newsmen he had great respect for, but others he felt, I think, were trying to trap him, and his pose—and this was only my impression—was to hand them back the sort of superficiality they were dealing out. He replied to me that it made him feel good to know someone liked what he wrote. He promised to send me an inscribed copy of his next novel on which he had been working for a year and ten days. This was March of 1940. But he asked me to remind him of his promise, because he intended to get fairly drunk when he finished it and might forget. He wrote that the book would have thirty-two chapters and he had finished twenty-eight of them and with luck it would be the best novel he had ever written. He asked me to wish him luck with the last four chapters. As it turned out there were many more chapters. This was *For Whom the Bell Tolls.* I didn't have to remind him of his promise. He sent me a copy—I believe it was one of his author's copies because it came to me several weeks ahead of publication. He wrote my name and "wishing him all good luck always" and then signed his name in full. I think it was his best novel as he had hoped it would be.

MILTON WOLFF: Robert Jordan, the character in the novel, is really a Jewish boy from the Bronx, Alex Kunslich, a communist who was the inspirational leader of the American group of guerrillas who operated behind the lines. They were made up of a Finn, Billy Aalto, and another Jew from New York, Irv Goff. Goff was a former vaudeville acrobat and a self-described health nut. Their main exploit was down south where they liberated a prison holding a number of leading Republican figures. Physically the description of Jordan is like Philip Detro, a battalion commander who was seriously wounded at Teruel and died of wounds, and Robert Merriman, who was a Berkeley professor and who was captured and executed in Spain by the fascists. I think the physical descriptions and the background of the character, Jordan, came from those two. Now, how they talk and how they screw and all that stuff, that's probably Ernest. But the action was the Jewish fellow, Kunslich. I later got Aalto and Goff into the OSS with me in World War II.

DENIS BRIAN: Hemingway made no attempt to portray André Marty in fictional camouflage; he gave the chief commissar of the International Brigades his own name and damned him as a madman with a mania for executing his own men. Philip Knightley wrote in *The First Casualty*: "The principal Communist hatchet man in Spain was André Marty. He admitted to some 500 executions; others would multiply that figure by five or even ten."[1] Is that accurate?

MILTON WOLFF: This is the first time I ever heard of Marty admitting to anything. I don't know if he killed anybody or had anybody killed. I do know Hemingway had a falling-out with him because Marty would not give him some special credentials other than what regular reporters were receiving. Hemingway considered himself more than just a reporter in Spain. This is why he took off after Marty. I've been hearing this for the past fifty years about Marty and who he killed and who he didn't kill. I just have never seen any proof of it.

[1] Phillip Knightley, *The First Casualty,* Harcourt Brace Jovanovich, 1975.

Let's forget André Marty for a minute, okay? I'd like to forget Marty for all time, because I know people who are making statements about him as though they are facts, and as far as I know it just has become a fact by constant repetition. I never met the man, never had anything to do with him, but I do know people who have and they said it was all bullshit—that he was a disciplinarian, that the Americans got on his case because he insisted that all the stuff the Americans were sending over to the Lincoln Battalion boys be divided among all the International Brigades. Because, obviously, the German antifascists, and the Italian antifascists, and those from Poland were not getting anything from home, and the Americans should not be in a special class. And that got a lot of people's asses burned, too.

DENIS BRIAN: Even the Russian writer Ilya Ehrenburg of *Izvestia* called Marty authoritarian and mentally sick and said Marty suspected everyone of being a traitor. Other leftists recall him as a butcher who had people shot for minor offenses.

GEORGE SELDES: Hemingway detested Marty, who had fought with the Red Army during the Russian Revolution. I think probably rightly. Marty was as brutal as any communist commissar has ever been and didn't hesitate to execute his enemies.

MILTON WOLFF: I know Hemingway thought Marty was crazy, but, you see, at the beginning of the war the French that came over to defend Madrid were the cream of the crop. After that, the French that came over were not so hot. Marty had a lot of trouble with them and, in spite of being a communist, he was a French nationalist and, as all Frenchmen are, a chauvinist. He was acutely embarrassed by the behavior of the late-coming French. You see, these things that are said out of context—like "Marty was crazy"—without any background to them sound weird. If you know what the situation was and the pressures, anything is possible. And Marty had a problem from the third echelon on. But they died in the hundreds in the defense of Madrid.

GEORGE SELDES: I only have this one objection to *For Whom the Bell Tolls:* he gives the impression to millions of readers that atrocities were *only* committed on the Loyalist side. Whereas for each atrocity on the Loyalist side of which there were some committed by people like Marty, there were probably ten, twenty, fifty on the other side. They killed all their prisoners and admitted it. Besides, after the war Franco executed ten thousand—he called them traitors. These were civilians who had defended Madrid. They were in the prisons and Franco emptied the prisons by executing in the first ten years at least a hundred thousand, maybe more. The ordinary reader, not knowing what happened on both sides and reading a man who wrote a great book, a man we can trust, gets the wrong ideas about Loyalist atrocities. But I think Hemingway was honest, as a known supporter of the Republic, to write of an atrocity committed by Republicans.

MILTON WOLFF: I would admire that, too. But I'd add the qualification that the qualitative nature of the atrocities was different. One was more vast than the other, as Seldes says, more impersonal than the other. The Republican government did everything to stop kangaroo trials, summary executions, the burning of churches and stuff like that, whereas the fascists had an organized policy of eliminating any even remotely suspected source of resistance. You should know two things about Hemingway's book. One is about the chapter on the alleged atrocities committed by the Republicans early on in the war in a village. After he outlined the book to Maxwell Perkins, Perkins was not enthusiastic, saying he didn't think America was ready for it. So Hemingway sent him a new chapter, and on the basis of that new chapter Perkins became very enthusiastic about the book. The second thing is that in Hemingway's published letters there's one to Bernard Berenson, the art expert, where Berenson marvels at the ability of creative writers to invent. And Hemingway cites that chapter of the atrocities committed by the Republicans as pure invention on his part. That was the chapter that incensed me, not because I thought there were no atrocities committed on the Republican side, but because Hemingway equated it with the organized terror that the Nationalists and fascists carried out, which was quite a different thing.

Aftermath

JOHN RYBOVICH, JR.: While Ernest had been in Spain covering the civil war, Rybovich & Sons installed a flying bridge and heavy outriggers on the *Pilar*. Nineteen thirty-eight, when he returned from Spain, was his last year in Bimini. His marriage to Pauline was on the rocks, and before the end of 1939 he left Key West to settle on a small farm outside Havana, Cuba. That year he was the first person to catch two whole blue-fin tuna. No one had ever brought in a whole tuna before that hadn't been attacked by sharks. You know, he never at any time entered a fishing competition—to compete against others. Perhaps this was to preserve his macho image, and not be among the fishermen that lose. There's only one winner in a competition and there's so much goddamn luck attached to fishing; it's not only a matter of skill.

TOM GLAZER: In the 1940s I roomed with a friend, Thomas Browne Bennett. He had fought in Spain and had met Hemingway. Tom told me that Hemingway paid his—Bennett's—way back here to the States. Bennett said that Hemingway told him he kept "union hours" as a rifleman in the Spanish trenches on the Loyalist side for several days, perhaps longer. Early one Sunday morning our phone in Greenwich Village rang and I sleepily got up and answered it. A gruff voice asked for Bennett. "Who's calling?" I asked testily. "Hemingway," came the reply. I woke up fast and called Bennett from his bed. I had thought Bennett's tales about Spain and Hemingway rather tall, but I became a believer pronto.

MILTON WOLFF: I didn't let that angry letter of Hemingway's calling me wet behind the ears get in the way of our friendship. I asked him to come to the tenth anniversary of the Lincoln Brigade and he sent up a recording he had made. I called him when he was living at the Finca in Cuba and I called him again when Dr. Barsky was put in jail and had a long telephone conversation with him.[1] This was after World War II. I had been in the OSS in Europe among other things. He asked me how many krauts I had killed. Here I was asking him to get help for Barsky and he wanted to know how many krauts I'd killed.

ALVAH BESSIE: I wish the hell I'd known Hemingway better. He was responsible for getting my book, *Men in Battle*, published. Maxwell Perkins said to him, "There's a guy here by the name of Bessie who's written some good short stories. He wants to write a book about Spain." And Hemingway said, "Grab it! It'll be the best book written by any of the guys in the Brigade." This was nice of him, and Perkins signed a contract with me just on Hemingway's recommendation. I was grateful to him for that. But Scribner's never promoted it. He was mad about that. When he wrote the introduction to Gustav Regler's book *The Great Crusade*, Hemingway mentioned I'd written a fine book but he didn't even mention the title. That was like him.

MILTON WOLFF: He was a generous man. He offered to share the proceeds of *For Whom the Bell Tolls* with the Lincoln Brigade, but I put

[1]Called before the House Un-American Activities Committee in 1950, Dr. Barsky refused to name contributors to an antifascist committee. Consequently he went to prison for six months.

the kibosh on that with my letter criticizing him as a tourist in Spain. But he helped us as individuals. He helped me, too, you know. He sent me $400 so I could help some guy who was in a mess with an egg business in Connecticut. The main thing was that Hemingway knew the score probably better than any of the other writers who went to Spain. It's not so much what he did, but what he didn't do. He could have made a tremendous contribution to left-wing literature and antifascist literature. I don't mean in terms of propaganda, but in the way Dreiser and Sinclair Lewis did.

MORLEY CALLAGHAN: Hemingway and his friend Dos Passos had a violent break over the war. Dos Passos thought Hemingway had fallen for the communist line and Dos Passos had reacted very violently against the whole left movement. Hemingway said dreadful things about him, calling him "a one-eyed Portuguese bastard." [Dos Passos was, in fact, illegitimate.] I had lunch with Dos Passos a year before he died. He simply said it was a political break; he went wildly to the right and Hemingway stayed on the left for a long time.

JOHN HEMINGWAY: I was in Havana when Dos Passos came through after World War II and Papa was so pleased to see him; they were as happy as bedbugs. This was after years of estrangement. The reason Papa was off Dos Passos—at least, the reason he told—was that during the siege of Madrid normally any of the correspondents, or anybody who got to leave the country, brought back goodies and necessities as well as luxuries to spread around for the guys who hadn't had a chance to leave. Because there was nothing available in Madrid. Apparently Dos Passos came back this one time, they all gathered around him expectantly and Dos, who was an absentminded-professor type, said, "Oh. Oh, yes." He pulled out some Hershey bars or something like that. And that was all he had. He hadn't really thought about it, and Papa thought that was unforgivable. There had to be more than that, although sometimes little things become gigantic. In times of shortage these things become terribly important. Politics may have had something to do with their break, but later, not then. Then Dos was very much in the civil war. He was there. There may have been something about objecting more vociferously than Papa to some obvious things happening with the Russians coming in.

DENIS BRIAN: The hurried, secret execution of José Robles Pazos was the more likely cause of their break. Pazos, a Loyalist colonel and a friend of Dos Passos, had suddenly disappeared. At first, Hemingway assured Dos Passos that Pazos was safe. Then Hemingway learned that the communists had suspected Pazos of spying [he had relatives on the Franco side], or of being too outspokenly critical of their growing influence, and had executed him. The details are still unknown. Instead of grieving with Dos Passos, Hemingway said something to the effect that the death of one man suspected of disloyalty was less important than the Loyalist cause. Dos Passos did not share his dispassionate, pragmatic attitude, and became bitterly anticommunist. Hemingway maintained that Dos Passos became progressively more right wing as he became wealthier.

Hemingway as War Correspondent

DENIS BRIAN: Did Hemingway fail as a war correspondent in Spain by suppressing the truth about atrocities committed by the Loyalist Republicans, and about communist persecution and summary executions? Phillip Knightley, a special correspondent for the London *Sunday Times*, records the information he maintains Hemingway neglected to reveal. He writes: "Some 60,000 people are said to have been killed during a period of Republican terror, including twelve bishops, 283 nuns, 4,184 priests, and 2,365 monks. A similar purge was taking place on the Nationalist side. It appears that the Nationalists murdered about the same number. The brutality of both sides was extraordinary, and on the Republican side it frequently had religious overtones. 'A crucifix was forced down the mouth of the mother of five Jesuits,' according to Professor Hugh Thomas. 'Eight hundred persons were thrown down a mine shaft. And, always, the moment of death would be greeted with applause as if it was the moment of truth in a corrida.' "[1] What do you think of that, Mr. Seldes?

GEORGE SELDES: We all knew there were atrocities in the first months of the war. The burning of churches, for instance, has been charged to Loyalist Republicans. Do you know who burned the churches? The Anarchists. They had five hundred thousand members, especially in Barcelona and Catalonia. Most of those early atrocities were committed by the Anarchists. They were never blamed, but the Reds have been blamed—which is ridiculous.

DENIS BRIAN: But what of Knightley's accusation that Hemingway suppressed the truth of communist persecution and summary executions? I notice Knightley doesn't name any correspondents who *did* report such events.

[1] Phillip Knightley, *The First Casualty*.

GEORGE SELDES: Knightley is mostly totally wrong in everything he says. Hemingway was not aware of the communist persecutions and summary executions, because it wasn't going on. The year and a half I was living in the Florida Hotel in Madrid, the same hotel as Hemingway, I don't know of even any rumor of atrocities for us to investigate.

MILTON WOLFF: There was early terror that took place on the Republican side—if you can call it that, because nothing [in terms of political allegiance] was settled in the first three or four months. The police were all gone, the army had defected, and political parties and peasants had a field day with priests and fascists and landowners, and whoever they imagined were their oppressors in the past. That was one form of terror Hemingway described in *For Whom the Bell Tolls*, and that's quite different from this continual barrage of insinuation that under Joe Stalin's orders the communists spent most of their time killing the opposition. That's what Knightley is saying. Hemingway never said that and he never knew it. If you read his play, *The Fifth Column*, it's quite a different story. It tells who was being killed and who was doing the killing. [In the play, Franco's rebels are bombing and shelling Loyalists in Madrid, and partisans on both sides behave brutally. Also, the Fifth Column in Madrid—fascists, monarchists, and Nationalists in hiding—snipe indiscriminately at people in the streets.]

STEPHEN SPENDER: In *For Whom the Bell Tolls* he tries to be fair. He does show there were massacres on both sides.

DENIS BRIAN: But that was a novel and published when the war was over and nothing could be done about the situation.

STEPHEN SPENDER: It's impossible to ask a reporter, when he's on one particular side, to report the atrocities committed by that side—or they'll throw him out of the country. It's very impractical, that kind of criticism. It's written by somebody who doesn't know the conditions at all.

DENIS BRIAN: Hemingway made the same point [*Ken*, September 22, 1938] when he said that if there had been terror or persecution to report a correspondent had two options: he could try to get the story through the censors and risk being kicked out of the country, or he could leave the country and write freely about it. He told of an encounter with Frederick Voigt, of the *Manchester Guardian*—though he didn't name him or the paper. Voigt had just arrived in Madrid and said he was writing about the terror in the streets and the bodies lying in the streets every morning. When challenged, Voigt admitted he had not seen one body, but was confident he was right. Hemingway conceded that in the first months of the war "uncontrollables" had killed people but said that now Madrid was as free from terror as any city in Europe. He admitted he knew of three people shot for spying in the course of a month. Had the atrocities persisted and had communist persecution occurred, certainly Hemingway should have known. Several of his news sources and friends in Spain were in high places and in the know, including Gustavo Duran, who commanded the 69th division, and Joris Ivens. Hemingway returned to the United States several times during the war so that—had he known of the atrocities—he could then have reported them free of censorship, though of course at the risk of not being allowed to return.

MILTON WOLFF: The Republic was strangled and the weight of superior arms won the war. Now, what the hell ever happened between the political parties and at the front, and who got shot, all that is bullshit to me. It had nothing to do with the fact that this was the beginning of World War II. Six months later Hitler marched into Poland. People lose sight of that. So it was just a continuation. I don't care about who was killing whom and why, because five hundred or five thousand dead is kind of crap, if it ever happened, and I doubt it. It did not decide the outcome of the war or the fate of the world.

DENIS BRIAN: But what of Knightley's charge that Hemingway's silence about atrocities—if he knew of them—was unforgivable in a war correspondent?

MILTON WOLFF: Hemingway was more than a reporter in Spain. He was a partisan of the Republic, and every time he came back to this country he came to rouse American opinion on behalf of the Spanish Republic, to get ambulances to bring back to Spain, and so forth. He considered himself more than a war correspondent in every war he covered. He was a poet. He was Byron. He took sides. If that bothers Mr. Knightley, tough shit.

PHILLIP KNIGHTLEY: Milton Wolff is right. Hemingway was more than a reporter in Spain. He took sides. He was a partisan for the Republic. There is nothing wrong with a war correspondent taking sides, providing he lets his readers know his stance and providing he imposes some limit to his support. For example, he should draw the line at writing lies to support his side. If he writes lies he ceases to be a war correspondent and becomes a propagandist. The Republicans, thanks to André Marty's spy paranoia, were executing hundreds of *their own loyal* supporters. Hemingway knew of the executions (including that of José Robles Pazos) but never wrote a word about them at the time because the Communist Party was the most active of the groups fighting for the Republic and Hemingway did not want to damage the Republican cause. This was a lie by omission. So, Hemingway was a propagandist in the Spanish Civil War and not a war correspondent. It is as simple as that.

DENIS BRIAN: There was strong support for Franco's rebels in America, especially among Catholics and that included Hemingway's wife, Pauline. It may explain why in reporting a Nationalist atrocity he used sardonic humor.

ARNOLD GINGRICH: When I was editing *Ken* magazine during the Spanish Civil War, Hemingway caused quite a controversy by his account of how infants had been killed. We had a news photo of a row of infant corpses in Barcelona after a bombing raid. The rebel authorities denied they were responsible for the deaths, saying their planes had not bombed Barcelona at the time the infants were killed. Hemingway wrote that as they were Loyalist babies it was not likely they had been bombed by Loyalists. And he concluded: these babies must have bombed themselves.

GEORGE SELDES: Hemingway was the most brilliant writer of us all in Spain, there's no question about that. He was a good war correspondent.

PETER DAVIS: In the 1980s I was making a documentary film about war correspondents who covered the Spanish Civil War and I asked Martha Gellhorn who she thought were the most reliable reporters of the war. She said Herbert Matthews of the *New York Times,* and Joseph North of *New Masses.*

DENIS BRIAN: As most I have questioned were pro-Republican soldiers or reporters, it has doubtless given a less-than-impartial view of the opposing sides in the civil war. Here's another opinion obtained by a free-lance reporter for the *Chicago Daily News,* Sheila Duff-Grant,: "I tried asking innocently whether the Franco [rebel] side was more law-abiding and well behaved than the government. The British consul in Malaga looked at me sharply, but his wife, quite unabashed, declared: 'Oh! They're all as ghastly as each other!' "

Truth or Trash?
Conflicting Memories

DENIS BRIAN: Poet Stephen Spender says that he and his first wife, Inez, had lunch with Hemingway and Gellhorn in Paris in 1936, during which Hemingway bragged of taking Gellhorn to the Madrid morgue every morning to toughen her up, and then showed Spender photos of war atrocities that he kept in his pocket. During a subsequent meeting with Hemingway in Spain, Spender says they discussed courage and cowardice. These recollections were part of a *Paris Review* interview with Spender.[1] Martha Gellhorn's response was published in a subsequent issue of the magazine.[2] She denied any knowledge of Spender having had a first wife, denied ever lunching with Spender and wife in Paris, said she didn't even know there was a Madrid morgue at the time—although she realized now there must have been one—and doubted the existence of the war-atrocity photographs. Believing she might be the sole surviving witness to a few years during the Spanish Civil War she hoped her testimony would intimidate "apocryphiars," as she termed them, and prevent scholars and biographers from repeating the fantasies of apocryphiars in mistake for the facts. According to Spender, Hemingway had said to him, "only if you actually go into battle and the bullets are screeching around you, can you know whether you are a coward or not. Mind you, you shit your pants with fear. Everyone does that." Gellhorn mocked this account, inviting *Paris Review* readers to visualize a whole army with soiled pants. She also vehemently disputed Spender's statement that Hemingway admitted he had come to Spain to test his courage rather than as an enthusiastic supporter of the Republic. She insisted that he was honestly committed to the cause, admired the men in the International Brigades and respected the Spanish people. He proved it, she wrote, by his actions.

STEPHEN SPENDER: I naturally resented Martha Gellhorn calling me a liar or apocryphiar. I never implied that Hemingway did not wholeheartedly support the Spanish Republic. But his lifelong concern about his own courage was something apart from that.

DENIS BRIAN: What is your evidence that you did have lunch with Hemingway and Gellhorn? Was your wife a witness to the conversation about taking Martha to the morgue to toughen her up?

STEPHEN SPENDER: That is probably the thing Martha Gellhorn is right about. Hemingway did, in fact, say this to me and I was young and took it seriously. But, of course, Martha's right; he couldn't have meant it seriously. She says I made it up, but one doesn't make up things like that—because one remembers them.

[1]*Paris Review* Winter–Spring 1980.

[2]*Paris Review*, Spring 1981.

DENIS BRIAN: He has such a deserved reputation for telling tall stories—Gellhorn also calls him an apocryphiar—it's surprising she doesn't now assume, as you do, that this was just another of his tall tales.

STEPHEN SPENDER: She wanted to use any old argument. The point is she wanted to deny we ever met, which is obvious rubbish.

DENIS BRIAN: Why?

STEPHEN SPENDER: She's that kind of person. I don't know her very well, but I think she just wants to be the only person who's ever met Hemingway.

DENIS BRIAN: You say that on the occasion he mentioned daily visits to the morgue he also brought out photos of atrocities.

STEPHEN SPENDER: Yes. Again, it's so long ago one never knows if one is remembering a memory. But since then I've heard that Hemingway was famous for carrying around these photographs.

DENIS BRIAN: In the now defunct *Ken* magazine there are several photos attributed to him of dead men and animals—war victims. In *Paris Review* you state that Hemingway and Gellhorn invited you to lunch in a Paris restaurant where they served things like steak and chips. Because your wife ordered sweetbreads and wouldn't drink you say Hemingway called her yellow. Then you say he made the comment about taking Gellhorn to the morgue.

STEPHEN SPENDER: That's what Gellhorn denies ever happened. She was probably so infatuated with Hemingway she forgot we were there.

DENIS BRIAN: But if Martha Gellhorn *was* there, why didn't she at that time say, "No, he doesn't take me to the morgue every morning. He never takes me to the morgue."?

STEPHEN SPENDER: With four people talking, I don't think she need necessarily have heard what he said. Or perhaps she understood it was an exaggeration. I don't think it was necessary she should have denied it at that time.

DENIS BRIAN: Did he have any purpose in showing you atrocity pictures?

STEPHEN SPENDER: He said it was to overcome my squeamishness.

DENIS BRIAN: Have you any independent proof of that Paris encounter?

STEPHEN SPENDER: Yes. That same day or the next, Hemingway and I jointly gave a reading at Sylvia Beach's bookstore. James Joyce was in the audience. There's also a published photo of the invitation to the Hemingway-Spender reading in an American literary annual for 1986.

And a friend, Muriel Gardiner, reminded me I had told her of our lunch with Hemingway and Gellhorn the next day. She had remembered because it was the same week that her brother, a passenger on the Hindenburg, survived by jumping from the burning zeppelin.

DENIS BRIAN: Did you consider Hemingway a great personality?

STEPHEN SPENDER: Yes, he was intoxicating just to be with. He was exciting. And I think in a way there was something very touching about him. He was a self-dramatizer, but he was very isolated within his own legend, wasn't he? When I was in Spain he was very nice to me. I was being abused very much because I was trying to save a friend who had deserted from the International Brigades, and there was a lot of talk about this because, of course, it was a rather terrible thing to have someone appear as a supporter of the government, as I certainly was, and at the same time be doing something so very inconvenient as to try to save a life. Hemingway, in fact, rather took the line with me, "You're too squeamish. You're too squeamish about the war. You're altogether too squeamish." Once someone came up when I was with Hemingway and started abusing me and when he went away, Hemingway said, "He's yellow. Don't be taken in by him. He's a coward himself." So in that way Hemingway was remarkably nice, because you would have thought he'd be the first person to attack me on these grounds.

DENIS BRIAN: Pauline had tried to save her marriage, once planning to confront Hemingway in Spain during the war. But he forestalled that trip by meeting her in Paris. A new hairstyle and her threat to jump from the balcony of their top-floor hotel room failed to win him over.[1] She gave him an uncontested divorce and he and Martha Gellhorn were married in a civil ceremony in Cheyenne on November 21, 1940. His marriage to Pauline had lasted thirteen years, though for the last three he had been involved with Martha.

LORINE THOMPSON: I think maybe Pauline sometimes felt guilty about having stolen Ernest from Hadley. She said one time something to the effect that she'd taken Ernest from Hadley, and Martha had taken him from her.

MRS. JOHN DOS PASSOS: My husband thought Pauline was a marvelous

[1]Bernice Kert, *The Hemingway Women*, W. W. Norton, 1983, and Carlos Baker, *Ernest Hemingway: A Life Story*, Scribner's, 1969.

woman. It puzzled and irritated him very much when Hemingway walked out on her.

JOHN HEMINGWAY: There was a great deal of bitterness between my father and Pauline. A lot of it was financial. Papa resented the fact that Pauline was extremely wealthy and still insisted that he pay; sort of punishment stuff. He did pay but he probably tried to get out of it as much as possible.

MADELAINE HEMINGWAY MILLER: Ernest got interested in Catholicism through a priest who was a friend in World War I.[1] Though when the boys, Patrick and Gregory, were brought up that was Pauline's business. Ernest donated a pipe organ to one of the Catholic churches in Key West in order to get dispensation to marry Martha. I don't understand it. We were raised Congregational. Ernest had to get fortified to go to confession. He got so fortified, he couldn't make it [laughs].

HADLEY MOWRER: When Pauline was Ernest's ex-wife too, I met her at the Algonquin in New York City and we seemed to be glad to see each other. Another time my second husband, Paul Scott Mowrer, and I were going down to Florida and we thought we'd see Pauline in Key West, not because she was in exactly the same situation she put me in, but because we really felt sorry for her. We stopped and had lunch in the awfully nice house Uncle Gus had given them, and Paul was the soul of tact and wisdom. It finally wound up by Pauline saying, and it gave me a great shock, "Boy, I hate him now!" I'm very happy to say I never learned to hate Ernest. I've been mad at him, but never hated him. But she was that kind of quick, hot, emotional woman.

DENIS BRIAN: As Hemingway and others predicted, the Spanish Civil War was the prelude to World War II. The civil war ended on March 28, 1939, when Madrid fell to Franco's forces. Britain declared war on Franco's ally, Germany, on September 3 of that same year.

---

[1]And Pauline was probably the catalyst. While she and the still-married Ernest were having an affair, Pauline told novelist Kay Boyle that she was converting him to Catholicism, adding, "The outlet of confession would be very good for him."

SEVEN

·

WORLD WAR II: COUNTERESPIONAGE AND OPERATION FRIENDLESS

THOMAS SHEVLIN: Ernest hankered for a more active role in World War II than being an ambulance driver or a war correspondent, but he couldn't have gotten into the army. Although he was a terrific shot, his eyesight wasn't any good. And he was shot up physically. But he did a lot of undercover work down in Cuba, where I was stationed for a time. Ernest impressed the American ambassador in Havana, Spruille Braden, that he was just the man to keep his eye on the many Spaniards in Cuba suspected of Axis sympathies. And he recruited several friends to work with him.

CONFIDENTIAL MEMO
FROM FBI AGENT R. G. LEDDY
TO FBI DIRECTOR J. EDGAR HOOVER
OCTOBER 8, 1942.

It is recalled that when the Bureau was attacked early in 1940 as a result of the arrests in Detroit of certain individuals charged with neutrality violations for fostering enlistments in the Spanish Republican forces, Mr. Hemingway was among the signers of a declaration which severely criticized the Bureau in that case. In attendance at a Jai-Alai match with Hemingway, the writer was introduced by him to a friend as a member of the Gestapo. On that occasion I did not appreciate the introduction, whereupon he promptly corrected himself and said I was one of the United States Consuls.

Mr. Joyce [Second Secretary of the embassy] made enquiries of Hemingway concerning his attitude toward working with us, without disclosing the reasons, and reported that his attitude appeared to be entirely favorable to the Bureau; that he was unable to remember the details of the Detroit incident in 1940, and that he regarded the Gestapo introduction as a jest. Consequently, early in September 1942, Ernest Hemingway began to engage directly in intelligence activities on behalf of the American Embassy in Havana. These activities he manages from his finca, with visits to Havana two or three times weekly. He is operating through Spanish Republicans whose identities have not been furnished but which we are assured are obtainable when desired.

At a meeting with him at his finca on September 30, 1942, the writer was advised that he had four men operating on a full-time basis, and fourteen barmen, waiters, and the like, operating on a part-time basis. The cost of this program is approximately $500 a month. The ambassador has noted that he likes Hemingway's approach and wishes to encourage him. Hemingway told me that he declined an offer from Hollywood to write a script for a "March of Time" report on the "Flying Tigers" in Burma, for which the compensation was to be $150,000, because he considers the work he is now engaged in as of greater importance.

One of the aspects of Mr. Hemingway's relationships with the embassy is to utilize his services for certain coastal patrol and investigative work on the south coast of Cuba. Hemingway, who has a wide reputation as a fisherman, knows the coastline and waters of Cuba very intimately; he has also engaged over a 12-year period in some scientific investigations concerning the migration of marlin on behalf of the Museum of Natural History, New York City.

[Line blacked out] has acceded to Hemingway's request for authorization to patrol certain areas where submarine activity has been reported. [Line blacked out] and an allotment of gasoline is now being obtained for this use. He has requested [line blacked out] and has secured from the ambassador a promise that his crew members will be recognized as war casualties for purpose of indemnification in the event any loss of life results from the operation.

With specific reference to the conducting of intelligence investigations on the island of Cuba, by Mr. Hemingway, the writer wishes to state that his interest thus far has not been limited to Spanish Falange and Spanish activities, but that he has included numerous German suspects. His reports are promptly furnished and he assures Mr. Joyce that his only desire is to be of assistance on a cooperative basis, without compensation to himself, and that he will be guided at all times by our wishes. So far no conflict has developed between his work and that which Bureau personnel is handling in Havana; and Hemingway told me that he wishes to be told where to limit his investigations whenever this is thought desirable.

CONFIDENTIAL MEMO
FROM FBI DIRECTOR J. EDGAR HOOVER
TO FBI AGENT LEDDY
DECEMBER 17, 1942.

Any information which you may have relating to the unreliability of Ernest Hemingway as an informant may be discreetly brought to the attention of Ambassador Braden. In this respect it will be recalled that recently Hemingway gave information concerning the refueling of submarines in Caribbean waters which has proved unreliable. I desire that you furnish me at an early date results of your conversations with Ambassador Braden concerning Ernest Hemingway and his aides and their activities.

CONFIDENTIAL MEMO
FROM FBI AGENT D. M. LADD
TO FBI DIRECTOR J. EDGAR HOOVER
DECEMBER 17, 1942.

Hemingway has been accused of being of communist sympathy, although we are advised that he has denied and does vigorously deny any communist affiliation or sympathy. Hemingway is reported to be personally friendly with Ambassador Braden, and he is reported to enjoy the ambassador's complete confidence.

Ambassador Braden, as you will recall, is a very impulsive individual and he apparently has had a "bee in his bonnet" for some time concerning alleged graft and corruption on the part of certain Cuban officials.

Agent Leddy has advised that Hemingway's activities have branched out and that he and his informants are now engaged in reporting to the Embassy various types of information concerning subversive activities generally. Mr. Leddy stated that he has become quite concerned with respect to Hemingway's activities and that they are undoubtedly going to be very embarrassing unless something is done to stop them.

Mr. Leddy has advised that Hemingway is apparently undertaking a rather involved investigation with regard to Cuban officials prominently connected with the Cuban Government, including General Manuel Benitez Valdes, head of the Cuban National Police; that he, Agent Leddy, is sure that the Cubans are eventually going to find out about this if Hemingway continues operating, and that serious trouble may result.

Mr. Leddy stated that he can point out to the ambassador that he, Leddy, has not checked any reports from Hemingway concerning corruption in the Cuban Government; that he does not feel that Bureau agents should become involved in any such investigations, it being entirely without our jurisdiction and a matter in which the Cubans themselves alone are concerned and something that, if we get involved in it, is going to mean that all of us will be thrown out of Cuba "bag and baggage."

Agent Leddy stated he can point out to the ambassador the extreme danger of having some informant like Hemingway given free reign to stir up trouble such as that which will undoubtedly ensue if this situation continues. Mr. Leddy stated that despite the fact the ambassador likes Hemingway and apparently has confidence in him, he is of the opinion that he, Leddy, can handle this situation with the ambassador so that Hemingway's services as an informant will be completely discontinued.

Mr. Leddy stated that he can point out to the ambassador that Hemingway is going further than just an informant; that he is actually branching out into an investigative organization of his own which is not subject to any control whatsoever.

CONFIDENTIAL MEMO
FROM FBI DIRECTOR J. EDGAR HOOVER
TO AGENTS TAMM AND LADD
DECEMBER 19, 1942.

Concerning the use of Ernest Hemingway by the United States ambassador to Cuba: I of course realize the complete undesirability of this sort of a connection or relationship. Certainly Hemingway is the last man, in

my estimation, to be used in any such capacity. His judgment is not of
the best, and if his sobriety is the same as it was some years ago, that is
certainly questionable. However, I do not think there is anything we
should do in this matter, nor do I think our representative at Havana
should do anything about it with the ambassador. The ambassador is
somewhat hot-headed and I haven't the slightest doubt that he would
immediately tell Hemingway of the objections being raised by the FBI.
Hemingway has no particular love for the FBI and would no doubt
embark upon a campaign of vilification. You will recall that in my conference recently with the president, he indicated that some message had
been sent to him, the president, by Hemingway through a mutual friend
[almost certainly Martha Gellhorn], and Hemingway was insisting that
one-half million dollars be granted to the Cuban authorities so that they
could take care of internees.

I do not see that it is a matter that directly affects our relationship as
long as Hemingway does not report directly to us or we deal directly with
him. Anything which he gives to the ambassador which the ambassador
in turn forwards to us, we can accept without any impropriety.

CONFIDENTIAL MEMO
FROM FBI AGENT LEDDY
TO FBI DIRECTOR J. EDGAR HOOVER
APRIL 21, 1943

The writer has been advised in confidence by an Embassy official that
Hemingway's organization was disbanded and its work terminated as of
April 1, 1943. This action was taken by the American ambassador without
any consultation or notice to representatives of the Federal Bureau of
Investigation. A complete report on the activities of Mr. Hemingway and
the organization which he operated is now being prepared, and will be
forwarded to the Bureau in the immediate future.

CONFIDENTIAL MEMO
FROM FBI AGENT D.M. LADD
TO FBI DIRECTOR J. EDGAR HOOVER
APRIL 27, 1943.

Mr. Hemingway has been connected with various so-called Communist
front organizations and was active in aiding the Loyalist cause in Spain.

Despite Hemingway's activities, no information has been received which would definitely tie him with the Communist Party or which would indicate that he is or has been a Party member. His actions, however, have indicated that his views are "liberal" and that he may be inclined favorably to communist political philosophies. At the present time he is alleged to be performing a highly secret naval operation for the Navy Department. In this connection, the Navy Department is said to be paying the expenses for the operation of Hemingway's boat, furnishing him with arms and charting courses in the Cuban area. The Bureau has conducted no investigation of Hemingway, but his name has been mentioned in connection with other Bureau investigations and various data concerning him have been submitted voluntarily by a number of different sources.

THOMAS SHEVLIN: The American ambassador in Havana, Spruille Braden, thought Ernest had done a great job with "The Crook Factory," and approved his request to continue his secret undercover work as captain of his own boat, the *Pilar*. He had a daring, if not suicidal mission—hunting German submarines in Caribbean waters. He named the operation "Friendless," after one of his cats. Ernest had that old boat of his loaded up with all sorts of RDF [radio direction finders], machine guns, and hand grenades. There were a lot of German sympathizers around that area and enemy submarines were active. His second in command was Winston Guest.

WINSTON GUEST: It was a rather exciting, romantic idea: to patrol the coast of Cuba. At the time, submarines were sinking our tankers and other ships off Cuba. They were coming up alongside *viveros*—those are boats that go out from Havana and other towns to catch grouper and snapper, with wells in the hold where they keep the fish alive, so when they go to market they're fresh. Submarines had been accosting a number of these *viveros* and taking off fish, chicken, bread, and sometimes fresh vegetables. Ernest thought we might, as a decoy, be accosted by a submarine in those waters.

THOMAS SHEVLIN: Ernest would get a triangular fix with shore base and his boat and maybe one of our boats, and one of these broadcast stations broadcasting shipping news to enemy submarines. Then he would close on it.

MALCOLM COWLEY: Spruille Braden, the U.S. ambassador to Cuba who authorized the mission, told me that it was extremely dangerous. The *Pilar* was disguised as a fishing boat though it was heavily armed with machine guns, a bazooka, and high explosives. The plan was to cruise off the coast of Cuba hoping to be ordered alongside by a German submarine. Then Ernest and his crew of nine would use their weapons to destroy it, at the risk of their boat being destroyed in the attack.

WINSTON GUEST: We did sight a submarine once. It was fairly rough and we'd been out all morning and we came in behind one of the Keys to have lunch, during which time we kept a lookout. The ship suddenly appeared two or three miles away. We couldn't quite make out what it was. It looked like a tug towing a barge. We got the glasses out and you could see immediately it was a submarine, I think 740 class. It was cruising slowly, not more than a few knots in the direction NNW. So we pulled up our anchor and went out and we fished out of the channel in the direction of the submarine. Luckily one of the boys had hooked a barracuda at the time. We were a little more than trailing speed going out there. We hoped to casually come alongside the submarine and then attack it with machine guns and hand grenades hidden on board. But it speeded up and went directly on the course NNW. And that was the submarine that ended up at New Orleans. I think they landed three or four men at the mouth of the Mississippi River, and I don't know whether they were apprehended or did some damage or whatever. But we didn't have any contact with them. So immediately what we did was go back to shore and get a car and drive as quickly as we could to Havana. Ernest made a report which was given a DF which, I believe, means "not credible," not a very high rating. About two days later they called him again and said he was completely, one hundred percent right, that it had been a submarine, that several tankers had sighted it on this course, due NNW, toward New Orleans. Then the story came out eventually about it landing men there.

MALCOLM COWLEY: Spruille Braden said Ernest had worked out the plan intelligently and, I believe, would have succeeded if he had made contact with an enemy submarine.

DENIS BRIAN: Martha Gellhorn thought Hemingway's exploits in Operation Friendless were just an excuse to fish and get extra gasoline in wartime when supplies were restricted.

CARLOS BAKER: Perhaps that impulse did come into it to some degree, but I think he was quite patriotic and the work was important. As Winston Guest says, they did in fact encounter a German submarine but it was going too fast so they never closed with it.

DENIS BRIAN: Ellis O. Briggs, stationed in Havana as an American diplomat, praised Hemingway and his crew for working with dedicated purpose. In his memoirs Briggs records the following conversation between Hemingway and a U.S. colonel that gives a marvelous picture of Hemingway's style:

> The U.S. Colonel: "Suppose the German submarine stands off and blows you and the *Pilar* out of the water? What then, Papa?" "If he does that," replied Ernest, "then we've had it. But there's a good chance he won't shoot. Why should a submarine risk attracting attention when the skipper can send sailors aboard and scuttle us by opening the seacocks? He'll be curious about fishermen in wartime. He'll want to know what kind of profiteers are trying to tag marlin in the Gulf Stream with the war on. If he recognized the *Pilar*—so much the better. Carry enemy sportsman back to Berlin to write dirty limericks about the Führer. Feather in the bonnet for *der Kapitan*. Fame and promotion for the crew. Why not? Those boys are suckers for publicity." "But even if you get ordered alongside," argued the colonel, "your Nazi skipper isn't going to pipe you aboard to have a glass of schnapps with him. He'll have men on deck, and they won't be holding slingshots." "That's right," Ernest admitted. "Along with the grenades we need a machine gun. I shoot a machine gun good, John. Practiced on my grandmother. Nazi soldiers won't know what hit them. Now how big is the conning tower and how wide is the hatch? But what I really want to know is, how much damage would grenades do inside a submarine?"[1]

DENIS BRIAN: While Ernest was out at sea Martha stayed at the Finca working on short stories. The male protagonists had convincing touches of Hemingway: an untidy character who spills coffee topped with whipped cream on the bed, a man who provides the female protagonist with his name and considerable fortune. One story, "Portrait of a Lady," is about a beautiful female war correspondent who uses her looks and charm to wheedle secret information from officers. Martha used her own experiences as a reporter during the Finnish-Soviet War for authentic details. It convinced Leicester, says biographer Jeffrey Meyers, that Martha had been unfaithful to his brother.[2] Now she was tackling a novel about an

[1]Ellis O. Briggs, *Shots Heard Round the World*, Viking Press, New York, 1957.

[2]Jeffrey Meyers, *Hemingway*.

unhappily married woman who is having an affair with a Frenchman. I never learned Leicester's response to that.

WINSTON GUEST: At one time on our cruise, we used to come in behind a Key called Cao Confite. There was a harbor there and every night the manuscript for the novel Martha was writing, *The Purple Orchid* or whatever, used to come in for him to read.

DENIS BRIAN: It was titled *Liana*.

WINSTON GUEST: Well, he'd sit up late with an oil lamp reading the manuscript and correcting it. In the book she writes about a man and his wife living in a place like the Finca—which was their home in Cuba. I just read extracts of the book. I didn't like it. The man was always barefoot and in shorts and this and that and the other. She was obviously painting a rather unattractive portrait of Ernest. I thought it was very gallant, very honorable of Ernest to do anything he could to help improve her manuscript, because he had a gift for writing second to none. Whenever we came back to Havana from one of these sub-hunting cruises, we used to have a live pigeon shoot. Ernest was very keen about people being athletically fit, and one afternoon he recommended that I go out with Martha Gellhorn to do some running: run up half a mile or a mile ahead, and then back to join her and walk with her for awhile, and then run ahead again.

I'll never forget Martha asking me what I thought of her choice of a husband. She explained to me that she'd picked Ernest because of his ability as a writer and possible remuneration from books. And I thought to myself, what a tough, mercenary bitch to discuss her husband with me, someone she hardly knew. She didn't imply that she loved him at all. She implied to me that she married him as a practical matter; it might help her improve her writing.

MARTHA GELLHORN: What rubbish. My "career" had started before I ever met Ernest Hemingway, perhaps my biggest success being a book of novellas about the unemployed. Ernest Hemingway did not help my "career." On the contrary. It should be noted that I never used his name or my association with him, not when I was married to him or ever after. So much for a calculated marriage. But you know, I was regularly blackguarded by Ernest Hemingway in the later years to anyone and everyone. I am used to my curious role as a monster in his life, and it doesn't matter much to me. I loved him as long as I could and when I lost all respect for him as a man—not as a writer—I said so and withdrew and that was that.

THOMAS SHEVLIN: Shortly after they first met, Ernest decided to go off to the Spanish Civil War and Martha said, "Fine, I'll go along with you." And then she got her correspondent's credentials from *Collier's* and wrote some books looking over his shoulder.

IRWIN SHAW: Lies! The things Guest and Shevlin say are absolute canards! They were playboys who were easily led by the nose by Hemingway. They were toadies. I'm very friendly with Martha; she has always been a good friend of mine. Knowing her as I do, it sounds absolutely improbable that she married Hemingway for her own advancement and without loving him. If you read *Travels With Myself*, one of her books, you'll see that even after all the horrible things he did and said about her, it's a very affectionate portrait of Hemingway.

DENIS BRIAN: In her book *Travels With Myself and Another*, Martha Gellhorn gives several endearing glimpses of Hemingway, including the time in China in 1941 when he took pity on a diminutive horse that had collapsed under him. Muttering about cruelty to animals, he put his arm over the saddle and under the horse's belly—and carried the little animal![1]

WINSTON GUEST: Martha wanted him to be more like his friend Gary Cooper. I knew Gary Cooper very well, but they were two different characters. Just because she married the wrong man is no reason for her to make derogatory statements about Ernest and be disloyal to him.

THOMAS SHEVLIN: She could never get him to look like Gary Cooper. He could go to the best tailor in the world and he still didn't look well-dressed.

WINSTON GUEST: Once she said to him, "Why don't you wash more, Ernest?" Well, it would have been so easy to make him take a bath, I should think, if she wanted him to. Just ask anybody nicely enough and I think they'd do that. Ernest was very fair, very helpful to Martha Gellhorn.

DENIS BRIAN: After completing her novel, *Liana*, Martha flew to Europe in the winter of 1943 as a war correspondent for *Collier's*, and watched air crews of the famous Dam Buster 617 squadron at Woodhall Spa, Lincolnshire, take off in their Lancasters for a bombing raid on Germany. In the spring of 1944 she went to the Italian front and visited the atrociously wounded at battalion aid stations. Ernest was lonely without her. His two younger sons were at school and Bumby had gone to Europe.

JOHN HEMINGWAY: I started off the war as a military policeman, then

[1]Martha Gellhorn, *Travels With Myself and Another*, Dodd, Mead, 1978.

transferred to the infantry. I think Papa was glad about that [laughs]. Despite his experience in the Spanish Civil War, he didn't give me any specific advice on fighting. What he had done was suggest books to read. He recommended the classics, *Clausewitz on War* and one called *Blitzkrieg* by a Czech, a simplified explanation of the theory of blitzkrieg. Papa knew I'd be adequately trained and that I was already familiar with the Thompson machine gun, for example. I had learned to take it apart and put it together when I was ten years old.

DENIS BRIAN: Martha returned to the Finca in March and resumed in person the thrust of her recruiting letters to him, saying he belonged in Europe at his old trade of war correspondent. She ridiculed his sub-hunting as a weak excuse to keep out of the real action and danger.

WINSTON GUEST: I knew him well for a year and a half in Cuba when I was his executive officer on the *Pilar* and I admired him enormously. He was a very fine shot, a very good sportsman, a good storyteller, a very good friend, and delightful company.

DENIS BRIAN: But not for Martha. She constantly reminded him he was shirking his duty. She did everything but call him a coward. They quarreled incessantly and not only about his absence from the European war front.[1] Hemingway was a master at finding subjects of contention. When Martha had their cats neutered to control the expanding population and one died, he raged as if she had killed it deliberately. Gregory thought Martha was blameless in the arguments he overheard, and that his father was entirely in the wrong.

WILLIAM WALTON: I know Martha Gellhorn well. It takes two to tango, you know. Martha was a wicked, wild bitch. Oh, the joint cruelties!

DENIS BRIAN: Hemingway capitulated. Telling Martha she would be to blame if he got killed, the two of them left for New York in April 1944, on their way to London. In Manhattan they met fellow writers in Costello's bar.

JOHN HERSEY: I came into Costello's in mid evening and went to the bar and Costello said, "There are some writers in the back. Why don't you go and sit with them?" There were Hemingway and Martha Gellhorn, Vincent Sheean and his wife, Paul DeKris, Joe Sayre and his wife; and one or two others. I had first met Hemingway when I was an undergraduate at Yale and he was sitting at the bar of a speakeasy in New York in

[1]Carlos Baker, *Ernest Hemingway: A Life Story.*

1936 or so—the 21 Club, I think it was. This was before he went to Spain. He was a hero in a schoolboy's eyes at that point, the first meeting. We had a few words with him and he was perfectly casual. After that I met him several times at the 21 Club and elsewhere. He was kind to me the few times I saw him. That night in 1944 in Costello's Hemingway left before the rest of us and we stayed in the back and heard nothing more of what happened until several days later. Costello gave me an account of what happened. While we were in the back, John O'Hara came into the bar and Costello said what he'd said to me and presumably others, "There are some writers in the back. Why don't you join them?" O'Hara said, "Who's there?" And Costello gave some of the names and O'Hara was then deeply offended that he had not been invited to what he thought must have been some party going on in the back and began to drink angrily at the bar by himself. O'Hara had brought an Irish blackthorn stick with him and Hemingway had come from the back, approaching O'Hara from the rear, and pounded him on the back, saying, "For Chrissakes, John, when did you start using a walking stick?" O'Hara had replied that it was the best piece of blackthorn in New York City. Hemingway said, "It is, is it. Then I'm going to break it." Then O'Hara is said to have put ten dollars on the bar and said, "Here's ten you can't." Hemingway is said to have put ten dollars on top of O'Hara's ten and said, "Here's ten I can do it over my own head," which he then proceeded to do. I can believe another account that Hemingway first put several napkins on his head before breaking the stick over it. Hemingway may have treasured his head; that is where he thought his stories were. When we emerged from the back room very late that night, O'Hara was waiting in the street to vent his anger on someone and did it by turning on us and saying sarcastically, "Nice people!" and staggering off into the night. I was in awe of all those people at Costello's.

DENIS BRIAN: Hemingway pulled strings and flew to London, Martha went on a slow freighter loaded with dynamite.

CHAPTER

EIGHT

•

WORLD WAR II:
NORMANDY
INVASION AND
HURTGEN FOREST

DENIS BRIAN: Hemingway was introduced to Mary Welsh soon after he arrived in London. She was a vivacious, attractive *Time* reporter.

WILLIAM WALTON: I was with the 82nd airborne as a *Time* correspondent. Hemingway and I met in London in May 1944, before the invasion of Normandy, at a party the photographer Robert Capa gave. I parachuted into France on D-Day, June 6, and landed in a tree. I knew Hemingway quite casually, so I was surprised after I was in Cherbourg, on June 24, when Ernest turns up and he had gone to press headquarters in London, collected all my mail, and brought it to me in France. This was such an unheard of courtesy, because I hardly knew the man. But he honestly was extremely attracted to me and interested in me and my parachuting experiences.

DENIS BRIAN: Shortly after, he wrote to his new friend Mary Welsh that he loved you, so that he got friendly very quickly.

WILLIAM WALTON: That's right. When he turned up in Cherbourg he wanted a place to stay and I had a house along with a couple of British officers in military government. We put him up overnight. Then we went off on a couple of trips together. He wanted to travel with me and he did quite a bit. Through the end of June and early July we were together a great deal.

JOHN CARLISLE [war correspondent for the *Detroit Free Press*]: I shared a tent with Hemingway for some time. We were with the fighting Fourth Division at the start of the Normandy push. I must have bored everybody in Detroit, Michigan, when I got back from Europe, talking about Hemingway. He was a delightful character, totally oblivious of the fame and acclaim that had been his. He wrote and talked as a realist. He was blunt and forceful, but everything was edged with a touch of subtle humor. During a long gabfest in the blackout at night in that big tent in the apple orchard with other war correspondents in their bedrobes, someone asked him why he left his beautiful home in Cuba for this. "Hell," he said, "I had to go to war to see my wife." She had gone ahead of him to cover the war for national magazines. In four days Ernie was a legend in the division. They were talking then about how Hemingway and Stevie captured a chateau. Stevie was Lieutenant Marcus L. Stevenson of San Antonio, Texas, an aide to Brigadier General Theodore Roosevelt, Jr., and divisional public relations officer. When Teddy died in Normandy, Hemingway cheered up Stevie, who had loved Teddy. I recall Hemingway with a captured set of Nazi binoculars around his neck and a captured Nazi map case slung over his shoulder. He was in his mid-forties then, but already had gray in his beard. Stevie used to call him Pop. The first day Ernie and Stevie went up to the front with a two-star general, a Jerry 88 shell exploded not many feet away. Hemingway just stood there, and the general never even turned his head to look at the shell crater. The general asked Ernie why he'd come to the war when he didn't have to. "Oh," he said, "I got war fever like the measles. Any chateaux around here? I love chateaux." When they came across one, Hemingway found the wine cellar and picked out the best wine for the general. We roomed together for about three weeks.

I got to know him bumming around with him all day long and all night long, sitting around getting plastered and having a good time. He was nothing the way I thought he would be. Remember that I'm stuck with fifty-five newspapermen and there's nothing so goddamn egotistical as a war correspondent. And I think Hemingway liked me because one morning at breakfast in the mess I stood up with a hangover and denounced them all as a bunch of arrogant, egotistical shits. I said, "Why don't you write about what the GI is doing, for Chrissakes, instead of writing about yourselves?" Some clippings had come in and all these guys were saying: "I was the first in Valognes. I was the first in Chartres." It was all, "I did this," and "I did that." What I loved about Hemingway personally—because I'd read everything he'd ever written that I could find—was that he was a real, genuine guy. He didn't talk about himself. He had no egotism that I could see at the time I was with him in France. He was a great companion, a real, marvelously interesting person. I fell in love with Hemingway like all the newspapermen did and it took me twenty years to recover.

WILLIAM WALTON: I loved him, too. I also admired him. He was marvelous company. You see, he wasn't always telling us about his life. We were telling him about our lives, too. He had a marvelous gift for extracting all kinds of tales from me of my childhood, of my parents, of my loves and adventures, and he remembered them all. If you told it again and abbreviated, he'd say, "Ah hah, no, no, no. *That* wasn't her name. *This* was her name."

JOHN CARLISLE: That was one reason I liked him: he seldom talked about himself. Mostly he talked about how well our guys were doing in the war. He was a great admirer of GI Joe. Hemingway always said this goddamned war was made for the GI. "He loves his rifle," he said to me. "You find this out. Hang around some time when our guys come out of the line. I'll bet you everyone of them asks for two toothbrushes." I didn't believe this. So one time I heard of a regiment that was pulled out; we always had one in reserve, you know. They'd been in the front lines for sixty-six days. I watched these guys after they got deloused, took a shower, and were lined up. Sure enough, every one of them had two toothbrushes, just like Papa said. I said to one of those guys: "Jesus Christ, you must take care of your teeth." He said, "Bullshit, I get the mud out of my M1."

He seemed to have a great concern for the wounded. He liked the fact that they moved the field hospitals up close. He talked to me about how great it was that they flew the wounded by airplane out of Omaha Beach right into those big hospitals in Scotland and England, and that they got excellent care, and they got blood plasma on the planes, people tending them. He liked Patton. He was the first to tip me off when Patton got any place. The first thing Patton asked about was food, Hemingway said. Later I got into a jeep with Patton and rode up to a company command post and the first thing he said was, "Where's the captain? Are you the captain of the company?" And the guy says, "Yes, sir!" "Are you getting hot food?" "Yes, sir!" Patton said, "You'd better be, goddamnit! If you don't get hot food, you let me know!" Hemingway said, "This old Blood-and-Guts Patton has a heart and people don't know about it."

WILLIAM WALTON: Ernest's voice, incidentally, was a little bit higher in the scale than he wished it to be, though not as high as George Patton's. He changed his mind about Patton, whom he eventually loathed. We all did.

DENIS BRIAN: Why?

WILLIAM WALTON: Because he was such a shit. Remember how he slapped the soldier in the hospital? I had brushes with him myself. He was absolutely insulting to me in General Bradley's presence. Bradley, in turn, gave Patton hell. Patton was a disturbed, egotistical brat.

JOHN CARLISLE: Hemingway said this modern war was made for the Germans and Americans: they understood it better because they both knew how to handle tanks, and how to coordinate planes with tanks. He understood tactics, which I didn't. He knew more about the goddamned army than I did. He was a walking encyclopedia on how the war was being fought. He thought the Germans were damned good soldiers and fought well even without air support. Everybody in the Third Army thought so, too.

DENIS BRIAN: Hemingway claimed to be very shy and said he needed to drink to be comfortable with people.

WILLIAM WALTON: He was enormously shy.

DENIS BRIAN: Did he help you with your reporting?

WILLIAM WALTON: Never. Not a word. He interfered and tried to prevent me from using material about experiences we had shared, because I could get it in print much faster than he could. He never saw a word of mine, except when he peered over my shoulder when I didn't want him to. I'd have to ask him, "Please leave me alone!" I couldn't write with him watching. He was terribly curious about my writing and didn't approve of it much. He didn't want me to write anything, so the facts would be left for him. But I was under contract to write once a week. Ernest wanted to save everything for his books.

JOHN CARLISLE: That explains why I rarely saw him writing news reports, and he always had time to talk. I enjoyed every minute with him because there was nothing phony about him, no "Why can't I be with people of my own class?" He knew I thought fishing was the greatest waste of time. He didn't care. I said, "It amazes me you having a hang-up about fishing."

He says, "Is that so? Did you ever go fishing?" I said, "Yeah, it's a waste of time." He never said boo. No argument or nothing. We used to sleep in sleeping bags and we had bunks right together. I could reach out and touch him. I said, "Papa, you had a great idea with Ingrid Bergman in a bedroll with the hero. I'd like to have somebody in a sleeping bag with me. That was a great idea! How do I get anybody in there?" He said, "That's your problem." He was easily amused and very amusing. He was not like the current generation where you go out to lunch and everybody tells these goddamned lousy stories. His were more anecdotes. I'd met some people who'd written books and they all had inflated, bombastic opinions of themselves. Hemingway was so goddamned genuine in the things he talked about. Like, one night I was in the doghouse with this commander of the friggin' press corps, a lieutenant-colonel who had been a flunkey in the Internal Revenue Service Washington bureau, and none of us who were what we thought topnotch reporters ever thought much of the IRS as a service. I couldn't stand him. So he put me in the outer-perimeter tent and Hemingway said something to him, barked at him, one day. So Hemingway wound up there, too. The other occupant of the tent was an English correspondent they were mad at. Somebody had turned him in for taking rings off a dead German, supposedly. I don't know if he did or not. Hemingway always had a bottle of wine. We'd lay there and he'd pass me the bottle of wine, but he wouldn't give anything to this English correspondent. He didn't like him. The surprising thing is that he was telling me all about the troubles he was having with Martha Gellhorn, which I didn't know anything about. The marriage was over and wherever he showed up, she ran away from him. He told me he really thought—I have a good memory for this—that at that point Hadley was the best of the lot. He said, "I never should have left Hadley." I saw Martha Gellhorn at some gathering at the University of London. For some reason I didn't take to her. I don't know why. He told me the night we were lying in this goddamned tent in this apple orchard in a little town called Mehou: "When I got to know Marty, I knew she collected things. She collected bric-a-brac, oriental rugs, paintings; and it took me some time to realize that I was part of the collection. She collected me." He didn't speak in anger about her, just talking. I wasn't particularly interested but I didn't have anything else to do but listen. Then we'd listen to the girls playing music for us on the radio and listen to German news reports. They said the Third Army was about to land at Brest, and here we were in Normandy just waiting to be committed to the battle.

JOHN HEMINGWAY: My father hated to be alone. I'm very fond of Martha and I'm extremely certain in my own mind that, far more than incipient rivalry as writers, the real reason for their breakup was that her trade meant enough to her that she would leave and go practice it rather than stay with him. He wanted a wife as a companion.

JOHN CARLISLE: When I first met him I thought about everything I'd read about him: that he was a loner, that he didn't go down to New York and run around with people. I used to wonder how can a man catch a thousand marlin? Didn't he ever get tired of catching marlin? I never asked him that, but I did ask him one thing—I told him frankly, because you could talk frankly to him, as a matter of fact he liked it—I said, "A man with your reputation, your caliber of writing, you have the smallest output for anybody of your class in the history of literature. You have produced very little." And he said, "Writing is not easy for me. I am too critical of my own stuff, so I constantly rewrite and rewrite and rewrite. And it's hard work." I'm not remembering his exact words. I'm trying to remember what I think he said. He asked me, "How come you never wrote any fiction? A lot of newspapermen try." "Well," I said, "I think the reason was I was satisfied with my by-line on the big stories I covered. Writing is hard work. You have to sit at that goddamned typewriter and you're alone with God. Half the time I'm dead tired from just collecting the information. There's a tug of war between being a reporter, getting too many facts, and then having to condense it and put it down and write it within the goddamn style of the paper I'm working for. And it's hard work." He said, "You're damn right. You know what you're talking about. It was always hard work for me." One time I was writing my head off and he came in and said, "Hiyah, Jack!" And I said, "All right." He stood there a while, then he walked away, because that was him. If you were busy he wasn't going to bother you. He'd come back a couple of times and say, "How are you doing?" I'd say, "I'm almost through." He came back a little later and pulled up a folding chair and sat there. And I said, "Well, I've got the goddamned thing done!" He said, "How many did you do?" I said, "I did six. I did a fucking series. I won't have to do anything for a week." He said, "Let me see one." He just looked at it and said, "You know, it's pretty good for the speed you did it." [Laughs.] I thought he was being kind to me, I had no illusions about anything I wrote. There used to be a guy sitting there and Hemingway knew I didn't like him, a guy out of St. Paul. I used to say to Papa, "Listen to the son-of-a-bitch. He's written it and now he's reading it out loud to

himself!" Then this guy would laugh and say, "That's damn good! That's
me at my best!" I said to Papa: "A son-of-a-bitch like that, they ought
to shoot him." Hemingway said, "Maybe they will." Wherever we went
we had tents and about two hundred fifty people took care of us. We had
jeeps, our own mess, our own cooks. We had our censors and we had a
radio station with us, a Maquis radio. At one time the Germans thought
it was Patton's headquarters and they bombed us one night because of all
the activity and the radio going. They knocked out army ordnance about
five hundred yards away; they didn't hit any of our own people.

Some said Hemingway had a secretive side. I can understand that. I'm
a Scot. My middle name is MacGregor and I'm a great believer in the
right of privacy; it's part of my heritage. But when I'm after a story,
nobody has any rights. Hemingway was a reporter at heart, too. One day
General Barton—he carried a little lightweight cane instead of a gun—
was standing in the middle of nowhere with us. Hemingway said to him:
"What the hell is going on from your point of view? Where are we and
where are we going? What are our objectives? When are we going to
move, or are we going to sit here and do nothing?" So the general took
his goddamn cane—and it had been raining—and in the mud he showed
us where we were, where the Germans were and what we were going to
do and how we were going to do it and when we'd start. All because of
Hemingway boring into him in a nice way. Sure, he said, "Where the hell
are we, general?" But he said it in a nice voice. Not like saying, "You
goddamned fat rummy! Now you're sitting on your ass!"—the way some
war correspondents treated some generals. I always thought the reason he
could write about people and make you feel these characters really lived
was that he must have met somebody and used part of their lives. He was
the greatest expert I've ever seen in getting people to talk when he wanted
them to. In trying to find out how you felt about things, he seemed to
show genuine interest in you, the guy who was in front of him. I never
heard him say anything bad about anybody unless he had it coming, He
once said to me, "I agree with you that our lieutenant-colonel is a toy
soldier playing at war." He was lusty [laughs]. He wasn't afraid of any of
the words and, of course, everybody in the army swore pretty good. I tell
you one thing, he could hold his booze, unlike a lot of newspaper guys
we were with. They'd completely change their temperament when they
got drunk and became quarrelsome and aggravating. But the Hemingway
I saw for that month was not quarrelsome. I never saw him even stagger
although we drank endless bottles of wine. And he was generous. When

I didn't have anything to drink, he'd say, "Come with me. I've always got a drink for you." And he'd give it to me. I remember him saying, "How are you feeling?" And I said, "Oh God, I've got the world's worst hangover drinking that friggin' Calvados with you and those Maquis guys. It tasted like something that was distilled in a wet mop that had been locked in a cupboard for weeks, and somebody wrung it out in a glass." He said, "I disagree. It's the greatest drink, the national drink of the Normans."

When I recovered he said, "You ought to see Mont St. Michel. It's a great historical town, thirteenth century." I said, "I'm sick of looking at historical towns. I don't give a crap about them!" But he said, "Jack, they have a place there, the Hotel de la Mere Poularde, where they make omelettes the size of birthday cakes."

When we got to Mont St. Michel the place was crowded. I saw a major from Intelligence, Third Army, and said, "Jesus Christ, they won't put us up!" The major said, "You're a friend of Papa's. Papa runs the hotel. He'll get you in. He's the boss." I said, "Shit, he's only been here three days." He said, "It don't make no difference. He runs the hotel now." So I saw Papa holding court at a table, talking and laughing, and said, "I can't get in." He said, "The hell you can't get in." He took me up and put me and Shoop on the second floor across the hallway from him. Being with Hemingway was a real break for me. Before I met him I'd spent seventeen days in ditches, ducking, and hadn't seen a damn thing. At Mont St. Michel he made me walk with him all the way up those murderous steps. I almost had a heart attack. He had amazing energy. We took a look at the church, then he said, "Let's go back to where the booze is, the wine." Finally, I sat down at the Hotel de la Mere Poularde and the omelette was beautiful, the size of those birthday cakes they give in restaurants with one candle on.

He was an exciting person. For example, I'd lose him somewhere and I'd figure, "I'm going to find Papa where the excitement is." And I'd walk down the street and hear his voice, "Bring me a bottle of your finest red wine, quickly!" I felt comfortable with him and thought he was a happy, fulfilled man. Honest to God, I thought he was one of the happiest men I ever knew, a guy with a great zest for life and who enjoyed every minute of it.

WILLIAM WALTON: He made me laugh more deeply than anyone else I'd known. He had such a sense of the ridiculous, and when he got a reaction he'd play on that same theme and carry it further, which made for great conversations. And there was a big streak of the ham in him. I missed all the unpleasant things that seem to have happened to a lot of other people.

John Carlisle: I was sometimes bored to death, half dead. I told him one time, "Goddamnit, you must have been born for war. I think you like war." I don't remember his reply. I thought he would go on and on, even if he was in a wheelchair. I even thought he could have a good time brushing his teeth over a helmetful of water. He brought excitement just by being there. He had a natural gift of getting along great with men. There weren't any women around, so I don't know how he got along with women.

Denis Brian: Hemingway became attached to the 22nd Regiment as a war correspondent and met its commanding officer, Colonel C. T. Lanham.

C. T. Lanham: I had known Hemingway only a short time when I ran into him on August 8, 1944. The following day was my twenty-fifth wedding anniversary. I had mentioned it to my staff and since we were supposed to be pulled out of the lines the next day, they decided to have a little party at the command post featuring roast goose, which I had never tasted. I asked Hemingway to join us at the party. He said he couldn't and that was that. In any event, the command post was heavily shelled and a number of men were killed and wounded. I was hit, but not seriously. This marked the beginning of the Avranches counteroffensive of the Germans. We were not pulled out of the lines for a rest. In fact, we never were. The next day I saw Hemingway and told him the story of the shelling. He said the reason he had not accepted my invitation was that the place had the stink of death about it. You may remember that this was Pilar's phrase in *For Whom the Bell Tolls*. Hemingway told me about his premonition after the event, and I said to myself that's coincidence maybe.

But for his second premonition I was right there. Hemingway and I had visited this battalion commander in his command post just before we launched our first attack in the bloody battle of the Hurtgen forest. His command post was in a dugout which seemed proof against anything but a hell of a heavy aerial bomb. I told Hemingway I might have to relieve this man because I doubted his leadership qualities. Hemingway said, "You won't have to relieve him. He's going to be killed." When I got back to my command post a few minutes later, my executive officer came to me and said, "So-and-so," the man I was going to relieve, "has just been killed." A shell splinter had penetrated a narrow space between the logs that covered his dugout and killed him. That sort of shook me. Hemingway would hate me to call it a "premonition" and I'm ambivalent about it. The rational part of my brain says it's crap and the other part says: "You know, you'd better not have any fixed opinions as of this time." I'm openminded about ESP. If you live long enough you see many things you can't account for. Hemingway hated such talk. I don't know what he really believed. He veered back and forth between believing in nothing and in being a half-assed Catholic.

WILLIAM WALTON: He was very superstitious. He always said, "I'm going to play everything, prayer, rabbit's foot, touching wood three times. We need all the help we can get."

C. T. LANHAM: At bullfights some years later he'd go to a Catholic chapel every day and by God he'd pray, and he told me he did, for Antonio Ordonez to get through the fight all right. It absolutely astonished me, because I'm a card-carrying atheist [laughs]. The chaplain and head doctor were always hounding Hemingway. He said to the chaplain, "Do you believe there are no atheists in foxholes?" And this guy says, "No sir, Mr. Hemingway, not since I met you and Colonel Lanham."

JOHN CARLISLE: Hemingway was absolutely fearless. I thought war didn't bother him a goddamn bit. I made him laugh by saying, "Papa, I don't know why they don't put me up on the goddamn recruiting posters in Detroit, with the words 'Jack Carlisle is living proof that an ordinary guy can't die of fright in the uniform of the United States Army.' " I told him, "I go through war scared to death all the time." He said, "Oh, crap!" Once when we were under shellfire, I said, "For Chrissakes, I don't think you can hear those friggin' shells!" He said, "To hell with them!"

Hemingway's Second Conquest of Paris

DENIS BRIAN: When Hemingway got wind of an Allied drive for Paris he told his jeep driver-bodyguard Red Pelkey to take him from Lanham's command post to as close to the French capital as possible without tangling with German armor. They stopped at Rambouillet, a small town some twenty-five miles southwest of Paris. Next to arrive was Colonel David Bruce, head of the OSS in France. Profiting from his "Crook Factory" experience in Cuba, Hemingway had already established an active intelligence service.

DAVID BRUCE: On our first day in Rambouillet, the people were very uneasy since the Germans had tanks just outside the town, which it was evident they could reoccupy at any moment. A truckload of French Resistance men attended Ernest and were devoted to him, accepting his leadership without question. By the second day, largely thanks to Ernest, we had formed a rather well organized if tiny H.Q. in a local hotel, from which Free French soldiers made sorties to attract enemy fire in order to pinpoint enemy concentrations. Ernest's bedroom was the nerve center of these operations—boys and girls on bicycles reporting from as far as Versailles. There, in his shirtsleeves, he gave audience to intelligence couriers, refugees from Paris, and deserters from the German army. Army gear littered the floor, revolvers of every nationality were heaped carelessly on the bed. The bathtub was filled with hand grenades and the basin with brandy bottles, while under the bed was a cache of army ration whiskey. By this time we had an imperfect but functioning counterespionage system. On the third day German fire killed one of our partisans and then there was a sudden influx of American and Canadian correspondents. The correspondents were very impatient, being newly arrived, to find no allied troops in Rambouillet en route to Paris. They managed to mitigate their dissatisfaction by disposing of the remnants of the hotel's wine cellar. There was considerable feeling displayed by a few of them against Ernest, apparently for having been first on the scene. He was obliged to push a couple of them around with the back of his hand, which, in addition to broken noses, resulted eventually in them lodging jealous charges against him that he had actively borne arms against the Germans thereby violating his war correspondent status.

DENIS BRIAN: Among the correspondents were Andy Rooney of *Stars and Stripes* and William Randolph Hearst, Jr., of the Hearst newspaper chain.

WILLIAM RANDOLPH HEARST, JR.: Hemingway was carrying a gun, sidearm, and he shouldn't have been. He was only a reporter the same as us, but he thought he was the Second Coming and acted like it. He took messages from army messengers, regular official messages from one headquarters to this headquarters. And I challenged him. I said, "You'll get those kids in trouble." Oh, he was very nasty. He was just as officious as all hell. I don't think anybody liked him, to tell the truth.

DENIS BRIAN: David Bruce did.

WILLIAM RANDOLPH HEARST, JR.: He had no reason to.

DENIS BRIAN: So did William Walton of *Time*.

WILLIAM RANDOLPH HEARST, JR.: Never heard the name before.

DENIS BRIAN: Another man who loved him was John Carlisle of the *Detroit Free Press*.

WILLIAM RANDOLPH HEARST, JR.: They can have him. All three of them can have him. He was a pain in the ass around us. I'm surprised at David Bruce. He had very fine taste, you know. He was a gentleman. Hemingway was not.

DENIS BRIAN: Bruce says some noses were broken.

WILLIAM RANDOLPH HEARST, JR.: I don't know of any broken noses, but he pushed people around. I didn't like Hemingway but I thought he was a hell of a good writer. No question about that. He started a new style.

ANDY ROONEY: Hemingway had taken over this little hotel in Rambouillet. It had about thirty or forty rooms. And he was working with the French Maquis and had stored hundreds of guns and other weapons in a lot of these rooms. The press corps arrived and was staging itself, getting ready to go into Paris with General Leclerc's Second French Armored Division. And a first-class group of American correspondents—Ernie Pyle and Hal Boyle, a wonderful writer for the Associated Press, among them—were there, maybe as many as forty of them. It got to be a shouting and shoving match, because we all wanted rooms in the hotel. Hemingway had about fifteen of the rooms, most with nothing but weapons in them. He had been going out on these forays on his own and locating the German gun positions. There weren't many of them, but it didn't take many to stop a column of tanks going into Paris.

JOHN CARLISLE: He discovered a barroom in this little town. He wouldn't tell us why he liked it so well. The guys in there spoke French; we didn't know who the hell they were. Finally, he told us it was the Maquis. These guys would come in there and make their secret reports and this is where Hemingway hung out until they went out again on missions. He spoke excellent French and the French people loved him. The Americans respected him, but lots of the French, I found, adored him.

LEICESTER HEMINGWAY: Papa was our reigning hero then, working with Colonel Bruce of the OSS on a voluntary basis. Papa was the guy who could do no wrong, knew both languages—French and English—perfectly, could make instant funny translations, and understood things we only vaguely guessed at.

DAVID BRUCE: I admired Ernest as an artist, friend, and a cool, resourceful, imaginative military technician and strategist. From what I saw of him, he was a born leader of men.

DENIS BRIAN: Although he couldn't get fellow correspondent Irwin Shaw to follow him into battle. Ernest had got hold of an enemy motorcycle and tried to persuade Shaw to join him in a ride toward the enemy lines to draw fire and so give their positions away. Shaw prudently declined.[1]

ANDY ROONEY: He had done a pretty good intelligence job, using maps to locate German gun positions. He had also organized French resistance in this hotel and they were conducting their own little war. When other correspondents got there, Hemingway wouldn't give up any of his rooms. Not a popular decision. So we were eating dinner in the hotel dining room that night. City editor Bruce Grant of the *Chicago Daily News* got into a fight with Hemingway in the middle of the dining room. It was the damndest thing I ever saw. Bruce Grant was taller than Hemingway, but thin and in his late fifties, or even sixty. And they started this brawl. Then Harry Harris, a good war photographer with the Associated Press, who was only about five feet four, got between these two giants. It was really comical. He stood between them like a little referee in a boxing ring. At this point, Hemingway stalked over to the French doors at the side of the dining room and went outside and yelled at Grant to come out. Grant didn't do anything. So about a minute later Hemingway threw open the door in a very dramatic way and said, "Hey, Grant, are you coming out to fight?" Well, I could never take Hemingway seriously after that. I'd always liked him as a writer, but this was such a schoolboy thing. It was really funny.

DENIS BRIAN: Next day Hemingway reverted to role of reporter when he saw Captain Hans L. Trefousse of the U.S. Army interrogating a line of German prisoners.

HANS L. TREFOUSSE: He saw me standing and talking in this field and came over and said, "My name's Hemingway." I said, "Ernest Hemingway?" And he said, "Yes, Ernest Hemingway." I said, "The last time I saw a picture of you, you had a beard." He explained he had recently shaved it off. There were French partisans with him and they told me he had been active in the liberation of Versailles—that he practically took it singlehanded. They were exceedingly impressed with him. He didn't introduce me to any of the partisans. They spoke to me on their own, but

[1]Jeffrey Meyers, *Hemingway*.

I didn't believe the story about his taking Versailles singlehanded. I didn't believe it then and don't believe it now [after the war Trefousse became Professor of History at Brooklyn College of the City University of New York]. Hemingway was very robust, in good health, and radiating confidence and warlike spirit. He stayed around and listened to me interrogating the prisoners. He was very much interested in the whole business. I was overwhelmed. Look, if you're twenty-one and you're approached by Hemingway you become very flustered. I'd read some of his books and I'd just graduated from college, and naturally admired him. So I was quite taken with the fact that he was there. He asked me a lot of questions. I explained that I had very little trouble getting information from the prisoners, except for the elite troops, the SS officers and noncoms. But they could almost always be made to talk by a simple trick: you'd put a tag around their necks with the word "Russia" on it, then lead them outside. Russia is similar enough to the German word for it. Then they'd ask the sergeant outside, "What does this mean?" The sergeant would say, "We have prisoner-of-war camps in Siberia and Florida. You're going to Siberia." And they'd ask why, and he'd say, "Because you didn't talk to the captain." Nine times out of ten, they'd fall for that—come back and tell me anything I wanted to know. There was another trick I told Hemingway. If you had a large number of prisoners you lined them up and told the noncoms to please report by unit. So you got the whole order of battle without their knowing what they were doing, because they would obey automatically. And that was precisely what we wanted to know. No physical force was ever applied.

DENIS BRIAN: Hemingway was no advocate of tender treatment for Germans.

JOHN HEMINGWAY: I know my father claimed to have killed 122 "krauts" as he called them, but I think that's what he probably wished he had done [laughs]. I suspect he killed some. His contacts with the OSS came up during the breakthrough to Paris and then anything was likely to have happened. It's possible he did some things he claimed to have done. I think it's authenticated that he threw hand grenades down into a cellar where they suspected Germans were.

DENIS BRIAN: But nobody I know of reported the results.

LEICESTER HEMINGWAY: Any number in excess of a hundred is really putting a little gloss on it.

DENIS BRIAN: But there's no hard evidence that he killed even one.

DAVID BRUCE: The French general Leclerc arrived on our fourth or fifth day in Rambouillet and Ernest, myself, and Mouthard—an invaluable and famous French secret service operator—gave the general's intelligence officer a detailed summary of German strength between us and Paris, along all routes, with sketches of obstacles to be expected.

HANS L. TREFOUSSE: When we set out for Paris, some twenty-five or thirty miles away, Hemingway followed in the jeep right behind me. The Free French weren't very strict about such things; there wasn't any fixed order in which you drove. I accompanied the combat division toward Paris in case there were more prisoners to be interrogated en route or in the city.

ANDY ROONEY: We started out for Paris on August 24, and correspondents had a choice of going with one of two points of operation. I happened to choose the one given less chance of getting to Paris first, because fewer correspondents were with it. Hemingway chose the same one. So we were eight or ten miles out of Paris and German guns had hit the lead tank. That was always a problem, because if the road was narrow none of the other tanks could get through and they might as well have knocked out all our tanks. We were trying to locate the German gun position. I was over by a farmhouse behind a stone wall, all alone, sort of nervous because all the rest of the guys are in tanks and I've parked my jeep. And I see this figure moving down along behind the stone wall. I'm nervous, because I think he may be a German. And it turns out to be Hemingway, alone. So the two of us crouched there behind the stone wall for more than an hour. He talked about where the German gun positions were and what he'd been doing. It was a strange little experience for me, I was impressed with how thoroughly he enjoyed the little bit of war he was having. He honestly was enjoying the whole operation. It was a toy war for him at that point. It was not yet dirty or muddy and the enemy was pretty well defined in front of us. The danger, while it was there, was not maximum. Not many were killed going into Paris. It has always confused my attitude toward Hemingway. I would have enjoyed his novels better if I hadn't had that little experience with him and Bruce Grant in the hotel. So childish!

Though I did have confidence that he knew what he was talking about. I had the feeling that he had been thorough in his attempts to find out where the dangers were ahead of us. But he was nervous. Well, I don't know about nervous, but we weren't sticking our heads up. He asked me who I represented. I was with the army newspaper *Stars and Stripes*. I had had some contact with Mary Welsh—I'd seen more of her than I had of him—and he recalled she said she knew me. But we were mostly concerned with what was happening in front of us. I was twenty-two and I'd read *The Sun Also Rises* and perhaps two more of his books. As someone who hoped to be a writer himself, I was quite impressed with his literary style. I suppose Shakespeare would have had childish moments that would have disappointed anybody who admired him as a writer. He was armed and none of the rest of us were. That was a big issue, too. The other correspondents were sore at him because he carried a pistol. It made them nervous, because their only protection was not being armed and having it established that correspondents were noncombatants. Hemingway was not my image of brave. It was admirable in a way, but he was like someone who either didn't understand the danger or was so taken up with his own image of himself he ignored the danger. A brave man, to me, is someone who commits an act with the knowledge he may be killed, and doesn't want to be killed, and has thought the whole thing over. I don't think in the classic sense that Hemingway was brave.

ROBERT CROMIE [*Chicago Tribune* war correspondent]: We were advancing on Paris and there was some shooting near us and I asked Hemingway about it, and he said "That's the Germans keeping their cards in the musicians' union. They're retreating, but they want to fire a few shots before they go." He was known for carrying a gun. I was a war correspondent on Guadalcanal, too, and a very funny picture of me appeared in the newspaper because they painted out the pistol I was carrying—which was illegal, of course.

BILL MAULDIN [cartoonist, writer]: That was perfectly excusable because the Japanese were not signatories to the Geneva Convention. I was in Vietnam in 1965 wandering around in a rice paddy and a helicopter pilot handed me a pistol and said, "You'd better keep this with you." I did—for a day, so I was carrying a gun myself under those circumstances. But the Germans in Europe followed the Geneva Convention, which protected correspondents who weren't armed.

DENIS BRIAN: Did they keep to it?

BILL MAULDIN: They did enough that it behooved us to follow it, too. I think a correspondent who carried a weapon in those circumstances was asking for trouble.

JOHN CARLISLE: Some of our guys claim they saw Hemingway taking off with some Frenchmen just before we got to Paris. He disappeared and somebody said they saw him coming back carrying a tommygun in the crook of his arm. I never saw that. It could well have been.

WILLIAM B. CRAWFORD: My father, Kenneth Crawford, was most flattered that Hemingway wrote to *Newsweek* mentioning him, and calling him brave as jumping off buildings. I suspect my father was brave [as a war correspondent for *Newsweek*], though he always denied it. You can take S.L.A. Marshall's account of Hemingway using Pa and another unknown correspondent and their jeep to draw fire on the approach to Paris as substantially true. Pa told the story often, saying Hemingway tipped him to a shortcut to Paris, that he and his companion were fired on briefly, and that Hemingway came along later in an elegant liberated vehicle, explaining that someone had to go first and draw fire. Far from holding it against Hemingway, Pa also recalled the incident with amusement. He regarded Hemingway as a childish man and a great literary talent.

HANS L. TREFOUSSE: Hemingway was following close behind my jeep as we crossed the Seine and entered Paris at Porte de St. Cloud. We were held up because the French had thrown some Germans into the river. It was an awful thing. I think they lynched them and then threw them in the water, which we didn't particularly care for. But, then, what could we do? Germans were firing behind us and then these self-propelled guns wheeled up and fired backwards at them. As we entered Paris together the cheering crowds were overwhelming. Liberation Day was a tremendous experience. While the French cheered, I said to some of them, "There's a very famous American writer right behind me, Ernest Hemingway." And the average person apparently had never heard of him. They weren't interested. We managed to get as far as the Arc de Triomphe where there was a huge crowd and we were taking some prisoners away when somebody threw an incendiary grenade in front of the Etoile. I fell flat on my face because there was shooting for the next ten minutes. When I got up, all the prisoners were dead. They had been shot. And I had been hit on my side by this incendiary grenade; my pants and hand were burnt. I got up and Hemingway said, "Oh, you've got to have that taken care of. It could become infected." He took me to a first-aid post nearby and that was the last I saw of him. I had a burn wound and at the first-aid station they said, "We can evacuate you to the United States." I said, "Don't be silly. I'm twenty-one years old and I'm in Paris and you want to evacuate me!" But I took Hemingway's advice and for the next three months my hand was bandaged afresh every day. I don't know for sure who threw the bomb. I hope it was the Germans or the French fascists, so that I was a hero rather than a fool. My friend later became

Bright-eyed baby Ernest displays his finery, a winning smile, firm grip, and no fear of heights.
(JOHN F. KENNEDY LIBRARY)

At sixteen Hemingway was a head taller than friends (from left) Morris Musselman, Lewis Clarahan and Proctor Gilbert. They were on a hiking trip in Michigan in 1915, when, said Clarahan, "Ernest used to make things exciting." (SUSAN LOWREY CRIST)

The imaginary becomes real. The Boy's Rifle Club at Oak Park High School existed only in Ernest's imagination, until he was challenged to prove it wasn't fictitious. Then, in 1917, he armed himself (left) and friends for this photographic evidence. (SUSAN LOWERY CRIST)

Lifelong fan Susan Lowrey (now Crist) with the object of her admiration in senior class at Oak Park High School, in 1917. Though Ernest looks glum, Susan remembers him as always laughing and carefree. (SUSAN LOWREY CRIST)

Grace under pressure: Despite painful war wounds, Ernest smiles in the Red Cross Hospital, Milan, Italy, in July 1918. His visitor is fellow ambulance driver John Cloud.
(HENRY VILLARD)

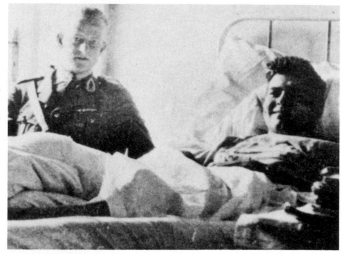

Nurse Agnes von Kurowsky and her patient, Ernest Hemingway. She was his first love and the model for Catherine Barkley in A *Farewell to Arms*.
(JOHN F. KENNEDY LIBRARY)

Convalescing from war wounds at Stresa on Lake Maggiore, Italy, in 1918, Hemingway met Pier Vincenzo Bellia and Bellia's vivacious daughter, Bianca. Sixty years later, Bianca claimed Ernest had proposed to her. (JOHN F. KENNEDY LIBRARY)

Wedding day for Ernest and Hadley in 1921, with (from left) sisters Carol and Ursula, mother, brother Leicester, and father. (JOHN F. KENNEDY LIBRARY)

Famed muckraking journalist Lincoln Steffens took an interest in Ernest when they were on a reporting assignment in Genoa in 1922. There Hemingway learned less is more through the succinct language "cablese." (JOHN F. KENNEDY LIBRARY)

Twenty-four-year-old EH drapes a fist over brother Leicester, eight. After the birth of son John (Bumby) in Toronto, Ernest made a brief visit to Oak Park, Illinois in the winter of 1923. (JOHN F. KENNEDY LIBRARY)

John Hadley Nicanor Hemingway sits on his father's lap in their rue Notre Dame de Champs home in 1924. Ernest was quite mad about the boy, Archibald MacLeish recalled.
(JOHN F. KENNEDY LIBRARY)

Henry (Mike) Strater who studied with Edouard Vuillard, did not please Ernest with this portrait. He thought it made him look too intellectual—like H.G. Wells.
(HENRY STRATER)

Strater's "Boxer" portrait of Hemingway in his early twenties met with the subject's approval.
(HENRY STRATER)

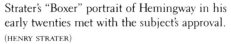

An excited crowd at Pamplona, Spain, in 1925 sees one man fall under the charging bull and another face it. That same year, the daredevil still on his feet, with beret, sweater, white pants and white sneakers, began to write *The Sun Also Rises*. (JOHN F. KENNEDY LIBRARY)

Brooklyn-born bullfighter Sidney Franklin and Ernest during their first encounter in Spain in 1929. Hemingway advised Franklin not to make killing the bull look too easy. (JOHN F. KENNEDY LIBRARY)

Novelist Morley Callaghan in 1935. Callaghan first encountered Hemingway in the offices of the *Toronto Star* during Ernest's brief but bitter association with the paper, and remained a lifelong admirer. (AP/WIDE WORLD PHOTOS)

Poet Archibald MacLeish who, with wife, Ada, were among Hadley and Ernest's closest friends in the twenties and early thirties. Although the men later quarreled, they eventually resolved their differences—at a distance. (CULVER PICTURES, INC.)

Key West portrait of the now famous novelist, by Henry Strater, in the early thirties. (HENRY STRATER)

Sister Carol Hemingway at the time of her engagement to John Gardner in 1933. EH disapproved and broke off all contact with Carol when she married Gardner. Her marriage proved more enduring than any of Ernest's. (CAROL HEMINGWAY GARDNER)

Bullfighter Sidney Franklin and EH share center stage with a giant marlin in Key West, August 1934. "You're looking bloody marvelous," said Hemingway. "I feel swell," replied Franklin. Last time they met, Franklin was being carried out of a Spanish bullring screaming in pain. When not fishing, EH was working on *Green Hills of Africa* and longing to return to them. (JOHN F. KENNEDY LIBRARY)

"Apple-Cored" Marlin: Henry Strater (behind Hemingway) caught the 500-pound fish, partially eaten by sharks, off the coast of Bimini in May 1935. EH, with a broad grin, took pride of place in the photo as if the catch was his. (JOHN F. KENNEDY LIBRARY)

Second wife, Pauline, gives a winking or grimacing Hemingway an outdoor haircut in Key West in the late 1930s. (JOHN F. KENNEDY LIBRARY)

Milton Wolff of the Abraham Lincoln Brigade in Spain in 1938. Ernest compared him with Abraham Lincoln.
(JOHN F. KENNEDY LIBRARY)

War correspondent Vincent Sheean of the *New York Herald Tribune* covered both the Spanish Civil War and Ernest Hemingway as subjects of compelling interest.
(AUTHOR'S COLLECTION)

Crusading writer-reporter George Seldes. (GEORGE SELDES)

Writer-reporter John Hersey. As a schoolboy Hersey hero-worshiped Hemingway. (JOHN HERSEY)

Robert Merriman, chief of staff of the Abraham Lincoln Brigade and journalist Martha Gellhorn chat with youngsters in Spain in 1937, during the Civil War. Merriman was one of the models for Robert Jordan in *For Whom the Bell Tolls*. Gellhorn became Hemingway's third wife. (JOHN F. KENNEDY LIBRARY)

William Walton (left) atop Time-Life's London office in Dean Street, with Dorothy Dennis (the office manager) and fellow war correspondent Bill White, in the spring of 1944. (WILLIAM WALTON)

Steel-helmeted Hemingway and an American sergeant with a line of German prisoners of war near Rambouillet, France, 1944, where Ernest learned the secret of making them talk.
(JOHN F. KENNEDY LIBRARY)

Ernest took this photo in Paris, August 1944, as the city was being liberated. Elena, a would-be resistance fighter, is at the wheel of the jeep; the regular driver, Captain John Westover, sits on the hood while the Army's chief historian in Europe, Brigadier General S.L.A. Marshall, stands between them.
(JOHN WESTOVER)

Hemingway and Colonel Charles T. (Buck) Lanham, commander of the Twenty-second Infantry Regiment, Fourth Infantry Division, examine captured German military equipment in September 1944. In those dangerous days Ernest woke happy every morning.

Psychiatrist Meyer Maskin, an expert on fear, had a provocative conversation on the subject with Hemingway, who mocked him to his face, praised him behind his back.

Papa Hemingway with son Patrick (by his second wife, Pauline) and his fourth wife, Mary at the Finca in Cuba shortly after World War II ended.

Mary faces fifteen Hemingway cats gathered at feeding time. Ernest sang and talked to his cats, explaining their great number by saying that one cat leads to another. He named some, to fit their personalities or appearance, Dillinger, Friendless, Uncle Wolfie, Good Will, Boisie, Tester, Thruster, Fats, Furhouse, and Nuisance Value alias Listless Kitty. (JOHN F. KENNEDY LIBRARY)

Rare photo of Ernest being interviewed. The scene: the Floridita bar. The year: 1953. Chilean woman journalist grins as Ernest parries a personal question, Thorvald Sanchez Jr., looks at photographer, and Mary (right) prepares to come to Ernest's rescue. (THORVALD SANCHEZ JR.)

Inspiration: Adriana Ivancich was Hemingway's model for Renata in *Across the River and Into Trees*, but the love scenes were wishful thinking. (AUTHOR'S COLLECTION)

Planning film of *The Old Man and the Sea*, in a Havana restaurant in 1953, are (from left) Roberto Herrera, John Hemingway, Ernest, Spencer Tracy, Mary, John's wife Byra (nicknamed Puck). (JOSEPH DRYER)

The Hemingways at Ernest's favorite bar in Havana, the Floridita, in the 1950s, with (from left) Mayito Meonocal Jr., Roberto Herrera, Taylor Williams, Joseph Dryer, and a friend. (JOSEPH DRYER)

Wedding witness (testigo) Ernest with Mary at the marriage of their friends Joseph and Nancy Dryer in the mid-fifties. (JOSEPH DRYER)

Bullfighter Luis Miguel Dominguin (right) sought Hemingway's advice in Cuba 1954. (JOSEPH DRYER)

Just recovered from a six-week bout with hepatitis, Hemingway greets fellow fishing expert and enthusiast John Rybovich Jr. in the Finca Vigia in 1954. (JOHN RYBOVICH JR.)

Hemingway's friend and editor at *Esquire*, Arnold Gingrich (right) discusses work with novelist Irwin Shaw in 1954. Ernest admired Shaw's writing until the novel *The Young Lions* appeared, lampooning him and brother, Leicester.

Ernest looks deceptively fit and carefree as he relaxes with his guests Toby and Betty Bruce at the foot of Galena Mountains, Idaho, in the fall of 1958.

Nancy "Slim" Hayward and Lauren Bacall enjoy a mostly hilarious three-hour lunch with Ernest in Spain in 1959. (LAUREN BACALL)

Malcolm Cowley and son, Robert, dine out near Malcolm's boyhood home in Pennsylvania in 1985. In 1947, when thirteen, Robert accompanied father to Cuba for a *Life* magazine profile of Hemingway and got a boy's-eye-view of the writer. (ROBERT COWLEY)

A book on either side of him and his beloved springer spaniel Black Dog on the floor nearby, "the closet intellectual" takes the news lying down, June 3, 1948.

head of all French firefighting services and he looked into the matter and said to the best of his knowledge a fascist had thrown it. Hemingway was totally sober all the time I saw him, and armed, although he wasn't supposed to be. What he did was wholly irregular, I was told afterwards.

JOHN WESTOVER [S.L.A. Marshall's driver-escort]: I was simply a graduate student who had gone on duty in the army. I first met Hemingway at Rambouillet when he was with a French partisan called Mouthard, who I understand was Louis Pasteur's grandson. I was impressed with Hemingway as I guess a starstruck kid would be with a movie idol. Here I was a nobody and I meet somebody extremely important and he was hail-fellow-well-met. The whole situation was a wildly chaotic one that didn't fit in with any military tactics I'd ever been involved in—and I was an experienced soldier by then. We were pinned down before we reached the Arc de Triomphe. When we reached it there was a lot of milling around. Firing broke out and the Arc was badly damaged. People were milling all over and Frenchmen wanted to kiss men on both cheeks. It was a wild situation. As a combat soldier I'd seen nothing like this in my life. It was intoxicating without drinking anything. There was a lot of machine gun fire and firing from a tank or tank-type armored vehicle. Some of the French might have thrown a grenade. People were crazy. At one time German prisoners were being kicked and beaten by some people coming out of the crowd and swinging a fist or kicking them.

JOHN CARLISLE: The last time I saw him was in the Ritz Hotel in Paris. Stevie [Stevenson] was with him and Pelkey, Ernest's sergeant-driver. Papa was barefoot and wearing a pair of khaki pants, and walking up and down the room with a good-looking gal [Elena] dressed in a khaki outfit. She had a German luger stuck in her belt, a bandolier of bullets around her, and a Free Forces of the Interior badge on her arm. And they were jibberjabbering. Papa said to me, "Pour yourself a shot of cognac." I had a hangover, so I poured a big shot. He said, "For God's sake don't drink it all!" While I was drinking they were jibberjabbering and it didn't sound like French. I found out later they were talking Spanish. I said to Stevie: "What the hell is going on?" They were now obviously having a violent argument, walking up and down the room together like they were on parade, waving their arms around. Hemingway stopped in front of me. He says: "Jack Carlisle, a woman never knows when it's over." Where he wound up with her, I don't know.

JOHN WESTOVER: Afterwards we celebrated. I have a slip of paper signed by various people including Hemingway. I introduced him to people like

Betty Ritz of the Ritz, the hotel owner's wife or the manager's wife. What impressed me was here I was, just a graduate student meeting all these world-famous people and in a world-famous place on a world-famous day. I was a young married man and I wrote long and frequent letters to my wife. She saved them and that I have some dependence on, because my written account is taken right out of what I was remembering immediately following the events, and it's very full, and I wasn't withholding details. When Slam [S. L. A.] Marshall was getting ready to do his article "How Papa Liberated Paris" he asked me to send material to him.[1] Then I got a request from Carlos Baker and I sent him my material. Baker replied, "I've got your account, I've got Marshall's account. I've got the driver Pelkey's account. Are you sure you were in the same war?" My view of it was from a totally different standpoint; factually, yes we were together and yes we got there. But who we saw and what we saw was considerably different in most cases.

DENIS BRIAN: According to the Colonel Marshall account in Baker's biography, Marshall, Westover, and a Spanish woman named Elena, who had joined them in Rambouillet, reached Paris together. Then they took cover behind a fallen tree as six halftracks and five tanks entered a large square near the Bois de Boulogne, firing machine guns at nearby buildings. When the armor moved on, the trio saw Hemingway stooping low and running across the third-story balcony of an apartment building. He called out in French, "The Germans are in the building behind us!" Elena translated and added, "We have to get out. The French are bringing up artillery." They hurried for the shelter of a doorway while Ernest covered their escape route with a carbine. Soon after, a tank sent a few shells into the building where the Germans were hiding.

JOHN WESTOVER: The Spanish woman, Elena, had attached herself to Hemingway. He called her a lovely girl from Bilbao. She was no beauty. She was a grown-up street urchin.

DENIS BRIAN: Hemingway and David Bruce arrived at the Ritz with a truckload of Free French soldiers carrying machine guns and were enthusiastically wined and dined.

JACQUELINE TAVERNIER-COURBIN [Professor of English at the University of Ottawa]: Accounts of the "liberation" of the Ritz differ, but according

[1]S. L. A. Marshall, "How Papa Liberated Paris," *American Heritage*, April 1962. "An eyewitness recreates the wonderful, wacky day in August 1944, when Hemingway, a handful of Americans, and a señorita named Elena helped rekindle the City of Light."

to the Hemingway tradition, after having "personally" liberated the Travellers Club, Hemingway, together with Colonel Bruce, Hemingway's driver Archie Pelkey, and some irregulars, made a dash to the Café de la Paix and then to the Ritz, which they found undamaged and deserted, except for the manager, "the imperturbable Ausiello." It was apparently that same day that Hemingway and Charles Ritz were introduced to each other by an ecstatic lieutenant of artillery. The tradition also has it that Hemingway and a group of resistance fighters, intent on chasing Germans, climbed to the roof of the Ritz and, blasting away with machine guns, brought down nothing but a clothesline full of Ritz linen sheets.

DENIS BRIAN: Mary Welsh got a reporting assignment to go to Paris soon after Ernest reached there and he was delighted to see her.

JACQUELINE TAVENIER-COURBIN: The affair between Ernest and Mary Welsh did not please everyone, in particular Mrs. Cesar Ritz, Charles Ritz's mother, who simply ignored Mary's presence, while bowing and smiling to Ernest. When Ernest returned to the Ritz after having been married, and thus had fulfilled the demands of propriety, Mrs. Ritz was charming to them both and they became good friends.

DENIS BRIAN: The official Ritz hotel version is that "when the Nazis conquered Paris in June 1940, they promptly requisitioned the Ritz. Goering installed himself in the hotel's Imperial Suite, ostensibly to coordinate his Luftwaffe's attacks on Britain, but also to supervise the plundering of art treasures taken mostly from French Jews. Other Nazis such as Goebbels and Himmler were frequent visitors. However inconvenient the stay of high-ranking Nazis, the presence of these officers permitted the hotel to make a small contribution to the French Resistance. By means of an elaborate code, used mostly to place fictitious food orders, employees of the hotel were able to pass along information on the location of key German personnel. An order for fourteen chickens, for example, might mean Goering was in residence. In August 1944, the Allies liberated Paris. If Ernest Hemingway was not the first to arrive at the Ritz, he was one of the first. A sweep of the floors failed to disclose any Germans. That done, he descended to the Cambon bar, where he was greeted with a glass of champagne."

A FRIEND: I was there at various times in Ernest's bedroom at the Ritz, where Jean-Paul Sartre and Simone de Beauvoir visited him. They sent Sartre home. They said, "Look, why don't you get going? We're going to stay here and do a little drinking and serious talking tonight." Although

Ernest was ill, she stayed all night. He described the experience to Charles Poore of the *New York Times* but in such scatalogical detail he knew Poore couldn't print it, especially in the *Times*. In a letter to Poore, Hemingway said de Beauvoir had wanted the literary experience of sleeping with him and he was willing but not sure if he was able, complaining of battle fatigue. He told her that the fighting had been as hard as at Gettysburg and when she asked him to spell Gettysburg, he said, "Make it Harrisburg."

LEICESTER HEMINGWAY: I saw Castor, as we called de Beauvoir, come out of the Ritz—the great hotel Ernesto liberated—the next morning. I had to report there regularly every morning to take notes, clear up stuff, run errands, and so forth. I was on detached duty from my unit and literally being his batman and secretary.

DENIS BRIAN: In a biography of reporter A. J. Liebling there's an anecdote about Charles Wertenbaker finding a missing $100,000 in *Time* magazine's Paris safe at this time. He was told the money had already been covered by the insurance company and he could spend it as he saw fit. Ernest heard about it, according to this account, and came for some of the spoils. Wertenbaker is reputed to have said: "I wouldn't give him the sweat off my balls! He's been trying to beat all our reporters by scooping stories and being the first to enter Paris."[1]

LEICESTER HEMINGWAY: Oh no, that's not true. He and Wertenbaker were two very great friends over there. And Mary and Wert were friends. I don't believe any anti-Hemingway quote by Wert. Of course, there was friendly rivalry, but, Jesus, he did incredible stuff helping *Time-Life* all during the war. He helped Willie Walton file more pieces to make *Life* look good, and he helped Mary file more good stuff with *Time* than anybody I know of.

WILLIAM WALTON: I agree with Leicester's point of view except for one thing. I don't think he ever went over Mary's copy at the time. And he never helped me, either.

JOHN HEMINGWAY: Paris wasn't all fun for my father. He was a little unhappy that Patton's Inspector General wanted to press charges against him for having participated in combat.

C. T. LANHAM: There were fellow correspondents who were jealous as hell

[1]Raymond Sokolov, *Wayward Reporter: The Life of A. J. Liebling*, Creative Arts Books, 1980.

of him, a couple in particular whom I subsequently met, and they had reported him to the authorities.

JOHN CARLISLE: Before I left Paris I said to him, "I'm going to do a story telling the real truth of what you did for the goddamn Third Army around Rambouillet, all the espionage you were doing." He said, "For God's sake, they're thinking of sending me home because I was playing soldier. Don't write it."

C. T. LANHAM: I wrote out a statement in which I said, "I have never seen him armed." And I hadn't. However, I was damned sure he usually was. And I'm sure his jeep was loaded with everything in the world it could be loaded with, but he was very careful not to let me see these.

DENIS BRIAN: Hemingway was officially interrogated by Patton's Inspector General in Nancy on October 6, 1944, for being a one-man army in and around Rambouillet [see Appendix A]. Fellow correspondents claimed through his activities he had impeded the progress of the military. This was a bitter and rare experience for him. He had to deny his heroic behavior to avoid being sent home to the United States—so that ever after people might doubt he had been a hero. He explained away all the evidence. Sure he had taken off his jacket with his war correspondent's insignia, but only because it was hot. He refused, he said, to lead Resistance troops, and merely gave them advice. Yes, they called him "Captain," but only as a term of affection. He agreed he had stored weapons and ammunition but only as a favor to the Maquis. Of course he had studied military maps and gone on patrols but merely to gather material for his articles. True, he had given orders to the irregular troops, but he was merely translating commands in English from the American colonel in charge. Not only was Hemingway exonerated, but General Barton wrote to him saying he was recommending him for a Distinguished Service Cross. And Colonel Bruce said, "If DSCs were awarded to all who truly deserved them, Ernest would have richly merited one for several exploits."

C. T. LANHAM: When asked afterwards about that episode when he had lied his way out of being a hero, Ernest's standard reply was "In the next war, by God, I'm going to have the Geneva Convention tattooed on my ass in reverse so I can read it in a mirror!"

DENIS BRIAN: After another trip to Paris to be with Mary Welsh, Hemingway returned to Lanham's division now fighting against a German counterattack in Hurtgen Forest. It was to become known as the Battle of the Bulge, one of the bloodiest battles of World War II.

Hemingway Confronts a Psychiatrist

DENIS BRIAN: In his biography of Hemingway, Carlos Baker writes: "His lifelong scorn of 'head doctors' reappeared in his mistreatment of a divisional psychiatrist named Major Maskin. One night the doctor invited himself into Ernest's billet and began to ask him probing, subtle questions. Ernest put on a sober face, saying that he needed Maskin's advice. He was troubled about his cats at the Finca Vigia. He had twenty or thirty and kept getting more. 'The little bastard was fascinated,' said Ernest. 'His eyes were bugging out.' 'Many people like cats,' said the doctor, adding that was no problem. 'With me it is,' said Hemingway. 'My problem is that I can't seem to stop having intercourse with them.' " Baker continues: "Dr. Maskin was discoursing about the nature of battle fatigue when Hemingway interrupted witheringly, 'Dr. Maskin, you know everything about fuckoffs and nothing about brave men.' William Walton, who was also present, traced some at least of Hemingway's scornful treatment of Maskin to anti-Semitism. The evening's debate, as he recalled it, was gross and cruel, both towards the doctor himself and the whole psychiatric brotherhood. It ended when the well-drubbed doctor shook a finger at Hemingway and predicted: 'You'll be coming to see me yet.' "[1] Dr. Maskin, what do you think of this account of your encounter with Hemingway?

MEYER MASKIN: It's all fiction.

DENIS BRIAN: Didn't Carlos Baker contact you and try to confirm it?

MEYER MASKIN: No, not at all. I saw Baker subsequently when I happened to be at Princeton and I called in and introduced myself, saying: "Would you like to see an incarnation of your fiction?"

DENIS BRIAN: Baker tried to separate fact from fiction but with Hemingway it wasn't easy.

MEYER MASKIN: Carlos Baker was very charming and we talked a bit and I got to like him very much. But his account isn't what happened at all. Baker got it from General Lanham—and he never had anything to do with me, nor I with him. I think Lanham simply put down in his memoirs what Hemingway had fantasized. Baker acknowledges that he never got

[1]Carlos Baker, *Ernest Hemingway: A Life Story.*

hold of me; maybe he tried, I don't know. I got a number of requests after the war to comment on my war experiences and I threw them all away. I didn't in any way want to benefit from the war, didn't want to take advantage, because I felt grateful that I had survived. So most of the people I knew never knew I had anything to do with Hemingway until Carlos Baker's biography appeared.

DENIS BRIAN: After that didn't any reporters or writers contact you?

MEYER MASKIN: No.

DENIS BRIAN: Isn't that rather extraordinary?

MEYER MASKIN: I think it is.

DENIS BRIAN: Fear and courage absorbed Hemingway in his life and work. Here's an account of his discussing them with a psychiatrist during a time of great stress, and nobody has checked up. How was the subject of courage brought up?

MEYER MASKIN: In a very incidental way and in a different context from the book's account. Hemingway said something very sensible after I'd shown him something I had written. It was pretty sad—fiction based on my experiences with infantry soldiers. Among other things, he said: "You know, you can't write like this," and he added, "Never start a war that you can't finish," which is not a bad proverb. The thing I had written was pretty defeatist. But that was the state of affairs. We were stuck in the Hurtgen forest. It was the first winter and very unpleasant. Everybody was getting frozen feet. I had written about the psychological impact of the war, especially at the infantry level. I was, after all, the psychiatrist for the division, which was a novel thing. As far as I can recall, Hemingway never referred to that at all. I don't even know if he *knew* I was a psychiatrist.

DENIS BRIAN: Did you consider him to be brave?

MEYER MASKIN: No, I thought he was silly with this machismo thing. I remember saying to him that if I had his talent and lovely home in Cuba, what the hell would I be doing in this mud? I recall now he said he drank less during the war than in peacetime. You see, he was playing soldier. The general was very concerned because Hemingway wanted to go out on infantry patrol and this meant other soldiers had to be told to guard him and risk themselves to protect him. The general couldn't tolerate an injury coming to Hemingway.

DENIS BRIAN: Baker indicates that Hemingway was possibly anti-Semitic, which might account for his attitude to you. Would he have known you were Jewish?

MEYER MASKIN: I look Jewish in an American sense. I'm a Mediterranean type. I'm also a psychiatrist and practically all psychiatrists at that time were Jewish. And there was my name, Meyer Maskin. But it never came up and he was never hostile to me. I never exploited our encounter; I never wrote it up. The first time I heard about it was when a friend of Baker's came around after the biography was published and I was in Florida already. So I went and bought the book. It was quite a surprise.

DENIS BRIAN: Baker reports that you shook your finger at Hemingway, saying, "You'll be coming to me yet."

MEYER MASKIN: That's very charming. I wish I had done it. It's a nice story and it indicates a great psychological prognostic talent. I wish I were that accurate all the time.

DENIS BRIAN: By using Baker's biography as their source subsequent writers could say that the irony is that, just as Dr. Maskin had predicted, Hemingway had to go to psychiatrists for treatment.

MEYER MASKIN [laughs]: *Major* Maskin, please, in that context. You know, it would have been a brilliant diagnostic feat with a twenty-five year range. [Closer to fifteen, in fact.] That's not a bad radar system.

DENIS BRIAN: Lanham calls Hemingway the bravest man he ever knew.

MEYER MASKIN: I wasn't preoccupied with bravery. The bravest man I knew was General Roosevelt, President Theodore Roosevelt's son, whom I talked to before the invasion of Normandy. I always thought a brave man was not one who acted appropriately in a dangerous situation—a lot of that is reflexes. I think it's the man who volunteers. That's what Roosevelt did. He volunteered to go with our invasion because he thought a general should be present with the infantry soldiers in an invasion. He went in twice—at Casablanca and Normandy on D-Day. Of course, Hemingway was brave in the same way—he volunteered to cover the war. I never stopped to think about that. The thing I was glad about in Baker's book is that at least there is no suggestion that Hemingway was saying I was cowardly in any way. After all, while the book says I brought cowardly characters out of the action, it acknowledges that I was there, at the front.

DENIS BRIAN: You never heard Hemingway say to you, "You know nothing about brave men, only fuckoffs!"

MEYER MASKIN: No. But his language was like that. So was mine.

DENIS BRIAN: And you agree now, that by your definition, Hemingway *was* brave?

MEYER MASKIN: Yes, I'll say that.

DENIS BRIAN: Did you show him your manuscript in a tent or in the mess?

MEYER MASKIN: I went looking for him. I was curious. I was less curious after I met him. I thought him kind of childish. Someone said he was frozen in adolescence. I'd accept that.

DENIS BRIAN: Being told that, Hemingway replied, "If you're going to be frozen, it's as good a place as any."

MEYER MASKIN: I would agree. I think that Hemingway, who was a great storyteller, made up the account of our meeting almost out of whole cloth, as he did so many of his stories. Although thematically what he said was consistent with his beliefs. In that sense, Baker is absolutely right. In other words, Hemingway's fantasy so much involved being a war hero, and there he was risking his life and upsetting the general who had to protect him so he could play infantry soldier. Obviously Hemingway had no respect for a psychiatrist who had to deal with what he called cowardly people who wanted to get out. So, in a sense, all of this was used properly by Baker. The theme is correct, I believe.

DENIS BRIAN: Do you think then the wild story about being sexually involved with cats is the sort of thing Hemingway wished he had said to you, but didn't say?

MEYER MASKIN: Something like that. I think a lot of it is *esprit d'escalier*. Although I don't want to make the same mistake of interpreting the dead after the fact. All I'm saying is that this didn't happen in my presence. So I don't know in what spirit it was said.

DENIS BRIAN: If he *had* said these things to you, you would have remembered them?

MEYER MASKIN: Certainly.

DENIS BRIAN: Suppose he had said them to your face, how would you have felt?

MEYER MASKIN: I'd have taken it as adolescent braggadocio or something like that.

DENIS BRIAN: Hemingway is dead and Maskin denies the incident occurred as reported in the Carlos Baker biography. But there is at least one living witness to the Maskin-Hemingway meeting: Hemingway's friend, war correspondent William Walton.

WILLIAM WALTON: My vision of the scene is a small hut in the Hurtgen forest and it is night and Buck Lanham is not there. The three of us are, and maybe Red Pelkey, Hemingway's driver, as acolyte. The conversation was quite long and not all rational—a lot of it was alcoholic. I don't remember the doctor presenting his manuscript, but perhaps he did. I could easily have gone in and out of the room when that took place. I never took a note of it. I have been asked about this incident dozens of times [although Maskin had not], because it was a crucial moment, crucial for Ernest obviously the way it turned out. I think Maskin's disclaimer is wrong. We can almost understand his motives. He looked stupid, and nobody likes to look stupid. Had he been asked earlier I bet his memory would have been more accurate. The line about "fuckoffs and brave men" could easily have been said when the doctor wasn't there. I easily remember the line, "You'll be coming to me yet!" That's what Ernest resented more than anything. And it was so true. But it was an angry retort; it claimed no insight into him. I got the overtones of the anti-Semitism or the anti-psychiatry even then. Ernest had often discussed his father's suicide with me. It haunted him and he terribly resented all psychiatrists. It wasn't just this man. A relative of mine was in an institution at that time and I discussed the problems with various psychiatrists—hers. And Ernest was very fraternal about it and sympathetic and supportive. He resented them all. At that time Ernest and I were living together day and night; we had no other choice. So we knew the same people. We didn't know this guy, but we both knew he was a psychiatrist. And this was a very black moment on the Western front. There were dismal, black, dripping woods. We all lived in it. God, we could have been losing the war at that moment—it seems inconceivable now—but men were cracking up in a way they never had before, at least in Europe. Desertions and shootings in the foot and everything else. It was a very creepy atmosphere. Everybody was talking about things they hadn't talked about before. Think of all those things as you focus on it.

DENIS BRIAN: Dr. Maskin, when Arnold Zweig requested permission of his friend Sigmund Freud to write his biography, Freud replied: "Anyone who writes a biography is committed to lies, concealments, hypocrisy, flattery, and even to hiding his own lack of understanding, for biographical truth does not exist and if it did we could not use it." Well, I'm trying to find and use biographical truth. You've heard William Walton's recollections. He says your line to Hemingway, "You'll be coming to me yet!" is accurate.

MEYER MASKIN: I'm fascinated by what Walton says. I won't disclaim that I may be stupid. I could argue that anybody who was there was stupid [laughs]. Once you get the correct atmosphere, what would anybody with any intelligence be doing there who didn't have to be there? In fact, if I free associate to that, I used to have discussions with my sergeant, because we were a screening operation for whether or not somebody could be sent to the rear echelon if they became neurotic, or had what we called combat exhaustion. We knew every way to get out: why didn't we apply it to ourselves?

DENIS BRIAN: Is it conceivable you said, "You'll be coming to me yet," as a joke?

MEYER MASKIN: If I said something like that I would only have said it jokingly. No clinician, nobody who takes himself seriously as a doctor, would offer that kind of prediction. So, if I said it, it's the way you would say, "You're crazy!" or "You're nuts!"

DENIS BRIAN: But as a psychiatrist, wouldn't you avoid using such an expression in a tense wartime situation, especially as Hemingway *might* have been cracking up?

MEYER MASKIN: You must remember I was practicing before going into a combat area. I had been working at a general hospital in Indianapolis before this position as divisional psychiatrist, for which I'd volunteered, by the way. That's not my style: I don't give people ominous prognoses.

DENIS BRIAN: And it wouldn't have been an angry retort, as Walton thought?

MEYER MASKIN: I don't remember that we got involved in enough conversations for me to get angry. Look, I went looking for him like looking for a national monument, out of sheer curiosity. I had no designs. This was not part of my life plan.

DENIS BRIAN: If Walton remembers it vividly the event is probably true, isn't it, but not as dramatic or as emotional an event as described in the books?

MEYER MASKIN: I'm willing to accept the fact that I may have said some of these things, or that they were said. If I'd had a sick relative, or if I had Hemingway's career and a suicidal father, I could have reacted, to any sentence spoken, differently. Since it was not part of my background and since I was a pro at this, that tends to routinize it a bit. I don't mean it makes me callous or indifferent, but these are not extraordinary events in my professional life. The first time I saw an operation in medical school I almost vomited. But after a while these become pretty routinized things. I was not an intimate. I did not discuss personal biography with anyone and therefore my statements weren't particularly measured. I could have been annoyed. I remember one episode that annoyed me. Hemingway got a bottle of wine and pulled out the cork with his teeth, took a sip, spat it out, threw the bottle against the wall and smashed it and made some obscenity. The wine was sour. I don't like that kind of behavior. Now I'm giving you a subjective reaction. That event had nothing to do with me. I also reacted a little bit, having heard from General Barton that he was apprehensive about having Hemingway around because he had to protect him. Since it was as miserable as Walton described it, I vaguely remember asking Hemingway something but I don't have a good conversational memory for exact dialogue. Everyone I talked to who was there hated it, myself included. We were miserable, especially that winter which was the worst time of the war. We were absolutely immobilized by the Germans because they'd mined the whole forest. Their artillery was exact, our casualties were enormous, and there was a lot of frostbite. The first thing on everybody's mind was: "When is this going to end so we can get out of here?" So it was remarkable to see people who volunteered to be there when they didn't have to be there.

DENIS BRIAN: This puts it in a much more reasonable context than the mystery of one man saying you said something which you deny having said.

MEYER MASKIN: When I read it in Baker's book it sounded much more melodramatic than anything I remembered. It may well be that these guys dramatized the event. We all process everything in terms of our own biographical data. And I was processing it as just a superficial conversation. They were processing it in terms of the events in their lives. But also I was meeting a man who even then was a myth. And that was another reaction: he was playing infantry soldier and he looked too old.

DENIS BRIAN: Were you drinking, too?

MEYER MASKIN: I don't drink. And you could use that if you will, that I'm prejudicial to drinkers, so to speak. But I can only add that my wife drinks. I once described myself as an unprincipled teetotaler. My not drinking is not a cause.

DENIS BRIAN: The Baker book has Hemingway saying of you, in response to his comment that he had sexual intercourse with cats: "The little bastard was fascinated. His eyes were bugging out." Weren't you insulted?

MEYER MASKIN: No, I was amused. Even that didn't excite me. I read it as an insulting remark, but not literally. I have patients who say all sorts of things to me.

DENIS BRIAN: But Hemingway wasn't a patient.

MEYER MASKIN: What I mean is I'm calloused enough so that I don't insult that easily. Probably what I must have done with that, if it happened, was not to take it literally, and simply to wonder what the hell he was so angry about. I don't think Hemingway knew me well enough that I would take any of this as serious appraisal of my competence. Therefore my reaction would be, "What's bugging him to exaggerate this thing to that degree?" Obviously, he was an angry man at this point.

Hemingway Confronts Martha Gellhorn

DENIS BRIAN: After his "confrontation" with Dr. Maskin, Hemingway faced one with Martha Gellhorn. Although they were now estranged and he had been living with Mary Welsh during several stays in Paris, Martha Gellhorn appeared at the command post of the 22nd Infantry on Christmas Eve, 1944.

C. T. LANHAM: She was a bitch from start to finish and every member of my staff who met her—and most did—thought so, too. I turned over my room to her and went out and slept in this icy trailer, and almost froze to death when I did get to sleep that night. You never had a thank-you, you never had anything from her. They hated her guts. She was rude, just plain country rude. I was sitting next to her in the jeep. I always let Hemingway ride in the front seat next to the driver. She went on in French thinking I couldn't understand it. Well, I'd gone to school at the Sorbonne in Paris in the 1930s, so I could speak French somewhat. She'd taken on what Hemingway always called "a big Christmas counterattack." He gave her hell and really made her just shrivel up when he turned on her and said: "Now you've gotten through with all the privacies in your life speaking in French, it might interest you to know that Buck speaks better French than you do!" That shut her up.

MARTHA GELLHORN: I'm sure that every word of Buck Lanham's is absolutely true. E.H. forced me to visit him at "his" division during the Battle of the Bulge. I had long left him, but we were not divorced and he had legal rights as it were to harass me. The form it took was to make such scenes that, from embarrassment, I did what he wanted me to do. He then stage-managed that disagreeable visit to put me totally in the wrong. The object, I think, was to justify his affair with Mary Welsh, of which I knew nothing. The division was in reserve and E.H. went on about how dangerous it all was, and since I'm a lifelong hater of lying—the apocryphal story being told under my eyes—I was far from jolly or pleased.

MILTON WOLFF: Hemingway accused her of some damn thing with a Polish officer and she claimed it wasn't true—while he was screwing around all over the place. Martha was very bitter about the breakup with Hemingway. She said she had bought the farm in Cuba and this and that, and she had to give it up.

DENIS BRIAN: Hemingway had more to worry about than his disintegrating marriage. He heard that his eldest son, John, who had been working for the OSS, was missing in action. In a letter to Archibald MacLeish, Ernest said that the news plunged him into a deep depression for several days.

JOHN HEMINGWAY: I was on an OSS mission in October 1944, with a Captain Justin Green, who was a neurologist, and a French partisan who we were hoping to infiltrate through the lines. But the Germans heard us and opened up. The French fellow was badly gutshot and died a couple of days later. Green was wounded in the foot and I was wounded in the shoulder and right arm. I had five bullet wounds and a bunch of grenade fragments. We were lying around when an Austrian lieutenant who spoke French looked at my dogtags and said, "Sprechen ze Deutsch?" And I said, "Non, je parle francais." Then he spoke French. He asked, "Were you ever in Schroons?" I said, "Yes, when I was a little boy." He said, "Do you remember anyone named Kitty?" I said, "Yes, she was my nurse." He said, "She was my girlfriend." He had known Papa and my mother and me when I was two years old, nineteen years before. He said, "Lieutenant Hemingway, do not be nervous. I know who you are and I am a great admirer of your father's work." That's all he said. We told our interrogators that we were lost and that the Frenchman had volunteered to show us the way back to our lines and he obviously didn't know the way. They bought that. I was a little nervous when I was taken prisoner that the Germans might treat me more harshly—now that I had been identified by the lieutenant—because of Papa's reputation as an antifascist. I had read, particularly in his forward to an anthology of war stories, *Men at War,* his recommendations about what should be done to SS men if we were ever in a position to do it, including, I think, castration or sterilization. I made several attempts to escape from the prison camp but was always caught. Within days of my capture there was a counterattack in the same area and the Austrian who had been my nurse's boyfriend was taken prisoner. They obtained details from him as to where I was likely to have been sent. When my father was told where I was probably held captive, he wanted to lead a rescue attempt.

WILLIAM WALTON: There was a lot of talk of trying to rescue John. It was serious *talk*, but there was always an awful lot of bombast going around our group. Derring-do. I guess there was a lot of derring but not much do. Ernest was often, as you can well imagine, living out his own legend.

C. T. LANHAM: If Ernest had had a suitable force to go with him and adequate support, he was just the type to try it. But I can't imagine anybody that would turn over, say, a battalion to him or a regiment for that purpose.

JOHN HEMINGWAY: As it turned out this Austrian lieutenant who'd spoken to me in French spoke English, too. The people who'd captured him discussed some things in front of him and he interrupted them—Papa told me this later—and he suggested that they not try to rescue me because my wounds were quite serious and it was unlikely I'd be able to accompany my rescuers, which was true.

DENIS BRIAN: General Lanham, you've called Hemingway the bravest man you've known. Was his continuing to eat his meal and refusing to wear a steel helmet or follow others to a cellar during heavy shelling an example of his courage?

C. T. LANHAM: No, that was an example of jackassery. On this business, the first 88 shells came through the wall of the place about three feet above our heads, I'd say. Of course, they might have exploded as they hit the wall, instead of going right through, and then they would have knocked everybody off in the place. It turned out—we later knocked them off—that they couldn't lower the gun. So Ernest may have felt that was why the shells went over our heads. Ernesto was battle-wise. He was just smart as hell on the battlefield. He didn't normally stick his neck out in these ridiculous things he's widely credited with doing. He went to a lot of jackass places. He went with me. He went in places he shouldn't have been, but by and large he knew what he was doing. He could have been killed in any of them, but he figured the odds were the other way.

DENIS BRIAN: Was he especially brave in Hurtgen forest?

C. T. LANHAM: I wrote to him about it after the war [May 7, 1946]: "You will be pleased to learn that our regiment received its second citation last week, the second one coming from Hurtgen. You were with us, or rather ahead of us throughout all of Hurtgen. Your influence on the break-through operation as far as the 22nd was concerned may not have been too heavy but by God you furnished just about three-quarters of the moral force of Hurtgen. My first on both citations turned on you. You shared in everything the Double Deucer did with damned few exceptions." And I wrote again [on June 15, 1948]: "One more thing Papa—something you gave me on the eve of Hurtgen and something I have never forgotten. I didn't have black ass [Hemingway's expression for being scared or de-pressed] on the eve of Hurtgen—probably because I had confidence and didn't know how bloody awful it was going to be on regiment, but I did have a bad feeling re catching one but was not unduly worried about it. Think sooner or later every guy in a lot of fighting gets that feeling—at least the Maskins say so and my experience in this war makes me think guys do—all of them. And how I mentioned the feeling to you the day before we jumped off after a few drinks of whatever we were drinking then. . . . Three or four hours later without any reference to me at all you brought up the old craperoo of 'premonitions' re something else. . . . And let me have it just where I needed it without once indicating dissertation was for me. It was good stuff. It was correct stuff. I have always been grateful to you for doing it and doing it the way you did do it. I never had any more 'premonitions' believe it or not—not once."

JOHN HEMINGWAY: It was quite a space of time when I met Papa after the war. He had already gone back to the States and to Cuba. That was when I first met Mary. He was out at the Havana airport to meet me. My wounds were pretty well healed by then. They were very impressive look-ing but not terribly damaging—all fleshy parts. We talked under the afflu-ence of ilcohol, you know, several times about what had happened to us and I'm sure I stretched my experiences and he probably stretched his a little.

C. T. LANHAM: People have told me what he told them about his wartime adventures, people of the utmost veracity, like David Bruce—and I know what Hemingway told me—and they're totally different [laughs]. It may have been the creative juices boiling in him. These things boiled around in his head all the time and then they fermented, and eventually a story came out.

IRWIN SHAW: Still, there's no doubt about Hemingway being very coura-geous.

DENIS BRIAN: I'm trying to find out what he actually did. In a 1950 let-ter to writer Arthur Mizener, which apparently he didn't mail because he thought it was too violent, he wrote of his killing 122 people and mentioned that the one that most distressed him was a soldier in German uniform riding toward the Nazi escape route to Aachen. Mr. Walton, were you in this area then?

WILLIAM WALTON: Sure.

DENIS BRIAN: Hemingway writes that he shot the German soldier with an M1 through the spine and the bullet came out through the liver. The young man was about his son Patrick's age, in his early twenties. Ernest says he laid him out as comfortably as he could and gave him his own morphine tablets. Is there any element of truth in that?

WILLIAM WALTON: I don't actually know but I'm doubtful. I was not with him through any events like this.

DENIS BRIAN: This is one of 122 he claimed to have killed.

WILLIAM WALTON: I think that's utter balderdash. He's fantasizing in one of his bad periods down in Cuba probably.[1]

DENIS BRIAN: What puzzles me is that he led such an adventurous life and had so many exciting true experiences. . . .

WILLIAM WALTON: Why did he need to embroider? He lost track of what was fantasy and what was real. I think at the time he probably believed these stories, but at the end it isn't really important. It's an index of what his mental state was but has nothing to do with his art.

DENIS BRIAN: Except that he said writing letters eased his way into writing fiction.

WILLIAM WALTON: Then it was part of the process perhaps.

DENIS BRIAN: In a letter to Scribner, Ernest wrote about shooting a German through the head and his brains coming out through his nostrils. Was he just showing off, Leicester?

LEICESTER HEMINGWAY: I think so. I did not know of any such incident taking place. A similar situation developed at Fourth Division while I was up there, but Ernest had nothing to do with it. It was something that happened at night and I was briefly involved and found all the brains in a helmet.

DENIS BRIAN: You didn't do the shooting?

LEICESTER HEMINGWAY: No. We found the body, the brains and so forth and I told Papa all about it and he was most impressed. And I think it maybe became part of shall we say his descriptive conversation?

[1] In postwar letters to Archibald MacLeish and Bernard Berenson, Ernest said he had killed twenty-six "Krauts" including a seventeen-year-old boy.

DENIS BRIAN: John, was your father eager to hear of your adventures?

JOHN HEMINGWAY: Oh, yes. They were coming out in bits and pieces. I think partly because of the starvation diet as a prisoner, details were very hard to remember then and even now aren't all that clear. We had an Australian lieutenant-colonel with us, a surgeon, who had been captured at Tobruk. He was a very fine old fellow and made sure the Geneva Convention was adhered to. He used to tell us, "I say, you chaps, you may have a bit of trouble with your memory as the diet is rather short on phosphorus. You may find yourselves repeating things. Don't let it worry you. As soon as you get back on a decent diet you won't have any problems." Then he'd go out and come back about half an hour later and repeat the whole thing. After I was operated on in Commar, Alsace, two of us were evacuated three weeks later to a prison hospital, accompanied by two old guards. I made a go for it on the way but I nearly split all my wounds open, shaking. It was freezing cold, too, in late November. A column from our Fourth Armored Division came into our prison camp and in essence liberated us. But we were still sixty miles behind the forward-most position of our troops and with quite a bit of the German army between. One of the big reasons for this attempt was to rescue General Patton's son-in-law, Colonel Waters, a fine officer, who was with us. There was a secret radio in camp that kept contact with the Allies. Anyway, there was a firefight and we took off. That night we rode with our rescuers and hid at several road blocks where various vehicles were hit. I was in the lead tank and it was hit in the front by one of these Panzer things, and I was knocked off the back. A couple of friends and I decided it wasn't a healthy place and took off on our own for a week before we were recaptured. We were taken to a big camp outside Nuremberg for about a week and a half and they began to evacuate everybody to the so-called redoubt area. During a ten-day march the same fellows and I escaped with an old German guard for a couple of days—and got caught again. But this time we were caught by kids with submachine guns who were very frightened. And I tell you, that was very spooky.

DENIS BRIAN: Did you say you escaped *with* a guard?

JOHN HEMINGWAY: Yes. Some of those guards were sixty-five to seventy years old and this one was close to his village. We asked him if he was going to go home, sort of kidding around. He had been talking about it. We said, "We won't implicate you." So he helped us get away.

DENIS BRIAN: John arrived at the Finca with Gregory and Patrick in June

1945. That was when he first met his father's future, fourth, and last wife, Mary Welsh. The couple married in March of the following year in a civil ceremony in Havana. Winston Guest was among the witnesses. Both Ernest and Mary were tense, and their sharp wisecracks escalated into a bitter verbal fight. Mary packed her bags prepared to call the marriage off after less than a day as Mrs. Hemingway. But she was tired and decided to wait until morning, when she changed her mind and stayed—for fifteen exciting and turbulent years. Two weeks after his marriage, Hemingway received a letter from his mother complaining that she had only learned of his fourth marriage through the newspapers. She hoped that *this time* he would have God's blessing, told him she had never stopped praying for him to have a great awakening before it was too late, and in her final sentence informed him that God's patience was infinite, embracing even the undeserving.

DENIS BRIAN: At about this time, he wrote a letter to his sister Carol Gardner, from whom he'd been estranged for thirteen years. The letter was never mailed, and went unknown until it was published in Norberto Fuentes's *Hemingway in Cuba*. Mrs. Gardner, did you know that in his house in Cuba there's a letter Ernest wrote to you in 1945 but never mailed? It's reproduced in the book *Hemingway in Cuba*.

CAROL GARDNER: I'd love to hear it.

DENIS BRIAN: Here it is over forty year late: He starts by calling you Beefy. He thanks you for your letters and photos, says his two younger sons are in school and that Bumby is a wounded prisoner of war. He says he liked having you as a kid sister and admits he bungled things badly but the only way out would have been to have shot John Gardner—which wasn't practical in New York.

CAROL GARDNER: [laughs]. Oh, my!

DENIS BRIAN: He admits that it's childish but says he hates John as much as he does Nazis and his feeling is as strong as something in a book by William Faulkner. He goes on to say that Leicester has grown up to be a good, brave guy and well liked. He says he could never look Leicester in the eyes because he looked so much like your mother but he could be friendly with him by keeping his eyes shut.

CAROL GARDNER: Les didn't really look like Mother, except he was blonde and blue-eyed like her, and the rest of us were darker.

DENIS BRIAN: He explains his breakup with Martha as his need for a wife in bed and not a competitor reporting some war. He says she had great talent but he taught her to write well in her own style and to shoot; and though he had loved her very much got cured of her and now hoped to have a happy marriage with Mary Welsh. And he writes of a letter from his mother curious to know who Mary Welsh is and assuring him that no matter how little he deserves it, God will look after him.

CAROL GARDNER: I'd love to have a copy of that.

DENIS BRIAN: I'll send it to you. I take it that you remember Ernest with love?

CAROL GARDNER: Of course. He was my hero, don't forget.

DENIS BRIAN: How did you see his two wives without seeing him?

CAROL GARDNER: I saw his first wife, Hadley, after they were divorced, when she came to visit us in Oak Park and she had little Bumby with her. I sometimes corresponded with her and liked her very much. Pauline was very friendly and kind and when I was living in Florida she invited me down to Key West—when Ernest was living in Cuba and was remarried to Martha Gellhorn. Pauline had always been very kind to me and treated me like a younger sister. When I went to Europe she helped me buy clothes and not only gave me the money, but gave me good advice. She knew what I'd need.

DENIS BRIAN: What do you think of his tall stories? Although he had many exciting experiences and did many brave things, he also told tremendous lies about things he'd never done.

CAROL GARDNER: Don't you think that's part of being a fiction writer? Everybody takes his work as though it was the gospel truth and it's ridiculous. He was writing stories. And I think when the conversation lagged, he made up stories. I think everybody is mistaken to imagine his stories are all autobiographical, because I know for a fact some of the people he wrote about—that little Prudence Boulton was a most unattractive little girl. I knew her and that Indian camp there smelled terribly. Ernest didn't enjoy going there much, but I suppose in retrospect he could make a story out of it.[1]

DENIS BRIAN: He wrote that she was his first sexual experience.

CAROL GARDNER [laughs]: I don't believe it. I don't believe it.

---

[1] In his story "Fathers and Sons" Hemingway wrote of Nick's [Ernest's] sexual encounter with Trudy [Prudy] in which she does "first what no one has ever done better."

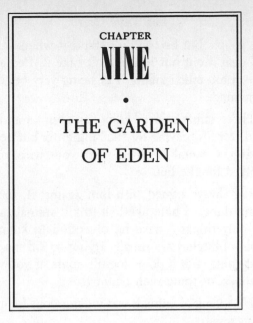

CHAPTER

NINE

•

THE GARDEN
OF EDEN

DENIS BRIAN: General Lanham thought Hemingway was magnificent in wartime, but in peacetime could be insufferable.

C. Z. GUEST [who married his friend Winston Guest]: I can't say lousy things about people and I won't. You can say lousy things about anybody in the world, even Jesus Christ.

DENIS BRIAN: But everyone admits there was a dark side to Hemingway, even those close to him.

C. Z. GUEST: To tell you quite honestly, I didn't like his character. Winston and I got married soon after World War II, and that's when I first met Papa. I feel quite detached about him. My husband adored him. They were great friends. Hemingway was a terribly strong man physically and he admired Winston because, I think, Winston was as strong as he was. There aren't that number of people big and strong in the world. I mean, when they come in, you say, "My God, look at the size of him!" I was in my early twenties when I met Papa and I didn't like him very much; I thought there was something cruel about him, a cruel streak. He used to needle people but he couldn't stand it whenever anyone teased him. He could dish it out but he couldn't take it. Perhaps he was cruel because he'd seen too much killing. I'm being very honorable about my thoughts about him.

DENIS BRIAN: He certainly enjoyed killing as a hunter and enjoyed watching bullfights. As for his praying for the bullfighter before the fights as he did, I understand, General Lanham, that your wife, on the contrary, would have prayed for the bull.

C. T. LANHAM: I always argued with him against it, too. I said, "I just can't bear killing things. I hate like hell to kill animals, a bird, anything like that. The only things I have no objection to killing are people—because the sons-of-bitches are usually trying to kill me. That's an altogether different thing. But a dove doesn't come at you with a gun, or a grenade or bazooka, or some such damn thing.

DENIS BRIAN: His killing of animals was incongruous for a man who loved cats and dogs so much.

C. T. LANHAM: Oh yes, absolutely. Anybody who laid a glove on any of his Cocksies as he called them, or old Blackie, his dog—hell, he would have killed them on the spot. When Blackie became virtually blind, Ernest always used the same soap to wash himself so that Blackie would know his scent and not be confused.

DENIS BRIAN: Your wife thought Hemingway was a male chauvinist pig.

C. T. LANHAM: My wife was not a good judge of Ernesto. She went down with me after the war to the Finca. She had never met Hemingway, he had never seen her before. And she got into a hell of a fight with him over some political views he expressed. She was furious. She weighed 124 pounds and 123 were straight wildcat and she turned to him and said: "You know, all you need is your umbrella. You fit the role perfectly." She was referring to British Prime Minister Neville Chamberlain who carried an umbrella, appeasing Hitler at Munich. And, God, Hemingway turned blood red. I thought he was going to kill her. He reached over and grabbed a bottle of wine and just glared at her and shut up, like that. From that time on he always had a reason when we got together—it was just going to be men and sorry, he couldn't ask my wife Pete. She just didn't like him. He wasn't her dish of tea.

C. Z. GUEST: In a way I think he was a sad man, but like him or not he was a star. When he went to restaurants, people crowded around for his autograph, and when he went to Abercrombie and Fitch the whole place was in an uproar. Women were nuts about him. He used to stay at the Sherry Netherland in New York and Leland Hayward's wife, Slim, and Dick Cooper's wife, both beautiful and bright women, were there and he obviously enjoyed their company and they enjoyed his. I could never forgive him for what he did. I was appalled after he almost shot Winston. He was standing behind Winston firing his gun over Winston's head and almost hitting him. It wasn't even his turn. It was during an international shooting match in Cuba. I expect he'd been drinking. He had a fabulous life and was a very competitive man and then, of course, he hit his head many times. That's very important. I've had several concussions from riding and competing, though nothing like he had. But you can't drink alcohol like that once you've hit your head very hard. Obviously he had a kind side to him, too. He was admired. He had to have something nice about him. He had something about him that was magnetic. You can't be a shit, you know, and be admired. Excuse my language. I suppose when people get older they change.

C. T. LANHAM: Before he wrote a book he'd go into training. That is, he wouldn't take a drink until noon. We'd be down there in Cuba and he asked us to come when he was ready to work on a book. I got down several times and spent a couple of weeks with him. He'd swim forty laps in the morning and forty laps in the afternoon in a huge pool. And he'd look at his watch every two laps, waiting for that clock to move around. When it was eleven on the dot, you could see his major domo come out of the Finca up on the hill and start down with this big tray and a huge shaker of martinis, what he called "Montgomerys." And old Hemingstein would look at his watch and say, "Well, Buck, it's eleven o'clock. What the hell, it's twelve in Miami, let's have a drink." And he would. But it was real discipline for him to go that long in the morning without a drink. He was disciplined about his work.

DENIS BRIAN: By the summer of 1946 Hemingway had completed many hundreds of pages of a novel titled *The Garden of Eden.*

LEICESTER HEMINGWAY: We all know what it's about. It's about a guy and gal changing situations.

DENIS BRIAN: Perhaps that's why Truman Capote in his book *Music for Chameleons* calls Ernest a closet everything.

LEICESTER HEMINGWAY: I know it. And I personally would like to quietly strangle Capote. Ernesto, I am willing to bet my life on it, was not homosexual. But he did have an enormous ability to care for both males and females, not in an erotic way but in a "You are a fellow human being," way. And in this, when he cared for somebody, he cared for them as completely as you can care for a fellow human being. Every writer tries to crawl into the skin of other human beings and to be them while he is writing from their point of view. That explains *The Garden of Eden*.

DENIS BRIAN: Here's a UPI account: *"The Garden of Eden* also deals with the themes of bisexuality, having Bourne and his wife attracted to the same woman, and androgyny, as the couple spends evenings pretending to exchange sexual identities." And Peter Griffin, author of *Along With Youth: Hemingway, the Early Years*, maintains that sexual behavior in the novel has its basis in Hemingway's life. "I know from conversations with Mary Hemingway that Ernest was involved in androgyny in more than one of his marriages," said Griffin.[1]

WILLIAM WALTON: Who was that? I haven't any idea. I would doubt it. Who knows? You never know what another man does in bed. This is a book. This is fiction. Don't take it too seriously. I think he should be given great marks for experimenting this way, that late in his career.

DENIS BRIAN: How did *The Garden of Eden* impress you?

WILLIAM WALTON: I'm glad the book was printed but it's not one of his major books. One can detect the origins of both women so clearly embodying certain characteristics of his first two wives.

DENIS BRIAN: Not of his sister-in-law Jinny?

WILLIAM WALTON: Well she's the most lesbian of the lot, but none of them is pure anybody. But, for instance, the destruction of the manuscripts in the novel is clearly based on Hadley's loss of his manuscripts.

DENIS BRIAN: Do you think both wives had lesbian tendencies?

WILLIAM WALTON: Oh no, not necessarily. Pauline maybe a little bit, but nothing serious. It's just imagination on Ernest's part, playing on an idea of a man and woman changing sexual roles.

DENIS BRIAN: Here's a synopsis of the book by William Robertson, book editor of the *Miami Herald:* "At its simplest Ernest Hemingway's *The*

[1]Curiously, at the Hemingway Conference at Northeastern University in May 1982, Patrick Hemingway said he was never allowed to visit his Grandmother Grace because, his father told him, she was androgynous. Another mystery is why Clarence Hemingway banned Ruth Arnold, the housekeeper, from his home as a danger to his marriage. After Clarence's death, Arnold became Grace Hemingway's companion.

Garden of Eden comes down to this; boy meets girl, girl becomes boy; girl goes crazy; boy meets another girl."

WILLIAM WALTON [laughs.]: It's *reductio ad absurdum.* You could say the book was far too full of recipes for drinks, for instance. There's so much emphasis on drinking and the interesting thing is nobody ever gets drunk. Ernest would never admit he was drunk and anyone who drinks that much all day would be ossified in the evening. None of the characters have real depth which he achieved in other books. We even have descriptions of their clothes, but we don't have anything about their ideas, or conversations outside of a little dialogue.

TOM JENKS [Scribner's editor of *The Garden of Eden,* quoted in the *San Francisco Examiner,* Dec. 18, 1985]: Those people who have scorned Hemingway for his machismo and a kind of brutality in his public life will have to reassess him because of the tenderness and vulnerability he displays in this book.

WILLIAM WALTON: That's certainly true.

DENIS BRIAN: Is it a reflection of himself?

WILLIAM WALTON: Oh, yes. He worked on the book at many intervals in his life, so it doesn't reflect one period. It does reflect his memories.

DENIS BRIAN: The publisher, Charles Scribner, Jr., would naturally be partial to the novel. He says, "It's really one of the richest novels I've ever read depicting writing."

WILLIAM WALTON: That's a thought. But I also felt that the character of the writer was so different when he went off to the writing room, and in a way we didn't participate in the mysteries of his creation. So that the reality was only in his life with these two women. This is a book. This is fiction. Don't take it too seriously.

EARL ROVIT: It's unfortunate it was commercially published because it's a rotten book. There are lovely things in it and the business of this unorthodox *ménage à trois,* and the haircuts, and what not. All struck me as personal material that a writer is getting rid of for his own therapy and is unable to universalize or make representative of anything other than his own peculiar warts and whims.

DENIS BRIAN: Did the novel surprise you, Mr. Plimpton?

GEORGE PLIMPTON: No, it's all in that short story "The Sea Change," that he wrote much earlier. It's something of a surprise to me that no one has made the connection between the two.

DENIS BRIAN: Anthony Burgess says there was a great deal more of the feminine and of his mother in Hemingway than people realized.

GEORGE PLIMPTON: I never knew his mother. She was a very tough bird. His mother was hardly a feminine person.

DENIS BRIAN: The novel showed an unexpected change from his anti-homosexual stance to a much more relaxed, even sympathetic attitude toward a lesbian. Jeffrey Meyers in his biography of Hemingway reveals that after she and Ernest divorced, Pauline had lesbian relationships.

MORLEY CALLAGHAN: I didn't know that. But I've heard it about so many women, I'm not surprised.

DENIS BRIAN: Hemingway indicated another source for "The Sea Change" and *The Garden of Eden* in a conversation with Hotchner. Ernest said that in his younger days at the Bar Basque, in Saint-Jean-de-Luz on the Atlantic coast close to Spain, he witnessed a quarrel between his pal Charles Wertenbaker and Wertenbaker's beautiful girlfriend. According to Hemingway the beautiful young woman left Wertenbaker for another beautiful young woman.

AARON LATHAM [author of *Crazy Sundays: F. Scott Fitzgerald in Hollywood*]: Hemingway's hero and heroine experiment with reversing sex roles. Catherine, the heroine, wants to become a man, and she wants David, the hero, to become a woman. She calls him "Catherine." And for some reason he calls her "Pete." [The name of General Lanham's first wife.] They talk about what they are doing as being "shameless." He feels guilty. She says she got the idea from a figure in the Rodin Museum—a statue which is half man and half woman. David worries about how easily Catherine changes from a woman into a man and then back into a woman again. He believes she enjoys "corrupting" him. And he is concerned about how easily he is corrupted. Of course, trouble invades Hemingway's "Garden." Short-haired David has an affair with long-haired Barbara. And then short-haired Catherine begins to crack up. One is left wondering if perhaps Ernest Hemingway and his first wife did experiment with exchanging sex roles way back in the twenties. If so, it would mean that Hemingway was fascinated by the woman in man and the man in woman from the very beginning of his career as a writer. And the experiments, which Ernest began with his first wife, were evidently continued with his last. On December 20, 1953, in a playful mood he took over her diary and wrote: "She loves me to be her girls, which I love to be. . . . Since I have never cared for any man and dislike any tactile contact with men . . . I love feeling the embrace of Mary which came to me as something quite new and outside all tribal law." In sorting out all these matters, Mary Hemingway wrote in [her autobiography] *How It Was:* "In our mutual sensory delights we were smoothly interlocking parts of a single engine, the big cogwheel and the smaller cogwheel. . . . Maybe we were androgynous."[1] Ernest Hemingway turns out to have been the kind of man who dreamed—and perhaps more than dreamed—about going out and shooting lions all day and coming home and making androgynous love. His personality was composed of unresolved opposites. He was not less than but rather *more* than a he-man.[2]

DENIS BRIAN: What was your impression of *The Garden of Eden,* Mr. Griffin?

PETER GRIFFIN: I have researched it, wanting to immerse myself in the nineteen twenties, for the upcoming second volume of my Hemingway biography. The manuscript of *The Garden of Eden* is almost sixteen hundred pages. It's incredible, much more audacious and feeling than his other works with the exception of *A Farewell to Arms.* What creeps in and spoils the published version is that the editor, Tom Jenks, had a conception of Hemingway both stylistically and of the man from the Carlos Baker biography, and so he produces a novel he thought Hemingway should have written. I'm told that Jenks is a hell of a nice guy and I've great respect for him because the manuscript is a mess and Jenks came up with a coherent novel. But it does not represent the whole *Garden of Eden* at all. It presents perversions or the *ménage à trois* as an enemy of creativity. And that isn't true in the whole novel manuscript. In that, it is much more subtle and much more exploratory. It's fascinating. It would have been wonderful if they'd published the whole damn thing and said, "Look, it's an unfinished work. Take it for what it is." There's stuff on aesthetics, on writing and painting that are wonderful. And they are left out of the published version.

DENIS BRIAN: Some critics say the book gives ammunition to those who think he was a latent homosexual.

WILLIAM WALTON: I don't think we'll dignify that kind of talk by seriously batting it back and forth.

[1] Mary Welsh Hemingway, *How It Was,* Alfred A. Knopf, Inc., 1976.

[2] Aaron Latham, "A Farewell to Machismo," *New York Times Magazine,* October 16, 1977, Latham read the manuscript of *The Garden of Eden* before its publication.

DENIS BRIAN: Would you say that if he was a latent homosexual, he was very latent?

WILLIAM WALTON: He sure was, right down to his shoes. But that kind of analysis of any sexuality is so boring.

DENIS BRIAN: Hemingway, who spoke and wrote of deviates with scorn and revulsion, now learned that a homosexual had been successfully impersonating him for years. The man, the psychotic son of a U.S. admiral, had toured American lecture circuits masquerading as Ernest, forging his autograph, and even entertaining young men in the Explorers Club in Manhattan.

CARLOS BAKER: It infuriated Hemingway; but he was never able to catch up with the impostor.

DENIS BRIAN: His friend, Archibald MacLeish, was angered, too, by speculation that because Ernest enjoyed war and to have a gun in his hand he was compensating for some sexual defect or inadequacy. In defense of his masculinity, Ernest had already wrestled with Max Eastman on the floor of their editor's office. Now, after years of war he was anxious to go to earth and concentrate on his novel. But would-be biographers and interviewers threatened to disrupt his work.

CHAPTER

TEN

·

HEMINGWAY
HUNTERS

**Malcolm Cowley, Irwin Shaw, Lillian Ross, Philip Young,
Charles Fenton, George Plimpton**

The hunter had become the hunted.

*At first he resisted most interviewers and all would-be biographers bent
on bringing him back alive. For a gregarious, outspoken, four-letter-word
man, he was unexpectedly reticent, even secretive about his own life. He
sidestepped personal questions from friends, as he had years before when
Scott Fitzgerald asked him if he had slept with Hadley before they were
married, and Hemingway had responded, "I don't remember."*

*Until 1948, when he was approaching fifty, he kept the most dangerous
at bay with threats. When ambushed by interviewers, especially on foreign
soil, he gave outrageous accounts of his life and loves he knew they could
not use. He had been a reporter; he knew the score. The bold and brash
he blasted with scatalogical dumdum bullets.*

Hemingway had good reasons for running scared: to avoid feeding

193

gossips with ammunition, to protect himself from libel suits, to preserve autobiographical material for his own use.

He had already been stung by malicious gossip. Publisher Robert McAlmon called him "a fairy" who had beaten his first wife, and deserted her to marry a lesbian. In fact, McAlmon was the homosexual or bisexual, and an alcoholic into the bargain. It was he who had married a lesbian, Bryher Ellerman. Bryher, a wealthy heiress, had left him to live with the wife of author Richard Aldington, Hilda Doolittle. Hilda was a former fiancée of Hemingway's mentor, Ezra Pound. Hemingway had responded to McAlmon's slurs by punching him in the jaw and calling him a half-assed, fairy ass-licking, fake-husband.

Then there had been the brouhaha over Ernest's first novel, The Sun Also Rises, a roman à clef, in which key characters had angrily protested his view of them. He feared that interviewers and biographers might ferret out more real-life models in his fiction—and there were plenty—who in turn would take him to court for libel or invasion of privacy.

Finally, he believed that living authors had a right to their own lives, for their own purposes and profit. Why give it away?

But all these motives could be expressed as one overriding need: to preserve the myth.

To the hunters closing in on their prey Hemingway resembled Lawrence of Arabia in seeming to back into the limelight. Why did he, for instance, avoid them and yet befriend gossip columnists, of all people, and bartenders? The answer was that he only confided in those he could tame or trust.

MALCOLM COWLEY

Malcolm Cowley was the first to run him to ground—in 1948. They were the same generation, with similar backgrounds. Hemingway and Cowley were both doctors' sons from the Midwest. After meeting briefly in Paris in the twenties, they had maintained an amiable correspondence. From 1930 to 1940, Cowley had been literary editor of the New Republic, which generally reviewed Hemingway with intelligent enthusiasm. In the 1940s, Cowley was a respected poet and perceptive literary critic and literary historian. He admired Hemingway's writing almost as much as Faulkner's, had read all Hemingway's published work and had informed and mostly favorable opinions of it. Cowley was known as a man of integrity who would not betray a confidence or, equally important, probe too painfully.

"By now he has earned the right to be taken for what he is, with his great faults and greater virtues," Cowley wrote in The Portable Hemingway

[*Viking, 1944*], *which he put together "with his narrowness, his power, his always open eyes, his stubborn, chip-on-the-shoulder honesty, his nightmares, his rituals for escaping them, and his sense of an inner and outer world that for twenty years were moving together toward the same disaster."*

Hemingway was lonely in Cuba after all the camaraderie during World War II. He told Cowley so in one of his occasional letters, and said he missed having someone around to whom he could talk shop. Who better than Cowley?

Life magazine made it possible. They'd finance Cowley's trip to Cuba if he could come back with what amounted to a minibiography of Hemingway. All Cowley had to do was get Hemingway to drop his guard.

MALCOLM COWLEY: In my letter to him I said it would help me out a great deal to have an interview with him in *Life,* and that the money I'd get for it would help to send my son, Rob, to school at Exeter, where he finally went—though I didn't need the money that badly and I wasn't very insistent. Ernest was a great deal more impressed by his generosity in agreeing to the interview than I was.

DENIS BRIAN: Although he did have a justified reputation for helping those in need.

MALCOLM COWLEY: That's true. So I went to Cuba in March 1948, and took my wife and son with me.

ROBERT COWLEY: I was thirteen then and we went down to Cuba during my winter vacation from grade school. It was the first time I had been in an airplane and it took us most of the day to get to Miami. Then we flew to Havana, taking off about sunset, an extraordinarily beautiful flight. You could see right down to the bottom of the ocean. You could look over the Everglades, see a small road and a single car going along. It was nothing like the way Florida's built up today.

The first meeting with Hemingway was at Havana airport during the Carnivale and he was waiting for us after customs. He was a celebrity there so he got us through customs in a jiffy. I remember this extraordinarily attentive man, who had the beard and the white open shirt in the best Havana manner, driving us at night through the Carnivale, past some of the most appalling slums I've ever seen. He treated my father as a great friend. They'd known one another in Paris and had corresponded. Relationships were always cordial; there was never any nervousness. We stayed in that marvelous hotel Ambos Mundos, in fact we lived in the room where I believe he wrote some of *A Farewell to Arms.* It was a very

European hotel. The old city of Havana reminded me of Palma, Spain: it was beautiful; houses built around courtyards and all that. We went out to the Hemingways every day of our stay of about ten days. One of the great old Lincoln Continental convertibles would come in and pick us up. The house was about twelve miles south of Havana.

MALCOLM COWLEY: He was very nice about giving the interview and we talked for a long time. This was all on a friendly basis.

ROBERT COWLEY: When my father interviewed Hemingway I'd spend a lot of time at the pool. Once a man came through the foliage and asked Hemingway for money. He said he had escaped from Devil's Island. Hemingway was wonderful with people. He had an utterly courtly manner when he was talking to women. My mother commented on that—a man with extraordinary good manners. You could also tell he was an extraordinary hater, because once sitting in the living room he read aloud to everyone there a letter from someone he utterly despised. He'd read a sentence and comment, read another sentence and comment. I'd never heard anything funnier or more vicious. He was funny. I can't remember the punch lines now; I was too young. He looked very directly into your eyes when he spoke to you and held that look and spoke very confidentially. He was an immense man, great broad shoulders, narrow hips, but a hell of a big gut. We'd be there for most of the day, through late afternoon. Sometimes, three or four times, we went into Havana. Once he took us all to a restaurant—you had to go up in an elevator. One of the stops was at a bordello on the way up. Hemingway pointed that out to my father and was very amused by it. Maybe my father went out alone to interview him a couple of times, then I wandered around the city during the day. One day we went out to a little town where he kept the boat. We went out about five miles and, oh God, it was a day with a high wind blowing and huge waves, a ten-foot chop. Up and down. Mary sat on the prow of the boat and she loved getting the spray—rather brave of her, because if she'd fallen off it would have been damned hard to retrieve her. They caught two or three barracuda. I got deathly seasick and whooped all over the top deck. Hemingway stripped off his jersey and wiped it up and threw the jersey into the sea—a man of action—and went on fishing. He tried to console me, saying we'd be going in soon, which we did. I was stretched out flat, I was so sick. There were no signs of his being mean or short tempered toward Mary as she states in her book, *How It Was*. No signs of his mental breakdown. But there had been the whole strange business of Patrick and Gregory being in an automobile accident, and Patrick going into a coma. Hemingway acted very much the concerned father and physician, staying night and day with Patrick. Gregory had been at the wheel of the car when they crashed and because of that Hemingway accused him of being responsible for Patrick's coma. For a time Gregory, as he said to me, took a bum rap for Patrick's condition. Then successful shock treatment exonerated him. Because if the coma had been physically induced—by the car crash—then the shock treatment would have turned Patrick into a vegetable [see Chapter 11, p.221].

DENIS BRIAN: None of this appeared in your father's piece, or the argument they had at lunch during your visit. Hemingway got mad at your father for disagreeing with Mary about red and white pines. Although your father was right, he gave in.

ROBERT COWLEY: I remember that lunch. My father is a great expert on pines—he's written on the subject. Everyone seemed to drink a lot when I was there but nothing out of the ordinary, but this might explain the heated argument. Hemingway was a man of heroic proportions. I've rarely encountered that quality with anyone else. It was not Falstaffian. There was absolutely no buffoonery. He was terribly witty and there was an aura of self-confidence, too, of absolute sureness about himself. He dressed casually, had casual table manners and treated the servants nicely. Hemingway was totally unexpected. I'd say he's probably the most extraordinary person I've ever met and that really goes a long way. But once you've accepted this extraordinary quality, there weren't, at that time, any surprises, such as the kind of rages into which he was supposed to fly. It was the personal magnetism—something utterly forceful about the man. It was the adventures he'd had and the people he'd known. And it was the manner he had with ordinary people he'd come in contact with; they all seemed to know him and pay him deference, more than the lord of the manor. In Havana he was a national figure, a national hero. I don't remember him saying a harsh word to anyone. He said it about people, not to them when I was there. The only other person I've met who had that quality was JFK, whom I met while I was at college and he was filming an Omnibus TV show at Harvard.

DENIS BRIAN: Hemingway made an equally strong impression on Archibald MacLeish, who said, "He was one of the most human and spiritually powerful creatures I have ever known. The only other man who seemed to me as much *present* in a room was FDR, and I am not excepting Churchill." What else do you recall of that visit?

ROBERT COWLEY: Hemingway's sister, Madelaine [Sunny] came down to the Finca with her son and her son kept calling him Uncle Ernie [laughs]. He hated being called Uncle Ernie. We went from Havana to Key West and spent one afternoon with my father there. Patrick was there, on an upper balcony and looking very wan. I think it was right after he had come out of the coma, and he didn't join us. My father talked to a lot of Hemingway's friends in Key West and to Pauline who was then very much alive. A nice woman. She was terribly gracious. For me, a thirteen-year-old lad, the great attraction was their swimming pool. My parents had bought me a pair of underwater goggles and that was all I cared to do—swim under water. I swam alone.

MALCOLM COWLEY: What Hemingway did was to say, "I don't want to talk about myself. But I'll tell you whom to get in touch with." So he gave me a list of people and I used what they told me. I had a great pile of correspondence about him, some of which is now at the Newberry Library in Chicago. In that respect my piece is extremely accurate in using what other people told me about Hemingway. He said it made him sick to talk about himself [laughs]. Of course, he was exaggerating.

MARY HEMINGWAY: Malcolm Cowley is really such an extremely nice and thoughtful and understanding man. Ernest didn't want to be put in *Life*, and he hated to sound boastful, so he put Malcolm on to people like General Buck Lanham, and people like that. You know, "You ask him. I don't want to tell you about this." Because it sounded so boastful. Most people think of Ernest as being a publicity seeker. It could hardly be less true. So it has always seemed to me.

MALCOLM COWLEY: The one inaccuracy Hemingway picked up against me, according to Hotchner, was that I said he carried one flask of vermouth and one of gin. And Ernest said, "Who would waste a whole flask on vermouth?" But this information came from, I think, Buck Lanham or John Groth [a war artist]; or somebody else made the error and I simply repeated it. I also got the account of his schooldays at Oak Park from other sources. He didn't want that used at all. But I very much calmed it down in the version I used, just saying that at Oak Park he was a literary boy, not a sports boy.

DENIS BRIAN: After reading all his books did you have a letdown on meeting him?

MALCOLM COWLEY: No, he lived up to his books. This is a very complicated question. He created for himself a persona, like Byron. I never had the pleasure of meeting Lord Byron, but Hemingway was an extraordinary person to meet. I regarded his persona as something rather different from the books he wrote.

DENIS BRIAN: Did he seem shy?

MALCOLM COWLEY: No. We had a grand time. We got drunk together and confided.

PHILIP YOUNG: While Malcolm Cowley was writing his famous profile for *Life*, Hemingway wrote to him, saying, "Malcolm, just say I got hit in Italy, got a couple of medals, and then stay away from it completely. Otherwise people will dig around in that area and I will get as sick as I was then." . . . I've seen that letter. It was clear Hemingway meant psychologically sick, because he added that in Italy he was really spooked and was scared that if somebody started digging around in there it would happen to him again.

DENIS BRIAN: Hemingway was also worried that someone else might read that letter. Cowley assured him that he didn't show Hemingway's letters around, but kept them in case Hemingway might want to refer to them in the future. No one else did get to see that letter, in fact, until Philip Young came across a copy after Hemingway's death. A subject Cowley avoided completely was Hemingway's hatred of his mother.

MALCOLM COWLEY: I never asked him the question. What would this be? You can see from one of his stories that she made a worm out of his father. She was one of those arty women who ruled the roost.

DENIS BRIAN: *Life* published Cowley's "A Portrait of Mister Papa," in January 1949. It boosted Hemingway's reputation to that of a larger-than-life uncrowned Emperor of Cuba, a genuine if unorthodox war hero, who was as devoted to his art as a priest to his religion. He must have liked it.

MALCOLM COWLEY: He was very pleased at first, then became less pleased, largely because of my saying he wasn't an athlete who became an intellectual, but an intellectual who became an athlete, which was absolutely true.

ROBERT COWLEY: After we left Cuba my mother talked about the enormous courtliness of the man. And my father and Hemingway kept up a regular correspondence. I used to make all the Christmas cards for my parents. My mother would sit me down for the afternoon every fall and I'd draw or crayon about a hundred Christmas cards. So my mother asked me to do a card for Hemingway. The picture I drew was a hillside with flowers, grass, birds, the sky, and some clouds. And just two feet sticking out of the hill, as if a man were sleeping there hidden by the grass and flowers except for his legs, which I thought in my childish way was a nice pastoral scene. But to my mother it looked as if the man might be dead. She said, "Oh God, you can't send that, because he's absolutely panicked by the idea of death!" So then I drew a picture of his boat the *Pilar*, a two-dimensional thing—and that was the card they sent him. It was obviously conveyed to me that his fear of death was strong, because I'd had my boyish drawing censored.

DENIS BRIAN: Part of Hemingway's do-it-yourself psychotherapy in controlling his fears of death and his nightmares of going insane, was to put them down on paper, to write about them obliquely in his fiction.

MALCOLM COWLEY: It's his short stories in particular that seem to give a clue to his inner life. In fact, candor about his inner life is one of the great things about his early stories. There he indicates that after his war injuries he was at times out of his mind. You get this in the short story in which he lies awake listening to silkworms eating and a dropping sound in the leaves ["Now I Lay Me"]. And also in that other story, "A Way You'll Never Be."

PHILIP YOUNG: I agree that "A Way You'll Never Be" is Hemingway's account of his mental breakdown after his war injuries. The story Hemingway gave—and he was a terrible inventor, an inventor of stories about his own life particularly—was that when he wrote that story he knew a young woman in Florida, maybe from his Key West days, who was in bad shape. He said the title was addressed to her, meaning: "You're never going to be as bad as this—as bad as I was." That's an anecdote. I wouldn't swear to it.

CARLOS BAKER: Hemingway completed "A Way You'll Never Be" as a sequel to "Now I Lay Me" while he was in Cuba in 1932. His explanation for the title was that the heat of Havana reminded him of life on the river Piave [where he was wounded] in 1918. Meanwhile, he said, he was watching a hell of a nice girl go crazy. Nick Adams [his fictional self] had been much crazier than this girl would ever be, continued Hemingway, and he gave the story its title, "A Way You'll Never Be," to cheer her up.

Malcolm Cowley's portrait of Hemingway had sustained and burnished the myth. Hemingway came off as a hell of a guy, a champion boxer, hunter, fisherman—even something of a record breaker in his four marriages—and a hero in two world wars who had topped it off by liberating Paris almost singlehandedly. The champion didn't stay unchallenged for long. An attack came from an unexpected source—novelist Irwin Shaw—who took great swipes at the heroic image.

IRWIN SHAW

Irwin Shaw's portrait of Hemingway is disguised as fiction. But the camouflage is superficial. In Shaw's 1949 novel The Young Lions, *the character Ahearn is unmistakably Ernest, a heavy-drinking* Collier's *war correspondent in Europe who is making a study of fear. [Scott Fitzgerald remarked that Hemingway's great theme is fear.] He sweats profusely—like Ernest—and talks obsessively about courage and the delights of war. Ahearn-Hemingway wins the Congressional Medal of Honor, but Shaw suggests he earned it not through bravery, but through stupidity. Ahearn has a younger brother, Keane—obviously and maliciously Leicester—a constipated, yellow-toothed oaf who takes sadistic delight in killing a young wounded Nazi soldier. There's also a less-than-flattering portrait of a Mary Hemingway surrogate.*

Shaw's first meeting with Hemingway had been after the Spanish Civil War. Shaw had recently completed a play, Bury the Dead, *and Hemingway remarked, "We make the dead and you bury them." Their most memorable encounter was in London during World War II, when Shaw was lunching with Mary Welsh. Shaw handed over or lost Mary to Hemingway, who subsequently married her.*

In The Young Lions, *Shaw's shots are funny and cruel, and few could fail to identify the real-life targets. In this book, Shaw proves himself more than Ernest's match in the popular art of literary manslaughter.*

But, though Hemingway may have been Shaw's clay pigeon, he was no sitting duck. Mary Hemingway explains, in How It Was, *what happened next. I read it out to Irwin Shaw for his response.*

DENIS BRIAN: "While we were dining with Harold Ross [editor of the *New Yorker*] and his blond, giggly wife in the bar at '21,' Irwin Shaw, my jovial friend who had been with me the day I met Ernest, came to the table and Ernest exploded. To my distress, he delivered himself of a violent, scarifying critique of Shaw, his character, his person, his writing, which caused Ross to wiggle on his seat and me to marvel that Shaw stood there failing to bleed from every pore." What caused Hemingway's outburst?

IRWIN SHAW: It's too personal to go into.

DENIS BRIAN: Correct me if I'm wrong. The picture I got was that Hemingway thought you had maligned him, Leicester, and Mary in *The Young Lions,* and that made him blow his top when he saw you.

IRWIN SHAW: That was a secondary consideration.

LEICESTER HEMINGWAY: I was disgusted with Shaw's portraits of Ernest and me in his book. But, what the hell! Irwin is not what we'd call the world's ace writer. He's simply a guy who is embittered because he knew that the Hemingsteins were running him a certain amount of competition in this world. He didn't like me, because I had been a little smartass in the same unit he was in during World War II. I don't know whether Ernest had threatened to punch him in the nose, as has been reported. I don't think Ernest would ever threaten to punch somebody in the nose. He would punch him in the nose.

DENIS BRIAN: In his novel, Shaw describes a man supposedly modeled on Leicester, who grins sadistically while killing a wounded Nazi soldier.

JOHN HEMINGWAY: That's ridiculous.

DENIS BRIAN: Might anything else have sparked your father's rage?

JOHN HEMINGWAY: Irwin Shaw was accompanying Mary Hemingway when Papa first attracted her attention, or vice versa. I think Leicester was also there. I'd suggest the possibility of some stupid jealousy.

LEICESTER HEMINGWAY: Shaw wasn't in love with Mary but he'd had an affair with her before she and Ernest met.

DENIS BRIAN: In your novel, Mr. Shaw, you have the character Louise, who seems obviously based on Mary Hemingway, asking you—in the fictional guise of Michael Whiteacre—to marry her. Did Mary Welsh, as she was in those days, ask you to marry her?

IRWIN SHAW: I prefer not to answer the question.

DENIS BRIAN: Are you still on affectionate terms with her?

IRWIN SHAW: Yes, I remained very friendly. I've nothing against Mary. But Hemingway was unreasonable and vulgar. He was paranoid about his friends. He had been very friendly with me. He turned on all his friends.

DENIS BRIAN: Did you read Mary Hemingway's autobiography in which she describes his attack on you?

IRWIN SHAW: I have it on my shelf and I've read some of the stuff she wrote about me—they're fictions. While in general it's a more or less accurate description of what took place, it leaves out material that might fill in the background. Hemingway had come to town and told a friend of mine he was going to punch me in the nose the next time he saw me. I guessed some of the reasons he gave Mary were part of them. I had just stopped into "21" on the way downtown from the hospital. My son had been born the night before and was on the critical list in an incubator, since he was born two months prematurely. When I saw Hemingway sitting at the table with Harold Ross [editor of the *New Yorker* magazine] I went over and said, "I heard you were going to punch me in the nose, Ernest, and here I am." He did not rise, but insulted me, calling me among other things "The Brooklyn Tolstoy." I left the table and went over and waited for him at the bar. He did not follow me, although Mary did come over to thank me for not making a scene. After I had a few drinks I left and went home. The next morning, Ross, who had been with Hemingway at the table, called me and said that just before I had come into the restaurant Hemingway had asked him who was the best fiction writer he had on the *New Yorker*. And Ross had said, "Shaw." Ross said to me that Hemingway had just grunted at this, and changed the subject. It was at that moment that I came in. I imagine Hemingway probably regretted it when he got sober the next day. I may leave something posthumously about the truth: I may write my memoirs or I may write a little paper.

DENIS BRIAN: Hemingway gave Mary a note next morning in which he said he loved her and did not wish to fight over his attack on Shaw, but "the Shaw thing had been an anger that I had like a boil for over a year. I thought what he wrote about my poor bloody unfortunate brother, you, and me was despicable. I had warned him to keep away from me. If you want to see Shaw because he is an old friend, that is perfectly o.k. and I understand."[1] Any comment?

IRWIN SHAW: During the war I had written a collection of short stories and Hemingway told me it was the best writing about the war. Even after he was very unpleasant to me, he was asked by the *New York Times* for the three books he would suggest to send as Christmas gifts, and he included a book of my short stories. I think his *Farewell to Arms* is a great book. I mean, I'm not going to let my personal feelings about a spat

[1] Mary Hemingway, *How It Was.*

between us, which is what it was, interfere with my admiration for what
he did for American literature.

LILLIAN ROSS

*Despite Shaw's low blows, Hemingway was not yet on full alert. And
reporter Lillian Ross's reverential attitude caught him napping or in a
manic mood. She had first visited him at his Ketchum, Idaho, home on
Christmas eve of 1947 and endeared herself to Mary by helping to wash
the dinner dishes. Then she was gathering information for her* New
Yorker *profile of Sidney Franklin, the somewhat eccentric Brooklyn-born
bullfighter, who had been Hemingway's friend and general factotum during the Spanish Civil War. Despite Franklin's comment after reading his
profile—"She [Ross] sits there like a little mouse, looking so cute, but
there's nothing but vitriol in her typewriter"—he apparently loved the
publicity and relished seeing his own wacky comments in print; among
them that he would never marry after seeing bulls breeding. Hemingway
seemed equally enthusiastic. For a time he was working on what he regarded as his masterpiece,* Across the River and Into the Trees. *But
when he was clear of that and Ross suggested a forty-eight-hours-in-the-
life-of-Hemingway piece, he readily agreed. Some think to his eternal
regret. Ross's approach has been called "the fly on the wall" technique,
where nothing is explained or interpreted. In fact, what she did was to
observe her subject carefully and, while he entertained friends in his
Manhattan hotel room, visited the Metropolitan Museum, and shopped
at Abercrombie and Fitch, she recorded almost every word, move, twitch,
and mutter of the master, excluding herself entirely from the printed profile. The result was extraordinary.* [1] *To some it was a vivid, accurate portrait of the man. To others it was a cruel travesty. To a third group it
seemed to chart the start of his fatal mental breakdown. Malcolm Cowley, whom Hemingway regarded as his best American critic, wrote to him
that it was malicious and the worst thing written about him, a strange
way for her to repay his kindnesses.*

MALCOLM COWLEY: I was very disappointed, because I thought it cheap-
ened Ernest. I was disturbed, but I thought that was his business, not
mine. That wasn't the way I had seen him, but nevertheless it was a
portrait.

C. T. LANHAM [in a June 15, 1950 letter to Hemingway]: For my part

[1]Lillian Ross, "How Do You Like It Now, Gentlemen?" *New Yorker*, May 13, 1950.

I would hate like hell to have any babe do a job like that on me. I found myself sore as hell a half dozen times while reading it.

WILLIAM WALTON: The way he spoke in the Lillian Ross piece was the extreme side of him. She was very accurate in that one, at that period which was one of his very low periods. Then he would talk in fake childish, or primitive terms, almost down to his accent. This was a piece of him.

JOHN HEMINGWAY: It was like a tape recorder. While all the things said were absolutely accurate, they don't sound the same written out, with the kidding around that was going on. I don't think it was her fault. She didn't know how to make it feel the way it really was then. Having listened to that kind of conversation, and knowing all the people involved, the funny thing is that if you could place the mood, this was the way it was during a nonworking period. My feeling was that he thought she didn't do a good job because she didn't capture the spirit, or explain the circumstances, but thought she was a fine woman and in no way blamed her.

A. E. HOTCHNER: She had no insight into the fact that Ernest had been working for a hard, long, arduous time in Havana on *Across the River and Into the Trees*, which he had just finished. So he came to New York and suddenly let loose. When he worked he was like a monk; he didn't drink and he didn't philander, and he stayed right with it. But when he came up to Manhattan with his manuscript it was a release, and he told her right off the bat: "I'm sick of sounding like myself with these interviews. I'm going to have some fun. The thing I like best is to sound like an Ojibway Indian, of which I'm part." So that was part of letting loose. She missed that. She missed the fact that he'd finished the book and wanted to have some fun. She missed the fact that he didn't want to make pronouncements and wanted to put everybody on, which he did. She didn't know much about a guy like Hemingway, that was the problem. She was honest and she reported everything as she saw it, but she just wasn't the person to do it. A good example of how she really didn't do a good job of reporting that which was *interesting*, to hell with accurate, *interesting:* Marlene Dietrich had come to the Sherry Netherland and a group of us, including Lillian, had spent the entire night talking—ten hours or so. The most fascinating and longest part of the discussion had to do with astrology. Dietrich was trying to get Ernest to give his vital statistics to an astrologer named Righter who lived in Hollywood and who ran her life, and still does. Marlene told marvelous stories of how she had tried to save Grace Moore, the singer, through warnings from this astrologer that she shouldn't be in an airplane. [Moore died in a plane crash.] Lillian didn't use any of that. And Ernest commented about how he didn't want to be run by the stars. And all that Lillian reported about the whole evening was a little reference to the fact that Marlene used towels from the Plaza to clean her daughter's apartment. Marlene called me up on the day the *New Yorker* came out. She was furious. First of all, she said, she hadn't know that Lillian was there in the guise of silent reporter in the shadows taking notes. She never would have talked so freely, she said, and certainly no reporter should have taken advantage of her. It gave her license to kill, she said. [Apparently she saw herself portrayed as a thief.] She was really furious; an uncontrollable tirade. Her fury was fanned hotter by her estimation of the way Lillian had written about Ernest, a man she had known over twenty years, and loved. Her anger finally choked her and she rang off.

MARY HEMINGWAY: Lillian recorded quite accurately everything that happened while we were staying at the Sherry Netherland Hotel. She is the most accurate interviewer of anyone I ever knew. There is no curtain between her and her subject whatsoever. She came the next morning—I was still asleep I think—and she and Ernest had a long chat. Everything she said in the *New Yorker* profile was entirely accurate.

DENIS BRIAN: What about Hemingway's comment to his publisher, Scribner: "She's made horses' asses of us both?"

MARY HEMINGWAY [laughs]: It's quite possible if someone is as clear as Lillian and as accurate as she is, everybody is a horse's ass. Hotchner came down after the thing was published, saying *"You are ruined!"* Idiot things like that. I remember saying, "No single profile—in any magazine—of Ernest can ruin him." Ernest subsequently wrote to Lillian saying, "You did a good job, daughter."

DENIS BRIAN: I think what upset his adherents, in the Ross piece, was they thought he was being pictured as speaking Indian talk all the time, that it was his normal way of talking.

MARY HEMINGWAY: Oh, no.

DENIS BRIAN: How often did he revert to Indian talk? Was this a joke?

MARY HEMINGWAY: Of course it was a joke. He had Bimini talk. For instance our conversation: just for amusement, we'd start out in French, and go into Swahili, and then into Italian and then Spanish and perhaps wind up in English, all in one sentence. You know, this is amusing. It brightens your day.

A. E. HOTCHNER: He was upset by the piece. Lillian always said that he thought it was marvelous. Well, that's ridiculous. What he really said was, "There's so much here that I don't know what to do with it, so I just said it was okay." According to to both Ernest and Mary, she sent the galleys and when they arrived in Havana it was the week the magazine was being published. So there wasn't anything to do about the galleys.

DENIS BRIAN: Here's a Carlos Baker reference to the Lillian Ross profile. It's on page 651 of the Notes Section of Baker's biography of Hemingway: "EH to author, Feb. 24, 1951, stated that the 'thing' was her idea. He was in 'full hold' of a novel and did not give a damn. But when he read it, while continuing to defend her right to say whatever she wished, he was 'shocked and felt awful.' "

MARY HEMINGWAY: He may have felt so without telling me. Lillian had said that she would send us galley proofs in time for us to make corrections and or suggestions. The proofs arrived so late that there was little time.

TRUMAN CAPOTE: I never met Hemingway, but I hated him. He was such a total hypocrite. He went on being a friend of Lillian Ross after she wrote that profile of him, so it doesn't matter. He was a total hypocrite and mean. I disliked him intensely. He was always writing little things about me when I was very, very young. I was about eighteen or nineteen and I thought, "My God, here's this man fifty years old, this famous man. What in the hell does he always want to be knocking me in the teeth about?" When Nelson Algren's book, *The Man With the Golden Arm*, came out, Hemingway gave him a quote which the publisher used: "All you Truman Capote fans get your hats and coats and leave the room. Here comes a real writer." "Well," I thought, "that really, I mean, is too much." When *Breakfast at Tiffany's* came out, Hemingway wrote a little note telling me how good it was, or how much he liked it. And I thought, "There's more of your hypocrisy for you!"

GEORGE SAVIERS: I thought Lillian Ross's *New Yorker* profile was rather amusing.

DENIS BRIAN: Arthur Schlesinger, Jr. told me it seemed to picture a man who had lost his gift and was cracking up.

MALCOLM COWLEY: I believe the mental breakdown was in operation at the time.

DENIS BRIAN: Lillian Ross said she was very fond of Hemingway and admired him, and that the profile was not meant to be brutal.

BENJAMIN DE MOTT [novelist, social and literary critic, and Professor of

English at Amherst]: Nevertheless, it is a piece of writing and if the person is cracking up and has lost his gift and so on, for him to be represented merely as a fool and not a person who had any quasi-tragic dimension is wrong. I don't care what the *intention* was. We all know about intention. Nobody means to do anybody in, but it comes forth in this way.

DENIS BRIAN: But in this instance, Lillian Ross didn't realize he was cracking up.

ARNOLD GINGRICH: The cruelest thing you can do to anybody is to quote him literally, with no selection, particularly anybody who is prone, as Ernest was, to feeling friendly with somebody and to relax and let his hair down and talk Indian talk, never dreaming that it would come out any other way than the way he felt about it. And actually feeling it was great when he first read it. He told her he thought it was marvelous. Afterwards, he wasn't too sure. When everybody said what a vivisection it was, he still thought, "Well, they're just jealous."

WILLIAM SEWARD: It did not depict the man I knew. In my opinion he was putting on a good act. It gave the impression of a trivial man and he was exactly the opposite. He was anything but trivial. I knew him as humble and going out of his way not to hurt people, and as an extremely shy person. When he was around photographers and newsmen he had a rather suspicious attitude toward them and simply put on a big show. The man I knew was far removed from the portrait in the Lillian Ross piece. He is the only important, so-called great man that I have ever met in whom I was not disappointed. And I have had occasion to meet over the years several U.S. Presidents, which may not be shooting very high, but I have never met a supposedly great man in whom there wasn't some disappointment. I saw Ernest in a number of circumstances and he always remained bigger than life. And I'm not a young kid with a great deal of hero worship.

MALCOLM COWLEY: If you take a stenographic account of what a man says at a certain time, that does not necessarily give you the impression of what the man was. Lillian's piece gave much more of the impression of a playboy and a snob than one ever actually got from Ernest. It wasn't a true impression. In other words, something much more was here. Hers was a trivial picture of the man. When I did my profile on Hemingway those weren't the things we talked about at all. As a rule he gave much more perceptive answers to questions than you got in her article.

CARLOS BAKER: I thought the profile was excellent.

DENIS BRIAN: Why do you think so many friends and admirers were shocked by it?

CARLOS BAKER: I suppose some felt it was a travesty, in that it showed Hemingway on vacation rather than the Hemingway they knew in daily life.

EARL ROVIT: My first impression on reading it was, "My God, did she do a hatchet job!" Then I got involved in Hemingway scholarship. She didn't think it was a hatchet job, and I'm not certain what Hemingway himself essentially thought of it. I suspect that when he originally read it, he was sufficiently monomaniacal that he thought it was a flattering portrait—until somebody told him it wasn't.

A. E. HOTCHNER: The whole thing was kidding. I don't think Lillian got any part of Hemingway. I mean, it came out he sounded like an old rummy. And she had no perspective, no balance.

Yet it is regarded by many as a classic of its kind. A result of the ensuing controversy was to put Hemingway back on guard against marauders intruding in his private life. Which was bad luck for Philip Young.

PHILIP YOUNG

PHILIP YOUNG: I'd written a Ph.D. thesis on Hemingway. William Gibson, a friend of mine teaching at New York University, asked to read it. He liked it and without asking me gave it to an editor at Rinehart, Thomas Bledsoe. He said if I'd rewrite it they'd publish it. I rewrote it. Then Malcolm Cowley, a free-lance critic, was given the manuscript at my suggestion to check it before it went to the printer. He did the job well and I took some of his suggestions. In the course of this he let Hemingway know about the book and Hemingway got suspicious and wrote Cowley that he was not happy about this. He didn't know who the hell I was, and so forth. It sounded very touchy and ominous to me.

DENIS BRIAN: Cowley described you to Hemingway as a well-intentioned admirer, "a bright, but not extremely bright" instructor and told him that if you went along with the changes Cowley had suggested, the book would permanently enhance Hemingway's reputation as a writer.

PHILIP YOUNG: Correspondence went on for months. Rinehart decided it would be better, my being an amateur, if they dealt with Hemingway and I said okay, thinking to myself, "I could do better, but if I screw it up they could say they didn't want to publish the book. But if they screw it up, I still have a contract." Selfish I guess, but smart. And it did get screwed up. I wrote him finally when he asked, "How come I never hear from Mr. Young?" And I said, "Here I go. It's my turn." And we corresponded for more than a year.

DENIS BRIAN: What made you persist?

PHILIP YOUNG: I was in the process of being fired, because I hadn't published anything. In fact I was fired from New York University because of it.

DENIS BRIAN: Publish or perish?

PHILIP YOUNG: Right. He worried that I was psychoanalyzing him and writing a full-scale biography disguised as criticism. I was out of a job. I had been let go by NYU because I hadn't published anything and I told him, "Hell, you let all these people write about you because they needed money. I just need to make a living." It was at that point I asked Rinehart, "Suppose he won't give me permission to quote him? We don't need it legally, anyway." Under "fair use" I could have quoted him in reasonable doses without his permission. I said, "Would you publish the book if I paraphrase him?" Rinehart said yes. So I wrote and told Hemingway I'm sure he would prefer his words to mine, but we were prepared to go ahead if he said no. I got a telegram back from him saying: "Go ahead!" I had tried to explain that I wasn't psychoanalyzing him, that I had simply quoted a couple of psychoanalysts. I guess he wanted that material out, but he never asked me to remove it, so I left it in. As for his fears of it being a full-scale biography, it wasn't of course. I didn't know anywhere near enough about him to write his biography, and a lot of what I knew wasn't true. Well, he not only allowed me to quote from his works but he gave up any payment due to him for the quotes and even offered to give me $200, which I declined. Finally, he said I was still free to call him a son-of-a-bitch if I wanted to. He turned right around and became very friendly.

DENIS BRIAN: In his book, Young, now a professor at Pennsylvania State University, suggested that Hemingway's World War I shell shock and traumatic wounding had a vital effect on his life and work. He also coined the expression "code-hero" to describe Hemingway's protagonists. According to author Max Schur, Freud considered that post-traumatic dreams like those Hemingway had after his being blown up were attempts "to master the stimulus retroactively, by developing the anxiety whose omission was the cause of the traumatic neurosis." Dr. Schur proposed another explanation, that "the repetition of traumatic events in dreams represents the ego's unconscious wish to undo the traumatic situation. This cannot be achieved without reliving the latter in endless variations." By writing of his war experiences in *A Farewell to Arms* and *For Whom the Bell Tolls* as well as *Across the River and Into the Trees,* and in several stories, he may also have been trying to master the stimulus retroactively. Hemingway endured recurring nightmares after both world wars. He described one in a letter to his wife, Mary. He was surrounded by Germans, then either pinned down or killed by a direct hit.

MARY HEMINGWAY: Professor Philip Young did a whole book based on the fact that Ernest had some terrible psychological wound from having been wounded, and pursued this thing and still does. It got him a doctorate in literature. All I can say to you, because I've said it to Philip, is I think it's horseradish!

PHILIP YOUNG: She never said it quite that way to me, but that's all right. I'm pretty confident of my theory. Although there have been times when he seems to have shown no sign [of the psychological wound] whatsoever, and I think there's something mysterious about it. At those times he appears to have conquered it so that he hardly knew it existed. On the other hand, he was dreadfully upset at times about discussing his wounding. There are still certain mysteries about Hemingway, such as how completely this psychological wound seemed to have disappeared in his personal life, and how he still remained absorbed with it in his fictions. That's really amazing in *Across the River and Into the Trees,* where he [the protagonist, Colonel Richard Cantwell] goes back to the place where he was hit and builds a little monument on the spot and defecates there. Well, my God, what's that? Thirty-two years later! That, to me, is impressive. I can understand perfectly why Mary would think it was horseshit, which is of course what she meant by horseradish. He doubtless didn't show it. But he did have this preoccupation with killing things. And Mary didn't always know what he was thinking. She knows that, of course. I quoted two psychoanalysts in my book about Hemingway: Freud, and Freudian revisionist Otto Fenichel, on traumatic neurosis as it's called. They have a theory about traumatic neurosis which sounded to me exactly what Hemingway had described. The other thing is that I came across this medical theory long after I had written the stuff, and I added the medical theory. It was a tremendous coincidence to have found these psychoanalysts confirming my views.

DENIS BRIAN: He wrote to you: "How would you like it if someone said everything you'd done in your life was because of some trauma?" and that he didn't want to be known as the Legs Diamond of Letters, being reluctant to go down in literary history as a clay pigeon.[1]

PHILIP YOUNG: He was amusing about it.

LEICESTER HEMINGWAY: The good thing about Ernesto was, in nine times out of ten instances the guy had an absolute emotional honesty. If a thing bothered him he'd say, "Look, this is what's really itching me." And he'd say it right out. If everything was going well and smoothly he'd say, "Goddamn, none of the things that used to bother me"—our bloody mother and the way she'd peck at us, or he'd cite various things that used to annoy him—"are showing up, and I feel wonderful." And he'd just plain out with it. All right, here's the thing. I don't think things that happened back when he was a teenager really did bother him a lot when he was in his forties and fifties. I think that somebody else might have tried to bother him and that this would have been Philip Young's forte. The only way Young might have thought he could get a rise out of Ernest was to say, "Hey, I think that first really bad time you got whopped, that scared you so mercilessly and really put the bejesus up you, is still bothering you, boy. Why don't you level with me and tell me about it?" At this point Ernest blew up and said, "Why, you dirty son-of-a-bitch you, don't try and go into this because, yes indeed, it could get me so infuriated it would bring it all up again."

PHILIP YOUNG: Hemingway wrote to Cowley, as a matter of fact, after he heard of my book and said he was really badly spooked back in those days [World War I] and if somebody started messing around with that business he was afraid it might come back, that he might get it again. I think this is the dead truth, that he was really worried about it.

LEICESTER HEMINGWAY: He might have, indeed, tried to put it away for thirty or forty years. But once you've put something away for forty years you don't want to bring it up again. I don't want to relive any youthful stupid escapades I had before I was twenty.

DENIS BRIAN: At the same time, having read the correspondence of a lot of people with your brother, I got the impression that Young was one of the most genuine and really admired him. Young has given up writing about him now.

---

[1]Jack "Legs" Diamond, a 1920s gangster, was so often riddled with bullets that he was known as "the clay pigeon." A rival mobster finally caught him asleep and blew out his brains.

LEICESTER HEMINGWAY: Gee, I hope so. Because, at one time, well after World War II, not necessarily when Ernest was very happy, we had a good conversation and he said, "All these people that keep picking on me and trying to dig under my fingernails, honest to Christ, Baron, it's enough to disgust a guy to the point of tickling his own throat and making himself vomit."

PHILIP YOUNG: I was only playing with the things Hemingway wrote about in his fiction and I never would have paid any attention to them or even known about them—that's my answer to that—unless Hemingway had focused on them. He's the man who wrote "A Way You'll Never Be," and so forth.

DENIS BRIAN: What do you think of the theory by a psychiatrist named Yalom that because Hemingway's parents rejected him, he scorned their rather narrow, middle-class views and created his own heroic alter ego. He then tried to live up to it, but constantly failed in his efforts. Does that make sense?

PHILIP YOUNG: Oh, yes. One thing I discovered later was the tremendous force of his rebellion against his parents and the enormous Victorian pressure placed on him, and his natural rebellion as a result. I now think that whole business looms just as big as the wound ever does. I didn't know that when I wrote my book.

CHARLES FENTON

Hemingway hunter Charles Fenton, a young Yale professor, followed hard on Young's heels, sometimes treading on them. For more than a year, from the summer of 1951 to the fall of 1952, Fenton fought almost frantically to land his big fish. He wanted to write a book about Hemingway's apprenticeship as a writer and to avoid his private life. In his letters hoping to get Hemingway's cooperation he reflected something of Hemingway's mercurial moods and suspicions.

Fenton said he empathized with Hemingway and realized how uneasy and irritated he must feel to know a sly pedant like himself was poking through Ernest's early writings. If Hemingway told him to drop dead he would understand. However—and this was the pacifier—Fenton assured. Hemingway he had no intention of writing his biography. That was one fear Hemingway could put aside. No personal revelation.

Hemingway had the jitters in the summer of 1951. All but the tame critics had ridiculed his Across the River and Into the Trees *as the pathetic, self-pitying work of a punch-drunk has-been.*

A sympathetic letter came from Fenton lambasting the critics as tiresome little fags or embittered scholars. And he apologized for bombarding Hemingway with questions, saying he felt like a lush baiting an aimiable stranger at the bar.

Hemingway was still wary. He wanted to know more of the professor's background. What he learned scared him.

Fenton left Yale in 1940 to join the Royal Air Force as a gunner. He wrote what he called a "lousy" novel that won a $4,000 prize jointly awarded by Doubleday and a movie company. The manuscript was never published nor filmed—an argument over the novel's ending—but Fenton kept the cash. The subject of the novel was life in an English military prison and the killing of a prisoner by a sergeant-major. Fenton mentioned that he had intimate contact with the military prison. Since World War II he had briefly and unhappily worked for the Luce organization before teaching at Yale. He was married with two children. Again he used the opportunity to stress that he was not going to write about Hemingway's private life, his own was too engrossing to spare the time for that.

Hemingway sensed disquieting ambiguities in Fenton's life story. An intimate contact with prison? Had Fenton himself been a prisoner? Had he killed someone? Speculating that Fenton had been imprisoned for some unspecified crime, Hemingway teetered between regarding Fenton as a jailbird or an FBI agent masquerading as a writer—both equally dangerous because they were out to get him.

MATTHEW J. BRUCCOLI: Hemingway was pretty paranoid in the 1950s. There were no mysteries in Fenton's life. He had volunteered for the R.A.F. in World War II, and had a distinguished record. He was shot down over the English Channel and floated around in a life raft before he was rescued.

PHILIP YOUNG: Hemingway was really savage about Fenton and treated him just as badly as he did me. And I think he had more reason to treat me severely than Fenton.

DENIS BRIAN: Then Hemingway read with alarm a biography of Scott Fitzgerald, *The Far Side of Paradise,* which exposed Fitzgerald's weaknesses, especially his physical and mental breakdown. Despite having fed some of this intimate information to its author, Arthur Mizener, Hemingway dreaded someone doing a similar job on him. He told Fenton so and Fenton replied: "You've got the wind up over the wrong guy." He repeated his pledge to steer clear of Hemingway's private life. He had already offered to avoid anything Hemingway considered forbidden territory between 1916 and 1926, and that included World War I and his marriage to Hadley. Fenton had located one of Hemingway's high-school teachers, and promised he wouldn't ask her if Ernest was queer for boys. As for Mizener, he knew him well, said Fenton, having studied under him at Yale. He characterized Mizener as a horse's ass, and an intellectual and social rube who was infatuated by literary people and the literary life. Fenton denied the urge to live vicariously through anyone else's biography and claimed to be resisting the urging of others to cram the book with Hemingway's marriages and blunders. He gave a warning that several writers were after just that kind of sensational material and offered to keep Hemingway informed about them. At times in his letters Fenton adopted Hemingway's vulgar, breezy style. In admitting that Hemingway's suspicions had made him angry, he wrote: "It burns the shit out of me." He concluded one letter by saying he'd briefly considered rewriting it in a calmer mood, but "I'm fucked if I'll rewrite it." Hemingway, surprisingly, caved in and cooperated. Fenton's book, *The Apprenticeship of Ernest Hemingway: The Early Years*, was published by Farrar, Straus and Cudahy in 1954. In his preface Fenton wrote, "Mr. Hemingway generously answered a number of troublesome questions at the beginning of the investigation, but I am even more indebted to him for the grace with which he endured the invasions of a project that held little appeal and considerable irritation for him." The irritation persisted after the book's appearance. Neither Young's nor Fenton's book pleased Hemingway, especially when the inevitable personal revelations found their way into magazines. Fenton may have tried to keep his promise but it was not possible to write the book without including "sensitive" information. But Fenton felt so confident that he had not antagonized Hemingway, that he agreed to introduce Professor Carlos Baker of Princeton University, an up-and-coming Hemingway hunter, to the master. It was not to be. Carlos Baker broke the news to Hemingway that Fenton had jumped to his death from a hotel window in Durham, North Carolina, in the summer of 1960. It was not known why.

MATTHEW J. BRUCCOLI: Fenton was a dear friend of mine. It was a great, great loss for American literature.

GEORGE PLIMPTON

GEORGE PLIMPTON: The year Fenton's book was published, 1954, I was walking down the corridor of the Ritz Hotel in Paris with a number of friends after a wedding reception. And I looked ahead, and there over at the bookstore in the long corridor of the Ritz was Ernest Hemingway. He was buying a copy of the *Paris Review* [Plimpton was an editor]. He was the first man before or since I've ever seen *reading* the magazine, which sobered me up quickly. It was the second year of this very small publication, but his interest was keen. Then I was introduced to him that same afternoon in the bar of the Ritz. I asked him very tentatively and nervously if he would submit to an interview for the magazine, and was surprised when he said he would. I think the reason he did was because there must have been a certain *nostalgie* there since that's how he started, of course, with small magazines. Here was the same sort of thing going on twenty years after he'd left Paris. He was on his way to Africa. This was before those two crashes and his being injured. A lot of the interview was conducted by letter and I think he was angry at having to stop his own work to answer questions. Also there are some questions that make writers impatient and unfortunately I asked a number of these. He was very sensitive about discussing technicalities and techniques. I asked him about something that always puzzled me, the symbolic white birds that appear in his sex scenes—which he was not very good at. In *Across the River and Into the Trees* and in other places, a white bird appears or flies around. When I asked him about it he was back in Cuba [after being injured in the plane crashes], on the dock, and he almost threw me in the water. His reaction was one of rage at the notion of my asking. He thought I was being critical and kept shouting: "Can you do any better?"

DENIS BRIAN: Did you use everything he told you?

GEORGE PLIMPTON: No, there were things he asked me not to put in. A lot of questions which fascinated him had to do with genetic possibilities. Why should he be a writer? Where did his ability come from? He talked a lot about his father and about his father's brother, an explorer who found the word "Hemingway" in China. I think in Chinese it means "the hunter of wolves," and he was very proud of that. And he felt this curious affinity with this odd uncle who was an explorer and led very much the life I think romantically he imagined himself following. The whole concept of tradition was very important to him. He talked about where does the great hunting dog get his honed ability to smell? He couldn't figure it out. His father was a doctor, so all of this was a puzzle to him. He felt it was somehow locked up in genetics.

DENIS BRIAN: Why would he ask you not to use this?

GEORGE PLIMPTON: I think he felt it was personal and he was unsure of it. Also, he told me that when we were in Madrid after he'd been injured in the two plane crashes in Africa, and he said he wasn't to be trusted at that time.[1] He said he was testing things. It was all right to talk about them but maybe you wouldn't want to have to stand for them if they were down on paper. He went over the interview and wrote a lot of it, so it's a literary document as well as an oral one, which he didn't really trust. He didn't trust his oral sense particularly as he was then in Madrid.

DENIS BRIAN: Sidney Franklin said Hemingway overreacted to homosexuals and once when they were together in Spain crossed the road to knock an obvious homosexual to the ground with a punch. Franklin told this story to Barnaby Conrad who told it to me. Do you credit this story?

GEORGE PLIMPTON: No. I sat with Hemingway and Tennessee Williams once. Obviously Tennessee Williams's tendencies were perfectly visible and I never saw anything but the greatest respect Hemingway had for him.

DENIS BRIAN: Did any of his letters surprise you?

GEORGE PLIMPTON: He used to have a lot of fun with his letters and a lot that seem perfectly appalling on the surface—for example his he-man letters that he wrote to Scribner, which some people take at face value. . . .

DENIS BRIAN: Claiming to have killed 122 krauts.

GEORGE PLIMPTON: Yes, and all that business about shooting Germans behind the head. He used to giggle, thinking of Scribner reading these things and probably believing them. He used to shift gears, depending upon to whom he was writing. Some letters were serious, some jocular, and some downright hyperbolic. He was a complex man. I've always been somewhat surprised by how seriously Hemingway was taken as someone of intense cruelty, someone who would take someone out in the middle of the night and knock him out.

DENIS BRIAN: Yet in your book, *Shadow Box*, you wrote that George Brown warned you that Hemingway was a dirty fighter who several times had tried to knee him when they were sparring. And you told of your own experience lunching at the Finca with Hemingway and Mary who were

[1]With good reason, according to Hemingway biographer Michael Reynolds. In *The Young Hemingway*, Basil Blackwell, 1986, he revealed that Hemingway's Uncle Willoughby was a medical missionary, not an explorer, although, of course, there's nothing to stop a missionary from doing a little exploring.

arguing about the number of lions they'd spotted in Africa on one day. He got up from the table, challenged you to show your boxing prowess, and gave you a hard left hook to your head that really hurt, his eyes small and furious like a pig's. You gave the impression that if you hadn't been able to stop his onslaught by smiling and asking him to show how he counterpunched he might really have hurt you.[1] Isn't that right?

GEORGE PLIMPTON: I can't answer that question, because it never happened. He probably would have pummeled me around a little more and then have helped me up and we would have had some drinks. I think he was just taking out his frustrations. He was a man of many parts. For me to admit that this was a typical string of characteristics on his part—that wouldn't be accurate at all.

DENIS BRIAN: Had he been drinking heavily at that lunch?

GEORGE PLIMPTON: No.

DENIS BRIAN: These occasional angry, aggressive outbursts seem to tie in with his depression and heavy drinking. You gave a similar account of a dinner at the Colony when he showed you what a fierce grip he had and left nail marks in your hand that lasted five days. Again you implied that if your girlfriend hadn't diverted him he might really have hurt you.

GEORGE PLIMPTON: It's very hard to conject something that doesn't happen. I think he probably would have squeezed until his strength ran out, but to purposely hurt me—no. It was a test.

DENIS BRIAN: How about George Brown's remark that Hemingway was no person to get involved with in duels of this sort?

GEORGE PLIMPTON: That's absolutely true. He was a very competitive man. He liked to show he was a good boxer, that he was very powerful. What the ultimate goal behind all of this was is very hard for me to tell. I don't think it was to hurt people.

DENIS BRIAN: When you were sparring it is possible he might have knocked you out?

GEORGE PLIMPTON: I don't think so for a minute. He would probably just have pounded me for a little bit. He tried it with everybody, even with Gene Tunney.

DENIS BRIAN: His Australian friend, Alan Moorehead, also a World War II war correspondent, judged Hemingway to be very serious behind his joking façade, and remarked that he could curse without malice, talk of

[1]George Plimpton, *Shadow Box*, Putnam's, 1977.

sex without being dirty and that anyone who called him a bully with a flare for publicity simply didn't know Hemingway. He also refuted the view that Hemingway was publicity hungry, saying that on the contrary he shut himself away, declining invitations to lecture or appear on TV or as a literary lion at parties. And Moorehead wasn't blind to Hemingway's faults; his violent temper, egotism and occasionally outrageous behavior. But he never found him boring. He witnessed the masterful thing Hemingway did with a German Shepherd in Italy. Two big dogs were fighting fiercely. Hemingway covered the German Shepherd with his jacket and threw the dog over a wall, stopping the fight, according to Moorehead.

GEORGE PLIMPTON: I doubt that story, to tell you the truth. How high was the wall? Did it go down five hundred feet? Was the German Shepherd killed?

DENIS BRIAN: It's funny you should doubt that story. Hemingway is supposed to be the tall-story teller, not his friends. But I'm inclined to trust Moorehead. Here's something that puzzles me about Hemingway. Did he write standing, because of his injuries?

GEORGE PLIMPTON: It was just a working habit. If he was injured, he'd be easier off sitting down, wouldn't he?

DENIS BRIAN: Unless he was injured in the rear.

GEORGE PLIMPTON: You mean he had boils on his rear?

DENIS BRIAN: Well, he called himself Ernie Hemorrhoid.

GEORGE PLIMPTON: I never thought of that. I never asked him. Thank God I didn't! But I'm sure he stood because he liked it and thought it was good exercise.

A. E. HOTCHNER: The minute you began to ask Ernest questions—and I think George Plimpton did it as well as anybody—he became stilted and formal and forced. He demanded that George give him a transcript and then very carefully rewrote it and edited what he had said. I don't think that gets very close to the man. I don't think it would have made Mr. Boswell's book very good. It's an interesting interview in that it elicited very measured and correct responses from Hemingway. But I don't think anybody can do a real job on anybody unless they're around them and then carry off, without any kind of editing, censorship, looking over the shoulder, or any kind of interference, their reaction to a person, their memory of conversation, behavior, smells, sights, foods, whatever it is—that's what works.

DENIS BRIAN: Do you feel the Hemingway interviewers put a lot of themselves rather than their subject into their interviews?

ARNOLD GINGRICH: Oh yes, completely. Cowley had quite an admiring attitude. Lillian Ross was commenting on the Emperor's bare behind while everyone else was oohing and aahing over the cut of his new clothes. Plimpton, I thought, was being rather elaborately correct with a difficult quarry, trying to bag him for the magazine and not scare him off.

CHAPTER

ELEVEN

•

"ACROSS THE RIVER AND INTO THE CAT HOUSE"

I went to Cuba on a fishing trip with Hemingway and the brother of Adriana Ivancich, the heroine of that dreadful book *Across the River and Into the Cat House.*—C. T. Lanham

DENIS BRIAN: Learning to drive a car in the spring of 1947, Gregory Hemingway hit an obstacle, and his brother Patrick, a passenger, bumped his head. Shortly afterwards Patrick had a mental breakdown that threatened his life. Mary was away caring for her sick father, and Hemingway nursed Patrick day and night for months. But Patrick didn't improve. Then his mother, Pauline, contacted psychiatrist Frank Stetmeyer, a German refugee living in Cuba. He gave Patrick electric shock therapy which immediately began to help and the patient was soon completely restored to health. Dr. Stetmeyer became Hemingway's exception. Marlene Dietrich was his one good German; "Stetski," as he called the psychiatrist affectionately, was his good psychiatrist. Ernest was so grateful that he gave Dr. Stetmeyer his prized Lincoln Continental as a thank-you present. It was a Hemingway habit never to sell cars he replaced but to give them away. In a benign mood of reconciliation—perhaps the psychiatrist had helped—Hemingway wrote to Archibald MacLeish the following year, suggesting they end their estrangement. As a "much improved guy" he proposed that they love each other loyally and with absolute mutual forgiveness for past "chickenshit." He said he loved Archie's wife, Ada, most of all his friends and had wanted to go to bed with her more than with any other woman, and not in order to read his books to her or recount his war experiences. He admitted that he had also wanted to marry Archie's daughter, Mimi, though he knew it was impossible. But Hemingway wasn't staying around for a reunion with his friends. A few months after his letter to MacLeish, he and Mary left for Italy on a strange mission. He intended to defecate on the spot where some thirty years before he had been traumatically wounded. When he arrived he changed his mind and, instead, buried a 1,000 lire note in the dark earth. It was, he explained, a symbol of the blood he had lost and the money spent in Italy. Duck hunting the following month he met eighteen-year-old Adriana Ivancich and became instantly infatuated. He warned Mary that his heart was "a target of opportunity" and "not subject to discipline." In *How It Was,* Mary referred to Adriana as their constant companion and foresaw that "from his romanticized memories of Italy in his young manhood, from his concept of the girl Renata he had created for the heroine of *Across the River and Into the Trees* and the enticements of proximity to Adriana herself, Ernest was weaving a mesh which might entangle and pain him."[1] On his return to Havana, Hemingway wrote Adriana frequent affectionate and paternal letters to which she responded. He believed he was immortalizing her in what he judged would be his greatest novel and doing the same for his World War II friend Buck Lanham.

C. T. LANHAM: One night Ernest and I were having dinner at Le Pavillon during one of his visits to New York City. He was staying at an apartment and insisted that I come back. Christ, it was one o'clock in the morning, and we sat there until three, and he said, "My God, you know Buck, I have immortalized you!" I said, "There's a job. How in hell did you do that?" He said, "I've got a whole bunch of short stories about you." He disappeared and came back with a manuscript and started to read it to me. Then he handed it to me, saying, "Here, I'll fix us another drink and

[1]Mary Welsh Hemingway, *How It Was.*

you read some of these." Well [laughs], my eyes just went closed and I never saw them all. They had to do with the 22nd Infantry and I think I was disguised in it in some way. I visited him several times in Cuba and once in Spain, but he never mentioned them again.

DENIS BRIAN: Joseph Dryer, an ex-marine, who had been a Dartmouth friend of John Hemingway, ran a farm in Cuba after the war and became a friend of John's father. He found that Hemingway's war experiences had left him with an implacable hatred not only of Nazis but of all Germans, except for Dietrich and Stetmeyer.

JOSEPH DRYER: Papa had a very strong personality that could be overwhelming. Although we never quarreled we didn't always see eye to eye. I was a friend of the family that organized the bomb plot against Hitler—the Stauffenbergs. Colonel Stauffenberg, who carried the bomb that exploded but only injured Hitler, was executed the day he was arrested. The mother, sons, and daughter—the children were very young—were all put in different prison camps. The plan was to kill them all *after* the mother had been interrogated. But when she was picked up for questioning, a doctor recognized her. He gave her a shot that put her in a coma and kept her in that state until the war ended. Because she couldn't be questioned, neither she nor the children were killed. One son was sent to Cuba to live with us—my brother and I had a farm there—and then other members of the Stauffenberg family came out and I got them jobs as interns in a bank. I did my best to persuade Ernest that there were some good Germans like these. He was very polite, but he was not about to be swayed. He'd say, "The only good German is a dead one," or, "The only good German is Marlene Dietrich." One of his favorite occupations was to show a movie after lunch. One time at the Finca, Ernest was showing *Casablanca* to several of us and at the part in the bar when Conrad Veidt and everybody else start singing *Deutschland uber Alles,* my brother and I also sang it at the top of our lungs. That incensed Papa who insisted that everybody else stand up and sing the *Marseillaise* at the top of their lungs. So as the movie was going on we were having fun. Once he was talking about "krauts" and somebody said how good-looking and well-preserved Marlene Dietrich was as she grew older. He said, "Of course. The answer is she's always had good quality sperm." Ernest was never drunk when we arrived at the Finca for lunch, but by the time we'd finished lunch we were all drunk.

DENIS BRIAN: Hemingway paid for his fun. He complained in letters to a friend in Spain that he was subjected by Mary to a nightly barrage of complaints that he was a heartless, selfish, stupid, spoiled, egotistical son-of-a-bitch. He wrote that although Mary was very dear to him she would not tolerate his writing interfering with her way of life, or her own writing career. And he dare not object to her decision to be neither his slave nor his cook.[1] In *How It Was* Mary wrote that it was apparent that Hemingway was trying to goad her into leaving him. She demanded a confrontation when she told him she intended to stay and run the Finca because, despite his behavior, she still loved him. He could only get rid of her by murder, or asking her to leave—when he was sober. She says that while sober he never again asked her to leave.

A FRIEND: She's saying, "I told him off and he really took it." But all she's really saying is, "I managed to hold my own. He didn't absolutely throw me out and make me stay thrown out." There were terrible times for her when she thought her marriage was doomed.

JOHN HEMINGWAY: It's not true to say my father didn't toe the line for any woman. I think he did [laughs]. He tried to do right, but then he did wrong. A lot. The woman that he was actually toughest on was Mary. There was no way he could be tough enough on her. Had any of his other wives been treated like Mary was, they would have left him.

A FRIEND: She was meeting all the people she ever wanted to meet in the world through him. I don't think Mary ever contemplated leaving Ernest because he was much too valuable to hang onto. Once she married him she knew that to stay married she had to shut up and take it.

JOSEPH DRYER: I'm sure Papa and Mary had arguments and I'm sure he drank too much. But he cared a great deal about her and there was real affection between them. At lunch her part was always to make homemade soup he particularly liked. Some days she'd have the soup ready at the right temperature and say, "Come and eat." He'd say, "I'm finishing my drink." "Come and eat now!" she'd say and get mad at him and he'd whisper, "We can't get her mad. We've all got to go and eat."

DENIS BRIAN: His angry outbursts were exacerbated by the almost unanimous thumbs down to his *Across the River and Into the Trees*. Apart from John O'Hara's extraordinary judgment that Hemingway was the greatest writer since Shakespeare and the strained superlatives of faithful retainers it was regarded as remarkably bad.

[1]In letters eventually put up for auction. The West German magazine *Der Spiegel* published extracts from them.

C. T. Lanham: I hope to Christ I wasn't the model for Colonel Cantwell in that novel. He told Leonard Lyons, his old pal the columnist, that I was, and it was duly published in Lyons's column. From then on whenever my name was mentioned in a paper in connection with some damn thing or another, it would always be, "the hero of *Across the River and Into the Trees.*" I couldn't abide the book. He had wanted me to go over the manuscript when I was stationed in Paris as Chief of Public Information, Supreme Headquarters Allied Powers in Europe. The very idea—to go over Hemingway's stuff and criticize it—appalled me. I wrote back to him, "Good God, Ernesto, who the hell am I to do a critical job on your manuscript? I couldn't think of it." So I was glad I didn't lay a glove on it. His books were singularly devoid of humor, but his letters to me were often screamingly funny. Much that he wrote was in the idiom we used between us. I always thought he didn't put it in his books because he didn't trust himself in the humor department. I later gave him hell for saying I was the hero of his book and said, "You know damn well I'm not." I added, "Ernesto, you are the hero of every book you've ever written." He said, "The truth is that the hero of *Across the River* is a composite of three people, you, an Irishman in the Foreign Legion, and myself." As for me, there's absolutely no resemblance until you come to the Hurtgen Forest—and he used a good bit of my idiom in that.

Robert Cowley: I remember my father getting the galleys of *Across the River* and sort of gulping and saying, "Oh my God, I've got to review this," and being, I think, much more gentle than he would have been ordinarily.

Denis Brian: What did you think of it, Mr. Cowley?

Malcolm Cowley: Very little. Actually, it was a rite of confession and absolution, but the confession stopped short. It didn't finish for the fictional character, because if you look at the book again, one thing Colonel Cantwell never tells is why he lost his star. If that had come in, it would have been a complete confession to Renata. Hemingway's imagination stopped there. If that had gone in, I think the book would have been rounded out.

Denis Brian: Welcome support came from World War I friend Dorman O'Gorman, who called the novel Ernest's best and too good for "lily-gutted be-testicled females who review books they could never attempt to write." Another sympathetic comment came from fellow novelist Raymond Chandler, who wrote, "He is trying to sum up in one character, not very different from himself, the attitude of a man who is finished and knows it and is bitter and furious about it."[1]

C. T. LANHAM: He had assured me he hadn't said anything bad about my friends in the novel. But when the book came out, he had torn some of them limb from limb. He'd done that to some senior officers who were good friends of mine, and to a certain extent he had celebrated some who were absolute pricks. When he didn't write to me for some time after the book came out, I wrote to him, "I finally came to the conclusion that you have not written to me for fear that our friendship may conceivably get me in a jam here, owing to some of your observations in *Across the River*. If that's what you're thinking, for Christ's sake, unthink it. If anybody wants to fire me because of my friends, they can fire me. And that goes double where you are concerned for you have been my number-one friend since 1944. I find that the ability to laugh and to wisecrack is as important here as it was in Hurtgen Forest. I have probably heard twenty or thirty people discuss *Across the River* at various times in the last two or three weeks. Only one had anything critical to say about it. A number thought it was the best book you have ever done but thought it could be appreciated only by highly intelligent people and, in particular, by people who have done a good deal of living. Colonel Whitelaw who is now Chief of Staff in Trieste, spent much of the evening eulogizing your book."

JEFFREY MEYERS: *Across the River* is underrated. First of all, it's not what everybody thinks it's about. It's not about Buck Lanham and Hemingway's adventures with him in World War II. So, unless you know what the novel's about you can't understand its meaning and judge it properly. Secondly, far from bragging and boasting about all these great things he can do in the guise of Robert Cantwell, it's a very, very self-lacerating, self-critical book where he's very hard on himself. In other words, it's completely the opposite of what everybody thought. It's about Dorman Smith, not about Lanham. It's very self-critical, not self-aggrandizing. And you have to judge it in the context of the fact that Hemingway hadn't had a book in ten years, the facts that Jones and Shaw and Mailer were coming out with big World War II novels, that he was physically sick before that and he had been quarreling with the critics. You have to take into account all kinds of other factors. To me, it's a very interesting book and the worse his novels are as art—that doesn't mean they're bad art, just that they're not great art—the more revealing they are about the man.

[1]Quoted in Norberto Fuentes, *Hemingway in Cuba*, Lyle Stuart Inc., 1984.

DENIS BRIAN: While smarting from the overwhelmingly negative response, Hemingway persuaded Mary to invite Adriana Ivancich and her mother to be their house guests.

JOSEPH DRYER: They came to Cuba and Adriana's brother, Gianfranco, followed. The family had financed a farm for him outside Havana. His father had been head of the Underground in his area during World War II, working with the Allies. In 1946 when they had their first general elections and the father was running for mayor of Venice, he was assassinated.

DENIS BRIAN: The arrival of Adriana enlivened Ernest and agitated Mary, who accused him of mooning over the young woman like a pimply teenager. Ridicule enraged Hemingway who threw Mary's typewriter to the floor, and in front of shocked guests flung wine from his glass into her face.

LEICESTER HEMINGWAY: Adriana was showoff material. You have to have somebody to show off to when you're doing your stuff; the old ego object.

DENIS BRIAN: Adriana later claimed she had revived his wilting creative powers. Do you think she inspired him, General Lanham?

C. T. LANHAM: I don't know about inspiration. He talked about her a lot and said how beautiful she was. Mary used to say, "You know, I feel I shouldn't be around because all of these teenagers fall in love with Ernest at first sight."

A FRIEND: And Ernest made sure she wasn't around. He sent Mary away from the house for several months and made her stay in a hotel in Havana. He said, "You must stay there. I demand my privacy. I am going to have house guests here. That's how it's going to be. Get used to it." She absolutely took it. She wanted so badly to keep on being his wife and to have the status of being the wife of a great writer that she'd do anything.

JOSEPH DRYER: Mary was very strong-minded and she could very well have said, "Either she leaves or I leave." Having the mother and daughter as house guests, Papa could have said, "If you don't like it, go to a hotel," or "go visit your family." Ernest had a bad temper and he could very well have said that. But to say "he kicked her out"—that I just don't know. I think Mary was concerned that a young woman, not much more than a girl, could enter the picture. Mary was a very different type: a dynamic, very self-reliant newspaperwoman who did everything to make Papa happy. At times, for example, she wouldn't go fishing with him—when she might have liked to—to give him the privacy of fishing by himself or with his friends. She had her own little boat and she and a man went out in it to compete against Papa for the biggest fish.

NANCY DRYER [Joseph's wife]: In Cuba, Adriana fell in love with Juan Verona, not Papa. She complained to me that Papa pursued her all the time and she couldn't stand it. She had great affection for him, but didn't love him. I had this from my friend Juan who was very interested in Adriana at the time and knew what was in her head probably more than anyone.

JOSEPH DRYER: We discussed Adriana and her relationship with Papa, with her brother Gianfranco. He had no criticism of it.

DENIS BRIAN: It's an echo from the Old Testament when dying old kings had young maidens to warm them and restore their strength.

C. T. LANHAM: I tell you, I had the feeling that in his condition there wasn't much he could do.

MADELAINE HEMINGWAY MILLER: I never heard of Ernest being impotent. He was always hoping to be the father of the whole world. He was proud of the boys he produced, but he always wanted a daughter.

NANCY DRYER: All the time I was with him, Papa was wonderful. He was considered an ogre by mothers of daughters in Cuba. They didn't like the talk that he and Mary swam naked in their pool [which they did]. It shocked Cuban society which is hypocritical and conservative. They didn't think it right for nice girls to visit the Hemingways.

DENIS BRIAN: Mary survived the gossip and the ordeal of Adriana's three-month visit.

A FRIEND: Yes, but Mary is her own best publicity agent and in her book she's talking about situations nobody else but Ernest is party to, where she can say, "He was magnanimous. He not only forgave me, he begged me to hang on." And she was telling him, "You're so abominable I can't stand you any more." And he'd say, "Stand me just a little longer. You know how I have these difficult days. I'm a writer, after all. You must understand." And it's not true that when he was sober he never asked her to leave. Because this thing that happened in Havana he didn't say when he was drunk.

DENIS BRIAN: Yet she claimed to have loved him.

A FRIEND: Maybe in the beginning, but not when he put her up at that hotel and moved that babe from Italy in.

CARLOS BAKER: Adriana made it quite clear in her book *The White Tower*, and in talking with my wife and me in Italy, that the *Across the River* portrait was quite false and exaggerated, and she herself had never even had an approximate sexual encounter with Hemingway.

DENIS BRIAN: If he couldn't have her in the flesh he could in fantasy. He consummated his love for her in the novel in which a battered ex-soldier remarkably like Hemingway makes love in a Venetian gondola to a young woman obviously meant to be Adriana. Hemingway kept in contact with Adriana over the years by writing her some two thousand letters, an indication of his enduring affection for her especially as she had been among those criticizing *Across the River*. Adriana married twice with Hemingway's blessing and wishes for her happiness.

NANCY DRYER: She had such a tragic end. According to my friend Juan Verano she had often talked about killing herself; this was something in her psyche that she evidently often thought of doing. She hanged herself.

Fun at the Finca and the Floridita

JOSEPH DRYER: Thursday nights Papa usually had about five friends to dinner. They'd all been involved with the International Brigades in Spain. Among them was Roberto Herrera, called Monstruo. He was a bald-headed, thin little guy, the brother of Ernest's doctor, Dr. Jose Luis Herrera. Monstruo acted as personal secretary and confidant. Anything Papa wanted done, Monstruo would do very exactly. He was a lot of fun. His brother had been battalion surgeon in the International Brigades during the Spanish Civil War. I asked Papa how Monstruo got his nickname and he said Roberto had been bitten by a shark and lost so much blood they called him "monster" because he survived. Then there was Juan Dunabeitía, called Sinsky, a tall, thin Basque who was captain of probably the most spotless tramp steamer that ever pulled into Havana harbor. And Father Don Andres, nicknamed Black Priest, a large, quite heavy man who had been sent from Spain to the smallest parish in Havana for being on the wrong side in the Spanish Civil War. Even though it was the poorest parish, he saved a little money to send back to people in Spain. They'd have dinner together at the Finca with a lot of wine and then sing songs of the Spanish Revolution, especially International Brigades songs. The Spanish Civil War was a favorite topic of conversation as well as what they'd individually been doing recently. They had a great deal of fun.

DENIS BRIAN: In her autobiography, Mary describes Father Andres as "a sweet, devout and innocent Basque who was also devoted to wine and food."

WILLIAM WALTON [laughs]: Father Andres was a priest who smelled so bad that whenever he came to the house he was required to take off his vestments and hang them outdoors and put on clean clothes that the Hemingways supplied.

DENIS BRIAN: How did Hemingway stand it?

WILLIAM WALTON: I don't know, but Mary drew the line. I remember when she and I were driving up the drive to the Finca, I said, "Look at that on the line outside the house." She said, "That means Father Andres is here. He now takes his clothes off and puts them out of doors automatically."

DENIS BRIAN: How did Hemingway behave among friends? MacLeish said he had an extraordinary presence.

WILLIAM WALTON: He did indeed. I agree with that completely. But he would never have been one for a stage or speaking career because his voice wasn't good enough.

JOSEPH DRYER: There was also an extremely gentle side to him, almost leaning over backwards to respect your privacy. In a good frame of mind and not preoccupied with a problem, he was very pleasant and easy to talk to. When I went to lunch or dinner he didn't discuss his own writing much, but he liked to talk about anything to do with military history. I had been in the Marine Corps with the Fifth Marine Division, and had a lung blown out by a sniper in Iwo Jima and Papa and I would occasionally discuss my experiences as a Marine. We discussed different campaigns in Europe, and Clausewitz and the philosophy of attack, the Marines' philosophy of storming beaches rather than pounding them with artillery. He was never boastful or talking about himself. He asked questions and tried to expand his knowledge, or just discussed a subject for the fun of it. He never discussed his personal experiences, although when I told him I had over a hundred pieces of shrapnel that could never come out inside one lung, I'm sure he said he had a lot of scars, too.

DENIS BRIAN: What was he like away from the Finca?

JOSEPH DRYER: Although his Spanish was not the best in the world he made a real effort, speaking slowly and carefully so as to be easily understood, which naturally the Cuban and Spanish people appreciated. At any bar people, mostly tourists, would come up to him. The Floridita was a big bar so he was better protected and the waiters there tried to protect him, too. The atmosphere was very pleasant and the food was outstanding. It was a very Spanish place with a high ceiling and a long bar of dark wood. They made the best daiquiris in the world, and created a special double-sized one for him with fresh lime juice and no sugar. But the principle reason he went to the Floridita was that he liked the bartenders.

DENIS BRIAN: What would strangers talk to him about?

JOSEPH DRYER: Usually politics. He was very careful about his political views, particularly in a country in which he was a guest. He was very happy in Cuba. I suspect he disapproved of Batista, but he didn't talk much about it. Sometimes the strangers would talk sports; sometimes all they wanted was to shake his hand and get his autograph. Quite often, someone who had been in the bar for a long time would find fault with something he had said or done and pick an argument with him. He didn't like that because he was very much a private person. He would usually sit at the end of the bar near the door—where it wasn't as easy to get to talk to him—with three or four friends. Still, about every two or three minutes someone would come up to say hello or to talk. Some were offended if he wasn't sufficiently polite, or wasn't giving them enough time to develop their arguments, or felt he wasn't paying enough attention to them.

THORVALD SANCHEZ, JR.: One day I was standing next to Hemingway in the Floridita and he said, "You know, your father made a big mistake." I asked, "What?" He said, "Because you'll never live up to your father. I never named any of my sons after me."

DENIS BRIAN: Perhaps he was joking.

THORVALD SANCHEZ, JR.: I think he meant it. He and my father were both heavy drinkers and big sportsmen and close friends. Hemingway wasn't a good sport. He was very competitive and he'd cheat. I guess he was determined to win. When he had drunk too much he was obnoxious and he drank something fantastic. Jeffrey Meyers interviewed my mother for his biography of Hemingway. She said he and my father drank straight gin and champagne chasers and just kept at it. This was during my father's fortieth birthday party and mother was furious at Hemingway because he went a little overboard and threw a lot of things out of the window, including her Baccarat crystal and God knows what. She never forgave him for that. It was a rough party. He and my father got along famously until he said he was in favor of Castro. That ended their friendship.

JOSEPH DRYER: If he'd had a bit to drink he could be short with people and he could be rough with those who had chips on their shoulders. But in the six years I knew him I never saw him get into a fight.

DENIS BRIAN: Mary did—over a dirty song. She tells in her autobiography how a fat tourist insisted on singing his own composition in Ernest's ear with his arm around his shoulder. Hemingway and a friend, Dick Hill, induced the man to accompany them to the men's room where Hemingway silenced him with "two left hooks and a little chop with the right." Mary reports that she and Ernest both hated dirty songs and dirty jokes.

JOHN RYBOVICH, JR.: Yet Mary Hemingway was the most profane woman I ever knew.[1] I met her at the Hemingway Billfish Tournament established by Cuban sportsmen after World War II. Ernest, as usual, did not participate, but Mary did from her own boat, *Tin Kid*. She won the trophy one year, which Ernest presented to her.

JOSEPH DRYER: Monstruo loved to go fishing with Papa and then at night to go hear a singer called Chori who was known throughout Cuba. He was very good and would sing his lungs out in some Havana dive for a few hours. One time Monstruo was in the Floridita—without Papa—and some huge six-foot-four Texan made a derogatory remark about Ernest. Monstruo said, "You mustn't speak about Papa like that." The Texan got up—and Monstruo was about five-nine and 140 pounds. He wagged his finger and repeated, "You shouldn't speak like that. I'm not going to allow you." The big Texan put one hand on Monstruo's bald head and pushed him down the bar, and told him to shut up. Monstruo came back swinging, and he was a very good fighter. Now the Floridita bar was very long and Monstruo punched him left and right all the way down the bar. The Texan never regained his balance, and went out all the way through the swing doors into the street with Monstruo following. There was a policeman outside and Monstruo ended up in his arms. Papa was delighted when he heard what had happened and went down to get Monstruo out of jail that night. Monstruo was probably the most loyal man you can imagine.

DENIS BRIAN: Absolute loyalty was a quality Ernest valued highly in his friends, which eliminated quite a few.

C. T. LANHAM: As far as I know, he never broke with anyone he met during the war years with me. And he spent most of the war with me

[1]Perhaps Hemingway's wives were driven to profanity. William Walton thinks Mary was no more profane than Martha.

before he came home. And, my God, he was crazy over all those people. They even made him an honorary member of my only wartime command. He broke with none of those. War seemed to bring out the best in him. In war, old Hemingstein, as he called himself, was magnificent. And in peacetime he could really be insufferable.

JOSEPH DRYER: I didn't see the insufferable side of him. When I knew him he was trying to write well and was very enthusiastic about what he was doing. I never heard him complain of his lack of action or his desire for adventure.

DENIS BRIAN: Tense moments in the Floridita seemed to be more than enough for him. Mary recounts in her book how a woman approached him there and suggested they resume the romantic encounter they had during World War II. Mary watched the muscles in his neck jerk—his distress signal.

THORVALD SANCHEZ, JR.: Mary usually rescued him from people like that. She was very good at protecting him.

JOSEPH DRYER: But such dramatic encounters were the exception. What he enjoyed was talking to his friends about anything that interested them, growing roses for instance. He'd sit and talk for hours learning all he could about growing roses.

DENIS BRIAN: He had another subject to discuss with friends when General Lanham wrote in a December 1, 1951, letter: "Saw a piece by a columnist on your brother Les and how to make wine in a bathtub from anything including soiled socks."

WILLIAM WALTON: He'd discuss almost anything, although he didn't ever tell me about his work in detail. But I read *The Old Man and the Sea* fresh out of his typewriter and I didn't have to ask him. He wanted me to read it. Had I asked, I'd never have read any of it. I was very excited about it. It was a beautiful little book, gemlike and perfect. He said he intended it to be one quarter of a book that included three other sections all with a connecting theme of life at sea. One of them became *Islands in the Stream.* He wanted me to read certain passages of that, so I did. He had been very pleased with my enthusiastic response to *The Old Man*, but very displeased with my response to his fictional account of his sub-hunting days. He made the protagonist in *Islands*, Thomas Hudson, a painter, who became a sculptor in the movie version. I'm a painter and when I stayed at the Finca Vigia I spent a lot of time painting. And he wanted me to read passages for veracity from the point of view of a painter. He disliked very much that I said the painter he had described was more a sports painter of "Dawn Over the Duck Marshes"—he was not Cézanne. Ernest hardly spoke to me for twenty-four hours because of that. And he took absolutely none of my advice about the book that I noticed.

DENIS BRIAN: Henry Strater had heard that Hemingway painted surprisingly well.

WILLIAM WALTON: I'm almost positive he didn't paint. He may have fooled someone by showing a Van Gogh as his, or some little Picasso sketches. There was a third-rate painter who lived near the Finca and Hemingway may have had two or three of his things around and as a joke pretended he had painted them. That was right down his alley.

DENIS BRIAN: Was he genuinely interested in painting?

WILLIAM WALTON: In one sense. Whenever we were in New York at the same time we'd always go to the Met. He had certain great favorites he wanted to check out—a beautiful Breughel, a half-harvested wheat field with the wheat very beautifully portrayed and sleeping peasants along one side. One of the great Breughels. He boasted among other things that he'd discovered the secrets of Cézanne. But he hadn't, really. He didn't understand modern paintings. He liked mine and I gave him a number of them that are now in the Kennedy Library. I did a little sketchbook for him of things around the Finca.

DENIS BRIAN: How did he and Gertrude Stein compare as art critics?

WILLIAM WALTON: She had more of an eye than Ernest and certainly in modern painting she had a great deal more education than Ernest did.

DENIS BRIAN: You weren't the only one enthusiastic about *The Old Man and the Sea*. General Lanham wrote to Hemingway on September 17, 1952: "It is truly one of the most breathless things I have ever laid eyes on or a ear to. It is knee deep in beauty and in all the values that mean so god damned much to jerks like you and me. It is written with an angelic pen and a heart as big as this lousy world." You can imagine Lanham's relief in being able to report favorably after having been evasive over *Across the River*. Buoyed by the ecstatic responses to his latest book Ernest was able to joke about the disastrous reception given to *Across the River*. When he wrote to Ada and Archibald MacLeish on October 5, 1952, he characterized the novel as a travel book on Venice liked by a small minority, including the owners and staff of the Gritti Palace Hotel, the owner of Harry's Bar, Mary Hemingway, and Bernard Berenson, the art critic.

A FRIEND: Of course he was pleased about the success of *The Old Man and the Sea*. It quickly sold tens of thousands of copies, fan mail came to Ernest by the thousand every few days. It was a great comeback after the failure of *Across the River*. He wanted to celebrate the success and get away from all the publicity by going on another safari in East Africa. Ernest had vowed that he'd never return to Spain as long as one of his friends was in a Franco prison. He got news about now that the last one had been freed. So he set off for Africa with Mary by way of Spain.

GEORGE SELDES: My wife and I started spending winters in Spain in 1953 and that's where I ran into Hemingway again. He advised me to stay at the Suecia Hotel in Madrid, which was small but excellent. There we heard the porters talking about room 211 being the Hemingway suite. And the maids told us all about the parties Hemingway had there. He spent 50,000 pesetas a month on whiskey alone for the parties. That was when he was there with the bullfighters Dominguín and Ordoñez. This amounted to $800, about twice the yearly salary of a Spanish worker. Franco more or less set wages at a dollar a day, so people making $350 a year got the going wages there. And in a month this man spent two years of their wages on whiskey alone. In those parties he had twenty to forty people in that suite of three rooms. But this was a terrific person, there's no question of it.

TWELVE

·

THE PHOENIX

DENIS BRIAN: Early in 1954 Ernest and Mary Hemingway were sight-seeing from a small Cessna 180. The pilot flew low over the Murchison Falls in Uganda, struck a wire, and crashed. None was seriously injured though Mary was in shock and the trio spent a miserable night on a cold hillside while elephants approached too close for comfort. Fortunately, next morning, a boat appeared on a nearby river and they traveled on it to a rough airstrip. Here they arranged for the pilot of a DeHavilland Rapide to fly them to Entebbe, the nation's capital. The takeoff was over bumpy ground. They never made it. The plane crashed and caught fire. Mary, the pilot, and the pilot of the previously crashed plane managed to squeeze through a smashed window to safety. But Ernest, too bulky to follow them, was trapped in the burning plane. The plane's metal door had buckled shut in the crash. Using his head and shoulder as a battering ram he forced it open and got out. He had suffered terrible injuries, including his tenth and near-fatal concussion, but he did not discover the extent and severity of his injuries until he was carefully examined several months later. A physician gave him primitive first-aid in a local bar by pouring gin in a hole in his head, from which cerebral fluid leaked onto his pillow during the night. Soon afterwards he joined a group fighting a bush fire. He stumbled and fell into the flames.

ARTHUR WALDHORN: Why does he throw himself into taking care of a brush fire in Africa after he's been in those airplane accidents? Here's a person who had an extremely heightened ego and he needed constant reaffirmation of his doubts about himself. Whatever he has done is still inadequate to the ultimate image he has of himself. He has to test himself further. It's as if people might think he hasn't proved himself. This is a regressive kind of arrested adolescent state, and of course you've got psychological problems, and to some extent his writing reflects it. On the other hand, he often gets a distance from that. In his "Big Two-Hearted River" the distance is remarkable, where he sees the young man's problem and he sees how one has to discipline and control it. And he makes the work the discipline.

WINSTON GUEST: Ernest told me about the first crash when they were flying over the Murchison Falls and hit telephone wires. It's a miracle they lived. That's his first accident there. Then another plane crashed on takeoff. That's when he came out with his famous statement about emerging "with a bunch of bananas and a bottle of gin." Not long before, poor fellow, he was in Italy shooting ducks and he told me a bit of the wadding backfired and he got an eye infection. He treated that as best he could with antibiotics and, I suppose, a certain amount of drink. If you have a concussion, you should never drink because it does irreparable damage to your brain besides what damage the concussion may have done. Oh, by the way, when he had his first injury to his head as an ambulance driver in Italy, he told me that during a shelling when he was in the trenches one of the beams covering the trench broke and fell on his head. And, to his dying day, he always covered the scar on his forehead where he received the wound.[1]

DENIS BRIAN: The Hemingways eventually made a leisurely return journey to Havana via Italy, France, and Spain. His injuries from the crash and flames sound like an autopsy report: in addition to the severe concussion he had crushed his liver, spleen and vertebra, his sphincter muscle was paralyzed, and his lower intestine had collapsed. Believing he could not

[1]The first and last time I heard this. Nor have I found it in any biographical work.

have survived, several newspapers wrote his obituary. He also saw double, his hearing came and went, and he endured constant severe pain.

JOHN HEMINGWAY: He had a personality change after those crashes; I don't think there's any question of it. I always tried to deny it and found excuses for it, but looking back I think there's no doubt about it. He was easily nasty after those crashes and really became quite a different person in those last years.

LEICESTER HEMINGWAY: The guy was feeling enormously bereft at the realization that his body was failing him.

JOHN HEMINGWAY: I was never aware of his being in great pain, but my father had become very dependent on drink. They had really cut him down on his intake because he had a bad case of hepatitis and was allowed just a little wine every day. And he was miserable. Not only that, he was also irascible.

JOHN RYBOVICH, JR.: I learned he had been very ill with hepatitis. Then in 1954 he invited me to Havana to pick up signed copies of *The Old Man and the Sea* for prizes for the new Old Man and the Sea trophy. This was his first day up in six weeks, but it was a delightful morning nonetheless. He was relaxed and charming. We traded fishes, he posed with me for a photographer and then gave me a tour of the farm. He wrote in the *Old Man and the Sea* book he gave me: "Dear Johnny, Hope you can read this light tackle treatise without too much pain. See you next year."

MARY HEMINGWAY: That year he had hepatitis, Ernest didn't drink anything for fourteen months. Before and after that we usually had two martinis before lunch and two or three martinis before dinner together with at least a bottle of wine, and depending on the number of guests, more bottles of wine. Ernest never took anything after dinner, or only on the rarest occasions. He would go to bed at ten-thirty or eleven and wake about daybreak without having had anything alcoholic since dinner. Of course, Cuba being hot, we always had thermoses of cold water beside the bed. I'm speaking of our normal life in Cuba. Some chickenshit professor who teaches English in Arkansas or Kansas listed him as an alcoholic, without ever having apparently made much of an investigation. It is *so* mistaken. I have been told by mutual friends that Faulkner used to go on week-long benders. Ernest never did that. I only once or twice saw him a little unsteady on his feet—in seventeen years. Once it happened to be in Cuba. On that occasion we stayed out, which was the *rarest* thing. We may have gone, in seventeen years, four or five times to nightclubs and had a few gin and tonics. And on *one* of those occasions, he was a bit unsteady as we got out of the car. I don't mean he fell down or anything like that, but that's the only time I ever saw him that way.

DENIS BRIAN: William Walton, Joseph Dryer, and others dispute this view of Hemingway as an almost moderate drinker, rarely even unsteady through drinking. After he recovered from hepatitis he resumed his visits to the Floridita.

THORVALD SANCHEZ, JR.: I was discussing Hemingway with a woman standing next to me in Harry's Bar in Venice. She was a Chilean newspaperwoman and said that she wanted to meet Hemingway more than anything else in the world. I told her I could arrange it if she'd come to Havana. It was one of those things you say, you know, that you never expect people to pick you up on. So I was quite surprised when I returned to Havana and she phoned me and said she was in Cuba and was taking me up on my promise. I said, "I'm not going to call Hemingway up, but if you'd like to come with me for a drink at the Floridita he'll probably be there and you'll meet him naturally." And he was there with Mary. Unfortunately this newspaperwoman began asking him very personal questions about his sex life. Mary came to his rescue, making a joke of it, and the woman stopped her questions. He gave me the galleys of *The Old Man and the Sea* and I took them to the Floridita for him to inscribe. One day I was broke in New York and I sold them.

JOSEPH DRYER: One of Papa's guests that year was the world champion bullfighter Luis Miguel Dominguín. After retiring he'd gone to the Sorbonne to educate himself and then into business. He'd had an affair with Ava Gardner and had acted in her film *Pandora and the Flying Dutchman.* He'd done a lot, but life was not satisfactory. So he came to Cuba to ask Papa what he should do with the rest of his life. He was there for about two weeks. Papa asked if my brother and I would take him out to parties at night, which we did. After about a week, Mary said to me, "Luis Miguel is asking Papa what he should do with his life. Papa is not going to give advice." Instead, Ernest would tell him stories about old boxers, baseball players, soldiers, and, of course, all of his stories would have a purpose. Finally, Mary said, "Gee, I wish he would tell him what he thinks Luis Miguel should do with his life—whether or not he should return to bullfighting." Now, that's a very difficult situation, when somebody has reached the pinnacle of his profession in the world. And if he continues, there's a very good chance he will be killed. Because Manolete had died in a *mano á mano* with Luis Miguel [in 1947]. So he had that memory fresh in his mind. I think Papa also used this opportunity to study Luis

Miguel and what made a bullfighter tick. Luis Miguel was a very attractive young fellow, nice-looking, and he had good manners; and the decision about what he was going to do with his life was naturally very important to him. I mention this as an example of the pressure put on Papa to give his opinion. I was then engaged to Nancy. She felt he was very protective and more of a second father than anybody she'd ever met and she could discuss anything with him and feel it would be a private conversation. She loved him. When Luis Miguel was there we were having dinner at the Finca and after a while I didn't know where Papa or Nancy was. And Mary and I and some other guests went out on the steps of the Finca and there were Papa and Nancy and Dominguín sitting on the steps in the moonlight, just finishing a bottle of champagne and Papa and Nancy were crying and Papa had his arm around her and he was being very emotional. There was warmth about him and a very real sincerity.

NANCY DRYER: That moonlit night Joe and I had just become engaged. That moonlight was very romantic. There I was sitting on the steps under a full moon with a great writer on one side and a great bullfighter on the other. Dominguín was extremely handsome and dashing and I had a crush on him.

JOSEPH DRYER: When we asked Papa if he'd be a *testigo* [witness] at our wedding—in Spanish or Cuban weddings a *testigo* is generally older than the bride or groom; it could be your parents' best friend or someone with whom you grew up—we were very pleasantly surprised when he said yes, and Mary said, "This is the first time I can remember Papa getting dressed up in a suit and tie, especially in the daytime."

DENIS BRIAN: And his advice to the bullfighter?

JOSEPH DRYER: He never gave it. He thought it best that Luis Miguel make up his own mind. And Mary was exasperated that he left Cuba and Papa had not told him what to do. He went back to bullfighting.

The Nobel Prize

DENIS BRIAN: Hemingway wrote to Archibald MacLeish on March 2, 1954, calling himself a bad brother and saying he loved Ada very much and loved MacLeish as if he were his brother. He predicted that he would never get the Nobel Prize as he was the only author who knew how to handle dynamite and make it out of nitroglycerine and sand. Less than three weeks later Hemingway learned his prediction was wrong.

C. T. LANHAM: Ernest phoned me the same day he heard he'd won the

Nobel Prize. He wanted to share the good news. I had just had a hernia operation. I walked along the hospital corridor to reach the phone and then spoke to him holding my gut in one hand and the phone in the other. He was tempted to tell the Swedish judges to shove it, he told me, because he suspected that no Nobel Prize winner ever wrote worth a damn after receiving the award. But the tax-free $35,000 was too much to resist. He was still too sick to go to the Stockholm ceremonies and still in pain from those plane crashes. So he recorded his acceptance speech in Havana.

GEORGE SAVIERS [Hemingway's doctor and friend in Sun Valley]: It did Ernest a lot of good to finally come back with *The Old Man and the Sea* after the early stuff he did in the twenties. I think he felt he was doing his best writing in those early days. And when he found he could do it again, that gave him a lot of joy and comfort.

HUGH BUTT [Hemingway's doctor and friend, later at St. Mary's hospital, the Mayo Clinic]: He made a comment to me about Faulkner. He said that anyone could write that way, it was verbose and wasn't in his opinion, good writing. He also said that the secret nobody seemed to have discovered was that *The Old Man and the Sea* was poetry written as prose. That's a lovely thought, isn't it?

DENIS BRIAN: There was no mention of his Nobel prize in an FBI report of July 20, 1955, which summarized his support of the Abraham Lincoln Brigade during the Spanish Civil War and his support for a rescue ship to be sent to help Loyalists escape after the war. Surprisingly the report also contained the following: "A confidential informant who has previously furnished reliable information reported that in September 1943, Ernest Hemingway was discussing certain newspaper articles which attacked the United States Army for refusing to admit to the Officers' Training School individuals who had fought in the Abraham Lincoln Brigade in the Spanish Civil War. According to the informant, Hemingway took exception and stated that the United States Army was perfectly justified in the action which was taken inasmuch as each individual who had been refused admission to the Officers' Training School was an out-and-out communist."

Dangerous Summer

DENIS BRIAN: Since the Nobel prize Hemingway had become a tourist attraction. Limousine loads came to see, touch, and talk. They ignored the UNINVITED VISITORS WILL NOT BE RECEIVED, or said they couldn't read

Spanish—in which the sign was written—or that they thought only Spanish speakers were verboten.

JOSEPH DRYER: Mary always did a tremendous amount of good in protecting Ernest from even well-known people who arrived, because their privacy was becoming important to them. She'd say he was working in the tower and couldn't be disturbed. He had a very definite routine of writing hours in the mornings. Still, he nearly always had house guests. A lot of people expected to stay with him, others wanted to invite him out for a meal.

DENIS BRIAN: Invited guests swamped the Finca in the spring and early summer of 1955, among them Sinsky [Juan Dunabeitía] and Roberto Herrara; Ernest's lawyer, Alfred Rice; his agent Leland Hayward, to discuss the projected movie of *The Old Man and the Sea;* Taylor Williams, a Sun Valley, Idaho, hunting friend who arrived with a smile and a broken ankle; Peter Viertel, who was to write the film script; the ever welcome William Walton who came, he warned them in a letter, "to eat mangoes, swim, paint bamboo, and talk endlessly," and Ernest's sparring partner, George Brown. In the fall, movie director Fred Zinnemann joined the group, then Leland Hayward's wife, and soon after that John Hemingway.

JOHN HEMINGWAY: This is very vivid in my mind. I'd been living in Portland, Oregon, and I was doing badly in business and I went down to Cuba for a visit and to borrow a little money. It was after all those crashes and Papa was in terrible shape. He wasn't supposed to be drinking, but he drank. And we were both a little smashed. We worked on a pitcher of martinis and then we had the boys put a dead goat on the roof of the tower. And then the buzzards started to come. And here we were up on the tower calling out, "Twelve o'clock high!" and shooting the buzzards.

DENIS BRIAN: John was followed by Mike Burke, an ex-OSS operative; Fred Zinnemann's wife Timmy; playwright Charles MacArthur and his actress wife Helen Hayes; writer George Plimpton; Bernard and Alva Gimbel; writer Alan Moorehead; Ernest's sister Ursula and her husband Jasper Jepson; photographer Earl Theisen and a friend—to name just a few of those welcomed and entertained. The uninvited included a group of midshipmen and chief petty officers of the U.S. Navy, who weren't sure what Ernest had written but thought he was a great guy. He ended up entertaining them at the Floridita. In the fall of 1956 Ernest and Mary escaped to Paris but didn't escape the crowds.

C. Z. GUEST: About the last time I saw him, he was at the Ritz in Paris and my husband and I happened to be there. Ingrid Bergman was in Paris, too, playing in Robert Anderson's *Tea and Sympathy*. Hemingway adored Ingrid Bergman. Well, let me tell you. After the show we all went to the Ritz, but the place was crowded. Finally, I don't know how they did it, they got us in. And Papa was going to have to sit at another table—with Ingrid Bergman. And there was a stampede of people to meet him, more than her. It was funny. So he had something magnetic about him.

DENIS BRIAN: Ernest and Mary went south from Paris to Pamplona to watch Antonio Ordoñez and others fight bulls. Their homecoming at the Finca was spoiled by a carload of Wall Street tycoons who arrived unasked, drank Ernest's whiskey and guffawed at his every sally while Mary groaned. As they were leaving she warned their driver that she'd shoot him if he ever brought another uninvited visitor. After a hot and humid Cuban summer in 1957 and a bitterly cold and wind-whipped winter, they looked forward to spending the fall and winter of 1958–9 in Idaho with black and brown bears for neighbors and no need for KEEP OUT signs. While duck hunting there, Ernest sprained his heel tendon vaulting over a fence. George Saviers, a Sun Valley physician, bandaged the heel and soon he was a regular guest at the Hemingways' home as well as a hunting companion.

GEORGE SAVIERS: He had more of a zest for life than most people.

DENIS BRIAN: Even after those plane crash injuries?

GEORGE SAVIERS: Yes. And he wanted to see that everybody around him in Sun Valley enjoyed themselves. I used to go with other friends of his to his place to watch Friday night fights on television. He would make book, and he had this marvelous propensity to make everybody win, whether they were betting on the black or on the white trunks. In those days TV was black and white. He was the bookie and *everybody* won. I know he felt competitive. Still, when he was hunting, he always wanted to see that friends got up first for the best shot. He was a very kind and friendly gentleman who couldn't get this through to many people, because he had this tough guy façade that was probably not his doing. I've met a lot of great surgeons, musicians, and artists and I would place him—and this is not hero-worship, although my ex-wife said that's what it was—as one of the greatest guys I ever knew.

DENIS BRIAN: Robert Cowley said the only other man he met who matched Hemingway's magnetic personality was President John Kennedy. You knew them both, Mr. Walton. Do you agree?

WILLIAM WALTON: They were not similar in personality but they had this quality in common—radiance, a sense of presence. Of course, once a man becomes president it seems to add to his sense of presence.

DENIS BRIAN: Back in Cuba in the spring of 1959, Ernest met Alec Guinness and his wife in the Floridita and invited them home to dinner. Guinness was filming *Our Man in Havana*. Other guests at the Finca that evening were writer Graham Greene, director Carol Reed, and actor Nöel Coward. After dinner, Ernest beckoned Guinness into his study and said, "I can't bear another minute of Nöel's insane chatter. Who's interested in a bunch of old English actresses he's picked up from the gutter? Not me. If he wags that silly finger once more I may hit him."[1] He glowered at severed heads of African game on the walls. "Lovely creatures," he said. "You love what you kill. I wouldn't kill Nöel—just dust him up a bit. Am I pissed?" "A little," Guinness said. Hemingway laughed and gave him a hug. Nöel Coward recalled the same evening in his diary entry for April 16, 1959: "Dined with Ernest and Mary Hemingway in that house just outside Havana and all got thoroughly pissed."[2]

JOSEPH DRYER: Papa spent the summer of 1959 with the matadors Luis Miguel Dominguín and Antonio Ordoñez, particularly Ordoñez and his wife, Carmine, getting material for *The Dangerous Summer*, just following the two great rivals across the country from one bullfight to another. He became very close to both men, maybe a little closer to Ordoñez, who is now probably Spain's most famous bullfighter.

WILLIAM WALTON: There's a certain sadness in the very last years. He was so patently failing and he had become a man twenty years older than his years, and his face was so sad.

DENIS BRIAN: Yet there were times when he could still display the old verve and energy. Both Mary Hemingway and actress Lauren Bacall gave accounts of their three-hour lunch with Ernest in Malaga, Spain in early July 1959.

MARY HEMINGWAY: Slim Hayward and Lauren Bacall came to lunch. They greeted Ernest as a long-lost friend and produced their man-capturing show for Bill [Davis] and Ernest. "Darling, you're so slim and beautiful," said Slim. "You're even bigger than I imagined," said Miss Bacall and Ernest puffed up. "It's so long, Papa, you never pay any attention to me," said Slim. Ernest looked contrite. . . . "Couldn't you teach me about

[1] Alec Guinness, *Blessings in Disguise*, Knopf, 1986.
[2] *The Nöel Coward Diaries*, Little, Brown, 1982.

bullfights?" asked Miss B., moving in very close, smiling up at Ernest.[1]

LAUREN BACALL: I was eager to meet this larger-than-life character. He really turned on the charm—calling me Miss Betty, saying he'd heard about me from Slim, and he'd admired Bogie, and my behavior during Bogie's illness made me okay in his book. Naturally I hung on his every word, and naturally Mary Hemingway, knowing him, was not too pleased. They were talking about hunting. She asked me if I was a good shot—leaned over, saying, "Maybe you'd like to come with us sometime," placing a bullet on my plate. I didn't blame her—obviously he'd given her a bad time in the past; just as obviously his ego required feeding.[2]

C. T. LANHAM: When I received an invitation from Ernest to attend his sixtieth birthday in Spain on July 21, I wrote back: "When I was a kid there was an expression in my section that was used when someone was going on a trip and couldn't sleep for excitement. The expression was journey proud. I've had it bad since your letter. I'm just plain country 'journey proud.' " I flew over and found him a very sick man trying to recapture his youth in Spain. It didn't work out because he was dreadfully sick and he was getting to be an old man, too.

DENIS BRIAN: Why did the inscription in the book *The History of the 22nd Infantry* cause him to burst into tears?

C. T. LANHAM: It was a brochure, put together by the chaplain I think. And I had written some sort of inscription. He just burst into tears and got up from the table. When he came back he damn near crushed my ribs. He was a bear of a man, you know. I wrote in the inscription what I thought his value had been to the combat team and what he meant to me.

DENIS BRIAN: This was the occasion when he violently objected to your accidentally touching the thinning hair that he had carefully combed across his scalp. Was he close to a physical or mental breakdown then?

C. T. LANHAM: Well, he was a sick man, I knew that. The plane crashes had ruptured his liver, and ruptured his spleen. And he had very bum kidneys that he was being treated for constantly. Of course, he was an absolutely incredible drinker. He could drink twenty-four hours a day. So he had a physical breakdown in all departments. He had lost a great deal of weight and was unhappy with himself. He was cursing his doctor every

[1]Mary Welsh Hemingway, *How It Was.*

[2]Lauren Bacall, *By Myself,* Knopf, 1979.

day, because although he was supposed to be with him the whole time, the doctor did a little sightseeing. I went into Ernest's room the morning I arrived to see if he was all right, because I'd heard he was ill the night before. And, my God, I looked around his room and there were bottles of urine in every possible place, all labeled and dated, waiting for the doctor to analyze them. Ernest was furious when I came in. He was sitting up, reading. He was never a hypochondriac, but now he was a very sick man. He couldn't write anything. Life had lost all meaning, all point for him. He might just as well have had terminal cancer and been in great pain. Some years earlier, in his letters to me, he'd set down his blood pressure almost day by day.

He found out about his hypertension by accident. A good friend of his was cursed with hypertension and told Ernest that he had to have his blood pressure checked before he could go hunting with him. And the guy was apprehensive about it, so to buck him up Ernest said he bet that his pressure was higher than his friend's. The doctor [José Luis Herrera] took the friend's blood pressure. It was high. Ernest then said, "Take mine." And the doctor took it and it was just coming out of the top of the tube. This really alerted him. Ernest wrote and told me about it. From that time on he began to be checked on that.

JOSÉ LUIS CASTILLO-PUCHE: Ernesto began the day [in Spain in 1960] waking up with a cramp somewhere or other, and often after he had gone to bed at night he would complain of peculiar sensations of some sort, and Mary would do her best to calm him down. He very often suffered severe attacks of anxiety or had terrifying nightmares, and acting as cross as a bear and swearing a blue streak were usually simply his way of asking for help. Mary was unable to work miracles, but fortunately she knew how to handle Ernesto and could usually get him back to sleep again.[1]

DENIS BRIAN: Back in Idaho for the winter Hemingway noticed lights on late at night in the local bank. He told Mary, "The FBI are trying to catch us. They want to get something on us." She put his fears down to being overtired. When they returned to Cuba—a country now ruled by Castro's revolutionary government—in the spring he seemed to have mastered his fears by concentrating on The Dangerous Summer. He invited his friend George Saviers to join him for a few days.

GEORGE SAVIERS: This will tell you what kind of guy he was. I had gone out fishing with Gregorio Fuentes and hadn't done very well. So Ernest

[1]José Luis Castillo-Puche, Hemingway in Spain.

quit his writing to take me out. Mary was with us. And I finally got my white marlin. We were heading back and we saw one of these floats with lanterns on it that fishermen use out there. They have a couple of lines down at different depths that float along at the edge of the stream. These floats mean almost as much as a boat to these poor fishermen. And this guy had lost his. And rich Cubans were running by it in their boats. We stopped fishing, pulled everything in, went out and picked up the float and found the fisherman who'd lost it and gave it to him. It took us about an hour to do it. He knew what it meant to the fisherman. And that's the kind of guy he was.

C. T. Lanham: Ernest returned to Spain in 1960 to get more material for *The Dangerous Summer*. Now he described bullfighting, his passionate interest for forty years, as corrupt and unimportant. He showed me the manuscript at one stage and I wrote to him and told him it was poorly written, prolix, tedious, and dull. He wrote back thanking me for what I'd said, agreeing with me. He said the book would never be published. But, Christ, they ran so much of it in *Life*. And when I told Mary what Ernest had said, she said, "I'm certainly glad you told me."

Denis Brian: Hemingway was still in Spain, lonely, bored, remorseful, suspicious, and on the edge of a mental breakdown. When he returned to Sun Valley he expressed fears that FBI men were tailing him, that he was going broke, and that his blood pressure was dangerously high. He resisted the suggestion that he consult a psychiatrist at the Menninger Clinic. "They'll say I'm losing my marbles," he said. But he agreed to fly to the Mayo Clinic in Rochester, Minnesota for a medical examination.

CHAPTER

THIRTEEN

•

SHOCK TREATMENT

MRS. LARRY JOHNSON: My husband was the pilot who flew Ernest Hemingway to Rochester. He had hypertension. I spoke to him before he left and he seemed normal, a little sick like some people are, kind of weak. To me he acted normal. He wasn't erratic. He never had any outbursts or anything all the way there and he didn't ever try to jump out of the plane as someone reported. And he didn't act like he was sedated. I think he had a bottle of wine with him. I think I saw one. Dr. Saviers went with him. My husband held regular conversations with Hemingway all the way to Rochester and thought he was a very nice, down-to-earth, old-fashioned gentleman.

DENIS BRIAN: Dr. Howard Rome treated his deep depression with electric shock therapy. Dr. Hugh Butt, a liver specialist, treated his physical problems: high blood pressure, an enlarged liver, diabetic symptoms, and the possibility that he had hemachromatosis, a rare disease. His friend William Walton persuaded John Kennedy to invite Ernest and Mary to his presidential inauguration. Hemingway was cheered by the invitation but not well enough to attend.

HUGH BUTT: I saw him more than daily for several months and got to know him quite well. Although he was ill mentally and physically he had happy times. At Christmas dinner [in 1960] with Mary and my family, my four children, he taught my daughter, Martha, to pull the corks from bottles. He was strong enough to pull them out, once you started them, with his fingers. He'd ask whether you wanted a loud pop or a little pop. Although I saw him when he was ill, he still had a great, great sense of humor. And he was great fun singing, he and Mary together, Italian and French songs. His voice wasn't anything great, but he was on key. They sang together. They'd obviously done it before. It was very pleasant. He gave me his book *The Old Man and the Sea* and I asked him how many times did he have to rewrite it. He looked at me and said, "Hugh, you go home tonight with this book and open it. Close your eyes and put your finger down on any page you come to. Then you sit down and try to shorten the sentence." I did that and for me—although I'm not a writer—it was impossible to shorten it and say what he said. He was implying, I think, that he had rewritten it many, many times.

TO: DIRECTOR, FBI, JANUARY 13, 1961
FROM: SPECIAL AGENT IN CHARGE, MINNEAPOLIS

Ernest Hemingway, the author, has been a patient at Mayo Clinic, Rochester, Minneapolis, and is presently at St. Mary's Hospital in that city. He has been at the clinic for several weeks, and is described as a problem. He is seriously ill, both physically and mentally, and at one time the doctors were considering giving him electro-shock therapy treatments. To eliminate publicity and contacts by newsmen, the clinic had suggested that Mr. Hemingway register under the alias George Sevier [sic]. [Blanked out] stated that Mr. Hemingway is now worried about his registering under an assumed name, and is concerned about an FBI investigation. [Blanked out] stated that inasmuch as this worry was interfering with the treatments of Mr. Hemingway, he desired authorization to tell Hemingway that the FBI was not concerned with his registering under an assumed name [blanked out] was advised that there was no objection.

WINSTON GUEST: I knew he'd gone to a hospital, but I was very naïve about it; I didn't know how ill he was. I'll never forget finding out who was the top psychiatrist at the hospital and I called him and said I wanted to talk to Ernest. I told him who I was. The doctor said practically, "Are you mad? Are you crazy? You can't talk to him at all." So then I guessed he must have been seriously ill, mentally ill. And I never saw him again after that.

MILTON WOLFF: He was being treated by a doctor in Cuba, I think, who was a great guy. He was doing all right there, but when he left Cuba and came here and saw some psychiatrists he just got worse and worse. I guess I heard from Diana Sheean, Vincent's wife, that Ernest was ill and in Rochester. I heard he was writing to everybody that the FBI was following him around and had a tail on him and was tapping his phones and reading his mail and that they were out to get him, he knew too much, and so forth. We were all incredulous—what the hell could he know that the FBI would be tailing him? Apparently, he was suffering from some form of paranoia. I wrote to him and his reply was a very upbeat letter. The last letters I got from him he said he was going to make it.

A FRIEND: He fooled the doctors into thinking he was cured and they released him. One day he told George Saviers he couldn't write any more. And he was crying.

C. T. LANHAM: Mary walked into their living room and found him with a shotgun in his hands, sitting on the couch. She spent an agonizing morning trying to talk him out of killing himself. Finally the doctors who were supposed to be there earlier showed up. They took the gun away without any problem and put him in a car and took him back to the head factory.

DENIS BRIAN: But before he was flown back to the Mayo Clinic, Ernest was given permission to return home to pick up a few things, escorted by nurse Joanie Higgons and Don Anderson, a strongly built six-footer. Ernest hurried ahead of them and loaded his shotgun.

JOANIE HIGGONS: It wasn't in my head that Hemingway was suicidal. He just seemed depressed and quiet. Hotchner described a terrible struggle for the gun and that Dr. Saviers had to help. Well, Dr. Saviers wasn't there this time, and it wasn't nearly as violent as Hotchner made it sound.[1] Though Ernest did have a ferocious expression on his face when he and Don wrestled for the loaded shotgun. After Don opened the breech, Ernest sat on the settee looking sullen. Then I telephoned Dr. Saviers, who came over to take Ernest back to the hospital.

[1]A. E. Hotchner, *Papa Hemingway*.

DON ANDERSON: He didn't put up much of a fight for the gun. He was pretty weak, so I didn't have a great struggle to get it from him. He was a different man in those last months, not completely different, but pretty much so. He had his good and his bad days. We all knew he wasn't well, but we weren't professional enough to qualify it. Hotchner's account was bullshit.

MRS. LARRY JOHNSON: On the second flight to Rochester he acted the same way: no problem at all. And he was telling my husband where there was a marijuana field not far from the airport and he was talking about several different things all the way to Rochester, how he fished in Wyoming and things like that. I think the trouble was that he was despondent because he couldn't think of anything to write, and because of the hypertension. [Larry Johnson was later killed when his plane crashed.]

DON ANDERSON: It's definitely not true that Hemingway tried to jump out of the plane in flight, as Hotchner wrote. I was sitting in the back seat with him and he talked on and off about hunting. He was a little bitter, saying he'd been shanghaied. I was apprehensive once when he grabbed a knife. I mean, when a person's that suicidal . . . I won't say I was scared. But then he just used the knife to cut his belt to make it shorter. There was no violence on the flight. No restraints on him at all during the trip. I wasn't there as his guardian. I guess Hotchner got his material out of the air.

GEORGE SAVIERS [also on that flight]: Hotchner's *Papa* was a bunch of crap. There are too many inaccuracies in it.

A FRIEND: Ernest and Mary were living together until the very last. He was literally a shell of himself and wondering whether he ought to try and mend the shell because his memory was going, or whether he should try and break the shell. Nobody knows what was in the man's mind, no one on earth. I have yet to meet the man who can tell me what was in Ernest's mind at any point in his life, it doesn't matter what he's saying or what he's writing.

C. T. LANHAM: Apparently he'd stopped drinking. They had him dieting. They had him doing everything. The only two dull letters I ever had from him were the last two. Both came from him while he was in the hospital. The last I recall writing to him was a plea, because I was beginning to get worried. I knew how sick he was. He had a drop where he sent his letters. because he was at that time still trying to keep people from knowing he was in the hospital. I told him this world would be a damned, empty, drab, lonesome place without him. And, for God's sake, not to do anything foolish—don't keep thinking those "black-ass thoughts" as he called them. His reply was very short and dull, and obviously dictated. It was perfectly rational, but noncommital in everything, not responsive. But after he had signed the letter he wrote in his own hand at the bottom— and this was a typical Hemingway expression: "Buck, stop sweating me out! Sweat out only flying weather and the common cold." And he initialed it. It was his jovial way of telling me not to worry.

LEICESTER HEMINGWAY: He had hemochromatosis. It's rare, but not a killer disease. It's a condition wherein the blood picks up more iron than normally and you eventually become more loaded with iron than a normal male. It's something that females almost can't get. They were undoubtedly doing the best they knew how, but I don't think they were going deeply enough into the chemical imbalance that probably was hitting him. They went heavily into shock treatment which they probably thought was going to fix him up immediately, and I don't think they did a good enough job of assuring him that his memory was going to come back. Because what scared the bejesus out of him was the realization it had wiped out so much of his memory. It just immediately erased it. He wasn't content to wait for three or four weeks for it to come back. A hell of a lot comes back in that time, and a hell of a lot more in four or five months, and probably in six or seven months you get everything back.

A FRIEND: Having persuaded his doctors that he was okay and eager to resume his writing, and after giving Dr. Rome his promise not to try to kill himself, Ernest left Rochester on June 26, 1961. His old pal and sparring partner George Brown drove him home to Sun Valley. It took five days.

C. T. LANHAM: They thought he was cured. Of course, like an alcoholic, he had stuff squirreled away everywhere.

DENIS BRIAN: On July 2, two days after his return home, Hemingway rose early, found the key to the basement where Mary had locked all the guns, picked up a shotgun and loaded it with shells he had hidden for this moment. He climbed the stairs to the foyer. Long before, he had written to his father how much better it was to die in a blaze of light than when old, worn, and disillusioned.

LEICESTER HEMINGWAY: So that nobody could sell it as a memento, one of his sons quickly destroyed the gun Ernest had used to kill himself. They cut it up, took it on a road, and rolled over it several times with a small truck, completely destroying it.

Inquest

Denis Brian: I'd like to ask you some questions about Ernest Hemingway.

Howard Rome [Hemingway's psychiatrist at the Mayo Clinic and nearby St. Mary's Hospital]: I've made it a practice never ever to reveal any of my contacts with Mr. Hemingway, because I gave him my word when he was my patient.

Denis Brian: I understand that, doctor. I don't want you to reveal anything secret between you two. But I'd like your response to this comment by psychiatrist Jonas Robitscher in his *The Powers of Psychiatry.* [1] He writes: "Hemingway complained that his course of eleven shock treatments erased his memories and made it impossible for him to function as a writer. . . . One month after the second series was completed and he was sent home cured for the second time, Hemingway died from a self-inflicted gunshot wound. If shock interferes with intellectual functioning—or if people who receive shock are convinced there is a detriment, whether or not it actually exists—the treatment can be the last blow in a series that makes life not worth living. Shock is a magical cure for some depressions; it has intensified the depressive quality of life for others." This psychiatrist is saying that Hemingway should never have had shock treatments, because it ruined his memory which was vital to his work.

Howard Rome: That's his opinion, and I don't know that Dr. Robitscher ever saw Mr. Hemingway.

Denis Brian: I don't think he did.

Howard Rome: Then that's his opinion, gratuitously.

Denis Brian: Have you read Mary Hemingway's account of the treatment at the Mayo Clinic?

Howard Rome: No.

Denis Brian: Tell me if you think it's reasonable. This is Mary Hemingway: "In New York I received an urgent call from Dr. Rome. Ernest was feeling so good that his sexual impulses were reviving. An interlude of privacy with me might do him inestimable good. . . . Dr. Rome said it would have to be in the locked, barred wing of the hospital. I had never been in a place like that before, and I mourned at Ernest's pitifully small collection of comforts, a few books, a few magazines, a few letters. No typewriter, no telephone, no pictures, no flowers. As we lay comforting

[1] Jonas Robitscher, M.D., *The Powers of Psychiatry*, Houghton Mifflin, 1980.

each other and friendly together in his single bed—'Like Africa,' I said—
other inmates pushed through the door, hollow-eyed men looking for
something we could not give them. Ernest seemed to accept them as part
of his incarceration, but they unnerved me. Our 'solitude' together was
not entirely satisfactory to either of us, and I was, maybe cravenly, relieved
to be let out of the locked ward. It was no solution for my husband either,
I reflected. But I had no solution for his problems."[1]

HOWARD ROME: I think that's a distortion of the actual facts.

DENIS BRIAN: What struck me as extraordinary was that other patients
were allowed to wander in and out of Hemingway's room.

HOWARD ROME: He was, too.

DENIS BRIAN: Hemingway was allowed to go into other men's rooms?

HOWARD ROME: He was given free access to the outside.

DENIS BRIAN: But what she says is that when they were alone in their
room together, perhaps trying to make love, inmates walked in and out
of the room.

HOWARD ROME: I don't know about that. That was an unusual case.

DENIS BRIAN: Would it have been possible for inmates to have gone into
their room?

HOWARD ROME: Possible? Oh yes, I think it was possible. The doors were
unlocked.

DENIS BRIAN: Do you think she gives a fair picture of what took place?

HOWARD ROME: It certainly isn't a fair picture of the way Mr. Hemingway was treated at St. Mary's Hospital.

DENIS BRIAN: How would you explain her account?

HOWARD ROME: She was upset. I don't think there's any question of that.

DENIS BRIAN: Was he allowed a typewriter?

HOWARD ROME: He was allowed . . . He never was . . . He lived in a closed
ward, but he had access to the outside. He went swimming, he did all
kinds of things on his own.

DENIS BRIAN: Oh, I see. He could have gone to another room for the
telephone or typewriter.

HOWARD ROME: He certainly could have.

JEFFREY MEYERS: The Mayo doesn't specialize in psychiatric treatment.
It's for physical illness. In fact, they treated Hemingway's illness as if it

[1]Mary Welsh Hemingway, *How It Was.*

were a somatic disease. They gave him shock treatment. There was no indication that Hemingway ever had psychotherapy. There was never any attempt to find out what the hell was wrong with him, what caused the illness. They just wanted to give him a zap with the electricity and try to jolt him out of it. I spoke to Hemingway's psychiatrist, Dr. Howard Rome, on the phone and he said something like, "My conscience is clear." I said, "It's very nice if you can feel that way after you're responsible for the death of one of the greatest geniuses of the twentieth century." I looked Rome up in a dictionary of medical writings and read a lot of papers Dr. Rome wrote and they show very little understanding for a psychiatrist: his whole attitude was to treat mental illness as a somatic disease, which seems to me completely the wrong way to do it. Shock treatment now is generally discredited and it's even outlawed in California.

DENIS BRIAN: Didn't it work effectively for some people with depression?

JEFFREY MEYERS: For some people, yes. But when it didn't work for Hemingway the first time, they tried it a second time. And when it didn't work a second time, they tried it a third time. Rome should have gotten the picture that with this patient it's not working. He just had one way of doing everything. If somebody came in to Rome with cancer or a hang nail, he'd probably get shock treatment.

DENIS BRIAN: I assume he's being satirical, Dr. Rome, with that last comment, but is what he says generally true?

HOWARD ROME: No.

DENIS BRIAN: Do you remember talking to him on the phone?

HOWARD ROME: No.

DENIS BRIAN: Is your conscience clear, as regards Hemingway?

HOWARD ROME: Oh, yes.

DENIS BRIAN: Is it true that you treated Hemingway's illness as a somatic disease?

HOWARD ROME: No.

DENIS BRIAN: Meyers says Hemingway had no psychotherapy.

HOWARD ROME: Of course he did.

DENIS BRIAN: When Jeffrey Meyers refers to your medical writings he's not referring to ones that would apply to Hemingway's treatment. He's just doing a small survey and not covering it all?

HOWARD ROME: You're right.

DENIS BRIAN: What about his statement that when shock treatment didn't work the first time, you tried it a second time and when it didn't work a second time you tried it a third?

HOWARD ROME: Unless you know the whole content of what he had. . . . But I choose not to talk about that.

DENIS BRIAN: So that generally you disagree with his conclusions?

HOWARD ROME: Absolutely.

DENIS BRIAN: And you don't even remember the phone conversation, but it is true that you feel your conscience is clear?

HOWARD ROME: Oh, indeed it is.

JOHN HEMINGWAY: I think a lot of the things Dr. Rome did are a little ridiculous. Pronouncing my father cured and letting him go home was one of the most ridiculous things anybody did.

DENIS BRIAN: What did you think of Dr. Rome inviting Mary to the hospital to try and spend a night of lovemaking with your father, and when she went patients walked in and out of their room? Even a healthy man wouldn't have been able to make love in those circumstances.

JOHN HEMINGWAY: No. And what woman could respond under the circumstances? It doesn't sound like the truth to me.

DENIS BRIAN: I suppose the room was kept unlocked for Mary's protection and maybe his, too, as he was suicidal. At the same time, they probably could have found an unlocked room somewhere in the hospital where people wouldn't wander in and out.

IRVIN D. YALOM [psychiatrist at Stanford University School of Medicine]: Hemingway struggled all his life with severe characterologic problems. In 1960 the accompanying signs and symptoms of depression—anorexia, severe weight loss, insomnia, deep sadness, total pessimism, self-destructive trends—became so marked that hospitalization was required. Electroconvulsive treatment is the treatment of choice for severe depressive illness, but is frequently ineffective in the presence of strong accompanying paranoid trends. He hated psychiatrists and openly mocked those he knew. It seems more pathetic than ironic that he was forced into the role of psychiatric patient during the last weeks of his life—a role which, according to Lanham, Hemingway must have considered "the ultimate indignity." The clinical picture of his final condition reflected a splitting asunder of the union of the ideal and the real Hemingway, a psychic system that, to survive, had become increasingly rigid and then, finally, brittle. Hemingway's idealized image crystallized around a search for mastery, for a vindictive triumph which would lift him above others. When the idealized image is severe and unattainable, as it was for Hemingway, the individual is flooded with self-hatred, which is expressed through a myriad of self-destructive mechanisms from subtle forms of self-torment to total annihilation of the self. These are excerpts from a study I wrote for the *Archives of General Psychiatry.* [1] It was intended as a psychological inquiry into some of the dynamics which help us to understand this great writer from a psychological standpoint. I attempted to interview Howard Rome, the psychiatrist who treated Hemingway in his final depression but he informed me, with a finger across his mouth, that before treating Hemingway he had been obliged to promise that his lips would be forever sealed. After my article was published a few individuals, who had some very strong feelings about the issue, wrote letters to the effect that I was belittling Hemingway. I think they have misread and misunderstood the thrust of my study, since I meant to do nothing of the kind. I have the utmost admiration for Ernest Hemingway as a writer and the utmost empathy for the anguish that was his during the very last part of his life.

EARL ROVIT: I spoke on the phone with the Reverend Wolfe who had been a fellow patient of Hemingway's at the Mayo Clinic. And he told me that Hemingway "was thoroughly disoriented and spiritually listless. Nor did he seem to be searching for a way out of his despair."

PETER DAVIS: Joris Ivens told me that even during the Spanish Civil War Hemingway talked about suicide from time to time. I think one occasion was when someone had committed suicide by putting a gun to his head and pulling the trigger, Hemingway said, "That's not the way to do it. It's to put the gun in your mouth."

THOMAS SHEVLIN: I knew Papa was very ill physically and had very high blood pressure which was enough to cause a mental lapse at times. And when he couldn't take it any more, why he just blew his brains out. I fully expected it.

SUSAN LOWREY CRIST: I wasn't surprised by his death, because I understood. He had been injured in so many ways, his head particularly, and he drank too much and cavorted, and he fought. He had all these things against him as much as he had for him. And I think what you have to come up with is his genius glows anyway.

[1] In the June 1971 issue, with Marilyn Yalom, professor of literature at Hayward State College.

LEWIS CLARAHAN: He'd had other accidents with rifles and shotguns. Everyone seemed to agree it was not an accident, that he had it figured out. I still think [1986] it was possibly an accident, but nobody agrees with me.

ALVAH BESSIE: I had been reading him all my life. And I knew he was fascinated with the whole idea of death. I knew that his father had committed suicide. I fully expected it.

GEORGE SELDES: Professor Karl Menninger of the psychiatric clinic told me that suicide is often a substitute for murder. Suddenly I thought of something. Do you know that in one of Hemingway's early short stories he tells of a man who put the gun in his mouth and tripped the trigger with his toe and blew off the top of his head? Reading one of his old stories, I saw that and thought: "Good heavens, in a 1924 story he wrote exactly what he did in 1961!"[1]

DENIS BRIAN: His biographer, Jeffrey Meyers, thinks Hemingway's suicide was an attack against Mary. Why, Professor Meyers?

JEFFREY MEYERS: I mean, you stand at the bottom of the stairs and you blow your brains out so your hair and your teeth and your eyeballs are splattered all over the place for her to come down and see a few minutes later. He knew she would wake up and find him in that state. And he'd also seen people in that state from the first World War and in Spain and the second World War and he knew what people looked like in that condition. In fact, with one of his articles he had a photo reproduced of a guy with the top of his head blown off. So he had seen what he'd look like immediately after he died.

DENIS BRIAN: But why did he stay with her if he hated her so much?

JEFFREY MEYERS: He didn't hate her. I think he was trying to get even with her for opening up the possibility of suicide for him. Also he resented his dependence on her. She didn't want to let him out of the Mayo Clinic and he wanted to get out, and she was right in that case. In many ways Mary suited him very well. She could take an infinite amount of abuse, she adored him. She was a good companion. I think the main trouble with Mary, apart from a streak of vulgarity and lack of intelligence, was the fact that she never understood what Hemingway was like as a serious writer and as a serious thinker. The evidence is there in her book,

[1]Even before 1924. In his short story "The Judgment of Manitou," published in his high-school yearbook *Tabula* in 1916, Ernest has his protagonist, caught in a trap, shoot himself with his rifle rather than wait to be killed by wolves. His heroes Robert Jordan, Harry Morgan, and Thomas Hudson also die violently.

How It Was, to show that she didn't have a clue what he was like.

DENIS BRIAN: It was strange that she left the keys around for him to get ammunition to kill himself.

JEFFREY MEYERS: She left them over the sink and when someone asked why she replied, "I think no wife has the right to deprive her husband of his possessions." That's a hell of an explanation! I had a long and strong passage about this in my biography, but I had to cut it out because of libel. Then Mary died afterwards and if my book had come out after her death I'd have been able to say much more about my feelings towards her.

DENIS BRIAN: You say she didn't understand him as a writer. But he did ask her to read his manuscripts.

JEFFREY MEYERS: Because she was the average reader, so to speak. She was no intellectual. I asked Hemingway's friend, William Walton, "How come Mary never went into Hemingway's motives and psychology in her book, or tried to work out how his mind functioned? What was the cause of his mental illness? And what was the best way to treat it?" Walton was rather witty. He said, "You guys want everybody to be a Jewish intellectual who's thinking out these great Freudian problems all the time, sort of a philosopher in search of the truth. But," he said, "an average Midwestern woman of that time didn't think of these things and didn't ask these questions."

DENIS BRIAN: But she did go to psychiatrists for help.

JEFFREY MEYERS: Yes, but she didn't take good advice. She got excellent advice from Dr. James Cattell, a doctor in San Diego, but she didn't take it. He told her that it would be much better for Hemingway if the newspapers printed the fact that Hemingway had gone into the Menninger for psychiatric treatment than if they printed the fact that he had blown his brains out after failure to be successfully treated in the Mayo.

DENIS BRIAN: He told her this after the fact?

JEFFREY MEYERS: No, he predicted exactly what would happen. Dr. Cattell had recommended that Hemingway either go to the Menninger or to the Institute for Living in Hartford where Robert Lowell, the poet, had been treated. [Lowell was a manic-depressive.] He said that Hemingway needed psychiatric treatment.

ARNOLD GINGRICH: In the early years he used to talk at great length about what an incredible thing his father's suicide was. How could anybody do such a messy thing? How could you leave a mess like that for somebody to clean up? Then he goes and does exactly the same thing. He was eloquent about it for years and years, that it was an unthinkable thing to do.

JOHN RYBOVICH, JR.: I think Hemingway's big disappointment was not being killed in action. That would have glorified him. He'd much rather have·died from some Nazi's bullet.

JOHN WESTOVER: It was in keeping with his character, that he would not want to live a life that was not a vigorous, active one. Originally they said it was an accident, and my comment to people near me at the time was that a man with his experience with weapons doesn't have such an accident.

JOHN CARLISLE: I was amazed when he did it, because I would have thought he was the last man in the world to do it, even though I have since read that there were suicide tendencies in that family.

WILLIAM WALTON: I was at the Finca in 1951 the night he got a telegram that his mother was dead. At the moment he was really estranged from Mary. And we discussed suicide, and his father's suicide. He blamed his mother for it, flatly, for henpecking and deballing—the operations she'd performed.

C. T. LANHAM: He never got over his father's suicide, and there was one letter I had from him after those terrible African plane crashes. He wrote that he was coming back on a slow boat across the Atlantic, and he said something like: "You know, Buck, I sit out here nearly all day at the stern of the ship and look at the wake of it—and, my God, how inviting it is!" And then he crossed this out and wrote in the margin—his letters were always filled with marginalia—in longhand, something like: "Don't worry, I will play out my stint." We used to talk about suicide in theory. I always said I'd do it with a forty-five, and he always said he'd do it with a shotgun.[1] But then he'd say: "I'd never do that."

JOSEPH DRYER: My father had been in the Marine Corps, too, and rejoined in World War II when he was fifty or fifty-two. But he overworked himself and got out of the Corps. In 1947 he was on the edge of a nervous breakdown but wanted to return to work. The doctor said he should either take a year off or have electric shock treatment. He chose electric shock treatment as a short cut. But the doctors warned us it could cause him to become suicidal. Now our house was crammed with guns. We were all brought up with pistols and rifles and everybody was a very good shot. So my father had electric shock treatment and we took all the

[1]Major General Charles Lanham died a natural death in 1978.

guns and razor blades out of the house. My mother thought he should stay at home where he'd get better care than in the hospital. Two or three months later there was no question he was better and we all went on a family trip to Mexico and then came back. Six months after those shock treatments my father went upstairs and shot himself. Absolutely no warning, or depression that we could see. He was getting ready to start a business. He had the money for that. And we boys were coming out of school to join him in the family business. We were later told that everybody was very sorry but they didn't know enough about electric shock treatment. And in effect we all have blamed his suicide on that treatment, because he was not suicidal in any way we'd ever seen. We think he'd be alive today but for those electric shock treatments. The doctor had warned us to strip the house of every possible weapon because the treatment could cause him to be suicidal for a relatively short period of time. But after we moved back from Mexico he seemed fine and the precautions were over and we moved everything back in the house. We were all home for Thanksgiving when evidently a black wave hit him and he blew himself away.

DENIS BRIAN: Did you ever discuss this with Hemingway?

JOSEPH DRYER: If I did, I don't remember it.

CAROL HEMINGWAY GARDNER: I wasn't terribly surprised when I heard Ernest had killed himself, because I had gone through it with my father, and knew he was depressed. And Leicester, of course, did the same.[1]

DENIS BRIAN: Hemingway biographer Michael Reynolds points out that Ernest "suffered from all of his father's ills: erratic high blood pressure, insomnia, paranoia, severe depression. Like his father, he wrote letters with fanatic intensity. Like his father, he worried about money when he had no worries. Like his father, he frequently behaved erratically, with rapid mood shifts and sometimes vicious responses. Under stress, real or imagined, the idea of suicide recurred insidiously. Like his father, he was caught in a biological trap not entirely of his own making. The blood line of Clarence Hemingway and Grace Hall has left us several books that will outlast all memory of Oak Park's fine families, but the cost was high."[2]

CAROL HEMINGWAY GARDNER: In all three cases, my father and two

[1]Leicester Hemingway fatally shot himself in the head on September 13, 1982. Suffering from diabetes and depression, he had undergone five operations and faced the possibility of the amputation of one or both legs. He was sixty-seven.

[2]Michael Reynolds, *The Young Hemingway*, Basil Blackwell, 1986.

brothers, my feeling was that their physical troubles were such that they couldn't handle them. My father had bad diabetes and was suffering from all kinds of severe headaches and I felt he thought it was a gift to everybody that he wasn't there. I know when Ernest came to my father's funeral he talked as though it was the last thing he would do. And the same with my younger brother, Leicester. He said he would never do it.

DENIS BRIAN: Then nominally a Catholic, Ernest told his eldest sister, Marcelline, that as a suicide their father was now condemned to eternal hell. Fortunately, no other Hemingway shared Ernest's belief. Do you assume, Mr. Cowley, that his physical illness caused the mental breakdown?

MALCOLM COWLEY: It certainly hastened it.

DENIS BRIAN: More than one person has said that when he shot himself he destroyed his own philosophy of grace under pressure.

MALCOLM COWLEY: I've never talked about that subject. But for the last two or three years he was really in a vast case of involutional melancholia and he had delusions. His self-destruction didn't seem to me in that case to have a bearing on his philosophy of grace under pressure.

DENIS BRIAN: Did you regard him as a Catholic?

MALCOLM COWLEY: I was fooled and wrong on that. I thought he was more of a Catholic even in later life than he admitted to be. But I was wrong, because suicide was not a Catholic way out.

DENIS BRIAN: But he didn't perhaps know what he was doing at the end.

MALCOLM COWLEY: Perhaps.

JOHN HEMINGWAY: After I left the army and was married, I was very depressed about what I was going to do, very gloomy. And Papa said, "You must promise me never, never . . . we'll both promise each other never to shoot ourselves." He said, "Don't do it. It's stupid." This was after quite a few martinis. I hadn't said anything about shooting myself, but I was obviously very depressed. He said, "It's one thing you must promise me never to do, and I'll promise the same to you." Of course, when I heard the news, that came back to me.

LEICESTER HEMINGWAY: He had an enormous number of problems. His friend Vanderbilt, and a great matador had just knocked themselves off. And various other things happened which broke his heart. And Fidel Castro had double-crossed him. Ernesto thought Castro was going to be the savior of the country and he turned out to be a communist.

MADELAINE HEMINGWAY MILLER: The morning of Ernest's funeral, I went to pray in a small church. And when I opened my eyes I saw a vision of his face with very sad eyes on the floor. I moved forward into another pew and looked again and his face was still there. It was a little frightening, but beautiful. I put my fingers to my lips and planted a kiss of goodbye on his face, and then went to get my sister Ursula. When we came back he wasn't there. Nothing like that ever happened to me before or since. I've been to church for Ursula's funeral, knelt and prayed and read the service in the Episcopal Church. I did the same for each of them. I did the same for Leicester. And nothing happened. And I was very *close* to Ursula. I am not psychic and I guess I'm not superstitious now that I think about it. Ernie and I were very much alike. And of the six children, I was the only one he wrote about. But I don't know what that vision of him meant. When I got home to Petoskey I told my minister about it and he said such things do happen.

MORLEY CALLAGHAN: I couldn't believe he was dead. When a reporter phoned me with the news, I said, "Don't worry, he'll turn up again." I meant it in the same way he'd survived the two plane crashes after he'd been reported killed. When I told my wife the news, she said, "No, it can't be." I described it as like hearing that the Empire State Building had fallen down. Edmund Wilson must have felt the same way about him. He wrote to me soon after, "He was one of the pillars of our time."

CHAPTER
FOURTEEN
·
HEMINGWAY
HUNTERS—THE
SECOND WAVE

A. E. Hotchner, Carlos Baker, Mary Hemingway, Norberto Fuentes, Jeffrey Meyers, Peter Griffin

A. E. HOTCHNER

What spurred Hotchner to write his Hemingway book was knowing Carlos Baker was launched on one. Carlos Baker, a professor of English literature at Princeton, the alma mater of Ernest's friends Scott Fitzgerald and Henry Strater, had written to Mary Hemingway saying he wanted to do a biography of Ernest and requesting access to his letters. Hemingway had previously given grudging approval to Baker's 1952 Hemingway: The Writer as Artist, *calling it "half good" with a number of factual errors, but with reasonable interpretations. Mary said Baker could read but not reproduce the letters because, shortly before he died, Hemingway had left a written request that they not be published.*

A. E. HOTCHNER: I had not intended to write about Ernest's last tragic years and death, but Mary came to me in the summer before I started to write my book *Papa Hemingway* and said: "Listen, Carlos is doing a book, as you know, and I want him to write the whole thing at the end as it was. Will you tell him everything and get him to talk with the doctor?" I said, "Mary, you mean you've come to the point that you're going to have it told [for years, Mary had maintained the fiction that Ernest's death had been accidental], but you're going to have it told thirdhand by somebody who knows nothing about it?" "Yes," she said. That's what decided me to write my book.

DENIS BRIAN: The blurb on the cover of *Papa Hemingway: A Personal Memoir* reads, "This is Hemingway as Hotchner saw him during those last thirteen years. At close quarters. Clearly and with love." The publisher, Bennett Cerf, remembers differently. He left this account in the Columbia University Oral History project, which was later incorporated in his autobiography: "Hotchner told me about his great friendship with Hemingway and said he wanted to do a story of his month or so with him when they took a trip together from the Italian Riviera to Spain. It was more or less parallel to the successful though cruel book Hemingway had written, *A Moveable Feast*, of a similar journey with F. Scott Fitzgerald. We could tell by what Hotchner said that this was going to be a rather mean book, too. I questioned the propriety of doing it, whether it would be in good taste. But, as Hotchner pointed out, Hemingway had written vicious things not only about Fitzgerald, but about Gertrude Stein, Sinclair Lewis and other friends of his. So why shouldn't it be done to Hemingway? In the last years of his life Hemingway had made a fool of himself with his 'Papa' routine, and Lillian Ross had inadvertently showed him up in her adulatory *New Yorker* piece. So we said, 'Go ahead,' and Hotchner's story expanded until it turned out to be a full-length book about Hemingway, ending with his dissolution and his finally killing himself after going quite insane."[1]

A. E. HOTCHNER: I don't know why he said that. It may just be his memory got a little distorted. It was not true that I told him it would be a mean or vicious book. It was never my intent. It was to be an account of a trip we took from Venice to Madrid, where we went, what he said, his reminiscences. There couldn't have been anything mean; nothing mean happened.

DENIS BRIAN: By "mean" I think Cerf meant your account of Hemingway's attitude to young women and his starting to go out of his mind.

[1]*At Random: The Reminiscences of Bennett Cerf*, Random House, 1977.

A. E. HOTCHNER: The original intention of the book was just an account of that trip across. Then a book or article came out about Hemingway saying he was accidentally killed by cleaning his gun. And I thought, "What a distortion." And having written the fragment, it washed back a lot of other things that I remembered. So I said to Bennett, "Listen, instead of just that trip, I'm going to write an account of the entire time that I knew him." That's all. Mary had put it out that his death was an accident, and it was being repeated. And there were a lot of rumors that he had been in the Clinic. I thought the time had come to tell what had happened.

DENIS BRIAN: You discussed Hemingway with the psychiatrist, James Cattell, who said he was suffering from delusions.

A. E. HOTCHNER: Yes, but I called him Dr. Renown in my book. I gave him an assumed name and I gave him the material I had written to read. He checked it over for accuracy. The shock treatment they gave him was primitive in the way it was administered. Today [1986], as I understand, during shock treatment the patient doesn't suffer like that. Then it was like sitting in the electric chair.

DENIS BRIAN: Yet shock treatment had cured Patrick of whatever was the matter with him.

A. E. HOTCHNER: Ernest thought it was meningitis.

DENIS BRIAN: Referring to you, Leicester Hemingway said, "Anybody who will hold a tape recorder on a man when he's drunk is not a friend."

A. E. HOTCHNER: I never had a tape recorder and he wasn't drunk.

DENIS BRIAN: Perhaps he meant a metaphorical tape recorder. All the accounts I've heard agree that he started drinking steadily after midday and kept drinking until he went to bed.

A. E. HOTCHNER: Ernest drank, but he'd taken drinks all his life so it didn't affect him that way. He could sit and have a couple of bottles of wine and talk and there wouldn't be any difference. His speech wouldn't be slurred, he wouldn't be drunk in any sense. I only knew him to be drunk on one occasion.

DENIS BRIAN: Dominguín, the bullfighter he attacked in *The Dangerous Summer*, said that after five in the afternoon you couldn't talk to him because he was insensible.

A. E. HOTCHNER: That's absolutely untrue.

DENIS BRIAN: Some people imply that Hemingway treated you less like a friend and more like a servant.

A. E. HOTCHNER: That you get from Jeffrey Meyers' biography of Hemingway. His nose was out of joint because I wouldn't see him, and I knew he was going to smear me.

DENIS BRIAN: General Lanham said that when he was in Spain for Hemingway's sixtieth birthday, you appeared to be suspicious of him and resented his friendship with Hemingway. Do you think a lot of his friends were jealous of his friendships with others and so would knock one another?

A. E. HOTCHNER: I guess so. The trouble with Lanham was that he was so foolish I couldn't tolerate him. He was just a foolish man. Hemingway thought, too, that he had turned foolish. He said that as a soldier when he knew him during the war he was a totally different guy. Something had happened to him, I don't know what. But he was just a terrible bore.

NAN TALESE [Hotchner's editor at *Random House*]: You must remember at that time Hemingway was a literary giant. I read the [Hotchner] manuscript and thought it was quite amazing and did not think it was gratuitously cruel to Hemingway, because it was clear that Hotch was enormously fond of him. It was an understanding of what had happened to this great writer in retelling the last days. And Hotch said that Mary Hemingway had said to him that the sons were grown up and it was time for the truth to be told. And that, I think, is what encouraged Hotch to go ahead, because he was very close to Hemingway in his last days. I think there was some discomfort on the part of Bennett, and Hotch needed encouragement, if I recall, in writing of Hemingway's suicide and the events that led up to it.

MARY HEMINGWAY: At no time ever did Hotchner give the slightest hint to Ernest or to me that he was making notes with the idea of producing a book about Ernest.

DENIS BRIAN: But as he was a practicing writer, it might have been expected.

MARY HEMINGWAY: No, he always professed himself to like Ernest, just for the fun of it, and all that.

DENIS BRIAN: I don't know if it's any consolation, but I think Hotchner was very fond of him.

MARY HEMINGWAY: I guess you're always fond of someone who can make you a million dollars. He wrote this book and made a great deal of money on it, as a totally traitorous thing to Ernest. If Ernest had known that he intended writing a book, he would never have seen him again, *ever.* This was a knife-in-the-back job, in my opinion. I'm sure Ernest would kill him, would have disposed of him.

NAN TALESE: Hotch adored Hemingway and is I think a great defender. If indeed Hotch said to Bennett Cerf, "Hemingway said vicious things about other people," he would have said it very much in a defensive way. It was a very delicate situation. I was absolutely sure this was the right thing to do. I was the youngest, least experienced editor there, but I was more passionate about this being the right thing to do, and I felt clearly suicide was something in those days that was never admitted, an unspoken subject, a great, lurid secret.

DENIS BRIAN: But it wasn't only his suicide, it was his behavior up to it, his drinking, interest in young women, being boastful and vainglorious and repeating himself; that's what I believe could be thought as a cruel thing to do to a friend.

NAN TALESE: Maybe it's not the most polite thing to do. It is the world, unfortunately, of writers, the way writers behave, and Hotch was not the first to do it. But I think the Bennett quote was said after the book was written, after people were still nervous. You have to put it in the context of his time. There was a great sense of ambivalence about how much should be told and I think Hotch needed support from his publisher that they thought he was doing the right thing. They were all finding reasons to do it. I have a very specific memory, not too clouded, because I was very new in publishing then. But I can't tell you anything about the conversations between Bennett and Albert Erskine, the editor, and why the book was signed up.

DENIS BRIAN: Did you know Bennett Cerf well, Mr. Erskine?

ALBERT ERSKINE: Oh, yes. I worked with him for about twenty-five years. I'm independent now but I still work for Random House. I don't trust Hotchner's memory any better than a lot of other people's.

DENIS BRIAN: Did you know Hotchner?

ALBERT ERSKINE: For a while. I haven't seen him now for twenty years, except maybe in a railway station or somewhere like that.

DENIS BRIAN: Can you speculate which man's memory is likely to be more accurate?

ALBERT ERSKINE: Not really.

DENIS BRIAN: This is a question partly about how biographers go about writing their books and in this case if the author intended to write a vicious book.

ALBERT ERSKINE: They are now beginning to remind me almost entirely of *People* magazine. What they mostly want is gossip.

DENIS BRIAN: Someone said that all literature is gossip, including Proust.

ALBERT ERSKINE: Could well be. Including Proust. I would start at the top on that one.

Reading the galleys of Hotchner's book gave her "a traumatic shock," Mary Hemingway claimed, and she wrote to publisher Bennett Cerf accusing Hotchner of "shameless penetration into my private life and the usurpation of it for money." Cerf and Hotchner agreed to some changes she demanded, but not to eliminate the chapter in which Hotchner tells how, fearing the publicity, Mary declined to take his advice and transfer Ernest from the Mayo Clinic to a psychiatric hospital. They also refused to take out the fact of his suicide. Mary sued in New York State Court for invasion of privacy. She claimed that the material Hotchner had used was in fact her property—as Hemingway's widow. Hotchner responded that Hemingway not only knew he was writing the book but had encouraged him to do it. He said that Mary's fear was that his book would detract from the biography underway by Carlos Baker which had her blessing. He chose august company in comparing Mary's action against him to someone trying to stop Plato from recording Socrates's dialogues, or to prevent Boswell from writing his Life of Dr. Johnson. *Judge Harry Frank ruled in Hotchner's favor. Mary appealed and lost. The book was published.*

DENIS BRIAN: Mrs. Hemingway, do you still feel as you did, in a 1966 interview with Oriana Fallaci, that "a writer doesn't belong to the public, only his writing does. Unlike a prima donna or an actress, he has the right to privacy if he wants it. No one should be authorized to tell the dissolution of a man, even less to tell it for money or sensationalism." And do you think a writer should be discouraged from writing all he can find out about the truth of a subject, if his aim is to paint a truthful, rounded portrait?

MARY HEMINGWAY: No, I certainly do not think a writer should be discouraged, if he has the approval of his subject and if, as you say, his aim is to paint a truthful, rounded portrait. But very, very few of us can do, or *do* do truthful rounded portraits, made with no motes in the eye, no imbedded preconceptions, no, or even few, possibly unrecognized or identified prejudices. In my experience, and reading, almost nobody achieves it. Hotchner's book, which cheated all the way, was full of exaggerations for the sake of sensationalism and royalties.

A. E. HOTCHNER: Who would determine just what things should and should not be kept from the public? This omnipotent censor of good taste. Who would it be? The author's wife? Well, Mary had her opportunity to set an example for all of us. Ernest had left a collection of chapters about his life in Paris in the twenties. One of those chapters recounted how Scott Fitzgerald had come to Ernest and confided to him his anxiety over the size of his penis, how Ernest assured Scott, after inspecting his penis, that it was normal by taking him to a museum and showing him the penis on a statue. I was helping Mary with this manuscript so I can tell you firsthand that the publisher suggested that in the interest of good taste this chapter should be eliminated. It was pointed out that this material would be particularly offensive to Fitzgerald's daughter, Scotty, and that it was not integral to the book. Mary was not to be deterred. It was her decision and her decision alone to print this chapter.

DENIS BRIAN: You're saying she had different standards for what should and should not be published about Hemingway?

A. E. HOTCHNER: I'm saying it's the widow's syndrome, a process I call widowfication. When Ernest was alive, Mary felt differently. She once wrote an article for a publication called *Today's Woman*, titled "My Husband, Ernest Hemingway," in which she confided such delicate intimacies as her fondness for kissing the soft places in back of his ear. [After his death] she wanted to control everything written about Ernest. Mary contended that my book was full of errors, but when under oath she was asked to enumerate these errors, all she could think of was that I had mismeasured their living room by four feet, called their chauffeur by the wrong name, and said on one occasion that Ernest came into the Floridita wearing khaki shorts whereas Mary claimed he never wore shorts in Havana. These three items were changed after the first edition. But Mary persisted in her various aberrations about the book—that I made a million dollars out of it and only did it for the money. It took me three years to write on an advance of a few thousand dollars. Money concerned Mary very much. It probably accounted for her decision to publish things like *Islands in the Stream*, which Ernest said he had to work on to make publishable. Long after her lawsuit was lost Mary continued to say Ernest had no idea I'd ever write about him, an act which she branded as a stab in the back. Mary didn't know much about writers' innards. When Ernest and I were in Spain together in 1959, having a good time traveling the bullfight circuit with matador Antonio Ordoñez, I had an amusing adventure going into the ring, on the occasion of a gala *mano a mano*, dressed as a matador. I was billed as Antonio's *sobre saliente*, the formidable El Pecas—the Freckled One. And it was a funny and perilous afternoon. Now I never dreamed that Ernest would ever write about that, but a month later there I was in prose and photo spread across the pages of *Life* magazine, my exploits described in detail under the by-line Ernest Hemingway. Mary didn't seem to realize that a writer is an undisciplined animal who will write about anything that touches his life.

DENIS BRIAN: Did you ever discuss it with her?

A. E. HOTCHNER: Mary was not given to discussion. She tended toward pronouncements. I think what bothered her most is what I left out of the book about her.

DENIS BRIAN: What's your view of Hotchner's book, Professor Seward?

WILLIAM SEWARD: I think the last few chapters are apparently very good fiction. I'm not saying that Hemingway's mind had not been affected some. Anybody that had as many accidents and had been as organically beat up, so to speak . . . I am convinced it was more physical than it was mental and Mary agreed with me. I had corresponded with him practically until a month before he killed himself, and I have combed through those letters to detect anything, without success. What I think happened was that he'd gotten physically beyond his point of return. He had incipient diabetes among a hundred other things wrong with him and he had lost weight and lost weight. He would apparently persist in drinking against doctor's orders and he could foresee himself as an invalid, lying in bed with people waiting on him, and he just couldn't take it—that's what the evidence points to.

WILLIAM WALTON: Hotchner's book made me throw up.

DENIS BRIAN: Too much imagination?

WILLIAM WALTON: Complete.

LEICESTER HEMINGWAY: He was not a good friend. I know that they were very close on a collaboration basis. But he began to distrust Hotch at some point in their relationship.

DENIS BRIAN: Although fellow Hemingway hunter Philip Young did not list Hotchner with the "vulture" biographers, writers of "obscene paperbacks appearing mysteriously from nowhere before [the] corpse [was] even cool," he has been the most informed and persistent critic in attacking Hotchner's book as largely fudged or faked.[1]

LEICESTER HEMINGWAY: I know that Hotch was in there closer than Laurel and Hardy, and yet Ernesto at one point was beginning to distrust everybody and certainly distrusted Hotch. And he was fucking right! Because Hotch is simply a journalist. He is not a good friend. A lot of the stuff is highly inaccurate. Hotch, for Chrissakes, created conversations and then reported them as having taken place. This helps make a book readable but it sure as hell is not truthful.

HADLEY MOWRER: I liked Hotchner's *Papa Hemingway*. It was very realistic, very lifelike.

ARNOLD GINGRICH: I always thought of Hotchner as being around in the phoniest period of Hemingway's life. We had *Papa Hemingway* in the house at *Esquire*. The boys brought it to me and I said, "Oh God, you don't want me to read this?" "Well, you may find it interesting." So I started out with very, very much a chip on my shoulder, and thought, "Hell, I wouldn't like this." If I liked it I wouldn't like it, don't you know? And then I began reading it and I came across the highly respectful references to *Across the River and Into the Trees*, which I thought was a Christ-awful book, and I thought, "This just shows this guy isn't worth reading." But I kept going. And, by God, I came to scoff and remained to cheer, because it became so evident that the stench of authenticity was all over every page, once the going got to get a little bad. So I just realized that that's the way it had to be. I believed it and found that it was pretty conclusively the truth. By the way, about the visit paid by Leslie Fiedler and a pal of his at Montana, where Fiedler used to teach: the winter before his suicide, they found Hemingway completely *non compos mentis*. It was a dreadfully cruel thing for them to print. It was after he got back from Mayo. I thought it was terribly indiscreet at the time. But I certainly believe they told it the way it was. Anybody reading that would realize— the man's off his rocker.

WINSTON GUEST: I only read excerpts from Hotchner's book, and I didn't approve of a person making friends with Ernest in his later days, after he'd had a couple of concussions from the two airplane crashes. [Hotchner knew him several years before those crashes.] Ernest wasn't himself after that. I prefer to think of him in full possession of his faculties. It's

[1]Philip Young, *Three Bags Full: Essays in American Fiction*, Harcourt Brace Jovanovich, Inc., 1972.

not fair to judge a man after those terrible accidents, particularly to his head.

C. T. LANHAM: I didn't know Hotchner well. I met him for the first time over in Spain at Hemingway's sixtieth birthday party. I flew over for that. And Hotchner hated my guts right off the bat. For some reason he looked on me as a rival. Christ, I wasn't running for sheriff or any other public office. He'd get off in a corner and whisper and whisper. It finally got to me. I just hated that sort of thing.

GEORGE SAVIERS: I was with Hotchner in Spain, too, at that party and I was there when Hotchner would come out to Sun Valley. Hemingway did everything to help Hotchner out and I think Hotchner wrote an inaccurate book. Hemingway's attitude towards Hotchner was a good field and no hit.

MALCOLM COWLEY: You know what Hotchner did? I could spot it because I knew the sources. When he wrote, "Hemingway said," actually he was quoting from Hemingway's letters to him. Because Hemingway's will said, "You must not quote from my letters." So Hotchner just put the letters in place of conversations.

JOHN HEMINGWAY: It wasn't accurate. To be quite frank I read the excerpts. My feeling from that was that he caught the character and the way it was to be around him better than any of the other books. But he was placing himself in situations where he wasn't, but he'd heard the details, which appeared to lend more validity to his testimony. There were a number of inaccuracies, but I don't think it was intended to be a scholarly work.

MALCOLM COWLEY: Although part of the book was faked, his vivid account of the last days is probably truthful. The early stuff was ignorant. I know enough about Hemingway's life to know that Hotchner got it all wrong in places.

ARCHIBALD MACLEISH: It was full of gas. Everything about it was slightly or wholly wrong—everything I knew about personally. Everything was fuzzy, as though told by somebody who'd heard it from somebody, who'd heard it from somebody, who'd heard it from the second cousin of the grandmother of somebody else.

A. E. HOTCHNER: Some of the things I used in *Papa Hemingway* were so wildly outrageous I didn't even bother to point them out or footnote them—like the anecdote he repeatedly told about meeting Legs

Diamond's girlfriend in the 21 Club and laying her on the landing after the restaurant had closed for the night. Hemingway loved to put people on, like lying to me about making love to Mata Hari. That was part of the fun of it, and you had to understand that. It was bullshit, of course. But fantasy and exaggeration were components of the delicate machinery that made Ernest what he was.

MADELAINE HEMINGWAY MILLER: Ernest had a wonderful imagination. You don't have to sleep with everyone you write about.

A. E. HOTCHNER: I wanted to recreate him as he was over the course of the fourteen years I knew him, let him say things he said as he said them, whoppers and all. I've done what I wanted to do—get Ernest Hemingway, as I knew him, on the page in moments of good going and bad, triumph and defeat, killing off old friends, befriending the friendless, working, drinking, joyful, and disillusioned.

Most critics gave Hotchner a standing ovation. "No biographer will be able to ignore it," wrote John Barkham; "Makes Hemingway live for us as nothing else has done," wrote Edmund Fuller. Orville Prescott called it "absolutely brilliant," and John Mason Brown believed "Papa himself, crusty, tender, shockproof, belligerent and sensitive as he was, would have approved it." The book became a best-seller.

CARLOS BAKER

Meanwhile, with Mary Hemingway's cooperation, Carlos Baker had been working on what Martha Gellhorn called "the King James Version" of Hemingway's life. Hemingway had been a hoarder of private papers, notes, unpublished stories and novels, thousands of letters, which Mary made available to Baker. Mary had not yet decided to publish Ernest's letters—which eventually she did despite his written request not to make them public. [1] *But Baker surmounted that problem by briefly paraphrasing many of them. He interviewed by mail and in person many people who had known Hemingway. Carlos Baker's* Ernest Hemingway: A Life Story *was published by Scribner's in 1969, and seemed to account for almost every moment in Hemingway's crowded life from birth to suicide.*

A. E. HOTCHNER: It's a compendium; like a repository of all the facts without a point of view, interest, or any real insight into the man.

HADLEY MOWRER: I thought Carlos Baker committed a miracle, covering the world, really, to get everything. I think it's wonderful.

[1]Carlos Baker, ed., *Ernest Hemingway: Selected Letters 1917–1961*, Scribner's, 1981.

JOHN HEMINGWAY: It made my father seem like a real son-of-a-bitch, which he wasn't. While strictly accurate, it's like taking testimony. Everybody gets to testify and this is the time that all the bastards get a chance to line up and give it to him [laughs]. Mr. Baker did a very fine research job, but I didn't think there was any warmth in the book. You didn't catch any feeling of the person.

MALCOLM COWLEY: I had also done research on Hemingway's life, and at times there were good stories and bad stories about what Hemingway did. I found Carlos Baker using the bad stories and leaving the good stories out, in cases where I was pretty sure that both were accessible to him.

DENIS BRIAN: Carlos Baker denied he had done that.

TRUMAN CAPOTE: The Baker book was bad all the way through. It was dull, it was uninteresting, it was badly put together, it had no selectivity, it was an atrocious piece of writing. Then, on top of the whole thing [laughs], considering how much the Hemingway estate backed him up and cooperated with him, it was a piece of duplicity, too. He was shoving the knife in there all the time. I never read a book in which I came away with the feeling that the author hated the man he was writing about.

DENIS BRIAN: Professor Baker, Truman Capote says that it's apparent from your biography of him that you didn't like Hemingway. Did you like him?

CARLOS BAKER: Yes, but people will say anything, as you know, whether it's true or not. I'm rather thick-skinned about this sort of thing. I don't give a damn. I could cite evidence that I liked Hemingway: the book I wrote about his writings, *Hemingway: The Writer as Artist*, which has gone through many editions. Some people got me over the barrel about it, for being too much in Hemingway's favor.

MARY HEMINGWAY: Carlos Baker did the most industrious possible job. And nearly all the facts are absolutely accurate. Professor Seward thinks the man is missing from the book. I think that would be quite natural, since they had never fished together, or hunted together, or chatted together. Baker did, I thought, a marvelous job of research, but didn't know Ernest and could not view him as a creature. Most people think of Ernest as being a publicity seeker, and I'm afraid Carlos sometimes gives that impression in the book, too. It just could hardly be less true. For example, when we were in hotels here in Manhattan, we sometimes went out side doors or back doors. Ernest didn't want to waste time with the press.

JEFFREY MEYERS: Baker's is an encyclopedia of facts and there is no interpretation in it, deliberately. He was writing to please Mary and Scribner and to propagate the official image of Hemingway. I think he went from hero-worship to disillusionment and he got fed up with Hemingway after ten years of writing the book. I think he felt Hemingway was on his back and taking over his life. As he saw Hemingway turning nasty towards the end of his life, Baker became severely critical of him. There were also a great many things Baker didn't know or couldn't say for fear of libel. He had a leaden prose style. Someone close to Hemingway said to me that Baker writing on Hemingway is like a virgin writing on sex.

WILLIAM WALTON: Baker gave a picture of Ernest as I knew him, within certain wooden limits.

DENIS BRIAN: I notice that with the Lillian Ross stuff, Carlos Baker didn't contact her. He just paraphrased her *New Yorker* article.

A. E. HOTCHNER: That's all he did with everything. He had all these marvelous letters and he just paraphrased them—which is against Hemingway's will. It was a thing Mary was suing about, yet there they all are. So, therefore, suddenly, the letters weren't so sacrosanct.

DENIS BRIAN: A. E. Hotchner wasn't so enthusiastic about the writer's freedom when a book came out in which he was described as—among other slurs—a "toady," a "hypocrite," and a manipulator and exploiter of Hemingway's reputation. These comments occurred in *Hemingway in Spain*, by Jóse Luis Castillo-Puche, published by Doubleday in 1974. Hotchner sued for libel and invasion of privacy. A jury awarded him $125,000 punitive damages and $6 as compensatory damages—one dollar for each slur the jury considered unjustified. A U.S. Court of Appeals reversed the decision in 1977, the three judges agreeing that "excessive self-censorship by publishing houses would be a more dangerous evil" than the possible defamation of individuals and that "in areas of doubt and conflicting considerations, it is thought better to err on the side of free speech." Judge J. Edward Lumbard, one of the three, wrote: "A writer cannot be sued for simply expressing his opinion of another person, however unreasonable the opinion or vituperous the expression of it might be. The evidence does not demonstrate that Doubleday had cause seriously to suspect that Castillo-Puche's opinions of Hotchner were without foundation."

A. E. HOTCHNER: I got a large award but the Court of Appeals said yes it was "reckless disregard" etc., but the First Amendment had to be upheld. So they overturned it on that basis.

DENIS BRIAN: The point being that free speech is more important than protection of the individual?

A. E. HOTCHNER: Right. I thought that was totally unreasonable. There has to be some limit on free speech, and the jury had found this was an excessive use of freedom. I thought this fellow [author Castillo-Puche] whom I had never met, was outrageous and that Doubleday was terribly negligent and the jury had agreed.

MARY HEMINGWAY

DENIS BRIAN: Mary Hemingway's 1976 autobiography, *How It Was*, with the inevitable exceptions was enthusiastically reviewed.[1] The *Chicago Sun-Times* critic thought it presented "Ernest Hemingway in a more intimate, more honest, more relaxed fashion than any previous book about him." *The Philadelphia Inquirer* reviewer agreed, calling it "the most authentic memoir about Ernest Hemingway so far published." And the *New York Times Book Review* approved of her dealing "lovingly with the good times, candidly with the bad."

LEICESTER HEMINGWAY: I couldn't stand it. I looked at the beginning of it and I thought, "Oh. Jesus, no!"

WILLIAM WALTON: Very pedestrian. Inadequate. She refused to submit to any editing. That's very unwise. She needed it desperately. She thought she wrote "good journalistic prose." I read her book with great interest, but it could have been much better.

DENIS BRIAN: Did it give a fair picture of him and their life together?

WILLIAM WALTON: She was a very poorly educated woman and had risen by her efforts, which is to be applauded. But she was extremely uncultivated and in this sense was a very inadequate wife for Ernest. Other wives, particularly Hadley and Martha, were ladies of great cultivation.

NORBERTO FUENTES

But Mary's hasn't been the most controversial Hemingway book since Hotchner's. That achievement belongs to a Cuban journalist, Norberto Fuentes. His book Hemingway in Cuba *was published by Lyle Stuart in 1984, translated from the Spanish. The Cuban government gave Fuentes*

[1]One exception was Jonathan Yardley, who called it "a genuinely dreadful book," though conceding that "absolute Hemingway freaks, the sort of people who like to know how long his cats' claws were, may love this book, but they had best be prepared to wade through a weed-clogged sea of petit-Papa prose in order to reach the goodies." *Miami Herald*, October 10, 1976.

access to all the material left in the Finca Vigia, including private letters to and from Hemingway.

DENIS BRIAN: Fuentes writes that in 1935 Ernest won all fishing competitions, beating such famous fishermen as Lerner, Farrington, and Shevlin.

JOHN RYBOVICH, JR.: No way. There weren't any competitions in 1935, other than keeping world records. Hemingway was not a competitive fisherman. Fuentes's idea of the Americans is a bunch of drunken bums. Of course, Hemingway would fit the drinking part very well.

DENIS BRIAN: Fuentes writes of Hemingway screening a newsreel over and over again showing an American marine sergeant waiting for Japanese soldiers to surrender on a Pacific island and then using a flame thrower to burn them alive one by one. Occasionally the sergeant turned around and smiled at the camera. When Father Andres asked why he kept screening it, and stopping it at that point, Doctor Herrara said, according to Fuentes, "Because we have sworn to kill that guy whenever we find him and Ernest wants us to remember his face well."

WILLIAM WALTON: That's just Ernest showing off.

DENIS BRIAN: Fuentes writes that Hemingway didn't turn on the air conditioning in his bedroom out of empathy for people who couldn't afford air conditioning. Mary, apparently, swore this was true.

WILLIAM WALTON [laughs]: They both often lied through their teeth, so I wouldn't put any credence to it. I think he hated air conditioning. I did, too. When I was at the Finca I never turned it on.

DENIS BRIAN: Fuentes quotes Dr. Herrara as saying Hemingway was under the protection of the Jesuits and could always count on their help or could hide in their monasteries if he needed to.

WILLIAM WALTON: He had commitments to the Catholic Church in a certain sense. He carried an amulet or two in wartime but rather as one carries a rabbit's foot. When people gave us good luck things nobody dared throw them away. Really, shot and shell were around us and Ernest often said, "I'd carry anything anybody gave me for protection." He did have admiration for the Catholic church in a funny, romantic way.

DENIS BRIAN: Fuentes says that Spruille Braden, then U.S. ambassador in Havana, and Gustavo Duran accused Hemingway of being a communist before a Senate committee during the McCarthy period. Although Hemingway was initially enraged, he later forgave Braden after the latter visited him. Duran, however, stayed in the United States.

WILLIAM WALTON: I would believe it all.

DENIS BRIAN: That they'd call their friend, Hemingway, a communist?

WILLIAM WALTON: I wouldn't be surprised at all.

DENIS BRIAN: Although we know Hemingway wasn't a communist.

WILLIAM WALTON: Uh-huh. I didn't know Braden, so I've no judgment about him. But that sounds absolutely kosher to me.

DENIS BRIAN: Duran might have done that?

WILLIAM WALTON: Sure.

DENIS BRIAN: It seems very forgiving of Hemingway.

WILLIAM WALTON: Yes and he was capable of that. He was vindictive but he was capable of great mercy, too.

JEFFREY MEYERS: I doubt if Gustavo Duran said Hemingway was a communist. Braden was scared and he might have said anything. Fuentes is totally, completely, and absolutely unreliable. This is Fuentes's way of getting someone else to say what Fuentes wants to say, namely that Hemingway was a communist, which, of course, isn't true. I think Gustavo himself was under tremendous assault, but he's the last man in the world to accuse someone else to save his neck. People did a lot of strange things in the McCarthy period. Almost everyone came out of it discreditably.

DENIS BRIAN: In one of his early letters Hemingway says something to the effect that, "We're all communists," but I think he said it in the way on St. Patrick's Day a non-Irishman would say, "We're all Irish."

JEFFREY MEYERS: Exactly. It's just like saying, "We all support the Spaniards in the Civil War." I made the point in my book that Hemingway was not like Edmund Wilson and Dos Passos and all the left writers of the thirties. He didn't swallow the communist line. And I argue that he was a lot more shrewd politically than anyone gives him credit for. Wilson is supposed to be the great political analyst and the great intellectual even though he'd gone to Russia when collectivism was going on in the early thirties, this slaughtering of *kulaks*—but he swallowed the communist shit. Wilson was in the country and didn't see a damn thing about it. Came back and said it was all great, just as Wells and Shaw did. Hemingway was a man with a kind of gut intuition, plus being on the scene in the Spanish Civil War. What you have to get very clear is that anything Fuentes says is both inspired by his desire to propagandize for the communists and secondly the fact that he's never been to America, he doesn't know English; his book was translated from the Spanish, and full of factual errors. He can't even get the names right, because he's unfamiliar with English names.

MICHAEL STRAIGHT [The late Gustavo Duran's brother-in-law]: Gustavo would never have called Hemingway a communist in those hearings. The hearings were behind closed doors. The transcript has never been released on them, if it was ever kept. It was before the [Senate's] Ferguson Committee up in the Federal Courthouse in New York, with Roy Cohn as counsel. They were closed sessions. Duran had a distinguished Republican attorney, Hiram Todd, advising him. It's inconceivable to me that Duran would call Hemingway a communist. He and Hemingway broke their relationship when Duran denounced as perfectly stupid Hemingway's expeditions with the *Pilar* looking for submarines while he was fishing. Hemingway recruited a lot of ex-Spanish Loyalists who were just layabouts and drunks living in Cuba and signed them on as members of the Secret Service. Duran, who had a professional background in that work, said, "It's preposterous. I don't want anything to do with it." And that led to his break with Hemingway. Duran was himself a victim of false accusations by people that he was a communist and it was the last thing in the world he'd try, to slough it off anyone else.

DENIS BRIAN: Do you agree that Hemingway was not a communist?

MICHAEL STRAIGHT: I know nothing about that. He wrote *The Fifth Column*, which was a fellow-traveling play, and he briefly sympathized with the Communist Party during the Spanish Civil War, as the only disciplined group around, as against the Anarchists and other groups.

DENIS BRIAN: Which presumably was also Gustavo Duran's attitude.

MICHAEL STRAIGHT: Yes. But I think that's the beginning and end of it. Hemingway spelled out his views precisely in *For Whom the Bell Tolls*. Robert Jordan is, of course, a Communist Party member. So he's sympathetic with it *under those circumstances*, but that's very far from being a member of the party and Gustavo never would have said that about Hemingway.

DENIS BRIAN: It seems then that Fuentes simply assumed Gustavo Duran made that accusation.

MICHAEL STRAIGHT: Heaven knows. That was a can of worms. The secret police in Spain were sending stuff over to the U.S.; Peron of Argentina was sending material here. The American military in Madrid was getting into the act. Gustavo himself was accused by all sorts of people of being a communist, including the socialist minister in Spain, which is why Gustavo was subjected to many loyalty investigations first from the State Department, then from the United Nations.

DENIS BRIAN: Mr. Cowley, according to Fuentes both Braden and Duran said before the House Un-American Activities Committee that Hemingway was a communist. There's no mention of this in the FBI files on Hemingway. Does it ring true to you?

MALCOLM COWLEY: I would hesitate to make a statement.

DENIS BRIAN: Was Hemingway a communist?

MALCOLM COWLEY: There's no question. Hemingway was not a communist.

GEORGE SELDES: Hemingway a communist? That's the biggest nonsense I've ever heard in my life. I think he was totally free of political feelings of any kind.

EARL ROVIT: The idea that Hemingway could have been a communist is laughable. Hemingway never joined *nothing!*

DENIS BRIAN: Nevertheless, Hemingway was uneasy about rumors that his name was being dropped by someone in connection with communism.[1] And he wrote to General Lanham that if called before the House Un-American Activities Committee he would deny ever having been a communist, state that in thirty years he had known only four honest congressmen and that he rated their fellow congressmen as slightly lower than snakeshit. He was never called. What may have been said about him before the committee might later have reached the FBI files. There are several pages in the mid-1950s completely blacked out.

JEFFREY MEYERS: But you can't depend on what Fuentes writes in *Hemingway in Cuba*. Just take the issue about the expropriating of the Hemingways' house. Fuentes says Hemingway gave it to the Cuban government. The Cuban government stole the house. Mary had to hand it over in return for getting part of her property back.

WILLIAM WALTON: Meyers is making that up, because he doesn't know what he's talking about. He thinks that it's probably true. It's implied if you're in diplomatic negotiations that you accept certain things, and

[1]In a November 10, 1954, letter to General Lanham, Hemingway wrote that Spruille Braden's talking while the Hemingways were in Africa was neither good for man nor beast and he would have to sweat it out.

behave accordingly. I told the president [John Kennedy] what the situation was and he called the State Department and said to arrange anything I asked on the subject. And he was very pleased with the results. The president was pleased with Mary's performance because she gave the Finca and its contents to the Cuban people, and not to Castro. She made that very clear. She thought it up herself. He thought that was brilliant. She got away with what she wanted from it. I call that a great success.

CARLOS BAKER: I interviewed Gustavo Duran and Spruille Braden and I didn't get the impression that they thought he was a communist.

DENIS BRIAN: Though Norberto Fuentes's *Hemingway in Cuba* is flawed, he provides unexpected insight into Hemingway by reproducing copies of letters left in the Finca Vigia. They include sixteen love letters to Mary Welsh, a long, probably unmailed letter to Martha Gellhorn after they broke up and a friendly letter from her, letters from Pauline Pfeiffer and from Adriana Ivancich. Adriana addressed him as "Crazy, good, sweet old lion," and signs off as "Your faithful daughter called, as always AI," and he writes that he accepts not seeing her as he would accept being in prison. Most unexpected was the unmailed letter to his sister, Carol Gardner, from whom he had been estranged since she announced her intention to marry John Gardner despite Ernest's vigorous opposition.[see pages 183-184.] Their estrangement had mystified his biographers, and Mary compounded the mystery when she wrote: "Over leisurely lunches in the empty dining room at Torvello my husband gave me a series of autobiographical sketches, each in such precise detail that I could never detect when he skidded off fact into fiction. . . . Carol was the most beautiful of the family. 'She married Jack Gardner. I was absolutely nuts about her. She looked as a girl exactly as I looked as a boy. No compromise, no change. We called her Beefy.' It was a love name, had nothing to do with beef."[1]

JEFFREY MEYERS

An experienced biographer—with Katherine Mansfield, Wyndham Lewis, and works on T. E. Lawrence, George Orwell and Robert Lowell under his belt—Jeffrey Meyers is Professor of English at the University of Colorado. He has taught Hemingway for twenty years and believes that Hemingway has had greater impact on other writers than any other American author of this century. "As for who's the greater artist, Hem-

[1]Mary Welsh Hemingway, *How It Was*, Knopf.

ingway or Faulkner, that's partly a matter of taste. It can't be proved. My taste is much more for Hemingway." Meyers' Hemingway: A Biography, Harper & Row, 1985, stirred British novelists Anthony Burgess, Anthony Powell, Iris Murdoch, playwright Tom Stoppard, and Proust biographer George Painter to write enthusiastic reviews or letters of approval. But many American reviewers enraged Professor Meyers, to put it mildly.

DENIS BRIAN: I'm going to be Devil's Advocate and quote your critics at you and give you a chance to respond. Leonard Butts of the University of Cincinnati in *Studies in the Novel* thought that despite your claims to have rescued Hemingway from his son-of-a-bitch reputation, you portray him as a cruel, selfish, sadistic, masochistic, and overbearing braggart who got what he deserved when friends and relatives rejected him and critics skewered him and his works.

JEFFREY MEYERS: I'm not trying to put down Hemingway. I'm trying to tell the full story of his life. What Butts never says is that anything negative that I wrote about Hemingway is false, exaggerated, or overemphasized. He never disputes my facts.

DENIS BRIAN: Here's Raymond Carver, poet and novelist, in the *New York Times Book Review*.[1] He says that your book bristles with disapproval of its subject [and praised rival Hemingway biographer, Peter Griffin].

JEFFREY MEYERS: I simply don't think it's true. Carver is no biographer, any more than Butts is, and Carver has no sense of what it means to do the kind of research and scholarship and discoveries that go into my book. Secondly, Carver made many statements in his review which did me a great deal of damage, because it was a prominent review and in some cases the only review anybody ever read. I refuted four or five points he raised, in a letter to the *New York Times*. You know Carver's response? Silence.

DENIS BRIAN: Professor Bernard Oldsey of Westchester University, in the *Philadelphia Inquirer:* "It can be rather disturbing to watch a prosecutorial biographer summon up a world-class novelist for moral chastisement every ten or fifteen pages."

JEFFREY MEYERS: Oldsey is a minor Hemingway scholar and his was a

[1]Raymond Carver, "Coming of Age, Going to Pieces"; *New York Times Book Review,* November 17, 1985.

more balanced review than the first two you read. It's much safer to be like Carlos Baker, to set the facts out and never state what you think. If you lay your cards on the line and take a strong position and have a moral stance of your own, you're bound to antagonize people who don't agree with you.

DENIS BRIAN: David L. Vanderwerken, professor of modern American literature at Texas Christian University, wrote in the Fort Worth *Star-Telegram* that you portray Hemingway as a beast and a terminal nasty "abusive to parents, wives, children, friends, editors, critics, fish, fowl and mammals," and says it's a wonder someone didn't kill Hemingway before he killed himself. Then he adds, "Meyers might as well have."

JEFFREY MEYERS: When you write a biography it's like being a whore: you spread your legs and anybody can come and fuck you.

DENIS BRIAN: Now you sound like Hemingway responding to his critics.

JEFFREY MEYERS: You pour out this work of serious scholarship into the world and any asshole who has some contact with a book review editor of a provincial newspaper can say whatever he likes. The level of incompetence in reviewing in America is unbelievable. With critics, you get absolute contradictions all the way down the line on every single point. John Leonard wrote a good, first, favorable review in the *New York Times*, but said I didn't carry psychoanalysis far enough and should have proved or stated that Hemingway was a secret homosexual, even though there was no evidence for it. Whereas other people said I carried psychoanalytical criticism too far. Some said the book was very well written, some said it was poorly written, some said it was very well organized, some said it was confusing. An English reviewer, Jonathan Keates, wrote: "Jeffrey Meyers is the Mother Teresa of literary biographers trying to resurrect lepers like Wyndham Lewis and Ernest Hemingway, and trying to make them out to be respectable, decent, and sympathetic human beings." I think that's getting much closer in a very witty way to what I was trying to do. All these assholes who think I'm too negative should read the next to last paragraph in my book.

DENIS BRIAN: I'll read it: "Hemingway described with unusual knowledge and authority physical pleasure, the natural world, violent experience, and sudden death. He portrayed the heroic possibilities and tragic consequences of war, the psychic dislocation in battle and the stoicism of survival. He created unsurpassed images of Italy, France, Spain, and Africa. As a man, he had intense idealism, curiosity, energy, strength, and courage. He attractively combined hedonism and hard work, was a great teacher of ritual and technique, carried an aura of glamour and power. As an artist, he wrote as naturally as a hawk flies and as clearly as a lake reflects."

JEFFREY MEYERS: I won't have to pay $50 an hour for my catharsis in this conversation, will I?

DENIS BRIAN: Every writer should have the chance to respond to critics. And that includes the Hemingway biographer you criticized—Peter Griffin.

PETER GRIFFIN

Peter Griffin is about a third way through an ambitious project—a subjective, novelistic approach to capturing Hemingway in four volumes. His first, Along with Youth: The Early Years, Oxford University Press, *appeared in 1985. It follows Ernest sympathetically from birth through World War I and up to his marriage to Hadley. It also includes five of Hemingway's youthful short stories—never published before—which Griffin found among the writer's papers. Raymond Carver called the book "wonderful and intimate."*

PETER GRIFFIN: Jeffrey Meyers criticizing my book in *National Review* was ridiculous.[1] Here he was a competing Hemingway biographer, published at the same time.

DENIS BRIAN: He wrote of your "limping" narrative, "unconvincing claims" and damns the whole books as seriously flawed.

JEFFREY MEYERS: I was writing a full life of Hemingway. Griffin wrote a life of him up to about age twenty-one. He was a very nice guy up to then, and not a particularly nice guy in the 1940s and 1950s. So it's very easy to be completely uncritical of Hemingway when he was a charming young fellow. You can't please anyone, unless you want to be as boring and simple-minded as Griffin is, where you kind of get down on your hands and knees and worship Hemingway as some kind of god. And this is called empathy. In fact, it's childish, naive infatuation.

PETER GRIFFIN: Sure, I expected that sort of comment. I think Meyers's book had an unpleasant flavor to a lot of critics. We started out both getting good reviews until the *New York Times* review by Raymond Carver came out. Then Meyers began getting negative reviews and mine were positive. Some of my early reviews were negative, I believe, because

[1]Jeffrey Meyers, "A Conventional Chap," *National Review*, January 31, 1986.

I presented a Hemingway that was different. Meyers presented a Hemingway everyone expected.

DENIS BRIAN: What started you off?

PETER GRIFFIN: My professor at Brown, Hyatt Waggoner, a leading authority on Hawthorne, didn't like Hemingway at all. He'd written a letter to Hemingway in the late fifties asking to use one of Hemingway's stories in an anthology he was doing. Hemingway said no and explained that his work was his legacy for his children and that he wasn't going to let it go for peanuts. Waggoner also wanted to believe with Gertrude Stein that Hemingway was yellow and I think he was convinced that Hemingway was a homosexual who had struggled against his homosexuality all his life and therefore was a hypocrite. The day I told Waggoner I was going to do my dissertation on Hemingway he said, "Of course, Hemingway was yellow, you have to admit that." I said, "I don't." And he got violent. This was in his house. He slammed a book down, stood up, and got red in the face. He had heart problems and his wife tried to calm him down. He was so emotional about it, he was on the verge of throwing me out of the house. "You have to state it, or you're lying!" he said. "You'll be doing a hagiography, a whitewash!" What turned him around was when Mary Hemingway gave me a chance to see Hemingway material at Waltham before the Kennedy Library was open. So I wrote an opening chapter of the book that was filled with new stuff and Waggoner called me up said, "This stuff is worth its weight in gold." All that kind of stuff. I wrote Mary Hemingway a note about my intention to write a Hemingway biography and she asked me to see her in New York City. So I went there. I really cared for this man and wanted to write an antidote to the Baker biography. She told me she had been to the publication party when the Baker biography came out and everybody had quite a bit to drink and a relative of Carlos Baker's told Mary that Baker detested Hemingway. I brought up [to Mary Welsh Hemingway] a girl that reportedly Hemingway had an affair with in the fifties, Valerie Danby-Smith, when he was doing *Dangerous Summer* over in Spain and who Gregory subsequently married. And Mary got furious with me. I thought she was going to slap my face. She said, "*I* was taking care of him!" implying there had been no affair. Despite what she had been through with him there was this terrific sense of loyalty and devotion to him. If everything she said about him in her book *How It Was* is true, and of course it's from her point of view, he did treat her roughly, yet she was protective of him and still thought of herself and Ernest as against everyone else. When I talked with her it was as if they were still a team, in a way, against outsiders. Jack Hemingway told me he was sure that the gentleness, sensitivity and vulnerability and compassion within his father at the period I wrote about—his early years—some of that remained with him to the very end.

I said, "I have great affection for your husband but that's not going to blind me to things he did when he acted like a bum. I'm going to say so, or I'll create the themes and images so people get that impression, but I'm going to do it in a parental sense where you're looking down at a kid you love and say, 'I love that kid but he's acting like a pig now and I'm going to tell him so.'" These meetings with Mary were over a period of about three months. My wife and I saw her in her apartment in New York each time and stayed longer each time. Once we stayed about six hours and she was very frank. If I said something stupid she didn't hesitate to tell me. She made me feel uncomfortable at first but later I appreciated it.

DENIS BRIAN: What did you learn from Jack Hemingway?

PETER GRIFFIN: When my wife and I were out in Sun Valley—we had flown across country, we were broke, and I was trying to get a job at a little private school there—I desperately needed money. I had to take any kind of job and Jack had said maybe there's a job at the school and used his influence to get me an interview. That night we had dinner with Jack and his family and had a wonderful time. I had known him on the phone for about four years so it wasn't as though I'd just met him. Next day when he picked us up to see some of the sights, he took us to the house where his father had committed suicide and we looked around. There was a caretaker there. I saw the place where Jack's father had shot himself and looked through some of the rooms and then he took us down by the grave. But that day as we were walking around Jack was angry, very hostile, and almost cruel to my wife and me. I had no idea why. Nothing had changed since the night before, except he explained it as a hangover. But then he said something when he took us to a restaurant downtown for lunch. He said, "That's the way we Hemingways are. We're nice guys one day and sons-of-bitches the next." Maybe that was the tendency in his father as he got older, to somehow change dramatically from being genuinely very friendly and decent to being a real bastard and then to change back again inexplicably. It seems almost to make you pay for the kindness. Maybe to keep testing you to see if you'll still be affectionate, even if you're not being treated well. A short story printed in my book, "Portrait of an Idealist in Love," is pretty autobiographical about Hadley and her sister. In it Hemingway writes that if you wanted to make friends with someone you earned their friendship by doing something nice for them. I thought that if you do that a lot you wonder whether people are in fact your friends or just reacting to your being nice to them. Maybe there'd be a tendency to think, "If I'm a son-of-a-bitch to this guy is he still going to like me?" So I'm going to be a prick to him today to see if he's a friend or just with me because I'm so careful to be good.

DENIS BRIAN: What did Mary think of your work?

PETER GRIFFIN: After I'd given her the first chapter of my dissertation, I phoned her on a Sunday morning and asked her how she liked it. She said, "Not much." I said, "Oh, Christ!" and hung up the phone. I told my wife, "My God, this may be the end. If she doesn't like my work, she's not going to let me use anything more." So we flew from Providence to New York and about two hours later I was walking into Mary's apartment to talk to her. She laughed and got a big kick out of it. It was a hot August and I was sweating like crazy. We sat down and had tea and she said, "I don't like what you're doing, but go ahead and see how it comes out." The dissertation which is entirely different from the subsequent book is a psychobiographical critical study of Hemingway's work.

DENIS BRIAN: I can see how that might have bothered her.

PETER GRIFFIN: In it, I do a Jungian interpretation of Hemingway and his work. I'd read all thirteen or fifteen of Jung's books in the Bollingen series, and in my dissertation I wrote of Ernest being motherbound. During my defense of my dissertation Professor Waggoner said, "You have found the key to Hemingway's career." And everybody at Brown said it was a big deal. But then, after speaking with Mary I realized she was right. Human nature is much more complex than that. Then I started to think of what made me care for Hemingway and why I was drawn to him. So I decided to tell the whole story and let my response to both the man and his work color everything I wrote about him.

FIFTEEN

•

HEMINGWAY
REAPPRAISED

DENIS BRIAN: Can you speculate how he would have responded if I asked him for an interview?

MARY HEMINGWAY: I think he would have done his best to put you off. That was his usual practice.

WILLIAM WALTON: He would scream and shout and be violent and then if he met you and liked you, he'd be very cooperative. In the late forties and early fifties academicians began to write about him and he held them all in great contempt, until one or two got through to him and he began to like them and cooperate with them. If he was in the mood, he'd lead them on with tall tales in a really heartless way.

DENIS BRIAN: Why?

WILLIAM WALTON: I don't see why you are so suprised that a man who has spent all his life inventing fiction keeps on inventing it in his private life.

DENIS BRIAN: Except that in his early triumphant writing days he was a news reporter, foreign correspondent, and a war correspondent in two wars, respected for his integrity and truthfulness.

WILLIAM WALTON: He was a schizoid, a double personality, as well as manic.

DENIS BRIAN: You think that explains it?

WILLIAM WALTON: Right. But I don't think you have to be all that solemn about it. I do think that a man who devotes his life to inventing stories doesn't suddenly turn that off when he leaves his study. I think Flaubert did it, too, and got totally confused about what was true and what wasn't.

DENIS BRIAN: Hemingway expressed his attitude to the truth in an unpublished manuscript in the Kennedy Library. He maintained that it was not unnatural for good writers to be liars, as lying or inventing is part of their trade, and that they even lie to themselves. He implied that he often lied unconsciously, and afterwards when he recalled having lied, suffered deep remorse. He found some consolation in realizing that all other writers are liars, too.

JOHN HEMINGWAY: As I was growing up I was never aware that my father, whose real life was very exciting, tried to make a myth of his life. It's only since his death, talking with my brothers, that it's become obvious that certain things were not true. But I held him in such high esteem that I could see him do no wrong. I suppose he had a rather useful tool for his overactive imagination. In a sense it's true, as Leicester suggests, that he wanted to be Superman's older brother. You see, he was very good at a great number of things which you people didn't give him credit for. Because when you're a writer, everybody thinks you wear thick glasses and smoke a pipe. But he was an outdoorsman, and a great shot, and he was a skilled handler of people in outdoor situations. He understood the minor tactics of a squad, of a platoon leader, of a company commander. He understood ground and how it should be used very, very well; unusually well. He learned it from others and from hunting from a very early age. As I became a man I could usually distinguish his tall stories from the facts, but as a child I certainly couldn't.

A FRIEND: He once said, "When other people tell lies it's no good, but if I tell them it's okay." This was a premise by which he went during his life. I know he prevaricated on various occasions, yet he always claimed to be an absolute model of probity. This was his blind spot. Every human being has blind spots concerning himself, doesn't he? I've never met anyone who didn't. The late man who could walk on water I'm sure had no blind spots, but I never got to meet him.

DENIS BRIAN: Can he be trusted then in anything where he is the sole witness or reporter?

CARLOS BAKER: That's a pretty large order. Like any novelist he is likely to over-elaborate, but to say he's not to be trusted in anything he says where he's the sole witness would be a very strong statement. Sylvia Beach in her own biography *Shakespeare and Company* put in a good many stories Hemingway told her that were not true. He was always doing that, and people were always quoting him as if they were true because he had a very convincing manner in conversation, evidently.

JOHN CARLISLE: When I read Carlos Baker's biography of Ernest I was surprised how many stories he told as the truth that were figments of his imagination. He might have been doing it to me, but I never thought he was. I actually thought he was one of the most truthful men I ever met.

DENIS BRIAN: What of the other picture of Hemingway as a violent man getting rid of his violence by hunting?

MARY HEMINGWAY: We hunted in Africa and many falls we hunted birds in Idaho. A great deal of the hunting was the pleasure of walking through African bush or Idaho sagebrush. He and I used to hunt ducks and pheasants in Idaho and *not* to kill ducks. Frequently the limit would be perhaps six a day, and we might have twelve in the deep freeze. We'd walk four or five miles in the fresh air looking at the country and smelling the wind, and come back home with two ducks. It was certainly not killing that engaged him. We did an awful lot of walking in Africa and of course if we found something that looked remarkably good in the way of a head we might possibly . . . But we passed up a great many animals who were just too sweet to shoot. Both of us did. For example, lots of people wondered why he never hunted elephants and Ernest said they were too important and dignified, too great as living things to be shot by a man. So this idea of a livid, wild killer, is not true at all.

DENIS BRIAN: Mr. Plimpton, you've said that the desecration of animal-kind makes you angry. How do you reconcile this with your admiration for Hemingway?

GEORGE PLIMPTON: The killing instinct is very difficult to talk about. Perhaps the thrill of the chase is an important emotion for some people—a primeval urge that is satisfied in hunting and killing.

DENIS BRIAN: One could say, then, that some men should be allowed to murder other men to satisfy a primeval urge.

GEORGE PLIMPTON: Well, that's a strong argument against hunting.

DENIS BRIAN: What do you make of his remark, "if I don't kill animals, I'll kill myself," Professor Young?

PHILIP YOUNG: I think it's an overstatement, but he did say it.

DENIS BRIAN: He also referred to the "gift of killing" when hunting animals. A strange expression.

PHILIP YOUNG: Yes, it is.

DENIS BRIAN: Ernest is quoted as saying to Janet Flanner, the Paris correspondent of the *New Yorker*, "I know it's probably bad, but I love to kill."

LEICESTER HEMINGWAY: It doesn't say *what* he loved to kill. Did it mean he loved to kill ants or doves or grouse or what?

DENIS BRIAN: I'm asking you. Did that include people?

LEICESTER HEMINGWAY: I've never known a person who really loved to kill people. I've known an awful lot of people who thought it a disgusting, disagreeable duty. Jesus, I love to shoot birds. Birds are wonderful eating.

DENIS BRIAN: Another statement of his was: "If I don't kill, I'll have to kill myself." Do you remember that?

LEICESTER HEMINGWAY: No I don't. Where do you get all these quotes?

DENIS BRIAN: From various books.[1]

MARY HEMINGWAY: Believing the printed word is a terrible mistake. The accounts of his bravado were mostly cartoons. Enormous exaggerations. It would be hard, though, to exaggerate Ernest's own—until he became ill—enormous enjoyment of life, which was so much greater than that of almost anyone. His enjoyment of *everything* and his *zest* for life, and his exuberance. Lots of people maintain he was a great, bravado boy, boastful, and a big, boisterous public figure. That would never be my opinion. What people saw as bravado could well have been disguise, an attempt to escape from shyness.

ALVAH BESSIE: Years and years after World War II when Martha

[1]One version was, "Since he was a young boy he had cared greatly for fishing and shooting. If he had not spent so much time at them . . . he might have written more. On the other hand, he might have shot himself." From Georges Schreiber, ed., *Portraits and Self-Portraits*, Boston, 1936.

Gellhorn was married to a guy who was then retiring editor of *Time* magazine, she came to a nightclub in San Francisco where I was working. And I walked up to her and said, "Aren't you Martha Gellhorn?" She said, "Yes." I said, "The last time I saw you was during the Spanish Civil War, when you gave me a chocolate bar. My name's Bessie." "Of course," she said. "What are you doing here?" I said, "I run the show here. One of the jobs I got as a blacklisted man." So she asked would I be kind enough to have lunch with her and her husband, which I did. Then she asked me if I'd show her some of San Francisco and Marin County, which I did. And we sat out at the pier at Sausalito, out there by the bay and I started asking her questions about Hemingway. I said, "What's your opinion of him as a writer?"—because Martha's a goddamn good writer herself. She said, and this must have been in the sixties: "I don't think anyone will be reading him in ten years." I agreed with her. But we were both wrong. They're reading him, all right. "But," I said, "he must have been a nice guy. Wasn't he?" A long pause. Then she said, "He was one of the cruelest men I ever knew and believe me I've known an awful lot of them." I understand it. He was a macho character, you know. It was very important for him to be a man. I suspect characters like that.

MARTHA GELLHORN: I'm sure I didn't say I'd known many cruel men, because I haven't. He was indeed cruel—in words—given to unpredictable murdering of people who had thought he was their buddy. I didn't give him much chance to be cruel to me, in any way. And I do believe he was not totally sane even as long ago as the forties.

CARLOS BAKER: It depends on how you define sanity. I think he had his moments of crazy impulsiveness like everybody else.

DENIS BRIAN: Would that account for his writing to magazine editor Ernest Walsh in 1926 that saints like Joan of Arc are "the shit of life" who develop wonderful publicity organizations after their death?

LEICESTER HEMINGWAY: He might have been showing off. You show off to people like Ernest Walsh, don't tell them all the truth. Walsh was the kind of guy whom everybody loved to pull the wool over the eyes of, and tell him, "Listen, we have something very big and mysterious and fantastic coming up and you'll be the first to know."

DENIS BRIAN: And what of his wanting to wear an earring to be like his African brothers?

LEICESTER HEMINGWAY: Ah, don't worry about it. A guy's entitled to any fripperies he wants, what the hell!

JOHN CARLISLE: There's a breed of cat now that is denigrating Hemingway, telling about how cruel he was and things he said to other writers, about which I know nothing. And what he's supposed to have said about Gertrude Stein, and about this one and that one who were famous, too. I don't know about any of these things. That is not the man I knew. This man was a gracious, decent human being.

MORLEY CALLAGHAN: He was probably my first admirer, the one guy in the world who knew about my work and liked it and spoke to others about it. Neither my wife nor I ever had an unpleasant scene with Hemingway, in spite of what people said. The guy must have changed an enormous amount the last ten years of his life, because I simply don't recognize the picture that people give of him. I often wondered what Hemingway would have been like if I had run into him in those late years. I always found him easy to talk to and straightforward. I've talked to other people who knew Hemingway in later years, Lillian Hellman, for example, and when I pointed out to her that he wasn't at all as she described him in that book of memories where she described meeting him and found him loud and boastful and swaggering, I told her she was just giving a stereotype of Hemingway. She quickly got off it and said, "Don't hold it against me. I don't really know him at all."

DENIS BRIAN: Diana Cooper, the wife of Duff Cooper, has a similar view of Hemingway, calling him a boring braggart or words to that effect.

MORLEY CALLAGHAN: I just can't imagine it, that's all.

DENIS BRIAN: Isn't it possible he was like that when he was drunk?

MORLEY CALLAGHAN: So other people say. Maybe through alcohol he was gradually going a little bit crazy and then he went completely crazy.

C. L. SULZBERGER [organized and ran the *New York Times* Foreign Service between 1934 and 1954]: I knew Hemingway in the late 1950s but never saw any sign of a mental breakdown although there is no doubt that he did drink too much—and he showed it often. On one occasion, I remember when he discussed the length of noses in relationship to courage I attributed this to his simply making slightly alcoholic conversation. I admired him greatly and found him to be sensitive and kindhearted. He was not overly modest but I do not agree with those who called him arrogant and a braggart. Though he did indeed have a certain vanity. He never spoke of his injuries in front of me or showed any signs of them, with the exception of a weakened back which forced him to do his writing in the latter years standing up with a portable typewriter aslant on top of a low bookcase. He was a man with immense qualities. His greatest genius probably was in creating an impact upon the English language. Since Hemingway's early stories and books, the language began perceptively to change—first in America, subsequently in England. On the whole I would say he was a likable, courageous man and a loyal friend. As Buck Lanham told you I had originally intended to publish several of Ernest's letters but his wife threatened legal action if I did so. Mary certainly made a nuisance of herself. I really have no affection for her but I liked Ernest extremely well. The story Buck Lanham told you [see introduction] is exactly correct. I was an innocent in those days, more than thirty years ago, and did not realize that letters belonged to the sender and not the receiver. I learned the hard way. [His book was withdrawn from the bookstores.]

The substance of what was in the Hemingway letters came out in *The Resistentialists*, a different version of the book, originally called *Unconquered Souls*. *The Resistentialists* was published ten years after the first one was withdrawn in 1973 by the Overlook Press. The story of Hemingway's friend is substantially the same as in the original version of *The Resistenialists*, but it lost a great deal by not being told in Hemingway's own words.

C. T. LANHAM: Ernesto broke with damn near all his friends. I lasted all the way to the end with him, and I disagreed with him on many things, but we were good friends in a whole series of different ways. He wrote me constantly and in those letters I know how many things he said about people who had been friends of his, which were adverse. This is why I would never give anybody permission to look at them. There are too many yellow journalists who want to get hold of this sort of thing. I suspect that was one reason Ernest decided his letters should never be published, even posthumously. Another reason is, I think, there were contradictions in letters to various people.

ARCHIBALD MACLEISH: He undoubtedly changed when he ran into psychiatric difficulties. I know nothing about that. But we became friends again after World War II and then had a long, long correspondence, and were very close to one another again. We met once in Havana in the fifties for an evening, but that was all. I knew better than to meet him again and I guess he knew better than to meet me.

DENIS BRIAN: When your daughter, Mimi, cried because Hemingway greeted her strangely, was he too aggressive or what?

ARCHIBALD MACLEISH: No. They were very close to each other when she was little and when she saw him again in America years later, he had a scar on his chin and she cried. She had gone to bed and she raced downstairs and ran to him, and stopped and stared, and cried, and ran back upstairs. He went up after a while and they talked for a long time. Worked it out. There was a story he said reminded him of Mimi, *Disorder and Early Sorrow*, Thomas Mann's story.

DENIS BRIAN: In a letter to Hemingway, General Lanham called him a "biological sport," and wrote "I don't believe any man regardless of age and condition could keep up with you for more than a few months." That was in 1959, less than two years before his suicide. Lanham also called them both "ever-blooming adolescents."

ARCHIBALD MACLEISH: Big boy, rather than adolescent.

DENIS BRIAN: Why was he so infuriated by Max Eastman's "false-hair on the chest" remark, implying Ernest wasn't all that masculine?

LEICESTER HEMINGWAY: He wasn't infuriated, he was simply insulted because Max Eastman not only knew he had hair on his chest, but Max was trying to make fun of the virility Ernest put into his writing. Hell, nobody deliberately puts virility into writing. He simply writes as the person he is.

ARCHIBALD MACLEISH: Eastman was a very big, very vain, rather empty man who had a considerable reputation in his early years as a writer. I think he even tried to write poetry once. Eastman went after Ernest. He and Ernest met in Max Perkins's office and Ernest hit him, he said, "not very successfully." Eastman fell over a chair and Perkins stopped them, and it was all very silly. Eastman was a good man to have as an enemy, a contemptible person.

DENIS BRIAN: How do you explain Ernest's passionate devotion to the young bullfighter, Antonio Ordoñez. When the man was injured by a bull, for example, Ernest sat at his bedside for hours. Spanish writer José Luis Castillo-Puche published these comments Ernest made in the summer of 1960: "On the way to Ordoñez's, Ernesto talked about him constantly, in the most flattering terms: 'He's a great kid isn't he? . . . He's stupendous. . . . He's very handsome and a very decent guy. . . . There's nobody like him. . . . I'd die if anything ever happened to him; but he's so good he doesn't deserve to have anything happen to him. . . . I'm so fond of him—he means more to me than a son.' "[1]

LEICESTER HEMINGWAY: Here's the thing. Ernesto was a great man for putting himself in the other person's position. In a sense he was trying to psyche himself into being able to write something where he was a young

[1]Jose Luis Castillo-Puche, *Hemingway in Spain*, Doubleday, 1974.

bullfighter, trying to get inside his skin. Ernesto had that absolutely incredible ability to give a damn, in a situation where he was learning as well as caring. On the other hand, if he didn't like a person he didn't give a damn.

GEORGE PLIMPTON: One can think of many of Hemingway's stories in which strong relationships between men exist, not homosexual, but friendship based on admiration and appreciation of skills. In his own life he had these strong attachments with a whole succession of males. Then he used to have almost petulant fallings-out with them. Archibald MacLeish was one, Ford Madox Ford another. These friendships finally broke down because Hemingway's friends were constantly being put to the test for some reason, as if friendship had to be tested. Which made it very awkward for everybody. Howard Hawks talks about a type of man-love, love that isn't sexual. All his great films, *Red River*, *El Dorado*, are love stories between men. In *Red River*, it's between Montgomery Clift and John Wayne. Hawks said he liked to make films about adventurers and since the world of adventure often gets cluttered up with a woman involved, he concentrated on the relationship played off between one man and another—the bond between them almost a love relationship.

MALCOLM COWLEY: My simple theory about Hemingway is that in Italy in World War I he found he was shell-shocked, and was guilty in his own eyes of cowardice of some sort. The one strong motive in Hemingway's life that led him to do most of the things he should have been ashamed of and was ashamed of, was that need always to be first in anything. Now, at the end of his life in the African safari there are a good many impossible episodes. He was yarning there. I think his breakdown went back a good deal further than 1959 and '60. I think he was beginning to have delusions after the African accidents in 1954. He admitted himself he was frightened to death. He told me in a letter that he finally recovered from a fear of death, in China in the early 1940s. I know some of the terribly mean things Hemingway said about people that I won't even repeat now. I'll repeat one of them. He said, for example, that Katy Dos Passos, the first wife of Dos Passos, was a kleptomaniac.

DENIS BRIAN: Was she?

MALCOLM COWLEY: I don't know. I don't think so. He made other remarks about people we both knew. Scott Fitzgerald's *The Last Tycoon* was "just written to get an advance, and never would have been finished." And other mean remarks. I'm sure he regretted them later, because he set high standards for himself. I think he really tried to create an ideal character and tried to live up to it, and failed every time, and every time he failed he was overcome with remorse. But his remorse seldom led to his making up to people for mean things he had done to them. We had an enormous correspondence. I sold his letters with Mary's consent. She asked me to hold up for six months to see whether the Kennedy Library would buy them, but they didn't have the money and after six months I sold them to Jonathan Goodwin, a private collector, for what seemed a fabulous price, $15,000. He put them up for auction at Parke-Bernet and they were bought by a San Francisco collector, a friend of Peter Buckley's, for $32,500. The letters had been shown to Carlos Baker and a few others. I saved one that seemed to me very revealing.

MORLEY CALLAGHAN: The *Washington Post* had me do quite a long piece on his letters [*Ernest Hemingway: Selected Letters, 1917–1961*. Edited by Carlos Baker, Scribners, 1981].

DENIS BRIAN: That's where you bring up the incident when the two of you were boxing. What's always puzzled me is your response when you drew blood and he spat in your face. And you apparently weren't offended.

MORLEY CALLAGHAN: I was astounded. But when he explained that's how a bullfighter showed his contempt of the bull, the thing became a sort of exotic piece of information.

DENIS BRIAN: You didn't mind his comparing you with a bull?

MORLEY CALLAGHAN: Oh well, he was just talking about gladiators. And he ruined my shirt. That was simply the way he was and I knew that one minute after this happened he was feeling great, so I never held it against him.

DENIS BRIAN: But then, when Scott Fitzgerald was acting as timekeeper and inadvertently let the round run one minute over time, for four minutes instead of three, during which you floored Hemingway, was that when your friendship with Ernest began to sour?

MORLEY CALLAGHAN: Yes. For a while, until it broke up, I had a very lovely relationship with him. The thing ended disastrously over Fitzgerald. We parted amicably, but it was a very difficult period, ruinous.

DENIS BRIAN: Hemingway never got over the false news account that you'd knocked him out in the first round and he suspected you'd planted the story? Which you hadn't.

MORLEY CALLAGHAN: Yes, that's exactly it. He was enraged about the long round, and was making a fool of himself. But it was understandable because his pride was hurt. He was just childish about his boxing.

DENIS BRIAN: It must have surprised you when you read his letters about the event.

MORLEY CALLAGHAN: It did, as you'll see in my review in the *Washington Post*. You can quote me. ". . . the many versions he gives of his boxing bout with me in Paris, with Fitzgerald acting as timekeeper, are strangely revealing and perplexing [in the same way that one wonders why he made up the story that the great middleweight Harry Greb stuck his thumb in his eye when it never happened]. In an early letter to Perkins, Hemingway explains how he slipped and fell when Fitzgerald let the round go on too long. Some years later, writing to Fitzgerald's biographer Arthur Mizener, he gives another version: now he is full of wine and Fitzgerald lets the round go thirteen minutes. A thirteen-minute round? Incredible! And he wasn't on the floor at all! Or is the daydream now the real thing? Was he always shaping and reshaping reality to suit himself, to soothe himself, carrying on conversations or fights or jungle treks in the night he wished he'd had? I don't know, but if this was the case, how terrible it must have been for him at the end, having a nervous breakdown, with his wild imagination working away, seeking the right end to his story, his life."[1]

DENIS BRIAN: Apparently Hemingway had strong feelings against psychiatrists and psychoanalysts, but never once mentions them in his hundreds of letters. There's not a word about Jung or Freud or anyone.

PHILIP YOUNG: That's interesting, isn't it? You're right. I think he might have been scared of that.

DENIS BRIAN: Mr. Waldhorn, did you ever know what the terror was that caused his nightmares and his attempts to ward them off by thinking about fishing and recalling all the girls he had ever known? Was this terror of death, and the unknown?

ARTHUR WALDHORN: It's a possibility. But there's no way in which, I think, one can make an allegory of that—you can't say this equals this.

DENIS BRIAN: He doesn't spell out his terror.

ARTHUR WALDHORN: No, and I don't think there's anything that enables us to spell it out. All we know is that there's terror. You know, Emily Dickinson knew what terror was and didn't always spell it out. And I don't think one can here, either. He told writer Arthur Mizener that he could not sleep in the dark—after his war injuries—and he told others that he was afraid that if he went to sleep in the dark he would never wake. There

[1]Morley Callaghan, "Everything He Wrote Seemed Real," *Washington Post*, March 29, 1981.

are hints of his nightmares in the Nick Adams stories, when Nick is talking to Paravicin and asks: "I don't seem crazy to you, do I?"

EARL ROVIT: When I wrote my book about Hemingway in 1962 this was long before there was very much public information and my interest was only peripherally biographical and I was personally shocked by the suicide, because to me like most people of my generation Hemingway was much larger than life. The ambivalent attitudes toward suicide—ranging in his work from complete contempt and disgust for anyone who would be such a coward, to a clear fascination thematically—even without what we know about the family relations who had committed suicide—piqued my interest. I think he's always going to be an enigma. There are very few private actions or reactions left in our well-reported world today. But to be certain that one is in the mind of somebody as complicated as Hemingway when he walks into that room with a gun, that's to take a kind of godlike arrogance. I think there are two questions. One I can't answer. Why does any man commit suicide? The other, which I do think is a legitimate question, is this: what various meanings does that act have, if any, on the validation or invalidation of work that has become public and has itself taken a kind of causative action in the world? I think the second question is really the question of biography, literary history, literary criticism, cultural history, and so on.

DENIS BRIAN: You have also said, "He was wonderfully hidden in the midst of his own creation."

EARL ROVIT: He was clearly, as I guess all humans have got to be—except he was more than most—a defensive-aggressive person, or an aggressive-defensive, however you want to put it. My hunch, which is no more true or false than anybody's intuition, which my work at that time made me believe, was that there was, I don't want to say a frightened or weak or scared character in this web: I guess we have the expression "running scared." I think he was running scared most of his life and long before the wounding at Fossalta. I think he was running scared when he was thirteen or fourteen. And one way to handle this was to pretend to be just the reverse. In a way, his talent was much, much more frail and narrow than anyone knew, except himself. Instead of what was current in the fifties, instead of upbraiding him for not taking chances as Faulkner and Gertrude Stein and many others did, they should have realized he was taking enormous chance on far less mileage.

DENIS BRIAN: Professor Young, did you know what was wrong with him at the end when he thought the FBI and the Internal Revenue authorities were after him?

PHILIP YOUNG: That's clear paranoia. I didn't know that at the time, but I did know that he was obviously in severe depression. That was clear from what people told me. He gave Leslie Fiedler who visited him in Ketchum in November 1960 the impression that he had the feeling that nothing he had ever written was worth a damn. I know a fair amount about depression and that's *entirely* characteristic; one's whole life seems a mistake. So you can see why I wasn't that surprised when I heard he'd killed himself, though I'm not saying I expected it.

DENIS BRIAN: Although he mentioned suicide all through his life.

PHILIP YOUNG: My God, yes. One of the old notebooks I found among his manuscripts, which goes back to the very beginning days in Paris as a young man before he had published anything really, speculates about different ways of killing yourself. This was a real preoccupation.

RONALD R. FIEVE [psychiatrist and author of *Moodswing*]: Ernest Hemingway's career illustrates the benefits and pitfalls of the creative manic-depressive. Hemingway's terrifically active periods alternated with his depressions. When he was depressed, self-doubt would overcome him. His heavy drinking during his adult life might be considered his own form of self-treatment. Hemingway had a sense of mission, or a sense of himself as the hero. In 1960 he was hospitalized. This must have been most difficult to accomplish since he had always hated psychiatrists. It is curious that manic grandiosity, when associated with people like Hemingway, Theodore Roosevelt, or Churchill, is grandiosity with a basis in fact. They *are* the biggest, bravest, and most powerful men in the world. For these few a delusion of grandeur coincides with the actual state of things; and if it does so, is it really a delusion? Psychiatry fails to provide the answer, since there is no psychiatric label for delusional grandiosity which grows into reality.

GEORGE SAVIERS: He considered himself a doctor and a surgeon [laughs]. I don't know whether it was because he was a doctor's son or whether he was just interested in the subject, but I'd give him medical journals to read and we'd often talk about medicine. He was definitely above average for a layman in his medical knowledge.

ARNOLD GINGRICH: In 1948 when Malcolm Cowley interviewed Ernest, his pose was to have utter contempt for all the log-rolling, lifted pinkie, tea-drinking, cookie-pushing, café, literary society. Then he found himself enjoying it and becoming an ornament of it. So he came full circle. He became that which he despised. It was, of course, a gradual process. The early pose—my wife was impressed when she heard Ernest had visited the White House by invitation and hadn't shaved—happened to coincide with his best work. But who's to say which was more sincere, the later pose or the early pose? They're both poses it seems to me.

DENIS BRIAN: Do you have any idea why he was so scornful of psychiatrists, Mr. Walton?

WILLIAM WALTON: Only the obvious one: his own problems. I think he was perfectly aware of his own strain of madness, that he was a manic-depressive.

DENIS BRIAN: And feared investigation of his own mental problems?

WILLIAM WALTON: Certainly. Anyone who suspected he needed psychiatric help was a threat. I think it's a common problem.

DENIS BRIAN: Hemingway seemed to have a premonition that he might die prematurely.

WILLIAM WALTON: He was haunted by the thought of death.

DENIS BRIAN: Did he threaten suicide and talk of death so often because he was a manic-depressive—and this talk was in his depressed state?

WILLIAM WALTON: Certainly. Absolutely. He was a classic manic-depressive his whole life.

DENIS BRIAN: Did you see him in deep depression?

WILLIAM WALTON: Of course.

DENIS BRIAN: Could you do anything to help him?

WILLIAM WALTON: No. You can't do anything for them.

DENIS BRIAN: Did drink help him?

WILLIAM WALTON: Not really. It helped a little bit.

DENIS BRIAN: And he was exuberant in his manic stage?

WILLIAM WALTON: Of course. And some of the silliest things he did were when he was up in a high.

DENIS BRIAN: Martha Gellhorn said she thought he was slightly mad long before his final breakdown in the 1940s.

WILLIAM WALTON: I would think so, too. The violent rages and wild drunkenness are all symptoms. But they don't exist all the time; they're periodic, you know. That pattern goes with the rise and fall of manic-depression.

DENIS BRIAN: Hadley and others downplayed any suggestion of manic-depression, saying he was occasionally depressed but usually with good cause such as being ill.

WILLIAM WALTON: I think it developed as he grew older.

DENIS BRIAN: Is it plausible that if he had faced up to his manic-depression and had taken lithium he could have lived a reasonably normal life in his last years?

WILLIAM WALTON: Probably not. I don't know enough about his symptoms. He had such physical problems, too—damaged liver and kidneys and all those concussions. All those internal ruptures would have had a chemical effect. You couldn't predict that lithium would have been the answer. In those days lithium was only in its experimental stages.

DENIS BRIAN: Leicester said Mary was responsible for a lot of Hemingway's emotional problems.

WILLIAM WALTON: In a sense, yes. She was an inadequate wife. She was, it's true, a very calming and sensible influence on him at times, supportive and admiring of his writing. She was not one hundred percent anything.

DENIS BRIAN: But didn't he need her in his last few years because he was so ill?

WILLIAM WALTON: No, because their conflict was so deep and so bloody. I think you could make a case for it being wise for them to separate.

DENIS BRIAN: You mentioned when you were at the Finca and Ernest was told his mother had died, he and Mary were estranged.

WILLIAM WALTON: A terrible estrangement over God knows what.

DENIS BRIAN: How about Mary encouraging him to go out with an attractive young woman and commiserating with him when it didn't work out? I thought Mary was jealous of other women.

WILLIAM WALTON: It's so unreal. He would talk about his affair with some African woman on that last trip to Africa and who knows how much was delusion and how much was reality.

DENIS BRIAN: Denis Zaphiro, the game ranger who spent several months with the Hemingways in 1953, said Ernest was probably drunk the whole time, though he seldom showed it except by becoming merrier, more lovable and more bullshitty. But when he wasn't drinking, Zaphiro found him to be depressed, morose, and silent.

WILLIAM WALTON: That's really good. That's the mark of a true alcoholic. I met Denis several times and thought he was a very bright, wise fellow.

DENIS BRIAN: In a letter to Adriana, Hemingway denied he was jealous but described Ingrid Bergman's husband Roberto Rossellini as a twenty-two pound rat who nevertheless made good children.

WILLIAM WALTON: This is vintage Hemingway.

DENIS BRIAN: He told Bernard Berenson that he was one-eighth Cheyenne Indian. Was he?

WILLIAM WALTON: I wouldn't take it too seriously. He'd like for it to be true because it would made him aboriginal—earlier than the Pilgrims.

DENIS BRIAN: In a letter to Berenson in 1954 he offered to be his son, said he gave and took no quarter, called himself lonely, bad, worthless. He said Berenson was his hero and wished Berenson would be his father if it was fun for him.

WILLIAM WALTON: That's absolutely genuine and he was probably high as a kite when he wrote it. You see, he longed for intellectual conversation and Mary couldn't provide him with one paragraph. And Cuba was an intellectual desert. He seized on any straw of this kind and he built up a romantic picture of Berenson, who was a snob. They were both interested in celebrityhood.

DENIS BRIAN: So he overcame his superficial anti-Semitism in wanting a Jew for a father.

WILLIAM WALTON: Well, yes. But, again, it's like wanting some American Indian blood. It's the same exact thing.

DENIS BRIAN: Despite his anti-psychiatrist stance he greatly admired Stetmeyer, the psychiatrist who cured Patrick of his mental breakdown. There's almost always an exception to everything he says.

WILLIAM WALTON: That's rather a nice rule of conduct for a person.

DENIS BRIAN: He said, "Never trust a balding man who brushes strands of hair across his bald top to cover it." Which is what he eventually did.

WILLIAM WALTON: [laughs]: Of course he did.

DENIS BRIAN: You laugh when you remember him. Because you had such fun together?

WILLIAM WALTON: We really did, we had enormous pleasure. Once or twice Mary and I went through his miscellaneous papers. We got into a vein of stuff and, God, we started reading it aloud to each other, laughing back and forth because it was *all* our lives. And it was very unembroidered or disguised.

GREGORY HEMINGWAY: I wish I could remember more of his humor. There were thousands of examples. Once we were sitting in a bar and this tall, very large, and stunningly beautiful girl came in. He caught me looking at her and shook his head, smiled with the side of his mouth and said, "Don't think about it, kid. Only God can make a tree." When we finally got a chaplain at Canterbury School, which is a Catholic school run by laymen and didn't have a chaplain until my last year there, he said, "Well, it's about time, for Christ's sake!" And then we sort of realized what he'd said and laughed. We were brought up Catholics, but he made it clear he didn't believe in an afterlife. He did, finally, believe in a superior being. He quoted to me one thing I thought was beautiful, and he was profoundly struck by the imagery. He recalled it as the saying of an old Indian Chief on his deathbed in the 1880s. "What is life? It is the breath of the buffalo in the wintertime, it is the flicker of the firefly in the night, it is the little shadow that runs across the fields and loses itself in the sunset." This was something he believed in but in organized religion, no.

ARCHIBALD MACLEISH: When I think about him now, there's not a word or phrase that recalls him to me. I think of the good days and the great achievement. One thing is now clear, and will be clearer when the present vogue of denigration ends—as it will. Ernest was the one great prose stylist this century has produced. He is part of the tongue and of few writers—very few—can that be said. And that's what remains of him for me.

MARTHA GELLHORN [in *Paris Review*]: He was a genius, that uneasy word, not so much in what he wrote as in how he wrote; he liberated our written language.

NATHAN ASCH: I hated the son-of-a-bitch and I loved him.

JOHN HEMINGWAY: I keep thinking what a wonderful old man he would have made if he'd learned how. I don't think he had faced up to becoming old.

A. E. HOTCHNER: There have been a few times in the years since he died when I have felt the sharp pang of missing him—a revisit to our haunts in Spain, a golden autumn day when the pheasants fly—and I have reread a chapter or two and I have found him there, just as he was.

LEICESTER HEMINGWAY: There were *uno, dos, tres* Hemingways in Spain getting free lunches and adulation and signing their names as Ernest Hemingway, some twenty years after the model died; his death reported in every major newspaper, often on front pages; on radio and TV, messages of condolences pouring in from among other places Moscow and the Vatican. You see, celebrity is so revered that phonies have only to claim celebrity to be accepted and feted.

WILLIAM WALTON: Reynolds Price wrote the best thing I've read about Ernest in recent years. I found his evaluation of him as a writer very rewarding and proper. As for his suggestion that Ernest was on the path to saintliness, the word can be applied to him. He was a masochist, too. He was asking to be crucified in many of the acts of his life, exposing himself to the danger of gunfire, of being hit. Oh, he was bucking for a sainthood. That would have been his term.

MALCOLM COWLEY: He had aspirations toward goodness, toward something close to saintliness. When he fell short of his ideal in a fit of professional jealousy or in one of his black rages, he blamed himself and sometimes offered contrite apologies.[1]

CAROL GARDNER: Half the people in Key West owed him for kindnesses. He didn't boast about it, but anybody who needed help he would volunteer. He wouldn't have to be asked by the fishermen and people who lived there. He was a very soft-hearted person.

DENIS BRIAN: How would Martha Gellhorn respond if told Hemingway's goal was sainthood?

WILLIAM WALTON: With a dirty word. And I would respond to her response with a laugh.

DENIS BRIAN: But how then would you justify your view?

WILLIAM WALTON: Well, look, he gave his Nobel medal to Our Lady of Charity of Cobre. There's a connection. He felt sometimes that he was worthy of sainthood; in his attitude toward his fellow men in the abstract, he felt his nobility should be rewarded. That was one side of him. He would justify the malicious, cruel side as something he had to bear. And he adored the small things in Catholicism, like wearing a scapular. It was part of his search for good-luck protection.

DENIS BRIAN: Though that wouldn't make him a saint.

WILLIAM WALTON: No, but it would have been peripheral.

MALCOLM COWLEY: I noticed that in his books priests are very seldom presented as being anything but admirable men.

[1]Malcolm Cowley, "Hemingway: The Image and the Shadow," *Horizon*, Winter 1973.

WILLIAM WALTON: I found his *Islands in the Stream* a very moving and fascinating book, and I read in it all kinds of feelings that I had never been aware of. So much of it was romanticizing his own life and problems, and I felt an earnestness in it.

MALCOLM COWLEY: That was a book he never finished. There were very good passages in it. Not the last passage, the chase. Havana before the chase, and some of the stuff that happened in Bimini were some of his best writing.

DENIS BRIAN: How do you rate him as a writer now?

MALCOLM COWLEY: I continue to rate him very high. My difference with many other critics is over *For Whom the Bell Tolls*, which I continue to think is a very important novel. *For Whom the Bell Tolls* is tremendously complex. One aspect of it is mystical, about conquering time. Hemingway has his character, Robert Jordan, have a mystical experience, turning time into an eternal present in which he lives in hours as much as he could in a lifetime. And, finally, to some extent he makes Jordan into a Christ figure. Hemingway still puzzles me. He was a man of extreme talent and one of the most charming people I've ever met. That contrast between the two sides of him, the side that was so charming and simple and candid, and the other side full of hatred and self-hatred is a very hard thing to bring together.

DENIS BRIAN: Did you ever see the hatred?

MALCOLM COWLEY: I got it in conversations with him, yes.

DENIS BRIAN: What aroused the hatred?

MALCOLM COWLEY: Usually rivalry.

DENIS BRIAN: Although he helped at least three potential rivals: Ezra Pound, Milton Wolff, and Alvah Bessie.

MALCOLM COWLEY: Yes, he could be very generous. Once, quite unexpectedly, he wrote to me enclosing one of his manuscripts as a gift. I had it valued not long after. It was worth $1,500.

WILLIAM WALTON: There's always a mystery about the creative personality and the creative act. It's shrouded in mystery and will always remain so. He's a character that interests me forever.

SIXTEEN

•

PSYCHIATRISTS'
VIEWS

To get the opinions of experts I discussed Ernest Hemingway with two psychiatrists: Philip Scharfer and Ronald R. Fieve. I hoped that they might solve some of the mysteries of his personality and behavior that puzzled even those close to him.

Dr. Scharfer is Chief of the Department of Psychiatry at Good Samaritan Hospital, West Palm Beach, Florida and is also in private practice. He studied at the City College of New York, attended medical school at the Université de Montpellier, France, and was in psychiatric residency at Long Island Jewish-Hillside Medical Center for three years and at Jackson Memorial for a year.

PHILIP SCHARFER: Do you know if any other family members suffered from depression?

DENIS BRIAN: His father committed suicide; he had diabetes and was worried by financial problems. His brother, Leicester, also fatally shot himself in the head—he was suffering from hypertension and diabetes and had undergone major surgery. His sister Ursula, who had cancer, is believed to have died from a drug overdose.

PHILIP SCHARFER: Besides shock treatment what other medical treatment did Ernest Hemingway have?

DENIS BRIAN: Medicine for hypertension was thought to deepen his depression so he was taken off it. Would you call him a classic manic-depressive?

PHILIP SCHARFER: I don't know that he had any of the manic symptoms.

DENIS BRIAN: He was the most exuberant, active, and enthusiastic man anyone met. His friend General Lanham called him "a biological sport" and said that no one could keep up with him. He was frequently arranging and going on safaris in Africa, hunting trips, fishing trips, following bullfights all over Spain.

PHILIP SCHARFER: A lot of people who suffer from what's called bipolar affective behavior—which is manic-depression—have classical manic episodes and during the interim their baseline is, maybe, hypomanic: increased energy and being a very exuberant and dynamic person. Usually, even these people have some phases where they become truly manic, not needing to sleep and being "high" almost as if they've taken some stimulating drug.

DENIS BRIAN: He suffered from insomnia and said that over a period of a month or so on one occasion he only had two or three hours sleep a night. Incidentally, he was at his best in World War II as a correspondent at the front in the midst of fierce fighting during the Battle of the Bulge.

PHILIP SCHARFER: Maybe the structured military situation helped—it might have been some help to a person who has a tendency to go off on tangents, and not using his energies in a focalized way. That may have focalized him.

DENIS BRIAN: Remember, he was a volunteer there. He didn't have to stay and he also behaved very independently by leading a group of the French Maquis, and breaking the rules for newsmen by being armed. Another thing, because of his machismo attitude, his extreme he-man stance, some regarded him as a latent homosexual.

PHILIP SCHARFER: From what I've heard, I wouldn't think he was a latent homosexual. There's no doubt, from the family history and from what you've told me, that he suffered from what we call "major affective disorder recurrent," recurrent depression. Also, there's a very excellent chance that he had a bipolar disorder or manic-depression. He may have been a borderline personality. This has nothing to do with manic-depression and can be a person's baseline level. It has to do with a person who is impulsive, at times acts in self-damaging ways, commits physically self-damaging acts, spending sprees, sex, gambling, drinking—physically damaging. A pattern of unstable but very intense interpersonal relationships—which he apparently had—the three divorces and the difficulty in retaining friendships. Intense emotions, difficulties in controlling his anger and other emotions.

DENIS BRIAN: Yes, he cried easily and had a quick, fierce temper.

PHILIP SCHARFER: These are all characteristics of a borderline personality disorder, with probably self-image problems. I don't know if he would sometimes ask, "Who am I, really?"

DENIS BRIAN: Not that I know. He was curious about why he should have become a writer and about where his ability originated. He felt it was something to do with genetics and also had what George Plimpton called "a curious affinity" with an odd uncle who was a missionary along the Chinese borders. Hemingway was proud that the Chinese for Hemingway meant approximately "hunter of wolves." Despite a Nobel prize and having frequently been brave and daring, he would tell way-out stories of fantastic deeds which his friends think he sometimes believed himself.

PHILIP SCHARFER: That goes along with quite a few things. Also the "affective instability"—marked shifts of mood, from depression to irritability to anxiety, each lasting a few hours; rarely more than a few days at a time without a return to normal. He may have been like this in between his severe depressions. Also, the tremendous depression when alone; his inability to tolerate being alone is one of the hallmarks of a borderline personality.

DENIS BRIAN: He despised his father for committing suicide, said it was cowardly and that he would never do it, yet even before his father's death, when depressed he had spoken of killing himself as if it was inevitable.

PHILIP SCHARFER: The depression itself changes totally a person's thinking. He was clearly very angry at his father for leaving him and was probably thinking of himself when he said "a coward's way out."

DENIS BRIAN: How do you explain his obsessive fear of death—apparently after being blown up and thinking he was going to die in World War I—and then his frequently attending bullfights and taking part in dangerous, death-defying activities?

PHILIP SCHARFER: Without knowing it, a lot of people relive a certain fear in the hope that repeating it and exposing themselves to it, will make it easier to face.

DENIS BRIAN: Freud and others said it was sometimes necessary for a person in dreams or under hypnosis to reexperience a trauma, in order to get over it.

PHILIP SCHARFER: And in the hopes that every time they survive the reliving, it becomes easier for them.

DENIS BRIAN: Hemingway's friend, William Walton, says that manic-depression is a curse and that there's no cure. Is that so?

PHILIP SCHARFER: Absolutely. But there's an excellent chance that with treatment a manic-depressive can live an otherwise normal life. The first line of treatment is lithium. When effective, lithium prevents future attacks of mania or depression and lessens excessively high or low moods. Most recently [1987], the last couple of years, we have tegrotal, which used to be used for convulsions. And shock treatment is useful as well.

DENIS BRIAN: Shock treatment didn't work for Hemingway.

PHILIP SCHARFER: It doesn't always work.

DENIS BRIAN: The consequent loss of memory was very damaging for him, because he was writing from his memories.

PHILIP SCHARFER: There is no neuronal damage, and loss of memory if it's due to the shock treatment is short term. He also had several concussions, so you wonder what brain damage if any may have contributed to any of his problems.

DENIS BRIAN: Can you explain why some say he was the nicest guy they ever knew, and others that he was an arrogant son-of-a-bitch?

PHILIP SCHARFER: He probably related to people based on transference and a feeling of who they reminded him of in his life. If they reminded him of a person he liked or was close to him, I think they would take on the same attributes [in his eyes]. It's also something found in borderline personalities where they regard people or occurrences as either totally good or totally bad; an inability to see the gray areas in life.

DENIS BRIAN: Right. He divided people into good guys or jerks. His first wife, Hadley, said that if people liked him or showed affection toward him, he would do anything for them.

PHILIP SCHARFER: It sounds as if he lived off that and when it was not available, would need to search for another source, almost a transfusion of whatever he needed emotionally.

DENIS BRIAN: I don't think he was given lithium. Should he have had it?[1]

PHILIP SCHARFER: Certainly I would have tried it. But would he have been receptive?

DENIS BRIAN: It doesn't always work?

PHILIP SCHARFER: No, it doesn't.

DENIS BRIAN: William Walton also said Hemingway was schizoid. Do you agree?

PHILIP SCHARFER: If he had a tendency to be avoidant and to lead a loner type of existence.

DENIS BRIAN: Quite the reverse. He couldn't bear to be alone.

PHILIP SCHARFER: Usually that's not schizoid, though there's a distinction between wanting to be with people and being able to be with people. A person who is schizoid prefers being by himself.

DENIS BRIAN: Do you think he could have been saved from his suicide?

PHILIP SCHARFER: If somebody wants to commit suicide, nobody can stop him if the person is firm and fixed.

DENIS BRIAN: Strangely, though, the guns were locked in the basement but his wife had left the key around in the bureau. She said a man should be allowed to make his own decisions.

PHILIP SCHARFER: I certainly wouldn't agree with that if there's any thought of suicide as a possibility. I would tell the family absolutely get rid of guns and ammunition, any possible weapons, especially if someone is impulsive and depressed. Sometimes the family doesn't listen, either.

DENIS BRIAN: He shot himself in the morning, literally under his wife's bedroom. There's a theory that suicide is often misplaced murder. Does this indicate Hemingway's suicide was anger at his wife?

PHILIP SCHARFER: Mornings are the worst times for depressed people. I think you'd be reaching to say it. It's speculative. Maybe.

DENIS BRIAN: Karl Menninger said that suicide is often murder turned against oneself.

PHILIP SCHARFER: Quite often it is. My number one diagnosis would be that he was bipolar—that's the term used in the past ten years for manic-depressive. At the same time and not exclusive of that, from what you say, he could have been diagnosed as a borderline personality.

[1]Lithium was being used only experimentally at the time of Hemingway's treatment. It was not approved as a prescription drug by the FDA until 1970.

DENIS BRIAN: He scorned psychiatrists and psychoanalysts, with the exception of the psychiatrist who cured his son, Patrick, of a mental breakdown.[1] He said his typewriter was his psychoanalyst. Friends thought his heavy drinking was an attempt to treat his depression.

PHILIP SCHARFER: That makes sense. Many bipolar patients have the onset of one of the phases where, suddenly, they have an increased urge to drink, and they do and it makes the episode worse. Other times, the drinking itself precipitates one of the shifts.

Ronald R. Fieve has already been quoted on Hemingway in the body of the book. Psychiatrist Fieve is internationally recognized as one of the world's leading experts on manic-depression and has made a study of famous men who suffered from it. He pioneered the use of lithium in the treatment of manic-depressives, and coined the word moodswing to characterize the mental illness. From 1959 until 1970 he was in charge of the acute psychiatric service of the New York State Psychiatric Institute. As well as running a private practice he is currently Professor of Clinical Psychiatry at Columbia University College of Physicians and Surgeons, and medical director of The Foundation for Depression and Manic Depression, 7 East 67th Street, New York, N.Y. 10021.

RONALD FIEVE: Depression is the most common psychiatric problem for which people seek help. When I began looking into the moods of great men who had been prominent figures of the past—political, literary, and financial—I found that many of these men had a common pattern of moodswing in their personal and professional lives. During their highs they were fascinating achievers, often worrisome but dynamic and creative leaders. During their lows, instead of being recognized as depressed they were viewed as "physically rundown" and fatigued. Many of the world's great artists have been manic-depressive. Their bouts of creativity almost inevitably coincide with a manic phase. These periods tend to be staggeringly productive. Golf for most manics is too slow. They would much prefer belting out a few good sets of tennis, trapshooting, or even bashing a punching bag. [Even that was too static for Hemingway who preferred shadowboxing.] And these men are twitchy; they're probably moving metabolically about a third or half again as fast as most of the

---

[1]Although Hemingway ridiculed the psychiatrist Dr. Meyer Maskin to his face, in a November 26, 1944 letter to his future wife, Mary Welsh, Hemingway wrote that he had just read a forty-two page informal report by the Divisional Psychiatrist [Maskin], much of it very interesting, and he judged the man to be good and kind.

people around them. The sleep-wake cycle is especially disrupted in manics who require less sleep, and depressives who are unable to sleep or who sleep excessively. One of the most common indicators of depression is a growing dependence on alcohol. But efforts to self-treat anxiety and depression with alcohol are largely wasteful. Instead of easing the problem they intensify and compound it. The first drinks provide a euphoric feeling but excessive amounts of alcohol lead to lethargy, sluggishness, and finally depression. Karl Menninger viewed alcoholism as "a disastrous attempt at a self-cure." I think of my own patients who sought help from alcohol first. In each case, unfortunately, the drinking was only the beginning of serious complications that followed.

DENIS BRIAN: Gertrude Stein suggested that Ernest Hemingway's hero was Theodore Roosevelt and that he tried to emulate him. According to your research, Roosevelt was a classic manic-depressive and consequently, to a large extent, Hemingway also being a manic-depressive couldn't help behaving like his hero. Could you describe how they were so much alike?

RONALD FIEVE: Henry Cabot Lodge wrote of Theodore Roosevelt: "His mere presence was so full of vitality, so charged with energy, that it was contagious, and seemed to bring all the possible joy of living as a gift or rather as an atmosphere to those who rode or walked beside him." He was always interested in nature, in the world around him. His high moods as a child were associated with overtalkativeness—a hypomanic trait that was to be present for most of his life and to worsen with time. Like many other hypomanics he too was attracted to and married a woman whom he could control, who did not frustrate his schemes or interrupt his goals and demands, and turned out to be his salvation because of her slower, steadier pace and more realistic judgment. The American West exhilarated him. Since a hypomanic must impose his will, he often tried to do so with complete lack of tact. He was refreshed and energetic after only a few hours sleep. He was at his desk by 7:30 A.M. He fell into frequent rages and tended to bully others. After battling verbally with visitors he would occasionally go a few rounds with a hired prizefighter. In only a few years he wrote 150,000 letters. At fifty-one he rode horseback over a hundred miles, then took a long, dangerous trip to Africa. Many thought he would not return alive, being middle-aged, blind in one eye, and overweight. [Almost an exact description of Hemingway.] The nation was fascinated by the newspaper accounts of his experiences killing lions and searching out adventure. He then toured Europe in an elated state. Is it possible to imagine him sitting still? He could not, in fact. When he left politics he had to go on safaris and tours of state through Europe, cowpunch, even organize his own small army to fight the First World War. [As Hemingway organized his small army at Rambouillet.] He is an extreme example of the hypomanic victimized by his own need for activity.[1]

DENIS BRIAN: It's extraordinary how alike they were. The big difference is that Roosevelt didn't kill himself. But here is something you wrote about hypomanics which fits both men perfectly: "One cannot say that such a person's judgment is not accurate. In fact, it is probably more acute than most people's, since the hypomanic individual is able to perceive the defects in others most rapidly and get to the core of the matter. He is able to convince people of what he believes. People will follow the hypomanic because of his energy and his enthusiasm. They are attracted by his vitality. He thinks big and he is generally able to seduce others into relinquishing their conservative scruples."

[1]More details about manic-depression can be found in Dr. Ronald R. Fieve, M.D., *Moodswing*, Bantam Books, Inc., 1976.

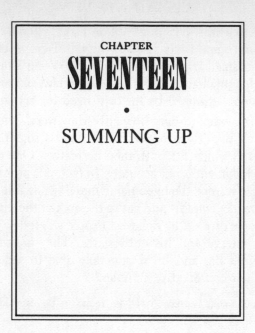

When he was three Hemingway's mother asked him what he was afraid of. " 'Fraid a nothing!" he replied. That wasn't true for long. As a boy he was often scared and never forgot the shame of overhearing an uncle call him a coward. Even more humiliating was witnessing his father's cowardice. Hunting or at work as a doctor he was a hero, but at home he was henpecked almost to enslavement by a demanding and domineering wife. Hemingway despised his father for this and his dread of becoming a replica of the demoralized man—for whom he felt love and contempt—spurred him to overcome his own weaknesses.

He was soon put to the test. Before he was twenty-two Hemingway suffered three traumas which had an enormous effect upon his life, his work, and his character. He only survived the psychic and physical wounds by developing a robust public personality that overwhelmed the weaker man beneath.

The role he played before the world, of a superman with almost magical powers of endurance and recuperation, sustained him.

His first trauma occurred on the battlefield during World War I. Although poor eyesight barred him from combat, at nineteen Hemingway drove a Red Cross ambulance on the Italian-Austrian front. He broke the rules to see the action, was severely wounded and won the Italian Silver Medal for courage. Exactly what he did to win it remained a mystery, even to him.

Effects of the wounding stayed with him for life in recurring nightmares that recreated the eerie terrain where he first realized that he was not immortal, and shifted to different nightmare scenes in later wars. His autobiographical short story, "A Way You'll Never Be," strongly suggests that in World War I he suffered what was then called shellshock, to the point of mental breakdown.[1]

He never received professional therapy (except in the last months of his life), but became a do-it-yourself therapist with his typewriter, and succeeded, to some extent, in subduing the terrors.

To his Oak Park neighbors Hemingway presented a cheerful front, the flamboyant war hero with a limp, and a yen to write. He concealed from them the symptoms of his shellshock, one of which was an irrational fear of the night. He believed that if he fell asleep in the dark he would never wake. So, for months he slept with a light.

He was still limping, supported by a cane, when he suffered a second shock. He had fallen in love with the nurse who had taken care of him in Italy and eagerly anticipated her return to the United States for their wedding. Then she wrote to call off the marriage. He tried to exorcise her memory by transforming her into a fictional character in three works, but the pain of losing her lasted long.

Hemingway's third shock came soon after: a further rejection, this time by his parents. Objecting to his carefree life after his return from the war, his mother forbade him the use of their summer home. His father backed her up. This banishment by his parents and their later condemnation of him for writing about "degenerates," permanently alienated him from them. Consciously or unconsciously, he made himself into their opposite.

---

[1]Hemingway scholar and critic Philip Young wrote to me: "I think the point is in what EH had written Malcolm Cowley, long before he heard of me: that he wanted no inquiring deeply into the Piave wounding for fear that would open up the whole nightmare, and then he might get sick all over again as he had been at that time." Professor Young, who first advanced the theory that Hemingway's wounds colored his life and work, now believes that his rejection by his parents on the heels of his jilting by Agnes von Kurowsky had at least an equally traumatic effect on him.

They were pious protestants. He became a sometimes Catholic with lapses into atheism. His father and mother were teetotal. Hemingway stepped up his occasional boozing until he was rarely without a drink at hand. His parents never divorced. He had four wives and many partners in adultery. His father was all but henpecked to death. Hemingway treated his women as if he were an uncrowned Henry the Eighth. His father spoke of sex reluctantly and with distaste. Hemingway was both romantic and ribald. His father seldom swore and then mildly. Hemingway took to Anglo-Saxon like a native, raised obscenity to an art form, and when forced by a timid editor to use caution, chose unambigious euphemisms such as "Fornicate the Illegitimates!"

It was not a complete conversion: he still shared his father's passion for hunting and, though few dared tell him, displayed his mother's dominating personality and unforgiving nature.

He took his fears and weaknesses to the fire as if to cauterize them—looking for danger, hunting lions, reporting wars from danger zones, boxing and brawling, driving a car over rough ground at breakneck speed, and sustaining an incredible number of injuries especially to his head.

In an effort to be the man he could respect, he had to dominate or deride all rivals or imagined rivals, going to such extremes that admirers still speak of him with awe. Even before his traumas Hemingway was eager to excel. After them, he had to.

As a wing shot, Hemingway was hard to beat. He was an exceptional hunter and first-rate fisherman with powers of endurance at the wheel of a ship that seem almost impossible. Some mock his boxing, downgrading him as a slugger. Others, who should know, rate him highly. Besides winning him the Nobel Prize, his writing has inspired generations of subsequent writers and still does. He was a good man to have around in an emergency. His knowledge of medicine, mostly self-taught, saved the life of his fourth wife after her doctors had given her up.

There is still something more to tell of Hemingway, confirmed by his friend William Walton, that helps explain why he hid from the world "the true gen" about himself.

At his best he was good-tempered, high-spirited, ambitious, confident, and courageous. He awoke each morning eager to face life. He invariably saw the humorous side of things and made fun of himself and others, displaying a talent for repartee. In conversation he held listeners spellbound with a dazzling mix of puns, expletives, flights of fancy, foreign phrases, snatches of songs, and bursts of laughter.

At his arrogant, aggressive worst he went around spoiling for a fight. He bragged outrageously, refused to concede he was ever wrong, ridiculed others—often with a searing wit—and believed he deserved special attention and recognition. When opposed he became irritable, even violent, threatening with the law those who thwarted his plans. He wrote intimate details of family affairs, not all of them true. He angrily fired a gun in a hotel room and threw objects from a window. At times he apologized for his behavior and was easily moved to tears.

In both good and bad moods he gave inflated accounts of his experiences, partly because that was how he perceived them and because his vivid imagination and need to excel caused him to distort events to the point of delusion.

He endured periods of deep depression throughout his adult life, when he felt people were tricking him, or taking advantage of him. Work, formerly a delightful challenge, required great effort. His animated expression changed to a sad stare and his normally resonant voice dropped to a monotone. It wasn't true, but he believed he was dangerously short of money and faced poverty.

Despite reassurances from friends and relatives, he was convinced he was being watched both on the street and in restaurants, and he claimed to have overheard strangers make threatening remarks. A passing car aroused his suspicion that someone was out to get him. Danger seemed to threaten from many directions.

What was his basic fear? That the authorities intended to hunt him down and punish him for some unspecified crime.

During those depressed periods he sat timidly on the edge of his chair or bed as if trapped. He lost weight and appetite, had insomnia, and became impotent. He believed he was incurably ill. When it became evident he might kill himself, those close to him took precautions. But he tricked them into thinking he had recovered from his depression—and carried out his carefully arranged suicide.

The preceding eight paragraphs are an exact description of Ernest Hemingway's personality and behavior. They are also an accurate synthesis of Emil Kraepelin's reports about his patients who suffered from manic depression. In his day, psychiatrist Kraepelin (1856–1926) was the acknowledged leading expert on that mental illness and Sigmund Freud's rival.

To all but a few, manic depression was a hidden fact of Hemingway's life.

The world knew only of his manic or his mellow moods when he encouraged the false image of himself as indestructible and unbeatable, a cartoon character presented as the real thing.

Times of depression reinstated the fragile, frightened, vulnerable Hemingway. Only his inner circle saw that side of him: his acute sensitivity, dread of being alone, an almost overwhelming sense of guilt and worthlessness, when he was tempted to end the torment by killing himself.

How did he survive so long?

Allowing for the effect of the three traumas, can his creative output also have been life-sustaining attempts to escape from his bouts of depression or Black Ass as he called it? To escape from the Hurtgen Forests in his mind?

To some extent perhaps, much as an irritated oyster produces a pearl.

He was not the first man of action to take to the pen. Walter Raleigh, Teddy Roosevelt, Gabriele D'Annunzio, Rudyard Kipling, and T. E. Lawrence among others led the way. But they never denied or belittled their interest in literature. Hemingway did, because for him it was a dangerous area. The secret core of fear and rejection stirred by the traumas of his early life was the wellspring of much of his writing. By transforming his fears into fiction he could distance and control them. Naturally he resisted those threatening to probe the source and to resurrect facts he had carefully buried.

To further steer the curious clear of his secret self, he left a trail strewn with innuendoes, evasions, hyperbole, understatements, and ambiguities. From these he built his alter ego. Over the years the mask or shield he had created welded so closely that, at times, it merged with the man. Perhaps he couldn't always tell them apart.

Both therapy and shield began to fail after he sustained brutal injuries in two plane crashes and a fire. Hospitalized with critical physical and mental problems, he was still able to fool his psychiatrist into releasing him. And, finally, the ultimate deception; he killed himself.

Despite everything, his was a life of far more pleasure than pain. Between his bouts of crippling depression he had an enormous zest for living, for writing, hunting, drinking, fishing, entertaining friends, watching bullfights, and reporting. And always he reveled in his role as master of the masquerade.

As a cat lover, he might have relished a picture of himself as the vanishing Cheshire Cat, watching from above with a fading smile as his hunters tried to bring him into focus and down to earth. No one brought Hemingway down to earth for long.

Twenty years after his death, Martha Gellhorn wrote of him in the *Paris Review:* "He was a genius, that uneasy word, not so much in what he wrote (speaking like an uncertain critic) as in how he wrote; he liberated our written language. All writers, after him, owe Hemingway a debt for their freedom whether the debt is acknowledged or not. It is sad that the man's handmade falsehoods—worthless junk demeaning to the writer's reputation—survive him."*

My aim has been to expose and explain these falsehoods. I now believe they fueled Hemingway's superman alter ego, a self-deception he needed in order to survive. A remarkable man still emerges, one seen by some as diabolical and by others as striving toward sainthood.

What is beyond dispute is this: he suffered. He created. His art endures. And that's the true gen.

Paris Review, Spring 1981.

A

·

THE MILITARY'S INTERROGATION OF HEMINGWAY IN WORLD WAR II

Not having previously fought in any war, Hemingway was understandably proud of his daring, effective activities as a military leader at Rambouillet in World War II. But when several unnamed men squealed on him and he faced an interrogation by General Patton's Inspector General—the rules forbid a war correspondent from taking part in the fighting—he had to lie to stay on the job. That was as he might then have said "a piece of cake," for him. At the same time he wanted the record to show he had done something more than tap at a typewriter to help his country. Here is a transcript of his interrogation.

October 6, 1944
Nancy, France

ERNEST HEMINGWAY, being questioned by Colonel Parks.

Q Please state your name, occupation and station.

A Ernest Hemingway, war correspondent, *Collier's Weekly*, APO 887.

Q I am required to caution each witness during an investigation of
   his rights with respect to the twenty-fourth Article of War. It is
   as follows:
   (The article of war was read.)
   Do you understand your rights as a witness?

A I understand them.

Q Were you in Rambouillet about August 22nd to 25th just before
   the French Armored Division entered Paris?

A I was.

Q Will you state briefly what you were doing there?

A On August 19th I stopped at the Command Post of the 22nd
   Infantry Regiment of the First Division just outside of Maintenon, in my capacity as war correspondent accredited to the Third
   Army, to ask for information on the front. This regiment was
   holding. The G-2 and G-3 of this regiment showed me the disposi-
   tion of their battalions of their main advanced outpost at a point
   a short distance beyond Epernon on the road to Rambouillet to
   be the Regimental Command Post. I was informed there was
   heavy fighting in progress outside of Rambouillet. I knew the
   country and the roads around Epernon, Rambouillet, Trappes,
   Versailles well as I had bicycled, walked and driven a car through
   this part of France for many years. At the official outpost of the
   22nd Infantry Regiment I encountered some French civilians
   who had just come in from Rambouillet by bicycle. I was the only
   person at the outpost who spoke French. These civilians informed
   me the last Germans had left Rambouillet at three o'clock that
   morning but that the roads into the town were mined. They
   reported that contrary to the information given me at the Command post of the 22nd Infantry Regiment there was no fighting
   in progress outside of Rambouillet at all. I started to return to
   regimental headquarters with this information which seemed to
   me necessary to be placed in the hands of the proper authorities
   as soon as possible, but after driving a short way down the road
   back to Maintenon I decided it would be better to return and get
   the French civilians and take them to the Regimental Command
   Post so they themselves could be interrogated and give further
   information.

When I reached the outside again I found two cars full of French guerrilla fighters, most of whom were naked to the waist. They were armed with pistols and Sten guns they received by parachute. They just came from Rambouillet and their story of the general withdrawal tallied with the information the French civilians had given. They also possessed additional information and I conducted them back to the Regimental Command Post of the 22nd Infantry where I translated their information on the town and the state of the roads to the proper authorities. I then returned to the outpost and in my capacity as war correspondent to wait for a mine-clearing detail and a reconaissance troop that were to make rendezvous with these French guerrillas who were to conduct them to the mined area which they had already reconnoitered.

I was proceeding toward Rambouillet as a war correspondent but would act as an interpreter for the troops which were being sent on mine clearing and reconaissance. After waiting for some time and no one coming up the French guerrilla fighters became very impatient. They had placed themselves under my command ignorant of the fact that a war correspondent cannot command troops, a situation which I explained to them at the earliest moment.

They wished to proceed to the mine field and establish a guard to prevent any American vehicles which might advance from running into it. I agreed that this seemed an intelligent thing for them to do and we were proceeding toward Rambouillet when we were joined by Lt. Irving Krieger of East Orange, New Jersey, of the 2nd Infantry Regiment. Lt. Krieger, aided by these French guerrilla fighters who placed themselves under his orders, cleared the mine field which was composed of a mixture of French and German mines. The field had been hastily made and many of the American mines were placed upside down. The source of the American mines was ascertained when examination was made of an American truck which had formed part of an American reconaissance unit which had been ambushed outside of Rambouillet by antitank and machine-gun fire two days before. The truck had been shot up and two jeeps had also been hit. Seven American personnel had been killed and were buried by the

French alongside the road. The leading car of the reconaissance unit had been allowed to pass before fire was opened on the truck and the two jeeps. Some American personnel escaped and some who were wounded were later recovered. I was never able to ascertain the names of these men, but during the time that we were in Rambouillet an officer from their unit came to town to ascertain the place of their burial and requested what papers had been taken from them by the civilian population when they were buried.

In addition to the mine field there were two German self-propelled antitank weapons in position to impede an American advance down the road. They were in the form of miniature tanks and I was informed by Lt. Krieger each one carried two hundred pounds of TNT in it and that they were controlled electrically. One was in the road pointing straight up the hill in order to take any column descending that hill head on. The other was on the left side of the shoulder of the road and as you looked uphill on the right side of the shoulder of the road looking uphill there was a high wall and any column descending the hill and encountering the first of these miniature tanks would have had to swerve to their right and would have been taken in the flank by the second of these self-propelled antitank weapons. This weapon is called by the Germans the Goliath self-propelled tank and was one of their vaunted secret weapons.

Lt. Krieger severed the wires controlling these tanks and placed a guard over them. After clearing of this road bog the French guerrilla fighters still wished to place themselves under my command. I explained that I was unable to accept this as a correspondent is forbidden by the Geneva Convention to command troops, but that I would be glad to give them the benefit of my advice on any matters that came up if I could do so without violating the Geneva Convention.

When my advice was requested by them I suggested they should aid in the preservation of law and order until the arrival of the proper constituted authorities. There was no disorder in Rambouillet of any kind. I also suggested to them that it might be useful for them to make a reconaissance of the two main roads beyond the town pending the arrival of the reconnaissance troop which was expected. This was done.

After the arrival of the reconaissance troop commanded by Lt. Peterson of Cleveland, Ohio, when the French guerrillas asked my advice as to what capacity they would be useful, I suggested that they might aid in screening the approaches to the town. Lt. Peterson was in sufficient force only to hold the center of the town at this time. This also was done.

After the arrival of Colonel David Bruce, CO, OSS, ETOUSA, I explained to him what had taken place in the town up to this time and offered my services to him in any way in which I might be useful provided that my actions did not violate the Geneva Convention or that any of them should in any way prejudice my fellow war correspondents. As senior American officer present in the town Colonel Bruce had a great many problems to deal with. These problems were greatly increased when the American reconaissance forces were withdrawn on the 20th, thus leaving the town which had been occupied by American troops without the presence of any troops except those who were there on special missions. These troops consisted entirely to my knowledge of British and Allied parachutists, agents employed on missions into enemy territory and other men engaged in secret intelligence activities.

After the withdrawal of the American combat units the problem arose of the disposal of this American personnel and whether there was a possibility of the town being screened or defended in order that the enemy should not reenter it when they became aware of the withdrawal of the American army reconnaissance units. This phase of the Rambouillet incident is covered by James W. Thornton, a Major AC, IS, 9 (WEA) American G-2 Division, SHAEF, APO 757. This statement is hereby appended.

Q That statement will be marked Exhibit C in this report of investigation. Please proceed.

A The following problems existed at this point. Presence of German troops in both small and large bodies throughout the forests of Rambouillet. Many of these troops had no desire to fight but wished to surrender. They were the residue of troops which had been defeated at Chartres. Other bodies of German troops were attempting to join the German forces which were intact between Rambouillet and Paris. It was necessary for the proper authorities to establish priorities for dealing with the problems presented by these different types of German forces.

Secondly, there was the problem of the possibility of the defense of the town.

Thirdly, there was a problem of obtaining precise and accurate information as to the enemy dispositions between Rambouillet and the Versailles road in order that this information might be delivered to the proper authority, if in case they advanced through this sector.

In all of these problems I served only in an advisory capacity to Colonel Bruce, who was the senior American officer present. I did not command troops nor give orders, but only transmitted orders given by a senior American officer who was occupied with multiple problems at this time.

In regard to the value of any information obtained, I offer the statements by Colonel Bruce, GSC, CO, OSS detachment and a statement by S. L. Marshall, Lt. Col. GSC, G-2, Historical Branch, who were in Rambouillet at this time.

All information received as to location of enemy mine fields, the implacement of any artillery and antitank pieces, the location of any radar antiaircraft batteries, the enemy defense lines, the strong points of which were blasted out the day before the arrival of the 2nd French armored column, and the number and movement of enemy tanks and troops in this area were evaluated, checked, and delivered by Colonel Bruce to the proper military authorities.

Q Were your activities observed or known by a number of other correspondents?

A My actual activities were not known to a number of other correspondents. My obvious activities as passing information, helping in the organization of the hotel, attempting to provide billets for the correspondents who arrived during the latter part of our tenure in Rambouillet were quite obvious, well-known, and frequently misunderstood.

Q In accordance with Paragraph 7, Army Regulations 20-30, it is appropriate that I acquaint you with the allegations which I am required to investigate. They are included in a report to the effect that Mr. Hemingway stripped off correspondent insignia and acted as a colonel, French Resistance Troops; that he had a room with mines, grenades and war maps; that he directed resistance patrols, which action is believed to violate credential rights of the correspondents. Is there further comment you desire to make with respect to those allegations?

A In reply to the above allegations I wish to state that all correspondents who were in Rambouillet can testify to the fact that I was wearing correspondent's insignia except at such times as I was in my shirtsleeves during warm weather. Correspondents are frequently seen in their shirtsleeves and even in their underwear without the proper insignia being exhibited. It is customarily worn on the blouse or on a great coat in bad weather.

In regard to being a colonel, if I were ever referred to as a colonel it was in the same way that citizens of the state of Kentucky are sometimes addressed as colonel without it implying any military rank, just as all Chinese who have followed the trade of war up to a certain age are always addressed as general. These forms mean nothing and one might be addressed affectionately as captain, colonel, or general without it having any military significance.

Any arms or armament seen by anyone in my room was stored there by French resistance men who were operating under the orders of the proper authorities and left these arms or armament in my room for security purposes. At this time various prisoners and suspects were being guarded in the courtyard of the hotel and it would be impossible to leave any arms or armament otherwise than in a secure place.

In regard to a war map, I don't understand this phase clearly. I have been accustomed to operate from maps ever since I have been an accredited correspondent. As I understand it, the only thing that correspondents must not do is to carry marked maps where they can fall into the possession of the enemy. I have never done this.

As far as the question of directing resistance patrols, I believe that has been covered in my previous statement.

Q Were there mines in your room?

A There were no mines in my room. I would greatly prefer not to have mines in my room at any time.

Q Did you tell any correspondents that you had removed your insignia so as not to prejudice them?

A I didn't tell correspondents that I had removed my insignia not to prejudice them to the best of my knowledge.

Q You accompanied the 4th Infantry Division for some time, did you not?

A I accompanied the 4th Infantry Division from the time of the breakthrough until the 25th of September of this year except for the short time that I was in Rambouillet.

Q Were you usually accompanied by a public relations officer from the 4th Infantry Division?

A I was accompanied by a public relations officer from the 4th Infantry Division or was in the company of other officers in that division.

Q Who was the public relations officer?

A Captain Marcus O. Stevenson.

Q Did you have one chauffeur most of this time?

A I had various chauffeurs during this time, but during the start of the time I was with the 4th Infantry Division Captain Stevenson usually drove himself and I accompanied him.

Q Did you at any time tell some correspondents that while with the 4th Infantry Division you removed your correspondent's insignia and fought with the men?

A I didn't tell correspondents this and didn't fight with the men.

Q With respect to your activity with the French resistance troops, do I understand that this consisted primarily of interpreting reports and orders and offering suggestions when asked for them?

A My activities so consisted. I also occasionally accompanied patrols in order to obtain direct information to aid me in evaluating information received and to give me necessary information for the writing of my articles. It is perfectly permissible for a correspondent to go on an infantry patrol.

Q Did you when in contact with the French resistance troops consider yourself or act in the capacity of a commander directing them?

A It was impossible for me to so consider myself due to the fact that I was an accredited correspondent.

Q Is there any other information you wish to add?

A Only the fact that in Rambouillet I wasn't armed, a fact which, as far as I know, has not been disputed. That is all.

Q Did you state to anyone at about this time, "I am no longer a correspondent."?

A I didn't make any such statement in a serious sense. I may have said jokingly, "I am now a hotel manager, the bouncer for this joint, the un-thanked billeting clerk, and general errand boy around the establishment," but in the serious sense that I was not a correspondent it would be impossible for me to make such a statement since I am an accredited correspondent for *Collier's Weekly* and am so earning my living.

Q Is there anything else you deem appropriate to add at this time?

A Nothing, unless there are any further questions you wish cleared up.

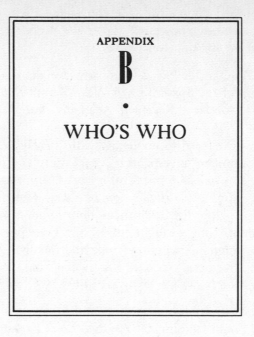

APPENDIX

B

·

WHO'S WHO

(To avoid repetition, "he," "his," and "him" refer to Ernest Hemingway alone.)

Don Anderson: Prevented one suicide attempt by wrestling the gun from Ernest's grasp, then flew with him from Idaho to Minnesota where he was hospitalized.

Nathan Asch: Friendly rival and admirer of Hemingway in Paris in the 1920s. Asch's experimental novel, *The Office,* was published by Harcourt Brace in 1925, the year Ernest began to write *The Sun Also Rises.*

Lauren Bacall: Actress and author of *By Myself,* Knopf, 1978.

Carlos Baker: His authorized biographer, who in *Ernest Hemingway: A Life Story,* Scribner's 1969, placates the widow and gives an encyclopedic but cautious account. Editor of *Ernest Hemingway: Selected Letters,* Scribner's, 1981, with Mary Hemingway's approval and despite

Ernest's expressed disapproval. He considered them "often libelous, always indiscreet, often obscene." Baker was Woodrow Wilson Professor of Literature at Princeton University.

Alvah Bessie: Adjutant of No. 2 Company, Abraham Lincoln Brigade, whose account of the Spanish Civil War, *Men in Battle,* Hemingway praised in the preface. Received Academy Award nomination for screenplay of *Objective, Burma!,* a 1945 movie. One of the "Hollywood 10" who refused to cooperate with the House Un-American Activities Committee investigating communist influence in Hollywood, Bessie served six months on a work farm in Texas, and wrote about it in a 1965 novel, *Inquisition in Eden.* After finishing prison term, sold Encyclopedia Britannicas door-to-door, then worked as stage manager at Hungry i nightclub in San Francisco announcing—out of sight—entertainers Lenny Bruce and Jonathan Winters. Other Bessie novels: *Bread and a Stone; The Symbol;* and *One for My Baby.* Several of Bessie's books are being reprinted by Chandler & Sharp.

Matthew J. Bruccoli: Publisher, author, and Professor of English at the University of South Carolina. Wrote *Scott and Ernest: The Authority of Failure and the Authority of Success,* Random House, 1978. Co-editor *Fitzgerald/Hemingway Annual,* 1960 to 1979.

David Bruce: Head of the OSS in France during World War II and afterwards U.S. ambassador to France, West Germany, and Great Britain.

Toby Bruce: Key West friend and general factotum who built walls for him, fixed and chauffeured his car, designed the dust jacket of *For Whom the Bell Tolls,* worked as his secretary and as the *Pilar's* mechanic.

Hugh Butt: Physician at St. Mary's Hospital concerned with Ernest's physical condition, especially his blood pressure. Mary called Butt "a genius and angel of character."

Elsie Byron: Helped her father run the Wigwam ranch in Wyoming where Pauline and Ernest stayed and he worked on *A Farewell to Arms.*

Morley Callaghan: Critically acclaimed novelist and short story writer. Fellow reporter on the *Toronto Star* and his friend and sparring partner in Paris until timekeeper Scott Fitzgerald let a three-minute round run to four, during which Hemingway hit the deck. Author of *That Summer in Paris: Memories of Tangled Friendships with Hemingway, Fitzgerald and Some Others*, Coward-McCann, 1963.

Truman Capote: Incensed by Hemingway's put downs and suspicious of his praise.

John Carlisle: War correspondent for the *Detroit Free Press* whose most memorable experience during World War II was sharing a tent and traveling with Ernest in Normandy.

José Luis Castillo-Puche: Author of *Hemingway in Spain*, Doubleday, 1974, in which A. E. Hotchner is described among other epithets as "a toady." Hotchner sued for libel and invasion of privacy. A jury awarded $125,000 punitive damages. In 1977, three U.S. Court of Appeals judges reversed the decision.

Lewis Clarahan: "I was his best friend in high school." They fished, fought, and hiked together.

Claud Cockburn: War correspondent for British *Daily Worker* during Spanish Civil War. Author of autobiography *I, Claud*, Penguin, 1967. Cockburn's novel, *Beat the Devil*, was filmed by John Huston. Contributor to *Punch* and the satirical magazine *Private Eye*.

Barnaby Conrad: Bullfighting aficionado and writer who was briefly Sinclair Lewis's secretary (as was John Hersey).

Robert Cowley: Accompanied his father, Malcolm, to Cuba for Hemingway interviews. Now senior editor at Henry Holt and working on own book about World War I.

Malcolm Cowley: Poet, critic, editor, literary historian. Encountered Hemingway in Paris in 1920s. Later, as literary editor of the *New Republic* usually enthusiastically reviewed his books and stories. Cowley's portrait of him in *Life* in 1949 gave him almost legendary stature. Cowley wrote *Exile's Return*, Norton, 1934; *A Second Flowering: Works and Days of the Lost Generation*, Viking, 1973; *And I Worked at the Writer's Trade*, Viking, 1978.

William B. Crawford: Son of the late Kenneth Crawford, *Newsweek* war correspondent covering World War II in Europe. Now senior producer CBS evening news.

Susan Lowrey Crist: Admiring Oak Park High School classmate. He was editor and she was associate editor of their school paper, *Trapeze*. She has avidly followed reports of his subsequent adventures and read most of his works.

Robert Cromie: World War II war correspondent *Chicago Tribune.* Long-time host of PBS's "Book Beat," when Cromie interviewed authors on TV. Now host of an author-interview show on National Public Radio.

Peter Davis: Documentary movie maker collecting material for a film about war correspondents including Hemingway.

Benjamin De Mott: Social and literary critic, and novelist. Mellon Professor of Humanities at Amherst College. Books include novels *The Body's Cage,* Atlantic Monthly Press, 1959, and *A Married Man,* Harcourt, 1968.

Mrs. John Dos Passos (Elizabeth): The second wife of the author, married in 1949 after first wife Katherine Smith was killed in an automobile accident.

Joseph Dryer: Dartmouth college friend of John Hemingway, who was wounded as a Marine fighting on Iwo Jima in World War II. Farmer in Cuba in 1950s when Dryer got to know Ernest.

Nancy Dryer: Joseph's wife who heard Hemingway called "an ogre" by mothers of girls in Cuba.

Albert Erskine: Random House editor since 1947, working with, among others, William Faulkner, John O'Hara, Robert Penn Warren, Ralph Ellison, and Eudora Welty. For the past decade, Erskine has been a consultant with the same publisher, and is now working with James Michener and Cormack McCarthy.

Ronald R. Fieve: Psychiatrist specializing in manic depression. Author of *Moodswing,* Bantam, 1976.

Lesley Frost: A publisher's editor and eldest daughter of the poet, Robert Frost. She worked for John Farrar, whom Ernest threatened to kill for calling his books dirty.

Carol Hemingway Gardner: Youngest of his four sisters. Though he was "absolutely nuts about her," when she defied him and married John Gardner he banished her from his life. She is still married to Gardner.

Martha Gellhorn: Journalist, novelist, and his third wife. They met in Sloppy Joe's Bar, Key West, and soon after were together in Spain reporting the civil war. Among her books are *What Mad Pursuit, The Heart of Another, Zoo in Madrid, A Stricken Field, The Trouble I've Seen,* and *A Psychiatrist of One's Own.* The titles might pass for a cryptic account of their stormy relationship. She gives her more tranquil view of Hemingway in *Travels with Myself and Another,* Dodd, Mead, 1978.

Arnold Gingrich: Founder and editor of *Esquire* magazine which printed many accounts of Hemingway's adventures. Gingrich, who married Jane Mason after Hemingway's affair with her ended, is the model for Professor John MacWalsey in *To Have and Have Not.*

Jane Mason Gingrich: A daring and beautiful society woman who had four husbands and numerous lovers—Ernest among them—and who underwent spinal fusion and psychoanalysis after breaking her back in a suicide attempt. Last marriage was to *Esquire* editor Arnold Gingrich. The model for Margot Macomber in *The Short Happy Life of Francis Macomber* and Helene Bradley in *To Have and Have Not.*

Tom Glazer: Roommate of Spanish Civil War veteran.

Francis Godolphin: Husband of Isabelle Simmons, his friend and next-door neighbor in Oak Park.

Peter Griffin: Thesis on Hemingway earned Griffin a Ph.D. from Brown University. Its reception encouraged him to write the first of four projected volumes of a Hemingway biography; *Along with Youth: Hemingway, The Early Years,* Oxford, 1985.

C. Z. Guest: Newspaper columnist and wife of Winston Guest.

Winston Guest: Polo-playing socialite, sportsman, airline owner, and Winston Churchill's cousin. Served as Ernest's second in command on the *Pilar,* used as a decoy to trap Nazi submarines off the Cuban coast during World War II. Ernest's unfailing admirer.

William Randolph Hearst, Jr.: World War II war correspondent for the Hearst organization; second son of the newspaper publisher.

Gregory Hemingway: His third son, born in Kansas City on November 12, 1931. Like Gregory's paternal grandfather, became a physician. Author of *Papa: A Personal Memoir,* Houghton Mifflin, 1976.

John Hemingway: His eldest son by first wife, Hadley. Wounded and captured as an OSS operative in Europe during World War II. Now,

Idaho State fish and game commissioner. Teaches French and Spanish in a Sun Valley school. Author of *Misadventures of a Fly Fisherman: My Life with and without Papa*, Taylor, 1986.

Leicester Hemingway: Worshipful younger brother who emulated him as newspaperman, adventurer, and author [a novel, *The Sound of the Trumpet*, Holt, 1953, and biography, *My Brother, Ernest Hemingway*, World, 1962] and also killed himself with a gun.

Mary Hemingway: His fourth and final wife. She started work in 1932 reporting for the woman's page of the *Chicago Daily News*. From there, Mary went to England as a London *Daily Express* reporter, switching in 1940 to the London bureau of *Time-Life*. Introduced to Hemingway by Irwin Shaw shortly after Ernest arrived in London as a war correspondent for *Collier's*, they met again in Paris soon after it was freed from Nazi occupation.

John Hersey: World War II war correspondent who wrote a novel, *A Bell for Adano*, based on wartime experiences in Italy; *Hiroshima*, a factual account of the atomic bombing of the city; and *The Wall*, a novel about the Nazi persecution of Polish Jews.

A. E. Hotchner: Novelist, playwright, and TV dramatist. His friend and traveling companion in the 1950s. Mary Hemingway went to court to try to stop publication of Hotchner's *Papa Hemingway: A Personal Memoir*. But she failed. Random House brought it out in 1966. The critics raved, Hemingway's friends were less than enthusiastic.

Joanie Higgons: A nurse in Sun Valley. Now married to Don Anderson.

Harry Hindmarsh: Son and namesake of the editor of the *Toronto Star* whom Hemingway threatened to kill.

Joris Ivens: Dutch film director who made documentary propaganda movie *The Spanish Earth* during the Civil War with Hemingway's help.

Tom Jenks: Scribner's editor by way of *Esquire* magazine, did a massive cutting job on Hemingway's 1500-page manuscript, *The Garden of Eden*, eliminating characters and about eighty percent of what Hemingway had written. The posthumously published 247-page novel appeared in 1986.

Mrs. Larry Johnson: Wife of pilot who flew Ernest to Mayo Clinic.

Phillip Knightley: Espionage expert. Special correspondent London *Sunday Times*, and author of *The First Casualty: From the Crimea to Vietnam, The War Correspondent as Hero, Propagandist, and Myth Maker*, Harcourt Brace Jovanovich, 1975. Coauthor *The Secret Lives of Lawrence of Arabia*, Nelson, 1969, and *The Philby Conspiracy*, Signet, 1969.

C. T. [Buck] Lanham: Commander of the U.S. Twenty-second Infantry Regiment, Fourth Infantry Division. Friends almost at first encounter, they endured the battle of the Hurtgen Forest together, admired one another, remained friends, and corresponded frequently after the war.

Aaron Latham: Author of *Crazy Sundays: F. Scott Fitzgerald in Hollywood*, Viking, 1971, and "A Farewell to Machismo," *The New York Times Magazine*, October 16, 1977, in which Latham previewed the then unpublished *Garden of Eden* manuscript.

Harold Loeb: Novelist and co-editor in the 1920s of the shortlived but superior little magazine *Broom*, whose friendship with Hemingway ended after Loeb was ridiculed as Robert Cohn in *The Sun Also Rises*. Loeb gave his view of Ernest in *The Way It Was*, Criterion, 1959.

Ada MacLeish: Professional singer and MacLeish's wife. She had great and lasting affection for Hemingway and he for her.

Archibald MacLeish: Abandoned law career to become poet and playwright. Close friend of Hemingway in Paris in the 1920s. Worked for *Fortune* magazine, was an assistant Secretary of State, and Librarian of Congress during FDR presidency, and finally a Harvard professor. Triple winner of the Pulitzer Prize, once for drama, twice for poetry.

Meyer Maskin: Psychiatrist attached to Fourth Infantry Division whose task was to decide which soldiers had become neurotic or suffered from combat exhaustion and should be sent to the rear echelon. After World War II, Dr. Maskin practiced psychiatry in Florida.

Bill Mauldin: Cartoonist and writer. Served with U.S. Army in World War II with the Forty-fifth Infantry Division and army newspaper *Stars and Stripes*. Acted in movie *The Red Badge of Courage*, 1950; author of *The Brass Ring*, 1971, and *Mud and Guts*, 1978.

Jeffrey Meyers: Professor of English, University of Colorado. Author of *Hemingway: The Critical Heritage,* Routledge & Kegan Paul, 1982, and *Hemingway: A Biography,* Harper, 1985.

John Miller: Met him when they traveled on the same ship, then train taking them to drive Red Cross ambulances in Italy during World War I. Visited him as fellow patient in a Milan hospital and joined him for ten days convalescent leave at Stresa, on Lake Maggiore.

Madelaine Hemingway Miller: Third born of his four sisters, nicknamed Sunny. He wrote of her in three stories and thought she played the harp like an angel.

Hadley Mowrer: First wife and mother of Ernest's son, John, nicknamed Bumby. She reluctantly agreed to divorce when he fell in love with her friend, Pauline Pfeiffer. A talented pianist and subject of a biography, *Hadley: The First Mrs. Hemingway,* Alice Hunt Sokoloff, Dodd Mead, 1973.

Benjamin Nehman: Relative of Hemingway's bullfighter friend, Sidney Franklin.

Olive Norquist: Owner of a dude ranch in Clark's Fork Valley, Wyoming, where he and Pauline spent a "second honeymoon," and where he corrected galleys of *Death in the Afternoon.*

Frank Platt: Taught Ernest English at Oak Park High School. Persuaded him on his return from World War I to talk of his war experiences to forty school boys.

George Plimpton: Admirer and emulator of the skillful and daring, Plimpton interviewed Hemingway for spring 1958 issue *Paris Review,* which Plimpton edits. Sparred and took part in contest-of-strength with EH. Author of *Out of My League,* Harper, 1961, *Mad Ducks and Bears,* Random House, 1973; *Shadow Box,* Putnam, 1976; *Open Net,* Norton, 1985.

Michael Reynolds: Author of *Hemingway's First War: The Making of a Farewell to Arms,* Princeton, 1976; and *The Young Hemingway: A Literary Biography,* Basil Blackwell, 1986. Professor of English at North Carolina State University.

Howard Rome: Psychiatrist who gave Hemingway a series of electric shock treatments at the Mayo Clinic.

Andy Rooney: War correspondent for U.S. Army newspaper *Stars and Stripes* in World War II. Now author, nationally syndicated essayist, and TV commentator on CBS' "60 Minutes."

Earl Rovit: Author of *Ernest Hemingway*, Twayne, 1963, and novel, *A Far Cry*, Harcourt, 1967. Professor of English, City College, New York City.

John Rybovich, Jr. Boat builder and fisherman who now writes column on sports fishing for *Boating* magazine.

Thorvald Sanchez, Jr.: Artist son of Ernest's drinking, fishing, and philandering buddy in Cuba.

George Saviers: His physician at Sun Valley Hospital who became a friend and hunting companion.

Philip Scharfer: Chief of the department of psychiatry, Good Samaritan Hospital, West Palm Beach, Florida.

George Seldes: Foreign and war correspondent in Europe for the *Chicago Tribune* and *New York Post* during the 1920s and 1930s, when he frequently encountered Hemingway. Crusading author of *You Can't Print That!: The Truth Behind the News*, Garden City, 1929, *Sawdust Caesar: The Untold History of Mussolini and Fascism*, Harper, 1935; and *Never Tire of Protesting*, Lyle Stuart, 1968. In 1940 Seldes founded and edited a weekly newsletter *In Fact: An Antidote for Falsehood in the Daily Press* [which was secretly funded by the American Communist Party, though, ironically, Seldes was an active anti-Communist]. It lasted ten years. At ninety-six, Seldes has published his memoirs, *Witness to a Century*, Bantam, 1987.

William W. Seward, Jr.: Chairman of the department of English, Old Dominion University, and author of *My Friend, Ernest Hemingway*, Barnes, 1969.

Irwin Shaw: Novelist and short story writer who had an affair with Mary Welsh before Hemingway met and married her. Shaw wrote less than flattering portraits of the Hemingway brothers in *The Young Lions*.

Thomas Shevlin: Sportsman, big-game hunter, and socialite.

Gordon Sinclair: Copy boy on the *Toronto Star* promoted to reporter in time to cover one story with Hemingway. Became one of Canada's most

loved-and-hated broadcasters, speaking three times a day over radio
station CFRB, and was a panelist on a TV show, *Front Page Challenge.*
Prime Minister Pierre Trudeau spoke of Sinclair's "wit, irreverent
bluntness and off-beat views." On a state visit to Canada, President
Reagan asked to meet Sinclair, who said to Reagan, then seventy: "It's
nice to see you younger fellows get ahead."

Agnes von Kurowsky Stanfield, Jr.: American Red Cross nurse who cared
for him when he was recovering from war wounds. He hoped to marry
her but she jilted him. He wrote of her several times especially as
Catherine Barkley in his 1929 novel *A Farewell to Arms.*

William Stanfield, Jr.: Agnes' second husband, who was more frank than
Agnes about her love affair with Hemingway.

Stephen Spender: Poet and critic who had a controversial meeting with
Martha Gellhorn and Ernest during the Spanish Civil War.

Samuel M. Steward: Chicago teacher and novelist [*Angels on the Bough,*
1936]. Friend of Gertrude Stein and of Alice B. Toklas who sent him
gossipy notes from France, such as "Cecil Beaton is desperately in love
with Greta Garbo and the Duchess of Kent equally so with him" as well
as giving him the "lowdown" on Ernest Hemingway. Author of *"Dear
Sammy": Letters From Gertrude Stein & Alice B. Toklas,* St. Martin's,
1984, Steward is now a professional tattooist in California.

Michael Straight: Speech writer for FDR. Editor and son of the founders
of the *New Republic.* Brother-in-law of Spanish Loyalist Gustavo
Duran. In *After Long Silence,* Norton, 1983, Straight explains a Communist past and the eventual unmasking with Straight's help of art
historian Anthony Blunt as a Soviet agent. From 1969 to 1977 Straight
was Deputy Chairman of the National Endowment for the Arts.

Henry [Mike] Strater: An artist who painted portraits of Ernest and
Hadley, and who boxed and played tennis with Hemingway. One of
three men pointedly excluded from his memoirs *A Moveable Feast.* Still
painting at ninety-one.

C. L. Sulzberger: Chief foreign correspondent for the *New York Times*
Foreign Service Worldwide, 1944 to 1954. Author of twenty-one books,
including *History of World War II,* American Heritage, 1966, *A Long
Row of Candles,* Macmillan, 1969, *The World and Richard Nixon,*
Prentice Hall, 1987.

Harry Sylvester: Journalist and novelist who sparred physically and mentally with Hemingway in Key West days. Contributor to *Commonweal*, a liberal Catholic magazine. Sylvester's novel *Moon Gaffney*, Ayer, 1976, covers the conflict a young liberal Catholic has with the political machine and his Church.

Nan Talese: Editor at Random House who worked with A. E. Hotchner on his *Papa Hemingway*. Now a vice-president at Houghton Mifflin.

Jacqueline Tavernier-Courbin: Professor of English, University of Ottawa. Author of *Ernest Hemingway: L'Education Europeéne de Nick Adams*, Paris, 1978, "The Mystery of the Ritz Hotel Papers," College Literature, Vol. VII, number 3, "The Paris Notebooks," The Hemingway Review, Fall 1981, "Fact and Fiction in *A Moveable Feast*," The Hemingway Review, Fall 1984.

Charles Thompson: His closest friend in Key West. Fishing and hunting companion. Co-owner of a ship's chandlery, an icehouse, cigarbox factory, hardware, and tackle shop. Appears as Old Karl in Ernest's *The Green Hills of Africa*.

Lorine Thompson: Charles' wife and Pauline Hemingway's friend. Head of Social Science Department at Key West High School.

Hans L. Trefousse: U.S. army captain in World War II who interrogated German prisoners. Was in jeep ahead of Hemingway during entry into Paris. Now Distinguished Professor of History, Graduate School of the City University of New York.

Henry Villard: Eyewitness to Hemingway-Agnes von Kurowsky romance who many years later asked her how accurate Ernest's account of it was in *A Farewell to Arms*. Became U.S. vice consul in many places including Teheran, Iran. Retired in Switzerland where Villard wrote "In a World War I Hospital With Hemingway," which was published in *Horizon*, August 1978.

Arthur Waldhorn: Author of *A Reader's Guide to Ernest Hemingway*, Farrar, Straus & Giroux, 1972. Professor emeritus, City College of New York.

William Walton: Artist, writer and World War II war correspondent for *Time*, who parachuted into France on D-Day. A close friend not only of Hemingway, but of his third and fourth wives, Martha and Mary;

who kept on good terms with all three—even more tricky than parachuting into enemy territory. From 1963 to 1971, chairman of U.S. Commission of Fine Arts.

John Westover: Captain in the U.S. army, driver-escort for Brigadier General S. L. A. Marshall, the Army's chief historian in the European theater.

Milton Wolff: Leading member of the Abraham Lincoln Brigade who fought against Franco and called Ernest and other war correspondents "tourists." Served with the OSS in Europe during World War II. National Commander of the Veterans of the Abraham Lincoln Brigade.

Irvin D. Yalom: Psychiatrist at Stanford University School of Medicine. Co-author with Marilyn Yalom of "Ernest Hemingway—A Psychiatric View," *Archives of General Psychiatry,* June 1971. He tried but failed to get information for the article from Dr. Rome.

Philip Young: Hemingway expert who originated the theory that his work was greatly influenced by World War I "traumatic neurosis," and who coined the phrase "The Hemingway Code Hero." Young's 1952 study *Ernest Hemingway: A Reconsideration* was revised in 1966 and published by Harcourt, Brace and World. Now Evan Pugh Professor of English at Pennsylvania State University, Young believes, referring to Hemingway biographers, that "best biographies [are] never known for politeness, never written to please publisher, widow of author."

INDEX

Note: unless otherwise identified, all works listed are by Ernest Hemingway.